LGDDM

TAMING THE
TROUBLESOME CHILD

Taming the
Troublesome Child

American Families, Child Guidance,
and the Limits of Psychiatric Authority

Kathleen W. Jones

HARVARD UNIVERSITY PRESS

Cambridge, Massachusetts

London, England

First Harvard University Press paperback edition, 2002

Library of Congress Cataloging-in-Publication Data

Jones, Kathleen W.
Taming the troublesome child : American families, child guidance,
and the limits of psychiatric authority / Kathleen W. Jones.
p.   cm.
Includes bibliographical references and index.
ISBN 0-674-86811-0 (cloth)
ISBN 0-674-00792-1 (pbk.)
1. Child mental health services—United States—History—20th century.
2. Child guidance clinics—United States—History—20th century.
3. Problem children—United States—History—20th century.
4. Problem youth—United States—History—20th century.   I. Title
RJ501.A2J64   1999
362.2'083'0973—dc21   99-11588

For Emily

Contents

Acknowledgments

This book began many years ago, when Jim Reed told me the work I'd planned on American motherhood was "not focused" and Gerry Grob asked if I had any interest in child psychiatry. As I have shifted from women's history to the history of medicine, and then back again, I have been fortunate to have had the guidance and support of good friends and colleagues who have helped to make it all worthwhile and financial assistance from several institutions to make it possible. It is a pleasure to acknowledge their contributions.

Gerry Grob has been unfailing in his support for this project. With his recommendation I received a fellowship from the History of Psychiatry Section at New York Hospital–Weill Medical College of Cornell University, which enabled me to do initial research. I also need to acknowledge the enthusiastic support of the late Eric T. Carlson, M.D., director of Cornell's history of psychiatry archives, and Jacques Quen, M.D., the program's associate director. They encouraged me to try out ideas in the Wednesday afternoon seminars and fed me helpful references at an early stage in my research. Many other librarians have provided assistance along the way, including David J. Klaassen of the Social Welfare History Archives, Peter J. Lysy at the University of Notre Dame, the staffs of the National Library of Medicine, the Schlesinger Library, and the Rockefeller Archive Center, and the reference and interlibrary loan staff at Virginia Tech.

I owe a special debt to Nancy Tomes, who pointed me to the files of the Judge Baker Foundation (and also read an early draft of the manuscript with great care). Staff at the Judge Baker Children's Center provided access to privately held scrapbooks. Richard J. Wolfe, then curator of rare books and manuscripts, and the staff of Harvard Medical School's Francis A.

Countway Library of Medicine, where the Judge Baker records are housed, made my hours of work there both comfortable and profitable. Carol Petillo and Wayne Cooper provided friendship, a room, and lots of encouragement during long research trips to Boston. Their generosity afforded me the time needed to understand the parents, children, and staff members who created child guidance.

Just as child guidance was a funded project, so too was this book. I have benefited from a Public Health Service National Research Service Award (MH 09308-02) and a National Institute of Mental Health postdoctoral traineeship at the Rutgers-Princeton Program in Mental Health Research under the direction of David Mechanic (MH 16242-09). This publication was also supported in part by grant number LM 05563 from the National Library of Medicine. Under the provisions of this grant I acknowledge that the contents of this work are solely the responsibility of the author and do not necessarily represent the official views of the National Library of Medicine. In addition, this project benefited from financial support during my year at the University of Manitoba and from a Virginia Tech Research Pilot Project Grant and Humanities Summer Stipend.

As I have moved from Rutgers to Manitoba and then to southwest Virginia, I have been fortunate to find colleagues who would read my scribblings, challenge my interpretations, force me to sharpen my positions, provide diversion from the task at hand, and even come up with just the right title. Andrew Abbott, Linda Arnold, Mark V. Barrow, Jr., Claudia Clark, Ellen Dwyer, Barry Ferguson, Dee Garrison, Natalie Johnson, Deborah J. Milly, Henry L. Minton, Heather Munro Prescott, James W. Reed, and Daniel Thorp all helped to shape this study in one way or another. Janet Tighe was a real cheerleader throughout the project, reading drafts and introducing me to Elizabeth Toon, Hans Pols, and the University of Pennsylvania writing group, who provided a critical reading of several chapters of the final manuscript. Four graduate students at Virginia Tech—Heather Harris, Sarah Mitchell, Dave Sheridan, and Anne Wohlcke—worked as research assistants, cheerfully tracking down missing citations and errant references. My editors at Harvard University Press, Michael Fisher, Ann Downer-Hazell, and Elizabeth Gilbert, smoothed over the rough spots.

Portions of several chapters were presented at various conferences and seminars, and I want to recognize the thoughtful comments of Janet Golden, Anne Harrington, and Steven Schlossman. An earlier version of Chapter 7 appeared as "'Mother Made Me Do It': Mother-Blaming and the

Women of Child Guidance," in Molly Ladd-Taylor and Lauri Umanski, eds., *"Bad" Mothers: The Politics of Blame in Twentieth-Century America* (New York: New York University Press, 1998).

A few people have been around for the duration. Paul G. E. Clemens has read so many drafts of this book, he must have much of it memorized by now. His critical eye has saved me from many mistakes. Since graduate school days I have shared many a discussion about the meaning of history (and the meaning of life) with Paula Baker, Carol Green-Devens, and Charlotte Borst. In late-night discussions and lengthy phone conversations they have helped me answer the questions "what's it all about?" and "why is it important?"

Family, who should be first in these lists of supporters and positive influences, always comes last. Frieda Shaull Jones has been a second mother, never failing to keep me working at the task. My parents, Donald and Anita Wildasin, and my sister, Rebecca Kahler, have been there when I needed to escape from myself to find balance. Finally, my daughter, Emily. Years ago, her own version of troublesome adolescence made the subjects of this book come to life for her academic mother. Now, as a clinical psychology graduate student, she is both friend and critic. I owe Emily the biggest debt; my greatest measure of appreciation goes to her.

Introduction

Fourteen-year-old Donald appeared before the Chicago Juvenile Court for the third time in 1909, causing the judge to wonder if perhaps the delinquent was "feebleminded." A gang of thirteen-year-old boys, truants from school, got caught jumping a Boston streetcar in 1920. During the same year, when Sophie defied her parents and stayed out very late, her family and the church child-saving agency thought her a "sex delinquent." In 1935 ten-year-old Tom absolutely refused to obey his stepmother and stole small items from home, twelve-year-old Josie threw temper tantrums when her parents wanted a say in how she spent her free time, and fifteen-year-old Malcolm was so moody and withdrawn that his mother wondered if the boy was becoming a homosexual. Just after World War II David provoked his father with defiant behavior, scorned schoolwork, and wanted to join the circus, while Ellen was apprehended for shoplifting. These boys and girls offended in different ways. Some were legally juvenile delinquents; others were merely young people who disrupted someone's regulations and moral values. They came from different backgrounds, some from families receiving charity and others from families living in middle-class comfort. Nonetheless they shared one common experience. The troublesome behavior prompted adults to turn for explanations and advice to experts in child guidance.

"Child guidance" is not a term familiar to most parents today. Although the words can still be found in the names of some community psychiatric clinics, in practice child guidance has been replaced by more specialized terminology—child psychology, child psychiatry, educational or vocational guidance counseling. In contrast, child guidance at mid-century was the best-known American contribution to the treatment of personality and

1

conduct disorders and, along with the juvenile courts, an integral part of delinquency prevention programs. Child guidance clinics could be found in most major American cities, and both Canada and England had similar evaluation and treatment programs.

What is child guidance? In 1940 a group of psychiatrists, psychologists, and social workers confronted this question in a symposium at the annual meeting of the American Orthopsychiatric Association (AOA). By that time the expression "child guidance" had been part of public discourse for close to two decades and the ideas behind it for at least a decade longer. The mental health professionals who belonged to the AOA used this opportunity to take stock of a multifaceted movement that seemed to be transforming both public policy and parent-child relations.

Those who spoke at the symposium often used "child guidance" as a synonym for specialized mental hygiene clinics for the treatment of problem children. While the clinic certainly defined the physical space of child guidance, child guidance meant much more to these AOA members than simply a network of institutions. By the 1940s the term designated a psychodynamic (and often psychoanalytic) interpretation of the behavior problems of children; a therapeutic approach to resolving the problems; the team of psychiatric, psychological, and social work professionals trained to work together to evaluate and treat problem children; and a critique of parental responsibility for troublesome behavior that was the wellspring of modern "mother-blaming." The mental health specialists who met in 1940 had no doubt that they were the authorities whose wisdom and advice could reclaim a child gone bad and prevent another from becoming an emotionally troubled or socially troublesome adult. "Child guidance," one of these experts boasted, "deals with all problems related to child welfare."[1]

While the term may not be well known today, the rhetoric of child guidance still frames our discussions of juvenile misbehavior. Child guiders[2] cast the troublesome child as a bundle of emotional needs that could be met only through the establishment of satisfying relationships with parents. If unmet, these needs resulted in disturbing emotional and behavioral problems and prevented a child from growing into a happy, independent, and self-supporting adult. For the child guiders an overt act of delinquency indicated a child with unmet needs, but so did the ordinary or everyday conflicts between children and parents. Through practice in the clinics and by speaking out in public forums, child guiders labeled the behavior problematic and offered advice on subjects as diverse as adolescent moodiness, bedwetting, truancy, discipline, the effects of divorce, the provision of allowances, and the use of leisure time. In 1945 Dr. Benjamin Spock, the twentieth century's best-known pediatrician, wanted to see the day when child guidance would be a part of every school system. Accessibility would enable teachers, parents, and children to "ask for advice on all kinds of minor problems as easily and as naturally as they can inquire about inoculations and diet and the prevention of physical disease."[3] Psychological services for children may not be available on quite this scale today, but public agencies and individual parents turn readily to the advice of child psychiatrists and child psychologists for help with the trials of raising children.

This book tells the story of the American child guidance movement during the first half of the twentieth century, the years in which child guiders accumulated public and private support for the ideas that all children are threatened with potential psychological problems which in turn can cause misbehavior and that mental hygiene professionals alone possess the special knowledge and the authority to help caregivers combat troublesome behavior caused by maladjusted personalities. The story of child guidance belongs to the history of childhood and to family history. It is part of the intellectual and institutional history of psychiatry. At times child guidance has been used to demonstrate the skewed outcomes of modern social welfare endeavors. The thread that weaves these histories together, the theme of this story of child guidance, is the problem of authority.[4]

The evolution and expression of professional authority can be narrated from many angles. One classic approach sets professional expertise within a model of internalist intellectual history, with changes often represented as scientific progress. From this perspective the story of child guidance is part of a transformation in thinking about behavior, initiated by psychiatrists and psychologists who might have been behaviorists, developmentalists, or psychoanalysts. These forward-looking scientists and practitioners declared that human activity was driven by universal needs, that childhood was marked by incremental stages of development, with personality patterns formed in youth and displayed throughout life, and that motives or explanations for behavior lay hidden beneath the surface manifestations of decision making. From an internalist perspective, the knowledge that shaped child guidance—the eclectic psychosocial framework of human development—becomes the vehicle through which to study its claims to the troublesome child.[5]

The emergence of child guidance paralleled chronologically the growth of child psychology and child development programs in American universities. In academic departments and child welfare stations, early twentieth-century researchers measured children against one another to find the range of physical and mental attributes of the "normal" child. The story of child guidance might well be subsumed in a broader study of the science of normal child development. To be sure, child guiders borrowed from the research and drew strength from this general interest in the scientific study of the child. Those engaged in the study of "normal" childhood believed they were replacing folk wisdom with scientifically verifiable truths about children. So did the child guiders. Their concern as clinicians, however, was not merely to trace the course of personality development but to direct and, if necessary, to change it. Where child developmentalists saw the child as a series of norms to be investigated through academic research, child guiders saw the child as a problem to be solved through psychological intervention. Although parallel, the two stories—of academic child psychology and of child guidance—have to be told as distinct tales of professionalism. Here I explore the ways a group of clinicians claimed authority to explain and treat the behavior of young people that, normal or not, troubled their elders.[6]

To build the story of child guidance as a tale of scientific progress in a broadly defined field of child psychology is a scaffolding difficult to reject. This is so in part because today we retain so much of the child guiders' worldview. When we consider that child guidance publicists represented each child as a unique personality, with emotional needs and a right to have those needs met by some adult family member—a view our modern emotional culture values and promotes—we are likely to see as almost inevitable the domination of child rearing by the scientifically trained professionals who first articulated those views. Yet such a theme of inevitability divorces the cognitive structure of child guidance from the social context in which a psychological understanding of the troublesome child developed. It would be a narrow approach to the question of professional authority.[7]

The story told here makes that social context central by bringing to center stage the practitioners and clients who together transformed the psychodynamic framework into the services and the prescriptions of child guidance. This is a book about the people of child guidance—the representatives of three aspiring professions (child psychiatry, clinical psychology, and psychiatric social work) for whom the emotional life of the child became the focus of clinical practice; members of the social service and child welfare communities responsible for the care of delinquent and dependent children; mothers and fathers of all social classes; and, not least, the troublesome children themselves. It was the exchanges among these players that gave meaning to child guidance and established the dimensions of its authority.

In studies of twentieth-century helping professions (those that work from a psychological model of emotional determinism and personalized casework and therapy), the relationship between practitioners and clients has been examined from both "top down" and "bottom up" lines of vision. Using the standpoint of the experts enabled some historians to point out the powerful hold of science on American culture, and to identify professional structures that have pulled together and protected communities of practitioners. These studies frequently condemned the "intrusive" nature of the professions, particularly the helping professions, and the victimization of their clients.[8] During the 1980s studies of charity and welfare began to question this denial of agency to subjects of professional intervention. The authorities may have been controlling, but why and to what extent, scholars asked, did people acquiesce to the control? Linda Gordon, Michael Katz, Molly Ladd-Taylor, and Mary Odem looked for the manipulation of welfare assistance to search out the meaning that services held for those served as well as for the service providers.[9] In medical history too, more than a decade ago Roy Porter urged historians to view the practice of medicine from the sufferer's perspective, as he wrote that a "physician-centered account . . . may involve a major historical distortion." Professional authority, it seemed, was a process of negotiation.[10]

Recently, however, attention has once again turned back to the experts, albeit in somewhat different fashion. JoAnne Brown, in a study of psychology and intelligence testing, would have us look away from the content and the organizational structures of professions to the language used by practitioners to create professional credibility. Brown offers a new way through the maze of professional authority, one that relegates arguments about social control to the historiographical ash heap even as it brings to the foreground the representatives of professionalization. Brown's study and Elizabeth Lunbeck's similarly Foucauldian outline of psychiatric knowledge and power in the early twentieth-century Boston Psychopathic Hospital have set new standards for inquiries into professional authority. In refocusing scholarly attention on the experts, Brown and Lunbeck remind us that the dynamic of power cannot be ignored in assessments of professional authority.[11]

Yet something is missing in this revival of the expert, and I do not mean simply a passionate condemnation of the abuse of authority implicit in earlier studies. Absent in these new studies is a calculation of the limits of authority—how far, how fast, and with what consequences experts acquired the right and the power to determine the causes and cures of a troublesome child's misbehavior.

In the history of child guidance the terms of professional authority were negotiated on at least three fronts. The protagonists in this story—the professionals, their lay supporters, the multifaceted clientele of child-saving agencies who required families to submit to a psychological evaluation, and parents who voluntarily sought out advice—intersected at the child guidance clinic. Progressive reformers gave birth to the clinic, imposing on child guidance a structuralist and environmentalist approach to delinquency prevention. The clinic was a precarious alliance of the reformers' ideology and the professionals' psychodynamic interpretation of behavior. For child guiders, negotiating an easy relationship with their lay supporters was one facet of professional authority. The clinic was also a workplace for the psychiatrists, psychologists, and social workers who functioned as an interdisciplinary team of experts.[12] Competing professional aspirations rent the team's unity, making conflict over professional territory one of the creative tensions in the child guidance clinic. Most important, clinicians and clients met at the clinic to negotiate diagnostic and therapeutic relationships. The confrontations and shifting alliances in the day-to-day operations of the clinic defined the limits of the child guiders' authority.

Children are the protagonists almost always left out of historical accounts of the child sciences.[13] Perhaps because the academic disciplines, from which child guidance drew, made the child an object of study, historians have easily adopted the same objectification. Moreover, children, as the child guiders sometimes observed, were always involuntary participants. Adults brought troublesome children for evaluation, often using deception to gain their cooperation. Age may have made them dependent, but it surely did not make them passive participants in the development of child guidance. To understand the intricacies that formed child guidance, the troublesome children, too, along with their adult supervisors, have to become integral actors in the story, included in any study of the limits of expert authority.

A caution about my use of "children" to refer to the objects of child guidance attention. Child guiders wrote about young people from infancy to late adolescence. In the clinics they felt equipped to address the problems of elementary school–age youngsters as well as those about to graduate from high school. Most of the youths whose stories I tell, however, found themselves at the child guidance clinic between the ages of ten and fifteen. The upper limit was dictated partly by court regulations—boys and girls older than seventeen or eighteen no longer fell within juvenile court jurisdiction. I have chosen to refer to the group collectively as "children," despite the adolescence of some of them and despite evidence that the clinicians sometimes responded with different treatment plans for the different ages. A distinct adolescent psychiatry developed only during the 1950s and 1960s; during the 1920s and 1930s the years of puberty and adolescence belonged to "child" guidance and "child" psychiatry.[14] Furthermore, "troublesome" is my adjective, not theirs. Throughout this book I have used the word as a descriptor for all the children of all classes and both genders who were, at one time or another, objects of professional concern, child welfare intervention, or parental anxiety.

Nonetheless, the social and economic class background of a troublesome child is a crucial variable in the story of child guidance, defining both theory and practice in the clinic. Nineteenth-century child advocates created the sickly, delinquent, and dull child, whose troubles symbolized the problems of America's economic underclass. The psychological clinic for children was a product of Progressive interest in these youngsters. During the 1920s and 1930s child guiders encountered a new class of clients and began to speak of the "problem child." Defined as "normal" (when compared with mentally, physically, and socioeconomically abnormal predecessors), the problem child displayed behavioral attributes that contravened some system of authority—usually school or family—and personality attributes that created tense relationships with parents, peers, and teachers. The problem child, unlike the earlier version of trouble, could be found in any economic environment. This homogenization of troublesome behavior proved to be an essential component of the authority claimed by child guidance.

To analyze child guidance only as a consequence of class interests leaves unexplored the important role of gender in this story of professional development and expert authority. As class distinctions receded in the child guidance lexicon, gender differences assumed greater importance. The highlighting of gender in child guidance work was, to be sure, a matter of relative emphasis. For the Progressive social activists who founded child guidance, class defined who was troublesome; gender described how they were trouble. Boys were truants and thieves; girls were "sex delinquents" and shoplifters. But both sexes were poor, and their poverty provided the key to their rehabilitation. Child guiders located trouble in all classes of children, expanding the word's meaning to include personality attributes as well as overt behavior. For the practitioners, gender identity provided a structure for their new diagnostic categories.

Gender can also help to explain the alliances at work in the child guidance clinic. Professional relationships in early twentieth-century social psychiatry, as Elizabeth Lunbeck has shown in her study of the Boston Psychopathic Hospital, depended on contemporary understandings of gender differences. Science and psychiatry were masculine; social work relied on sentiment and was, therefore, feminine. The respect and authority attached to each profession were rooted in the gendered perceptions of their labors, as was the working relationship forged between psychiatry and social work.[15] A similar pattern is evident in child guidance, where gender differences contributed to tensions between child psychiatrists and social workers. Here, however, the masculine (and often male) psychiatrists found themselves in a dubious position of authority, claiming expertise in the traditionally female prerogative of child rearing and intruding on the privilege of a maternalist social work tradition. In allying with social workers in the clinic, child psychiatrists propelled both professions forward. Yet that alliance was maintained at the expense of the other women of child guidance, the mothers of the troublesome children.

By 1940 child guidance was synonymous with mother-blaming. Though not a child guidance professional, Philip Wylie captured well their critique of motherhood in his 1942 work of social criticism, *Generation of Vipers.* Wylie's "good old Mom" was a suffocating presence in her children's lives, "the corpse at every wedding and the bride at every funeral."[16] Child guiders began during the 1920s to popularize a harsh critique of overprotecting and rejecting mothers whose emotional limitations seemed to account for the vulnerable personalities of the children. In the clinic, treating these flawed or "pathological" mothers became a prerequisite for changing the troublesome behavior of their sons and daughters. Rooted in intellectual constructs from psychology, psychiatry, and psychoanalysis, mother-blaming was also a practical mechanism for assigning professional responsibilities in the workplace. Social workers talked to mothers and psychiatrists worked with the children, and by dividing the patients mother-blaming sustained the alliance of professionals.

It is impossible to tell the story of child guidance without giving an account of its attack on mothers. The child sciences generally devalued maternal traditions, which they derisively called "instincts." Yet there is more to the critique of motherhood than what can be seen from the standpoint of the professionals. For some women the clinic's mother-blaming provided an outlet for frustrations unrelated to a troublesome child; others, however, resisted the bad-mother diagnosis and condemned their condemners. The records of rebellious mothers help to clarify the limits of child guidance authority, even in the face of public support for the establishment of more clinics. Resistance to the message of child guidance was local, unorganized, and had no overt political agenda, but it was, nonetheless, real and threatening to the professional child guiders. Resistance represented the authority of families to decide when and if to incorporate the advice of experts into their child-rearing philosophies. Mothers were often the obstructionists, but fathers, and children too, placed limits on the influence of child guidance.

The story of child guidance is a labyrinthine tale of combinations and confrontations—professional and professional, medicine and social reform, expert and family, parent and child—and the age, class, and gender tensions of the early twentieth century that gave meaning to these connections. It is a story best reconstructed from inside the clinic, where these relationships were raw and intimate. I have grounded this study of child guidance in the experiences of professionals, parents, and children at one clinic, the Judge Baker Foundation (JBF) of Boston.

Founded in 1917 by the Boston philanthropic community, the Judge Baker Foundation was a memorial to Harvey H. Baker, Boston's first juvenile court judge. Under the direction of William Healy, a physician from Chicago, and Augusta F. Bronner, a Columbia University–trained psychologist, the clinic quickly became a model for others interested in improving juvenile justice through psychological testing and mental analysis. This was not the first such psychiatric clinic to work with troublesome children. With the patronage of Progressive child welfare activists, Healy had created the prototype in Chicago at the Juvenile Psychopathic Institute. When in 1922 planners at the Commonwealth Fund (a privately funded philanthropic foundation) wanted to design a national delinquency prevention program, Healy, Bronner, and their Boston clinic were in the thick of things. The Commonwealth Fund moved quickly to add nondelinquent emotional and behavior problems to the caseloads in the fund's demonstration clinics, and the Judge Baker Guidance Center (JBGC; the new name was adopted in 1930) followed suit. Although Healy and Bronner remained leaders primarily in the field of delinquency research, practice at the JBGC included both individual treatment for self-referred families and diagnostic services provided for courts and agencies.

A local study always raises questions about the representativeness of the institution, organization, or town chosen for investigation. I will not claim that the Judge Baker Foundation was exactly like all other clinics. Because of its history and its directors the Judge Baker staff saw decidedly more delinquency cases during the first two decades of child guidance work than did, for example, the clinic in Philadelphia. The Judge Baker remained a privately funded clinic, unlike the St. Louis clinic, established by the Commonwealth Fund but with permanent financing dependent on the local government. Its caseload consisted of very few African Americans, reflecting the Boston population but unlike the clinic in Richmond, Virginia.[17]

At the same time, the Judge Baker clinic was held in high regard by leaders in the field. Eminent psychiatric practitioners, including Erik Erikson, Helene Deutsch, and Franz Alexander, spent weeks at a time working with the clinic's staff. The JBF was also a training institute for child guidance, supporting Commonwealth Fund fellows in psychiatry and social work students from nearby colleges. The diagnostic procedures Healy devised in Chicago and carried to Boston shaped procedures in clinics nationwide. The division of labor among the clinic's team members paralleled that of other clinics. I have tried to set the Judge Baker staff within the general context of child guidance professionalism, and connect Boston patients to the broad reordering of class, gender, and age relationships that took place in the early twentieth century. Nonetheless, the individual case records of the Judge Baker clinic—the stories of Boston families and the Judge Baker staff—are the foundation for this study. Only with a local study can we begin to gauge how, and how fast, the authority of child guidance reached into American families.

Through a close reading of records from 1920, 1935, and 1945–46, I have reconstructed the relationships that gave meaning to child guidance authority and to the psychological representation of the troublesome child. Each file consisted of the reports of psychological tests and medical examinations of the children, along with a social, economic and physical profile of the family called a "social history," and the records of interviews with the children and the parents. The juvenile court and charity agencies routinely added their reports to the clinic's records. In addition, individual files held letters between parents and the staff, between children and psychiatrists, and between the clinic's directors and juvenile justice and welfare agency representatives. Occasionally the files yielded pictures or other personal mementoes sent by patients. About half the records from 1935 included follow-up material collected during 1940 and 1941.

Using all the cases from a solitary year starkly displays the changes in the clinic's practice and in the clientele and gauges the clinic's status in the local community. The cases from 1920 show the clinic's operations three years after opening, before the Commonwealth Fund began its juvenile delinquency initiatives. These records highlight the modifications to Progressive child saving as Healy, Bronner, and several social workers constructed a psychological frame for delinquency. The year 1935 was chosen to represent the mature clinic, with a much larger staff including, in addition to Healy and Bronner, one part-time and two full-time psychiatrists, several psychologists, a social work director, and a group of social work students from nearby colleges. By 1935, too, the clinic had treatment as well as diagnostic programs in place. Furthermore, because they occurred several years into the Depression, the year's cases illustrate how the families and the clinicians integrated economic want into their psychological interpretations of problem behavior. The postwar cases offer a measure of the extent to which child guidance succeeded in psychologizing the troublesome child. In all I examined over a thousand of these richly detailed files.[18]

Healy and Bronner produced several statistical studies of the Judge Baker cases. While I have used their statistical compilations for categorizing the clients during these years and for comparing cases from 1920 and 1935 with the clinic's averages, I have chosen to focus on the stories and the rhetoric of the cases, the texture of the material rather than the quantity. When I refer to individual patients I have given them fictitious identities, but I have tried to remain faithful to the stories told by the parents and the children and recorded by the Judge Baker staff. The reference numbers I use in the text correspond to the case numbers assigned by the clinic. Each of the records in the Judge Baker files is an incomplete story, a piece of a life for which we can know neither the beginning nor the end. Often I rely on "snapshots" from these stories, snippets from the many conversations that built a child guidance case. One case record, however, helped me to see both the lifespan of an individual patient and the developmental stages of child guidance. I first encountered the story of Janet Landis on a bleak summer afternoon following days of reading case after very repetitive case of Boston's juvenile delinquents. Unlike other files, the three fat folders of notes about Janet spanned most of the years covered by this study; this one story serves as a lens for focusing all the others.

Janet was a different type of client for the Judge Baker Foundation of 1920; not yet a delinquent, Janet, and her mother, had been referred to Boston's preeminent child-saving institution by a church social worker. From September 1920, when the Judge Baker staff first examined this fourteen-year-old girl, to December 1943, the date of the file's last entry, Janet maintained steady contact with the clinic. Her record recapitulated the growth of the clinic and mirrored the interplay of age, class, and gender in the history of child guidance.[19]

As an adolescent Janet Landis was both strong-willed and defiant, but the social worker and Janet's mother were far more distressed by the girl's recent sexual experiences with a young neighbor. Janet's lack of remorse for her actions and her carefree attitude toward her blossoming sexuality led them to the Judge Baker Foundation. Although this case was one of the few private referrals in the records from 1920, Janet's form of misbehavior, termed "sex delinquency," was a common one in the records of the girls seen by the clinic for the juvenile court or local welfare agencies. Janet's "social history"—her family background—was also typical of the clinic's other cases. Raised by a single mother, Janet lived in less than luxurious surroundings although the family was not truly destitute. Janet might be considered part of Boston's large class of working poor.

After tests and interviews, the Judge Baker team labeled Janet a normal adolescent—no signs of "feeblemindedness" and not psychopathic. Finding Janet and most others in her cohort of delinquents to be normal adolescents was a crucial step in the accumulation of child guidance authority. Mental retardation and psychopathy, at the time both signs of constitutional degeneracy, offered little hope for rehabilitation and made institutionalization the only alternative. Moreover, both diagnoses were ringed by class and ethnic stereotypes. In classifying Janet and others like her as "normal" Healy and Bronner were opening the path for child guidance to move beyond its social welfare beginnings and extend its precepts to encompass all classes of children. While Janet's sexual experiences were not to be taken lightly, her behavior seemed to reflect an ordinary adolescent desire for excitement, independence, and adventure. In 1920 the staff was less interested in the dynamics of the mother-daughter relationship than they were in Mrs. Landis's homemaking abilities and the economic situation of the family. The staff recommended a boarding school to give Janet more supervision of her adolescent emotions.

Most case files from 1920 ended at this point. In and out, an examination lasting several hours, a staff conference, and a typed summary with recommendations to forward to the responsible agency or court official or share with the parent. The clinic had little contact with most of the children once the diagnosis was completed, although the staff sometimes tried to schedule follow-up visits. The church social worker occasionally brought Janet in to chat when the girl was home from school, but the clinic did not attempt further treatment of the adolescent Janet Landis.

Toward the end of the 1920s, however, Janet, now married and a mother of two children, voluntarily contacted the Judge Baker Foundation. Janet's story as a wife and mother exemplified the successful popularization of child guidance. When her first child proved difficult to discipline, this young mother wrote to Augusta Bronner, the clinic's psychologist, asking for suggestions. Janet wanted to raise her children according to "modern" methods, and needed ammunition to counter her mother's antiquated advice. Bronner replied with a reading list of texts by mental hygiene experts and recommended a consultation. A few years later Janet again contacted Bronner, this time criticizing the clinic for sponsoring lectures at fees she could not afford. Bronner supplied her with two tickets to the series of talks by prominent child experts. Finally, in the midst of the Depression, with the family showing signs of financial strain, Janet called at the clinic to set up an appointment for one of her sons. The staff ordered an evaluation, but now, twelve years after Janet and her mother first visited the Judge Baker Foundation, the clinic team believed that both parent *and* child might benefit from counseling.

Janet still fought with her mother, and the clinic thought the boy's trouble stemmed in part from this continuing mother-daughter conflict, or possibly was attributable to tensions in Janet's marriage. While her son had a few sessions with one of the clinic's psychiatrists, Janet kept regular appointments from 1932 to 1934 with a staff social worker. Over the course of her therapy Janet revealed a desire to leave her husband and live with another man, a path she chose to follow. Regular therapy ended when the social worker left the clinic. Since the boy's misbehavior abated during

Janet's therapy, the experts felt justified in blaming the mother's emotional problems for the son's trouble. Although no longer in treatment, Janet continued to contact the Judge Baker clinic from 1934 to 1943, whenever she was in need. She appealed to the clinic for help with an unplanned pregnancy and asked the clinic to intercede on her behalf with local welfare agencies. Living with one man, not yet divorced from another, with five children and her mother as part of the family, Janet was one of the victims of these years of economic stagnation. Often her pleas to the clinic were requests for introductions to agencies giving relief. Augusta Bronner responded with sympathy, pointing Janet toward various organizations that might help and even supplying Janet's daughter with a dress for graduation. But unlike Janet's notes to the clinic, Bronner's were rather formal. Although Janet saw the clinicians as friends, the Judge Baker staff had begun to view its self-referred adult clients not as partners in the pursuit of the child's mental health, but as patients in need of psychiatric counseling.

Janet survived her years of parenting. The last document in the file was a Christmas card and letter, dated December 1943. Janet's note confirmed the general return of prosperity during the war years. Her new husband had steady employment at last, and Janet was engaged in volunteer war work. With greater economic security, greater personal satisfaction in her marriage, and the beginning departure of her children from the family home, Janet no longer appeared to need the services of Boston's first child guidance clinic.

Child guidance had changed over the years of Janet's consultations, a change that can be traced in the clinic's response to Janet, the delinquent, and to Janet, the mother of a troublesome child. This book is the story of that change in child guidance—from an eclectic interpretation of behavior dedicated to a program of delinquency prevention to a more narrowly focused psychodynamic explanation of misconduct directed toward the problems of "normal" youths; from a diagnostic service that left treatment in the hands of other social agencies to a treatment program for both parent and child; and from a program in which children were the primary objects of concern to a therapeutic setting that made adults the focus of "child" guidance. Janet, of course, was prompted by her direct experience with the clinic, but others of her station, families with children who failed to live up to expectations of deportment and tried the patience of their mothers and fathers, also began to listen to child guidance experts and sometimes turned to the clinic for help with their modern troublesome children. Through the study of cases such as Janet's I have examined the meanings of these developments for the child experts, the parents, and their children.

Chapter 1 surveys the construction of a "troublesome child" by the precursors of child guidance. In 1899 the nation's first juvenile court brought together some of the medical and reformist thinking and applied it to poor immigrant urban children who best personified the nineteenth century's definition of trouble. Chapter 2 examines the efforts of Progressive era reformers to tap the knowledge of psychology and psychiatry for their child-saving programs. William Healy is the chapter's protagonist, the individual whose work at Chicago's Juvenile Psychopathic Institute laid the intellectual and institutional groundwork for the delinquency prevention programs renamed in the 1920s as child guidance. The procedures followed at the clinic and their relationship to the professional development of psychiatry, psychology, and social work are explored in Chapter 3. By going inside the clinic I examine the rituals of practice that clarified the work of each profession even as the procedures also created a single voice of child guidance.

The volume of that voice is the subject of Chapter 4, which looks at the various sites from which child guiders presented their message to the public. Crucial to the process of popularization was the normalization of juvenile misconduct. Popularizers transformed the troublesome child from the poor immigrant delinquent youth of the social reformers to the ordinary annoying youngster who challenged the authority of parents from any social caste but particularly those families who could claim to belong to a broad middle class. Chapter 5 examines why the message of the child guidance popularizers resonated with these families. In Chapter 6 I single out the children and explore their unique relationship with the clinic's psychiatrists, while Chapter 7 looks at the women of the clinic and the bond between mothers and social workers forged by the child guidance critique of motherhood.

What was child guidance? As it was constructed by the professionals, parents, and children at the Judge Baker clinic, child guidance became a framework for the reordering of class, gender, and above all, age relationships in the first half of the twentieth century, and a symbol of the ambivalent acceptance of psychiatric authority in modern American life.

1

Constructing the
Troublesome Child

In 1909 the Swedish feminist and author Ellen Key predicted that the twentieth century would be the "century of the child."[1] Historians often quote Key's phrase when they want to recognize the sensitivity of modern society to the welfare of the nation's young. It was during the previous century, however, that an urban bourgeois culture, largely Protestant and white, invested childhood with the qualities of a separate and special stage of life. Innocence was a principal component of that construction, a change from the Calvinist doctrines of predestination and the sinfulness of human souls young and old. Discussions of the innocence and purity of children appeared in Enlightenment philosophical writings, and the ideas flowered in the nineteenth century. Novelists, many of them women, described the purity and vulnerability of children, who were at once dependent on adult protectors yet also, because of an inherent goodness, able to instruct grown-ups in important lessons of character. This was the message in the romanticized life of Little Eva, the slaveholder's daughter memorialized by Harriet Beecher Stowe in *Uncle Tom's Cabin*. In the popular Horatio Alger novels the young male heroes bristled with spunk, but their energy was circumscribed by respect for the bourgeois values of honesty and hard work. Although sometimes on their own in the harsh world, still these boys acknowledged their debt to the adults who helped them along the path to a secure and happy life.

If nineteenth-century parents found these fictional characters' real-life counterparts not always quite so perfect, the child of popular culture none-theless often epitomized the nation's youthful goodness and developmental possibilities. Religious writers and storytellers used the good child as a symbol of self-regulated personal behavior and orderly social relations in an emerging industrial economy. Vulnerable, protected, and respectful of authority, the children in these writings exhibited the values this culture preferred in its dependents. Scientific observations of the child, in particular the child study movement led by the psychologist G. Stanley Hall, did little to dismember this perspective. The unique, special, and good qualities of childhood found representation throughout the culture.[2]

This good child generated its opposite. During these same years physicians and child savers, arguing for hard-nosed notions of science and not literary sentiment, began to construct the qualities of the not-so-perfect child gone astray. To nineteenth-century mental asylum superintendents and neurologists a spoiled and self-indulgent child was an omen of the insane adult. For the most part, however, practitioners in these fields had little to say about children. The troublesome child of the nineteenth century was constructed largely by lay reformers, who saw in many of the nation's children not goodness but signs of the ailments of a rapidly changing society—generational stress, urban living, industrial poverty, ethnic diversity, and multicultural standards of behavior. This child frequently broke the law, was usually poor, and often appeared to be mentally deficient. Superintendents of training schools for the "feebleminded" and specialists in the new field of pediatrics confirmed the emerging definition of trouble. The image of the good child—vulnerable, dependent, and malleable—mediated public responses to these other children. The troublesome child could be salvaged, and doing so would relieve cities and states of burdens caused by adult dependency, crime, and insanity. The juvenile court movement of the early twentieth century was the capstone of nineteenth-century thinking about the need to save the troublesome child.[3]

ALIENISTS AND NEUROLOGISTS: DOCTORS OF THE MIND

For all of the attention paid to the child in the nineteenth century, "alienists," or physicians who directed public and private mental asylums, expressed only limited interest in the possibility of childhood insanity. However, evidence among the young of behavior believed to be preconditions of mental illness caused alienists and, later in the century, doctors from the new specialty of neurology to speak out about the perils of a mismanaged childhood. Although often at odds professionally during the last years of the century, these two medical fields agreed that a child whose bad habits developed without correction could look forward to a lifetime of personal misery.

Throughout the nineteenth century alienists had little to do with children. In part their disinterest stemmed from a belief that the mind of the child was immune to insanity. Benjamin Rush, the Philadelphia physician whose ideas about medicine influenced many American practitioners during the early years of asylum building, held that "the reason why children and persons under puberty are so rarely affected with madness must be ascribed to mental impressions which are its most frequent cause being too transient in their affects, from the instability of their minds, to excite their brains into permanently diseased actions."[4] To be sure, the changes of puberty seemed to excite older youths to emotional imbalance, but early nineteenth-century physicians agreed that the unformed, pliable nature of the young mind protected the child from the signs of insanity.

Practice in the asylums must have confirmed these beliefs. While the population in these institutions grew in number and grew more diverse over the years, children were not a significant part of the new clientele.[5] S. V. Clevenger, a pathologist from the Cook County (Illinois) Insane Asylum, recorded only six cases of childhood (under age seventeen) "insanity" under his care in the early 1880s (and ten that preceded his time). He added to that number another fifty older patients whose case histories hinted that they could perhaps have been diagnosed insane as children.[6] Recent studies of individual asylums have generally corroborated Clevenger's assessment. Maris Vinovskis and Barbara Rosenkrantz identified the presence of very few young people in antebellum Massachusetts institutions for the insane. Neither Ellen Dwyer nor Nancy Tomes, both of whom examined the records left by asylum keepers, found the presence of girls and boys in these institutions a meaningful aspect of asylum development. Dwyer and Tomes concluded that families dictated the terms of asylum admission for adults.[7] It seems likely that bizarre behavior in the young rarely appeared to be important enough, or threatening enough, to warrant such a drastic measure as commitment to an asylum. During the nineteenth century the new institutions for the insane did not draw children out of their families and into public scrutiny; consequently the superintendents had little direct contact with the troublesome child.

Published reports from the asylum keepers also neglected childhood. Nineteenth-century physicians often submitted accounts of their most interesting or unusual mental cases, but few of these narratives from American alienists were about children. When Clevenger attempted to review the literature he discovered that most of the available stories came from European sources. Only a few American physicians found their young patients intriguing enough to publish case histories, and few of these articles appeared in the *American Journal of Insanity,* the primary newsletter of the asylum superintendents.[8] Childhood insanity was not unknown, but until quite late in the century professional publications paid scant attention to the topic.

One exception to asylum keepers' general indifference was William Stout Chipley's interest in girls with eating disorders. The identification and naming of "anorexia nervosa" occurred in England and France in the 1870s. Just over ten years earlier in Kentucky, however, Chipley, then the enterprising superintendent of the Eastern Lunatic Asylum, tried to call attention to a condition he called "sitomania." A few families had brought adolescents to his institution because they recoiled from food, refused to eat, and had not responded to treatment from family physicians. The girls were more well-to-do than the average patient admitted to public asylums. Chipley knew that for their families, the asylum was a last resort, chosen because alienists were familiar with the practice of force-feeding inmates. In 1859 Chipley's article did not garner much attention from his colleagues, and the stigma of institutionalization probably overrode Chipley's medical advice to the public. Girls from this social class could seek alternative, and presumably more fashionable, treatments for their troublesome behavior—health spas or extended visits to kin, for example. Non-eaters from lower social classes, if they existed, either were not visible to Chipley and his colleagues or, as Joan Jacobs Brumberg has shown, they may have made such public spectacles of themselves that their symptoms were discredited quickly as fraud.[9]

While sitomania did not elicit much professional interest, alienists from mid-century on did express concern about behavior in the young that warned of insanity in later life. Alienists, joined later in the century by specialists in neurology who had begun to treat emotional and physical ailments with no apparent physiological basis, singled out both masturbation and intellectual precocity as particular threats to the mental stability of young people.[10] Although they found evidence of each behavior in both boys and girls, physicians noted that the diseases were for the most part gender-specific. Masturbation was thought to be particularly problematic for adolescent boys, who seemed prone to a unique form of "masturbatory insanity." Girls were known to suffer dire physical as well as mental effects from overstimulation of the intellect.

The behaviors identified by these physicians were especially troublesome since each represented evidence of self-indulgence unrestrained by parent influence. This was an era in which obedience, ambition, and self-control were character traits valued by the middle classes as necessary for success in an expanding urban economy; along with the preservation of innocence, these were qualities the extensive new advice literature on child rearing urged parents to encourage in children.[11] Certainly in their casebooks and annual reports asylum superintendents listed "defective education" and "injudicious early training" as factors contributing to the insanity of their adult patients.[12] Neurologists, seeing private patients who complained of the vague nervous disorders often diagnosed as neurasthenia or hysteria, also feared that masturbation or precocity might have precipitated the ill health.

American commentators often cited Henry Maudsley, a British physician and author of a treatise on childhood insanity, when they sought an authority on the consequences of masturbation. According to Maudsley, the instability of the years surrounding puberty could be exacerbated to an extreme, or a "mania of pubescence," if boys masturbated. The American neurologist Edward C. Spitzka, whose study of the categories of insanity also warned of the effects of unrestrained "self-abuse," was an indigenous authority on the subject. Maudsley and Spitzka, both eminent men in their fields, worried that in the young the habit produced an unwillingness to work, impudent behavior toward parents, and morbid periods of depression. Maudsley told of one adolescent who "spent most of the day leaning against a door post or wandering about in a vacant and abstracted way," and others who found all forms of meaningful work quite unsuitable to their talents, all because of a "sort of moral insanity" caused by masturbation. Spitzka described a youth who stayed in bed for days on end, and observed that "the obtrusive selfishness, cunning deception, maliciousness, and cruelty of such [masturbatically insane] patients render them the curse of their home."[13]

Thus aware of masturbation's supposed potential for harm, physicians developed techniques to break the habit and cure the disease. Spitzka went to great lengths to help one patient whose lack of enthusiasm for work seemed a consequence of "self-pollution." His prescriptions included constant observation and the use of a straight jacket. When this boy eventually began to show an interest in his father's business, Spitzka pronounced the disease had been cured. Others advocated even more drastic measures, including castration and clitoridectomy. Although the medical narratives usually told of the heroic physician who cured his patients of the dreaded habit, the stories also contained a strong admonition that prevention, through vigilance and careful upbringing, was a parent's responsibility.[14]

Nineteenth-century physicians sometimes linked masturbation to another disturbing trait associated with excess and mental instability. Precocious intellectual and emotional development seemed to threaten the well-being of many of the nation's middle-class young. Indeed, physicians such as Spitzka believed that masturbation or sexual precocity could be induced by mental precocity, or too much studying.[15] The community of alienists and neurologists was not alone in alerting parents to an apparent epidemic of precocity; throughout the century, foreign visitors commented unfavorably on the uppity behavior of young Americans, their cleverness, independence, and assertiveness.[16] Alienists and neurologists, however, spoke of consequences deleterious to health instead of mere annoyance. Isaac Ray, superintendent of Butler Hospital in Rhode Island, chastised parents and teachers for overeducating the young, because pupils pushed beyond the point of diligence in their studies might suddenly reel from an epileptic fit, "like a clap of thunder from a cloudless sky." Too much schooling, Ray charged, threatened the child's mental stability, and might eventually result in hospitalization.[17]

"Defective training" was the problem, according to the thirty-ninth annual report (1857) from the McLean Asylum for the Insane. Intellectual precocity was only one sign of "appetites indulged and perverted, passions unrestrained, and propensities rendered vigorous by indulgence, and subjected to no salutary restraint," all of which represented untoward nervous development that could lead to insanity.[18] A writer to the *American Journal of Insanity* cautioned in 1859 that "instead of being cherished by parental pride [precocity] should give rise to a watchful anxiety; and especial care should be taken to retard the early growth of this dangerous element." Parents were responsible: too many fathers were "strangers to their children," and while some mothers took up the burden with "self-sacrificing love," too many others gave little thought to the "infinite responsibilities resting upon them."[19]

As with masturbation, children of either sex might suffer from the effects of intellectually precocious behavior. Many physicians, however, seemed to find the disastrous consequences of precocity most often in young girls.[20] In 1854 A. O. Kellogg related the tale of two sisters, both encouraged by their father to develop their minds, both given books to read, both sent to a prestigious girls' seminary. The moral of the case: both sisters succumbed to scrofula during their teen years.[21] Edward H. Clarke's diatribe against female education, *Sex in Education: or, A Fair Chance for the Girls* (1873), described the breakdown of patients after intensive intellectual exertion during adolescence. Puberty was widely believed to be an especially dangerous time for a girl's health, and Clarke was as concerned about the weakness of a girl's uterus as the instability in a girl's mind.[22]

Other critics of the early and extensive education of females drew connections between youthful precocity and the onset of the "female disease" of hysteria. The girl whose "nervous sensibilities" were overtaxed by excessive intellectual exertion progressed to a bedridden hysterical state as a mature woman, showing symptoms of paralysis, fits, and depression with no apparent organic cause. If not a full-fledged hysteria, surely neurasthenia, the late nineteenth-century disease of an overtaxed, overstimulated mind and body, might result from a young girl's precocious behavior.[23]

The nineteenth-century medical community generally agreed that hysteria could appear as early as adolescence. By the end of the century some physicians had identified this disorder in even younger children. In his essay for a medical encyclopedia the neurologist Charles K. Mills remarked that manifestations of hysteria at an early age were not so severe as the symptoms in an adult, but "even the gravest form of the disease may occur in childhood." As with adult cases, Mills cited evidence of its more frequent occurrence in girls, and he concluded that most knowledgeable physicians thought inappropriate educational methods contributed to the onset of hysteria in childhood.[24]

Through their discussions of the twin threats of masturbation and precocity, nineteenth-century practitioners who studied and treated mental diseases had begun to construct a troublesome child in psychological terms. They based their conclusions on the experiences of the adults they saw in the asylums and the neurologists' examining rooms. Parents and teachers who thoughtlessly mismanaged the tasks of child rearing exposed their offspring to a heightened risk of emotional instability and an increased chance of institutionalization later in life. In these medical writings the pathological manifestations of masturbation and precocity did not threaten all children equally; for nineteenth-century physicians the class and sex of a child were good predictors of the cause of troublesome behavior.

Though widely observed, the symptoms seemed to appear with greater certainty in economically comfortable families. The children of the rich and of parents who were, as Charles K. Mills observed, "willing to sacrifice unduly in order to over-indulge their children" seemed to be especially susceptible to hysteria.[25] When Isaac Ray and others spoke of precocious children, they described young people from families able to afford educational advantages for their offspring and willing to commit resources equally to their daughters and their sons. The young masturbator, too, was likely to represent a bookish youth whose family fortunes enabled him to avoid hard physical labor. For alienists and neurologists, then, the troublesome child was most often a product of an economically untroubled family.

In promoting childhood as the age for learning self-restraint, the community of medical professionals tapped into some of the anxieties about social identity that nagged at middle-class, upwardly mobile families throughout the century. An intangible good character was as surely a sign of status as were those more visible symbols of success—housing, dress, and etiquette. The best indicators of a good character were physical well-being and mental health.[26] The consequences of the unrestrained or exaggerated behavior of middle-class boys and girls, according to the alienists and neurologists, lay not so much in the present as in the implications of this behavior for future health and happiness. A lazy boy consumed by autoerotic behavior or a studious girl with body and soul racked by the symptoms of hysteria could not anticipate an easy transition to the adult role of wage earner or housewife.

Although the first decade of life held significant perils, the time surrounding puberty was the critical period for recognizing signs of physical and mental degeneration rooted in lack of self-restraint. Incidents of masturbatory insanity peaked between the ages of eleven and twenty-three, Spitzka reported in his classification of insanity.[27] Just as a lad was expected to settle with determination into a path to marriage and adult vocation, the masturbator veered off, out of control, toward an unpredictable future. For girls too, puberty was a dangerous age. The neurologist Bernard Sachs cautioned that adolescent hysteria could have "an important bearing upon the entire life of the child." Particularly at the age of puberty, Sachs warned, girls who were "over-ambitious and eager to pass their school examinations" could "keep up under the excitement of the examination, but immediately thereafter, whether successful or not, would become irritable, excitable, sleepless, would have laughing and crying spells by turns, would refuse to take nourishment, and eventually would either recover under proper treatment, or else pass into a condition of typical acute mania with absolute loss of reason, with intense excitement, and confused delirium." When in the throes of study-induced mania or hysteria, young girls put up a mighty show of rebellion. "'I can't' is the pet phrase of all hysterical subjects, or still better, 'I will not,'" Sachs reported. "It is not so much a direct lack of power to exert the will, as a tendency to exert it in perverse fashion." [28] Boys without will power and strong-willed girls turned nineteenth-century gender distinctions topsy-turvy.

Through their discussions of masturbation and precocity the alienists and neurologists acknowledged the centrality of both class and gender in definitions of the troublesome child. In labeling some childhood behavior as troubling, these physicians also reaffirmed the importance of children in the nineteenth-century bourgeois family. The minds of children were vulnerable to corrupting influences. As did lay writers and other professionals, alienists and neurologists represented childhood as a time to direct the formation of character and thus prevent future ill health. In the records left by nineteenth-century students of nervous and mental disease, the troublesome behavior of bourgeois children sometimes warranted direct professional intervention. Sachs, for example, proposed "absolute separation of the child from the family" and ordered use of the "rest cure," popularized by the Philadelphia neurologist S. Weir Mitchell, for young people suffering from hysteria.[29] For the most part, however, alienists and neurologists wrote cautionary tales to warn of potential danger. Theirs was only one facet of the troublesome child's identity. Significant because it replicated popular anxieties in medical language, their troublesome child was also a private problem, one that could and should be handled in the family.

The alienists and neurologists of the nineteenth century were not child specialists. Indeed, they showed less sensitivity to the special nature of childhood than did other professional groups. Their interpretation and treatment of childhood mental diseases continued to be filtered through the concerns of professionals who cared mainly for emotionally disabled and dependent adults. Even Bernard Sachs, whose text *A Treatise on the Nervous Diseases of Children* (1895) represented the most advanced word on the subject and who is now considered a founder of the field of child neurology, wrote more extensively about adults.[30]

PEDIATRICIANS AND CUSTODIANS OF THE "FEEBLEMINDED"

By the last two decades of the nineteenth century two groups of medical practitioners were not as reluctant as alienists and neurologists to channel their energies into the study of children. "Pediatrists" specializing in the treatment of children and superintendents charged with caring for people with mental retardation also based their views on their separate institutional practices. Unlike warnings from alienists and neurologists, however, this perspective located the identity of the troublesome child in the lower classes and determined the cause of troublesome behavior to be a deficiency rather than overindulgence.

According to L. Emmett Holt, medical director of New York's Babies' Hospital and one of the country's first pediatric authorities, it was "not so much that the diseases in early life are peculiar, as that the patients themselves are peculiar."[31] By the 1890s, when Holt wrote these words, the notion that a child had special needs and was not just a "miniature adult" had gained some credence in medical circles. Early in the century childhood illnesses had been lumped into the study of obstetrics and gynecology. During the 1880s a few physicians, including Holt, Thomas Morgan Rotch, and Abraham Jacobi, began to specialize in the study and treatment of young children. These new specialists argued that diseases in children exhibited distinct symptoms and often followed courses separate from the same diseases in adult patients. Some of them, like Holt, headed charity hospitals for infants and children. Though few were able to maintain practices limited to children, they organized the American Pediatric Society in 1887 to represent their professional interests. Children and adults, they believed, could not be treated identically; children needed doctors of their own.[32]

The notoriously high infant mortality rates from gastrointestinal illnesses, particularly among the urban poor, led these nascent pediatricians to conceptualize the troublesome child as indigent. Urban physicians watched as the babies brought to their hospitals died of summer diarrhea and other "wasting diseases." The families who turned to these charity hospitals were often immigrants, living in densely populated neighborhoods with few sanitation amenities. The new specialists concluded that many infants died because parents did not understand the rules of good nutrition and fed their babies spoiled or contaminated milk. Thomas Morgan Rotch, for example, developed a system of complex formulae to modify cow's milk for infant consumption; other pediatrists published popular guides for the proper feeding of infants and children. The doctors recognized, however, that carelessness alone did not account for the high mortality figures. Mothers in these urban settings often could not find pure milk for their babies. Leading pediatric activists set out to regulate the milk industry and make disease-free or pasteurized milk available to urban families.[33] To be sure, middle-class mothers, through their clubs and individually, looked to the baby doctors for advice about how to keep their children healthy.[34] The public activism of pediatricians, however, targeted the families of the lower classes. For these doctors, the troublesome child was sickly and most often poor.

As they built a medical specialty around the age of their patients the pediatricians assumed responsibility for the nervous diseases of children. L. Emmett Holt firmly maintained that factors trivial for an adult could "produce quite profound nervous impressions" in a child. By the late nineteenth century, physicians such as Holt believed that the rapid growth and immaturity of the child's brain made it more susceptible to dangerous stimulation. Holt noted the stress of city living and lack of sleep as causes of pediatric nervous diseases, along with "overpressure in school." Masturbation was an "injurious habit," but one that was often a sign of epilepsy, idiocy, and insanity, and a consequence of poor heredity.[35] In keeping with the emphasis on feeding, this pediatric specialist concluded that the nervous conditions were always "very much increased by all disturbances of nutrition."[36]

While age made children more susceptible to nervous diseases, age also helped them recover. Even unusual cases of juvenile hysteria appeared to respond to treatment much more quickly than adult cases because the causes were not so deeply rooted.[37] Intervention should be firm, Holt advised. For hysteria, the prescription included outdoor life and regular exercise, education in moderation, and, of course, a plain, nutritious diet.[38] Only for cases of true insanity, defined as a "change in a mind previously sound" and "very rare," did Holt refer students of his text to the authority of a neurologist.[39]

Pediatricians writing in the 1890s knew of recent developments in the care of children labeled "idiots," "imbeciles," or "feebleminded," changes that had begun to collapse juvenile idiocy, epilepsy, insanity, and juvenile delinquency into one comprehensive category of antisocial behavior related to hereditary defect. Superintendents of "schools" for children who showed signs of mental retardation, usually medical men by training, had become convinced that people with diminished intellectual ability could not be taught the skills needed for independent living and would require life-long custodial care. Indeed many thought care was essential because idiocy seemed so closely connected to the pressing social problems of alcoholism, insanity, criminality, and, in women, illegitimate births. According to the superintendents, "feebleminded" children also posed a particular problem for their families, since the care required by such children often sapped the financial and emotional strength of parents. Pioneer hereditarians did not regard the signs of degeneracy as irreversible, but social humanitarians, vocal in the National Conference of Charities and Corrections, began in the 1880s to question the effectiveness of training for life outside the institution. Although the "feebleminded" were not yet the "menace" they would become in the early twentieth century, children with this affliction were beginning to be targeted as the source of many urban social ailments.[40]

Caretakers of the "feebleminded," though not precisely child specialists, had ample direct experience with young people in state-supported and private residential "training schools." The training school had its origin in the same antebellum asylum-building optimism that established hospitals for the insane. Samuel Gridley Howe, a founder of the movement to institutionalize the "feebleminded," believed they could be trained and returned to the community able to care for themselves. By the end of the century, faith that the schools could return their charges safely to the community had begun to wither under the weight of hereditarian ideas. Isaac Kerlin, superintendent of the Pennsylvania Training School for Feeble-Minded Children, was a particularly outspoken advocate of life-long institutionalization for children with mental retardation, especially those he designated "moral imbeciles" because their mental disability left them with no sense of right and wrong. Moreover, some of these children Kerlin diagnosed as suffering from a particular "juvenile affective insanity" in which behavior alone, without the stigma of mental retardation, defined the child's condition.[41]

A few parents may well have turned to the Pennsylvania Training School and other quasi-educational facilities for assistance with a child whose behavior destroyed the family's tranquility, even if there were no signs of mental deficiency. Kerlin cited illustrations from his casebook: Bessie was destructive, and when placed in an institution, "it did not pain her to see her mother leave"; Tom was an "incorrigible boy" with an ability to acquire knowledge, but "full of mischief and deceit"; Anne's mother was "flushed with exasperation while telling her trials"; and an unnamed little girl "of precocious intelligence" had exhausted "the family means to control this child in her violent explosions of temper." In 1879, when he reported these cases, Kerlin still regarded the children as salvageable with proper education. By the 1890s, however, he and most of his colleagues had changed their views; their troublesome child had become a mental and moral defective who seemed to require permanent custodial care.[42]

As states began to adopt compulsory education standards at the end of the century, the slow or backward child presented a problem in the public school as well as in the family. Slow learners in the classroom may not have needed the institutionalization Kerlin recommended, but their presence in public schools disrupted a teacher's educational goals. Children who did not keep up with the class were often behavior problems as well. In 1896 a desperate Philadelphia teacher sought help for one of her charges at the University of Pennsylvania laboratory of the psychologist Lightner Witmer. Witmer, who represented a new force in psychology, was interested in the clinical and applied aspects of what was still primarily a philosophical discipline. The fourteen-year-old boy brought to Witmer was a "chronic bad speller." Witmer diagnosed bad eyesight rather than the suspected mental retardation and prescribed glasses. The student returned to school much improved, and Witmer went on to establish a clinic in which psychology and medicine might be applied generally to children who defied the norms of the classroom.[43]

Academic psychology was at a crossroads in the 1890s; traditionalists disapproved of Witmer's efforts to create an applied psychology and to tie the field to medicine and to education. But others soon began to see a promising future in psychology devoted to school problems. Through the work at his Psychological Clinic Witmer proposed a multifaceted approach to children's intellects, using medical examinations and casework studies of the children's backgrounds as well as forms of mental testing. As with the first poor speller, Witmer found that when a child's physical ailments were treated and the home life improved, the student often returned far higher scores on the psychological tests. His clinic was, however, an unconventional institution for the identification of troublesome children, and the superintendents of training schools continued to find that the vast majority of "feebleminded" children came from parents who were themselves idiots, paupers, criminals, or insane, without possibility of regeneration.[44]

The social consequences of failing to address a child's ill health or school disabilities framed much of the professional debate over malnourished children and children with mental retardation. Although aware of the effects of grinding urban poverty on child health, pediatricians and their public health allies were optimistic about the results of providing mothers with a pure milk supply and information about feeding requirements. Training school superintendents had, by the end of the century, lost much of their earlier optimism about the promises of special education for their inmates, but they idealized the custodial institutions as places where these special children could grow up safe and secure and the family's hereditarian taint would not be passed to a new generation. They designed training schools to protect these special students from themselves and from the barbs of a callous community, and to safeguard society from the social consequences of "feeblemindedness."

A troublesome child for these specialists was, therefore, a child in trouble through no fault of its own. Blameless itself, the malnourished or "feebleminded" child was an offspring of family heredity and parental mismanagement. Innocent and fragile, both groups of children required special protection if they were to grow up to be productive members of the community who would not drain public resources. These end-of-the-century medical specialists made some forms of troublesome childhood quite visible social and professional concerns.

CHILD SAVERS

Physicians did not act alone in the construction of the turn-of-the-century troublesome child. They had a great deal of help from organized social welfare. Nowhere was the notion of a child's unique qualities, both the potential for trouble and the possibility of prevention, more clearly at work by the end of the nineteenth century than in the efforts of charities and the corrections community to combat juvenile delinquency. No image better represented the troublesome child than the street urchins and ragamuffins who roamed the cities unsupervised and eluded efforts of the law and the schools to control their independence. In the 1890s Jacob Riis, a New York City reporter, captured their faces on film and elicited public sympathy with his graphic portraits of the lives these children led. The urban child he photographed—poor, dirty, often from an immigrant family, malnourished, and usually in tattered clothes—was not always a delinquent, but by the end of the century, the juvenile delinquent was invariably presumed to be an urban child with many of these qualities.[45]

As the cities grew so did the perception that American society faced serious present and future problems because of the wretched conditions in which these children were reared. Recreational activities sponsored by settlement houses and playground associations, municipal programs to support probation officers, and state-funded reformatories to separate young people from adult criminals were among the many plans from turn-of-the-century "child savers," the reformers who made careers out of the redemption of distressing, disturbing, and annoying children. For many child savers, however, the paramount antidelinquency and crime prevention program was the juvenile court, a separate institution combining models of treatment and punishment and created to adjudicate only the cases involving young offenders.[46] The century-long concern with rowdy youths gave troublesome behavior social and legal definitions as well as medical ones.

As early as the 1820s "juvenile delinquency" presupposed a combination of poverty and youth that drew antebellum humanitarians to action. By establishing age-segregated reformatories, the planners hoped to correct misbehavior while protecting the innocence of young offenders from the immorality of adult criminals in jails and prisons. Massachusetts reformers helped lead the way, opening the Boston House of Reformation in 1826 and, in 1848, an alternative institution, the State Reform School for Boys, for delinquents who seemed not quite as hardened as those at the state's first reformatory. In Chicago, a much younger city, a reform school similar to those in Massachusetts opened in 1855, followed in the 1880s by the creation of "industrial schools," for troublesome children not actually convicted of criminal behavior.[47] In his study of Boston reformers Eric Schneider has connected this determination to institutionalize children separately from adults to a desire in public welfare circles to divide the poor into worthy and unworthy categories.[48] In light of the bourgeois sentimentality surrounding childhood, what more worthy, more blameless creature than a child?

By isolating delinquents in separate institutions away from immoral families and beyond the influence of adult paupers and criminals, nineteenth-century social reformers hoped to salvage lives and prevent more trouble and social burden when the children were grown up. Even in the heyday of industrial growth after the Civil War, when activists turned for explanations of delinquency and dependency to the hereditary principles of the Social Darwinists, humanitarians still hoped to lift young paupers out of dependency and turn young delinquents away from a lifetime of crime by putting them in a new environment. Aggressive child savers used the quasi-public Children's Aid Society and the Society for the Prevention of Cruelty to Children to remove youngsters from miserable family situations.[49]

Still other concerned Americans took their middle-class ideas about childhood, family, education, and industry directly to the slums. They lived in neighborhood settlement houses and provided local residents with both material and spiritual resources to combat the problems of turn-of-the-century cities. The story of Jane Addams, founder of Chicago's Hull House, was similar to that of many women of her age and class who participated in the settlement house movement. Although college-educated, they found limited opportunities for public expression of their abilities, so they created their own. Taught that motherhood was the epitome of women's self-sacrificing nature, many of these women, including Addams, rejected biological maternity for a social motherhood through which they hoped to rear a whole class of poor urban immigrants. A faith in the goodness of their impoverished neighbors contributed to what would become a uniquely Progressive contribution to the salvation of the troublesome child. These reformers proposed to guide the families so that, instead of being institutionalized, children could learn middle-class values at home.

Settlement house workers discovered that children suffered and were troublesome because the families of the poor often seemed to be in disarray. Charity men and women cared for families devastated by the effects of alcohol and for single-parent households in which fathers had deserted. In some cases illness kept parents from working, and poverty denied families even the most basic needs. But in many instances wages from work simply did not stretch far enough. Families turned to the charitable organizations for help when all else failed, and young children went to work to keep from going hungry. While aware that the causes of these family problems were rooted deep in the industrial capitalist economy at the turn of the century, the child savers nonetheless continued to equate family failure with moral shortcomings. In this tension between structural and moral explanations of social problems that was so much a part of the Progressive era of reform, saving the family often translated into service programs for the mothers.[50]

First at the settlement houses and later through the federal Children's Bureau, reformers fixed their gaze on the deficiencies of working-class mothers (their basic ignorance of current feeding, hygiene, and child-rearing standards, their failure to supervise their children, and often their "immoral" behavior).[51] Day nurseries, visiting nurses, and child-rearing classes were among the solutions proposed to improve the quality of mothering, strengthen families, and prevent the formation of troublesome children. Jane Addams observed first-hand the differences between immigrant culture and American middle-class family values that often brought children into clashes with the law. In *Twenty Years at Hull House* (1910) she recorded some examples:

> The honest immigrant parents, totally ignorant of American laws and municipal regulations, often send a child to pick up coal on the railroad tracks or to stand at three o'clock in the morning before the side door of a restaurant which gives away broken food, or to collect grain for the chickens at the base of elevators and standing cars. The latter custom accounts for the large number of boys arrested for breaking the seals on grain freight cars. It is easy for a child thus trained to accept the proposition of a junk dealer to bring him bars of iron stored in freight yards.[52]

In this environment the solution to juvenile delinquency lay in reprogramming parents directly, by teaching them the importance middle-class Americans attached to an unburdened childhood and, indirectly, by passing laws to regulate child labor.

The juvenile court movement brought together many of the ideas about reforming delinquent and dependent children. Although in turn-of-the-century medicine the child was no longer just a miniature adult, in the law the same standards still applied to anyone over age seven. When adult sentences seemed too harsh for a young person, the courts dismissed cases rather than punish with the strict standards applied to older criminals. For many jurists both options—harsh punishment and dismissal—were unsatisfactory. As it was practiced, the law fit neither the image of the good child nor the perceived needs of the troublesome one for training and rehabilitation. Midway through the nineteenth century, judges in Boston and New York began experimenting with separate court sessions for children and with probation programs to monitor children found guilty but not incarcerated. Boston had a self-proclaimed probation officer as of 1841; the court in that city began hearing juvenile cases separately in the 1870s. Independently in Denver, Judge Ben Lindsey, known as the "children's judge," reinterpreted the city's truancy law in order to hold special hearings for all young offenders, with the children required to report weekly to Lindsey himself. These programs, however, were improvised affairs.[53] Illinois lawmakers, spurred on by Chicago child savers, were the first to establish a regular "juvenile" court with separate informal sessions, indeterminate sentencing, and probation.

The story of the founding of the juvenile court movement has been told many times. In 1891 the Chicago Women's Club, a public-spirited group of child savers imbued with a faith in the possibility of remaking the lives of delinquent boys and girls, set out to legislate separate judicial hearings for youths. Club members achieved their goal on April 14, 1899, when the Illinois legislature approved the first juvenile court law, "an act to regulate the treatment and control of dependent, neglected and delinquent children." Other state legislatures, also caught up in the spirit of Progressive era child saving, soon followed the Illinois model. Within a decade ten states and the District of Columbia had established age-segregated courts. Although in Massachusetts Suffolk County courts already held Saturday juvenile sessions, the state legislature, spurred on by Boston civic organizers, created its own version of the Chicago juvenile court in 1905.[54]

In one piece of legislation the juvenile court acts consolidated nineteenth-century medical and charity definitions of the troublesome child. The Illinois law, modified in 1907, defined a "delinquent child" to be

> any male child who while under the age of seventeen years or any female child who while under the age of eighteen years, violates any law of this State; or is incorrigible, or knowingly associates with thieves, vicious or immoral persons; or who, without just cause and without the consent of its parents, guardian or custodian, absents itself from its home or place of abode, or is growing up in idleness or crime; or knowingly frequents a house of ill-repute; or knowingly frequents any policy shop or place where any gaming device is operated; or frequents any saloon or dram shop where intoxicating liquors are sold; or patronizes or visits any public pool room or bucket shop; or wanders about the streets in the night time without being on any lawful business or lawful occupation; or habitually wanders about any railroad yards or tracks or jumps or attempts to jump onto any moving train; or enters any car or engine without lawful authority; or habitually uses vile, obscene, vulgar, profane, or indecent language in any public place or about any school house; or is guilty of indecent or lascivious conduct.[55]

Creators of these laws never intended the juvenile court to try children accused of committing serious crimes. These cases were quickly relegated to adult court sessions. Joan Gittens, in her study of Chicago child welfare, calls the "crimes" for which the court was appropriate "cultural misunderstandings" and "childish misjudgments."[56] The law codified an image of juvenile delinquency as behavior more annoying than violent, more socially offensive than criminal. The juvenile court system of informal hearings and personalized justice with heavy reliance on supervision was supposed to catch the young offender early and forestall further criminal conduct through active intervention with the child and the family.

Juvenile court judges from Denver, Chicago, and Boston dispensed individualized justice, designed to fit the nineteenth-century child, not the offense. The system depended heavily on information collected by community agencies and eventually by probation officers. The hearings were informal affairs. Judge Harvey H. Baker in Boston preferred to sit on a raised platform to command respect, but other judges, particularly Lindsey in Denver, wanted to present themselves as a friend of the accused. Lindsey expected to develop a special relationship with each delinquent, and he encouraged his boys to report their progress or new transgressions to him each week in sessions he called "snitching bees."[57]

Lindsey's personalism, shared at least in theory by his colleagues in other juvenile courts, was a blend of justice, religious conversion, and therapy. The judge heard confession, divined prescriptions to cure the causes of delinquency, and meted out sentences. In this context, delinquency could be viewed as the actions of good children with poor models and poor training. After a juvenile court "trial" it was the probation officer who supplied both model and training for the young offender. When Lindsey created the special court in Denver he acted as his own probation officer, but as the juvenile court movement took hold, paid probation officers moved between the court and the child's family, working to put in place the judges' recommendations.

Jane Addams recorded in 1910 that four-fifths of the children at Chicago's juvenile court were the "children of foreigners." Peter Holloran's survey of the Boston court from 1907 to 1927 confirms Addams's count. In 1917, the mid-year of Holloran's survey, 52 percent of Boston's delinquents came from Irish, Italian, or Jewish families. Holloran also found that 50 percent of the children came from families with fathers working at semi-skilled or unskilled occupations. Another 5 percent of the fathers were unemployed.[58] Poor and the sons and daughters of recent immigrants or perhaps immigrants themselves, these young offenders did not share the cultural heritage and class background of the framers of the juvenile justice system. As Eric Schneider has concluded about the Boston court, the juvenile justice program was a device that "remained mired in the class and cultural conflicts it was supposed to rise above."[59]

There is no doubt that class control motivated the child savers who created the juvenile court, but it is equally important to recognize the determination to regulate behavior based on conceptions of age. A reading of the list of offenses in the juvenile court act suggests that lawmakers believed behavior not necessarily illegal but inappropriate for the age of the "offender" was to be the target of juvenile justice. The fact that four-fifths of the children seen in the Chicago juvenile court came from immigrant families suggests the environment in which they grew up—the same neighborhoods with pool rooms, saloons, and railroad yards. Of course the court was designed to instill middle-class values in urban, working-class youths, but the court's definition of misconduct was so broad that, as social conditions changed in the twentieth century, its brand of social control and particularly its definition of "trouble" could just as well be applied to youth from any class.

Expectations for the juvenile court ran high; it was the cornerstone of the child-saving movement. The court combined the child savers' vision of a malleable troublesome (poor, immigrant) delinquent and the medical professionals' commitment to the prevention of future personal ills and social problems. Child savers assumed that through use of the court's great discretionary power, the judges and probation officers would treat the child's misbehavior, provide child and family with a guiding hand, and see to it that the trouble did not recur during childhood and did not evolve into an even bigger (adult) social problem. Having defined the troublesome child as amenable to change through judicial intervention, the coalition that pushed forward the juvenile court had little recourse when its efforts failed, or, as the Progressives put it, when juvenile justice met up with the delinquent "recidivist." The recidivist, or repeat offender, sparked criticism of the juvenile court movement, but the court's apparent failure with some children did not lessen enthusiasm in Progressive circles for juvenile justice. The juvenile court and its personalized justice for children remained the mainstay of relations between young people and the legal system until legal challenges in the 1960s questioned the constitutionality of its proceedings and forced reform.[60]

Ellen Key's promise that the upcoming century belonged to "the child" reflected decades of public and private concern about children, and years during which childhood underwent a process of dichotomization. The "priceless" child, the child as consumer rather than producer, the innocent, vulnerable, dependent child who needed gentle nurture to become a conscientious adult, these were the children created in middle-class families, mothers' clubs, and sentimental novels.[61] Bourgeois Victorian culture identified childhood as a separate, special time of life, a time for guidance and for pampering, at least by the standards of previous centuries. While compelling, these images were only a partial representation of the nineteenth-century child. Along with the cherubic goodness so generously depicted in Victorian fiction and promised in ladies' magazines came its antithesis—the troublesome child. As Victorian cultural standard-bearers painted a picture of "the child," their medical and charitable counterparts designed filters through which to view "the other."

There were many different models of troublesome children at the end of the nineteenth century. Some practiced bad habits; others were physically ill or emotionally troubled; still others were children with signs of "feeble-mindedness." Some were stubborn, annoying, strong-willed, independent, and often transgressors of the law. Whatever their specific identifying traits, the troublesome children of public discourse shared a few common characteristics. First, troublesome children usually came from a specific social background. The children who regularly contravened public mores were poor; they came from families of immigrants; and they usually lived in cities. The troublesome child was an urban problem flourishing among the lower classes. This is not to deny ongoing concern about middle-class children. Mothers' manuals and records of mothers' clubs throughout the century attest to that concern. In these presentations, however, as in the discussions of the alienists and neurologists, the troublesome child was a private peril whose plight contributed little to the public discourse of child saving. In popular discourse, troublesome children came from impoverished homes and they were emblematic of the anxiety-producing economic and social changes brought on by industrial capitalism.

Second, the trouble these children caused was not horrific. It may have disrupted family tranquility or challenged middle-class ideas of personal morality or social order, but the troublesome child was not on the same scale as a Jesse Pomeroy, the fourteen-year-old who tortured young boys and in 1874 murdered a neighborhood girl and hid her body in the basement of his mother's shop.[62] As Ellen Key's century of awareness opened, child savers emphasized the troublesome child's age as well as the trouble he or she caused. Child savers surrounded these children with the same sentimentality that enveloped middle-class childhood.

Finally, this symbol of social upheaval also held out a solution to the many problems tackled by Progressive reformers. If left to grow up without restraint and supervision, troublesome children promised to become the nation's burdensome adults—the criminals, defectives, and dependents who drained the public treasury, threatened class warfare, and made urban life so unpleasant. Child savers, however, believed troublesome children could be reformed and made middle class through wholesome programs and education, designed with consideration paid to the child's youthfulness. At its worst, trouble could be contained through institutionalization. In either case, troublesome children (and the social conflict they represented) would be shorn of the power to produce social chaos.

These troublesome children—poor, delinquent, sickly, possibly "feebleminded," with bad habits created by a bad environment or reflecting a flawed hereditary makeup—were the ones inherited by the reformers who launched the child guidance movement. When the specially designed programs failed to change the life course of some delinquents, a group of Chicago child savers led by Ethel Sturges Dummer cast about for the means to improve the effectiveness of their new juvenile court. Their efforts, the subject of the next chapter, established the theoretical framework for a psychological interpretation of juvenile delinquency and the institutional model for a professional diagnosis of the causes of troublesome behavior.

2

William Healy and the
Progressive Child Savers

Psychiatry and psychology, sometimes referred to as the new "sciences of human conduct," entered Chicago juvenile delinquency work through the research investigations and clinical practice of the Juvenile Psychopathic Institute (JPI). Progressive child savers created the JPI as an agency from which the juvenile court could seek medical and psychological evaluations of its most perplexing cases. The opening of the institute in April 1909 signaled the frustration of local activists with their juvenile justice system. Despite the court's intervention many youths reappeared a second, or even a third, time in the judge's chambers. Fearing that these youths might be mentally "abnormal," Chicago child savers hoped to apply new insights from disciplines devoted to investigating human behavior and the human mind. Their effort to incorporate the broad field of psychology into the search for an answer to the problem of juvenile crime is the substance of this chapter.

The story of the JPI belongs to two individuals: Ethel Sturges Dummer and William Healy. Committed to the traditions of Progressive reform and wealthier than many of the activists with whom she worked, Ethel Sturges Dummer provided both inspiration and financing for the JPI. William Healy was the institute's first director and author of the clinic's major research study, *The Individual Delinquent* (1915). An 800-page interpretation of the causes of delinquency based on the records of youths examined at the clinic, *The Individual Delinquent* became a standard reference for American criminologists and a guide for later child guidance practitioners.

Because of his part in the success of the Juvenile Psychopathic Institute and the influence of his efforts to study the individual psychology of delinquents, William Healy is widely regarded by psychologists and psychiatrists as one of the fathers of American child guidance. If so, then Ethel Dummer is surely one of its mothers, and both parents contributed to the genesis of the child guidance movement.

The labels attached to these two figures—Progressive, professional, maternalist, and child saver—provide a context to the story of their Juvenile Psychopathic Institute and the origins of child guidance. No single definition of Progressivism satisfies all historians, but I use the term as a general description of the spirit of dis-ease that motivated many activists to look for new ways to come to terms with the social and economic changes of the early twentieth century. The moral overtones of Progressivism have been well documented. Yet the Progressives' approach to reform was usually pragmatic, and much of their activism demonstrated a broad environmentalism. Moreover, the Progressives discussed in this chapter regarded scientific research as a tool for social betterment. As Jane Addams, director of Hull House, told reporters in 1909, the founders believed that Healy's work at the JPI would "get at the root of the exact causes of why children go wrong." With evidence collected at the clinic, Progressive reformers expected to combat urban crime with publicly funded child-saving programs.[1]

"Child saver" is a title more politically charged than Progressive. Among historians who interpret early twentieth-century activism as a form of social control, the term "child saver" has come to signify the social service agent who believed in the righteousness of middle-class family values and set out to disrupt and "Americanize" working-class and immigrant cultures. To "save" the children was to rescue them from circumstances the reformers considered inferior and corrupting. Here I employ the term with less opprobrium, to describe the awareness of some activists that young people were particularly at risk in an era of dramatic social upheaval. Child savers took steps, some more culturally sensitive than others, to mitigate that risk.[2]

Maternalism is also a word with significant political baggage. Feminist studies of social welfare characterize as maternalists the women activists who remade the American welfare system by designing programs specifically for women and children. The historians Seth Koven and Sonya Michel note that these women "transformed motherhood from women's primary *private* responsibility into *public* policy," hence the designation "maternalist." The Chicago women discussed in this chapter—Jane Addams, Julia Lathrop, Edith Abbott, Sophinisba Breckinridge—have been singled out as purveyors of this perspective. After achieving positions of authority, often in government agencies, maternalists acted as powerful patrons of other women, creating, as Robyn Muncy has argued, a "female dominion" in Progressive reform.[3]

In practice, precise distinctions among the terms are difficult to maintain. Early twentieth-century social activists of both genders, whatever the label, shared a commitment to the value of scientific investigation (even if they were not scientific investigators themselves). Many displayed a sensitivity to the social or environmental aspects of dependency and delinquency, even when they chastised the morals and manners of the lower classes whom they tried to save. And Progressives in general pursued a legislative agenda. I have reserved "maternalism" for activities specifically directed toward support and service programs for women and children, and I have adopted the more general term "child saving" for any form of activism with childhood as the focus.

Ethel Dummer certainly qualified as a maternalist; her sympathies were often captured by educational programs for women and services for economically disadvantaged children. The dominion she helped to create through her patronage of the Juvenile Psychopathic Institute, however, was a professional one that would diminish the Progressive agenda. In the context of early twentieth-century child welfare, the title of "professional" is as difficult to confer as are the labels of reform. Maternalists could (and did) claim as much knowledge about child behavior and as much authority to deliver regulatory programs as those certified with academic degrees in psychology or medicine. Scientific investigation was valued by both camps. Some reformers were respected researchers, and some practicing physicians and psychiatrists were best known as reformers. The task here is to examine why Ethel Dummer and her Progressive allies expected the sciences of human conduct to improve the work of the juvenile court, and to examine the efforts of William Healy to meet the Progressives' challenge at the Juvenile Psychopathic Institute. Child guidance was a product of cooperation between these two perspectives. Through Dummer's support of Healy and the clinic, child savers added a psychological component to their interpretation of juvenile crime. As Healy undertook the research sought by child savers, he blended the Progressives' sensitivity to environmental factors into a study of the child's mind. Their combined efforts created a place in the work of child saving for the clinical child behavior expert and a new "individual" persona for the troublesome child.[4]

PROGRESSIVE PATRONAGE AND THE JUVENILE PSYCHOPATHIC INSTITUTE

Born in 1866, Ethel Sturges Dummer was for much of her life an activist on behalf of women, children, and mental hygiene. The daughter and wife of bankers, she used her position and wealth to support a broad range of philanthropic projects. In 1906 a magazine article on child labor drew her into the Chicago Juvenile Protective Association, where she became an eager child saver and energetic supporter of the new juvenile court.[5] Many years after the opening of the Juvenile Psychopathic Institute, Dummer recalled that she had been especially troubled by "children who without rhyme or reason repeated some one symptom of delinquency, either stealing, lying, or sex offense."[6] When the court placed young offenders on probation, about 20 percent of the boys and 45 percent of the girls soon committed new offenses. Judge Merritt W. Pinckney of the juvenile court organized a small "research committee on delinquency" in 1908 to study the problem of recidivism. Ethel Dummer was one of the participants, along with Julia Lathrop, the Chicago settlement house worker soon to head the federal Children's Bureau, and William Healy, a local physician. This committee conceived the plan for the Juvenile Psychopathic Institute.[7]

For Progressive era child savers, delinquency was a complicated problem that could be profitably explored from many different angles. Passing legislation to create a juvenile court was only a first step. As noted in Chapter 1, some juvenile court supporters attributed the high recidivism rates to a lack of separate facilities for young offenders, and they set about creating a detention center and a reform "school" for Chicago's delinquents. Hull House sponsored recreational clubs to keep boys and girls off the streets and out of saloons and dance halls. Advocates for the National Playground Association found sympathetic ears among the Chicago reformers.[8] In a memoir Dummer explained that by creating the Juvenile Psychopathic Institute she and other members of Judge Pinckney's committee wanted to understand why some children seemed impervious to the "right education" and the "interesting activities" offered by existing programs.[9]

At the time Dummer believed all recidivists were "abnormal" or "mentally inferior," a view held by many in the field. The group named their new clinic the Juvenile Psychopathic Institute to designate this belief, and turned to the medical and psychological sciences to provide direction for the undertaking. "Psychopathy" sometimes referred to a mental disease without a neurological base, but increasingly in the early twentieth century the term diagnosed a condition or state of mind that lay somewhere between normality and insanity. It was this latter definition that the committee employed.[10]

To direct the new project, the group hoped to find "a physician with special experience in mental and nervous diseases in children and with an understanding of the methods of modern psychology," as Dummer wrote in an announcement about the JPI.[11] Locating such a child specialist would have been a difficult task in the early twentieth century. Both pediatrics and child study (the component of psychology devoted to research on children) were new fields with few practitioners. Changes in the practice of psychiatry, discussed in more detail later in the chapter, helped focus the committee's attention on practitioners from that specialty. After its first choice, Dr. Harry Linenthal of Roxbury, Massachusetts, rejected an offer, the committee eventually selected one of its own, William Healy, the Chicago physician who had helped the committee with its preliminary investigation of existing psychological clinics.[12]

William Healy was an unassuming forty-year-old medical practitioner when appointed director of the Juvenile Psychopathic Institute in 1909. His biography reads like a "luck and pluck" story by Horatio Alger. Born in 1869, Healy was the son of poor tenant farmers from Buckinghamshire County in central England. When the boy was nine, he and his family left England for the United States, settling first in Rochester and then in Chicago. The family's economic fortunes did not improve quickly in the new country, and poverty forced Healy to leave school at thirteen. While working in a bank Healy educated himself and, with help from friends in the Ethical Culture Society, made his way to Harvard University and Harvard Medical School (although he finished his medical training at Chicago's Rush Medical College in 1900). In 1906, following in the footsteps of many other physicians of his generation, Healy journeyed to Europe for a year of postgraduate work in research laboratories. Returning to Chicago a year later, he joined a private practice in neurology.[13]

Several reasons probably accounted for the committee's choice of William Healy to head its project. Both Healy and his wife, Mary Tenney Healy, belonged to the circle of Chicago child savers. Healy had taught a course on the psychological aspects of delinquency and dependency for charity workers at the Chicago School of Civics and Philanthropy (where Ether Dummer was a trustee). Although he had no special expertise with children, Healy was a physician with Progressive leanings and an interest in the problem of criminal behavior. As a participant during the project's planning stage, Healy avidly endorsed the proposed institute. In a letter to Julia Lathrop, Healy predicted that the resulting study would "be as classical as that of [Italian criminologist Cesare] Lombroso . . . and a thousand times more practically beneficial." Moreover, he had the support of the Harvard philosopher William James (with whom he had studied) and the noted Johns Hopkins psychiatrist Adolf Meyer, whose work was already redefining the outlines of that specialty. With backing from such men Healy promised to bring the new institute the respect of the medical and psychological research communities as well as a commitment from local child savers.[14]

The founding committee posed two tasks for the institute's new director—he would be both researcher and clinician. On the one hand, the clinic was to be an extension of the judge's chambers. Through medical and psychological examinations of young offenders, Healy would assist the judge in adjudicating cases of recidivism. When announcing the opening of the Juvenile Psychopathic Institute Jane Addams predicted that once Healy had studied a delinquent "we will then be in a position to know exactly the status of the child's case and how to deal with it."[15] On the other hand, the Chicago child savers believed in the value of scientific research, particularly if it was designed to find explanations for the problems plaguing early twentieth-century cities. Dummer and her allies wanted Healy to determine the "root" cause of juvenile crime from the data collected about the medical, psychological, and social backgrounds of seemingly incorrigible, repeat offenders. From the research Healy conducted at the Juvenile Psychopathic Institute, the Chicago child savers intended to devise new ways for the community to attack the problem of juvenile delinquency.[16]

In correspondence with Ethel Dummer during and after his tenure at the JPI, Healy acknowledged his personal indebtedness to the Chicago activist and child saver. The director justified the clinic's expenses, apprised her of his work, promised results, and cleared staff appointments with her. Dummer responded with encouragement, sent copies of books and articles meant to educate Healy, and paid the bills. Through her patronage Healy began a career as a clinician and a delinquency research specialist, work that would continue for more than thirty years. More important, through the patronage of Dummer and her allies, Healy constructed the research scaffolding for child guidance professionalism.

THE INDIVIDUAL DELINQUENT

Healy fulfilled the research component of his assignment in 1915 with publication of *The Individual Delinquent: A Text-book of Diagnosis and Prognosis for All Concerned in Understanding Offenders*. He dedicated the book to his patron, Ethel Dummer, and the influence of the Chicago Progressives was evident in the attention he gave to social and cultural determinants of behavior. Yet in the same volume Healy also began to establish an independent perspective on the causes of delinquency, one that emphasized the individuality of each child, the multifaceted causes of delinquency, and the emotional content of the child's mind. Ultimately there would be little room in this new, professionally driven, psychological explanation of juvenile crime for the delinquency prevention work, the environmentalist interpretations of conduct, or the advocacy of broad-scale legislative programs so familiar to Healy's sponsors.

In *The Individual Delinquent* Healy rejected the popular reliance on overly simplistic, deterministic theories of causation, holdovers from nineteenth-century interpretations of dependency and delinquency. No child, he argued, should be approached with a priori assumptions about the causes of delinquency; broad generalizations such as "crime is a disease" seemed "dubiously cheap" in light of investigations at the JPI. He also questioned the relationship between delinquency and psychopathology implicit in the name Dummer and her allies had given to the clinic. Instead, the study of recidivists appeared to prove that categories of "normal" and "abnormal" could not be used to predict delinquent acts, and Healy did not have "the slightest inclination to place delinquents as such in the list of abnormal individuals."[17] In 1914, when the Cook County government assumed financial responsibility for psychological examinations of delinquents, Healy's admonitions registered in the clinic's new name—the Institute for Juvenile Research.

At the turn of the century the psychopathological interpretation of crime often merged with hereditarian explanations of conduct. Those who followed the criminal anthropologist Cesare Lombroso looked for (and usually found) "stigmata of degeneracy"—the inherited, physical and mental signs of criminality—in juvenile delinquents. During the Progressive years these ideas were ensconced in a popular eugenics movement that hoped to improve the social order by applying hereditarian principles to reproduction. Though once holding membership in a eugenics society,

Healy by 1915 had begun to reject the theory that criminal tendencies were inherited. At times it was only a qualified rejection of these hereditarian beliefs, but in a specialized study of the role of inherited traits in a thousand repeat offenders, Healy and coauthor Edith Spaulding emphatically concluded that "the idea of bare criminalistic traits, especially in their hereditary aspects, is an unsubstantiated metaphysical hypothesis." At the JPI, juvenile delinquents were made, not born.[18]

Likewise, Healy questioned the common assumption that juvenile delinquents were inevitably "feebleminded." Test findings from the JPI did not support the more extreme views of Healy's psychologist colleague Henry H. Goddard from the Vineland, New Jersey, Training School for Backward and Feeble-minded Children. In 1915 Goddard's name stood for the belief that "delinquent" and "moron" (a term applied to the high-functioning "feebleminded") were interchangeable labels. Goddard's genealogical study, *The Kallikack Family* (1912), made quite an impression on the social welfare community. Supporters easily found evidence in prison populations to uphold the belief that "mental defect" accounted for criminal behavior. Although acknowledging that some delinquents at the JPI showed signs of low intelligence, Healy argued that "one rarely finds personal characteristics [such as low IQ] as a sole causative factor of criminalism."[19]

Healy called these contemporary theories "interesting and even seductive, intellectually," but also found them fundamentally flawed. Since they were based on aggregate data, none of the theories could explain every delinquent Healy examined at the clinic.[20] In their place, Healy offered a complicated web of "causative factors" unique for each child (see Figure 2.1). The specific set of factors might include a delinquent's heredity or mental ability, but no one factor was a sufficient explanation and the cause of delinquency could be uncovered only by thoroughly examining the physical status, emotional life, intellectual capacity, and environmental background of each child. "It disturbs us little to find the array of facts [in each case] too rich to permit the use of hard-and-fast lines of classification," Healy wrote in *The Individual Delinquent*. "Indeed, it is often by perception of the issues which emerge from the interweaving of factors that the greatest hope for the whole situation in handling the offender arises."[21] The causes of delinquency were complex and multifaceted; if the problem were to be understood at all, it would have to be at the individual level.

In *The Individual Delinquent* Healy presented twenty general categories of "causative factors," and provided an abundance of specific illustrations for each. For example, one chapter was titled "Physical Conditions: Peculiarities, Ailments," and in it Healy discussed "ocular ailments," "syphilis," and "undernourishment" as circumstances that might contribute to delinquent behavior. A case from that chapter was typical of Healy's approach to crime. Healy described the offenses of a fourteen-year-old boy as begging and being "quite unwilling to work at any honest occupation." The physical examination revealed an inflammation of the eyelids that caused tears to run down the boy's face. The parents, living in poverty, had sent their son out to beg, using his tears to elicit sympathy and alms. As Healy reformulated the problem, poverty, poor parental management, and an infection combined to create this particular delinquent.[22]

"Causative factors" in *The Individual Delinquent* ranged from love of

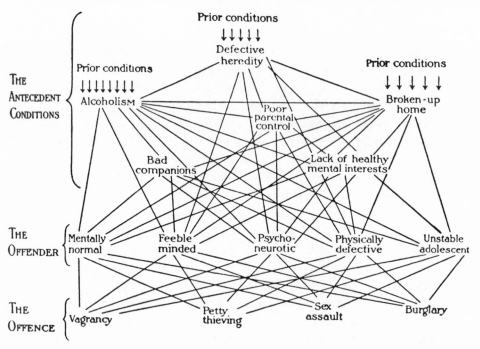

DIAGRAM OF SEQUENCE OR CONJUNCTION OF SOME SIMPLE ANTECEDENTS AND
CONSEQUENTS

Figure 2.1 Healy's web of causation, demonstrating the complex nature of juvenile delinquency. William Healy, *The Individual Delinquent* (Boston: Little, Brown and Co., 1915), p. 165.

adventure to home conditions, mental retardation, masturbation, "mental conflict," social suggestibility, adolescence, epilepsy, tea, cocoa and coffee, "incompetent parental control," movies and "pernicious stories," poverty, parental neglect, bad companions, and more. The causes of delinquency were developmental, physical, environmental, and psychological, and most often Healy found that only a combination of factors would fully explain a specific case.

As he did with all general theories, Healy advised against overemphasizing environmentalism to the exclusion of other important "causative factors." Still he devoted two complete chapters of *The Individual Delinquent* to "defective home conditions." The category signified both the moral worth of the child's family and the material circumstances in which the child and family lived, a dual meaning also evident in other contemporary studies of juvenile offenders.[23] Healy found that the influence of an alcoholic parent contributed to delinquency, as did parental quarreling, nagging, or teasing. Poverty, however, both directly and indirectly, also explained juvenile crime. "After all," Healy wrote, "respect for parents, and for the integrity of family relationships, and for the human body itself, is largely the basis of the morality of our civilization, and nothing so easily militates against it as crowded living conditions [caused by economic need]." Other negative environmental influences came from schools that placed students in inappropriate classes, from theaters and newspapers depicting lurid tales of crime, from peers with delinquent interests, and from "social allurements," a phrase referring to saloons, dance halls, and the fine, but for many youths unaffordable, clothes displayed in store windows.[24]

The shallowness of Healy's environmentalism is evident, however, when his work is compared with studies from other Progressive delinquency researchers. Three years before the appearance of *The Individual Delinquent*, Edith Abbott and Sophonisba P. Breckinridge also published a study of Chicago delinquents, *The Delinquent Child and the Home* (1912). As social researchers and directors of the Department of Social Investigation of the Chicago School of Civics and Philanthropy (where Healy had once lectured on crime), these women had intimate ties to the community of maternalist Progressives in Chicago. Much more so than Healy, the two activists spoke the language of class and culture when discussing the troublesome behavior of young people.[25]

On the basis of their study of juvenile crime in Cook County, Abbott and Breckinridge concluded that most delinquents grew up in "delinquent families" residing in working-class and immigrant communities. A working mother was one common symptom of a delinquent family, but, the researchers concluded, "there is no phase of family misery which is not illustrated in [the] fearful picture of a bad child's progress." To prevent delinquency, every child needed "the same conditions: homes of physical and moral decency, fresh air, education, recreation, the fond care of wise fathers and mothers." These were the elements Abbott and Breckinridge found missing in the families whose sons and daughters repeatedly made their way to the juvenile court. As a result, the two researchers found entirely "baffling" the relatively rare instances of middle-class delinquency encountered during their study.[26]

Because they thought the environmental sources of delinquency the most difficult to overcome, Abbott and Breckinridge called for a method to handle neglected children that would "take into account not an isolated child, but a child in a certain family and amid certain neighborhood surroundings." For these Progressives no single institute or court could be expected to "instantly produce from chaos" the "essentials" needed to transform a delinquent family into a nondelinquent one.[27] To bring about change required fundamentally new interventions, and it was maternalist reformers such as Abbott and Breckinridge who pushed successfully for passage of mothers' pensions laws, for example. If poverty forced widows to work outside the home instead of supervising their children, direct financial assistance from the state enabling mothers to stay home was one possible solution to the problem of juvenile delinquency.[28]

In contrast, Healy's examinations uncovered families with many children only one of whom was accused of delinquent activity, leading him to conclude that juvenile crime was best understood by examining individual reactions to a specific environment. In 1915 Healy named his approach "characterology"; how a child responded to the circumstances of his or her life, whether "mental defect" or environmental influences, was unique to that child and depended on idiosyncrasies embedded in the child's mind. "He who would know the sources of misdeeds," Healy advised, "must study the quirks and turns and conflicts and disabilities of the human mind and what causes them."[29] "Quirks and turns" led one child into a criminal career while another from a similar background with similar handicaps followed a more law-abiding path to adulthood. Healy did not discount a relationship between social environment and delinquency. Instead, as he indicated in the title of his book, his was an approach that assumed "the dynamic center of the whole problem of delinquency and crime will ever be the individual offender."[30]

Healy presented *The Individual Delinquent* as a work of general principles and procedures that might apply to "either a young offender or an older criminal."[31] Crime was the subject, not developmental age. In his first major publication Healy felt compelled to justify a model of criminality based solely on an examination of *juvenile* delinquents. Criminal careers usually began in youth, he reminded readers. The "disingenuousness of the offender is a barrier [to the study of causation] . . . [and] for this reason it is important . . . to approach the delinquent in the years of naiveté." And of course "the best rewards of therapeutic efforts" could be achieved by working with a young offender.[32] Everything was so much closer to the surface in a child—newer, more raw. The opportunities to uncover the "quirks and turns" of the mind were therefore much greater in the young, and also much greater was the possibility of straightening the kinks. Despite the patronage of the Chicago child savers, in 1915 Healy presented himself as a student of childhood by default. When, however, his criminology research was combined with the child savers' fervent desire to keep young offenders from becoming recidivists and with their investment in the institutional structure for the study of juvenile delinquency, Healy's work at the JPI helped to make the mental processes of children significant in their own right.

In sum, both the JPI and *The Individual Delinquent* were evidence of the unique Progressive blend of scientific investigation and practical application that often motivated reformers to turn to the medical sciences for help with social problems.[33] William Healy met the expectations of Dummer and her associates by compiling the characteristics of Cook County delinquents. Healy's troublesome children came from poor neighborhoods, had few Progressive-approved recreational opportunities, and perhaps displayed physical or intellectual weaknesses. Healy proved to the child welfare community that the delinquents were "normal," not psychopathic and usually not "feebleminded." Thus he gave the Progressives reason to hope that the social welfare programs they sponsored could prevent young people from committing crimes.

Yet as he buttressed the maternalist impulses of his patrons, Healy also psychologized the problem of juvenile delinquency. The individual delinquent was a mind at risk, one with unique personality characteristics that filtered and interpreted a situation in such a way that misbehavior was the outcome. A few of them showed signs of emotional conflict. The specific act of delinquency did not indicate the "causative factors" involved or suggest how seriously maladjusted a child might be. Minor infractions were often just the surface manifestations of deep-seated problems. After publication of *The Individual Delinquent* child savers faced the prospect that only a thorough investigation of the individual child, the family, and the community would uncover the explanation, or diagnosis, because the causes of each child's wrongdoing were idiosyncratic. There was, Healy replied to the child savers' request, no single "root" cause of juvenile crime.

INTELLECTUAL MENTORS: HALL, MEYER, AND FREUD

Healy constructed his views on crime—the importance of the individual diagnosis and the value of a scientific study of children—in the intellectual environment created by broad changes taking place in the fields of psychology and psychiatry. When Healy argued that complex mental processes determined each delinquent's behavior he demonstrated his debt to Adolf Meyer and Sigmund Freud, two figures whose ideas transformed American psychiatry in the early twentieth century. It was the psychologist G. Stanley Hall, however, whose devotion to the scientific study of childhood did much more than Meyer or Freud to give credibility to inquiries about the minds of young people. By the time Healy published the results of the JPI investigations, Hall's reputation as a researcher had declined significantly, but from the 1880s to the early 1900s the name G. Stanley Hall stood for psychological research about childhood. Hall called the field "child study."

Hall trained as a psychologist in the European laboratory of Karl Wundt, whose experimental approach to psychology distinguished his students from those schooled in an older philosophical study of the mind. In 1882 Hall assumed a post at Johns Hopkins University, where he was among a handful of academicians for whom the study of psychology meant scientific research in the laboratory. Imbued also with an interest in pedagogy and a firm belief that evolutionary biology could explain developmental changes in the individual child, Hall began his child study career with a project on "the contents of children's minds." First Hall wanted to know what knowledge young people possessed when they began school, but he did not stop with the factual content of their minds. His research also explored beliefs and feelings. The results, published in 1883, brought him the immediate acclaim of American educators. For a few years after this article's publication Hall's career took him in other directions. Then, during the 1890s, Hall returned to the study of children with renewed enthusiasm. Hall and the students he trained at Hopkins and later at Clark University in Worcester, Massachusetts, made a place for children in the research agendas of experimental psychologists.[34]

To be sure, Hall was not the first nineteenth-century scientist to make the child an object of psychological or developmental study (although he was one of the first to turn the study into a career). Contemporary developmental psychologists usually locate their historical roots in the work of Charles Darwin, the father of evolutionary biology. After publication of *Origin of Species* in 1859, Darwin turned to observing the instinctive behavior and emotions of children. In *The Expression of the Emotions in Man and Animal* (1872), Darwin pointed out difficulties in studying adult emotions and suggested that observations of children (or the insane) might provide greater insight. Darwin's stature in child studies, however, is more often credited to the publication in 1877 of a "Biographical Sketch of an Infant," a record of the physical and psychological development of his son. Drawn by Darwin's work, the German physiologist Wilhelm Preyer also closely traced his son's development and offered his observations as commentary on the psychology of childhood. Published as *The Mind of the Child* (and translated by Hall in 1889), Preyer's work stimulated a rash of similar "baby biographies." Prior to these publications some parents probably kept private diaries of their children's emotions and behavior. It now appeared, as the historian Alice Boardman Smuts has written, that with the blessing of G. Stanley Hall and child study, "such records were not only of personal interest but possibly also of scientific value."[35] Children, it seemed, could be observed and studied as part of efforts by physiologists, psychologists, and philosophers to understand the causes of human behavior.

In delinquency studies, the name G. Stanley Hall is less often associated with studies of infants and young children than with his survey of adolescent emotions published in 1904 as *Adolescence: Its Psychology and its Relation to Physiology, Anthropology, Sociology, Sex, Crime, Religion, and Education.* For Hall the two-volume *Adolescence* represented the culmination of his thinking about the relationship between psychology and biology. Scientifically rigorous experimental psychologists who came after Hall, including William Healy, called *Adolescence* more philosophy than science.

Yet even though there are few direct references to G. Stanley Hall in *The Individual Delinquent*, his presence is evident in the very possibility of a scientific investigation of the mind of the adolescent delinquent. Moreover, professional skepticism did not diminish Hall's popularity with the public. New York City mothers formed a "child study" group, an idea that later spread nationwide. *Adolescence* became required reading for parents, teachers, and recreation directors.[36] During the JPI years Healy worked in the shadow cast by G. Stanley Hall's psychological studies of the child.

In contrast to Hall's oblique influence, the psychiatrist Adolf Meyer directly shaped both the work of the Juvenile Psychopathic Institute and the design of *The Individual Delinquent*. While Hall represented new interests in pedagogy and psychology, Meyer symbolized a new dynamic psychiatry, one wedded to the promotion of mental health rather than to the custodial care of the mentally ill. When the Chicago child savers asked Healy to undertake delinquency research, Adolf Meyer was already considered one of the eminent men of American psychiatry. Meyer settled in Chicago after arriving in the United States in 1892 with a medical degree from the University of Zurich. During his years in Chicago, and later at the Illinois Eastern Hospital for the Insane, Meyer began to question somatic explanations of insanity and to apply, instead, a holistic approach to mental illness. In 1908 Meyer became director of the Henry Phipps Psychiatric Clinic at the Johns Hopkins School of Medicine, and from that position he influenced at least two generations of practitioners.[37]

"Psychobiology," Meyer's interpretive framework for psychological problems, repudiated mind-body distinctions that had driven late nineteenth-century psychiatrists to search for somatic explanations. Meyer urged psychiatrists to study instead the "whole man," and he dismissed dogmatic "systems" of explanation in favor of a method that integrated social, psychological, and physical aspects of human life. The dynamic psychiatry advocated by Meyer located the cause of mental illness in a lack of fit, or maladjustment, between the individual and the environment. According to Meyer maladjustment could be caused by many factors, including heredity, social and family background, physical health, and personality characteristics; in some instances he accepted the notion that the maladjustment could be "psychogenic" (originating in instinctual conflicts). Healy's understanding of the relationship between misconduct and mental processes was built on Meyer's approach to mental illness.[38]

Psychobiology also drew attention to the relationship between mental illness and troubling social problems. Meyer's dynamic psychiatry directed psychiatrists to move out of asylums to gain closer contact with community life. "One of the most important lessons of modern psychiatry is the absolute necessity of going beyond the asylum walls and of working where things have their beginnings," Meyer told an audience at the New York Academy of Medicine in 1909.[39] The expansive climate created by these views led to the establishment in several cities of new types of institutions for psychiatric practice. Some were out-patient dispensaries added to traditional nineteenth-century asylums; others were independent psychopathic hospitals. Within both institutions psychiatrists expected to address problems early, before the symptoms degenerated into mental illness. The dispensaries and hospitals permitted short stays for observation and treatment while psychiatrists assessed the need for longer periods of commitment. Most important, as Elizabeth Lunbeck has shown, the new institutions brought under the psychiatrists' gaze problems of marriage, work, and sexuality previously considered outside the bounds of psychiatry.[40]

Childhood was one of the first "problems" discovered when Meyer asked his colleagues to look beyond the asylum. Families, schools, and social service agencies appealed to the staff of the new outpatient facilities for help with obstreperous youth. For example, during its first five years of operation (1913–1918), 40 percent of the patients at the Boston Psychopathic Hospital were children or adolescents. Likewise, the dispensary of the Phipps Psychiatric Clinic at Johns Hopkins Hospital, opened in April 1913, treated 236 youths under sixteen years of age out of a total of 708 patients. Children were "by far the largest group seen," according to dispensary director, C. Macfie Campbell. When Meyerian institutions brought children into psychiatric practice, attendants often found that the rigid classifications of traditional psychiatric textbooks did not fit the facts of childhood. Dispensary practice, therefore, forced psychiatrists to think about the need for a "child" psychiatry.[41]

The significance of childhood was also fostered by the work of the National Committee for Mental Hygiene (NCMH), founded in 1909 by a former asylum patient, Clifford Beers. This committee initially brought together social welfare advocates (Julia Lathrop was a member) and psychiatric leaders (including Adolf Meyer) for the purpose of improving conditions in mental hospitals. Led by Adolf Meyer these reformers gradually developed both a broader vision of the uses of psychiatry and a commitment to the promotion of mental health as well as to the detection and cure of mental illness. Childhood was the "period *par excellence* for prophy-laxis," according to William A. White, the superintendent of St. Elizabeths Hospital in Washington, D.C., and a leader in the mental hygiene move-ment. "If we are to produce a better race of adults, we must be able to control the influences which go to mold the adult character." Through its studies and publications, the mental hygiene movement, with Meyer as its figurehead, made the mental health of an adult contingent upon the behav-ior and personality of the child.[42]

Healy's allegiance to Meyer was both personal and philosophical. The eclectic or holistic approach to diagnosis, the stress on individual differ-ences in adjustment to the environment, and the faith in the prevention of future criminal behavior through intervention in childhood, all evident in *The Individual Delinquent,* marked Healy's intellectual affinity with the new psychiatry. Meyer had also recommended Healy for the JPI post, and after the clinic opened Healy continued to seek his guidance, requesting help about everything from research design to the format for patient re-cords. The debt Healy owed to Freud was initially less apparent than the influence of Meyer and the mental hygienists. Nonetheless, James Jackson Putnam, an early Boston Freudian, found impressive Healy's "attention . . . [to] the newer researches in the direction of individual psychology (psy-cho-analysis)." It was through Healy's study of juvenile delinquency that Freudian concepts first were applied to the nation's troublesome children.[43]

Freud came to America, as the story goes, in 1909, the same year Ethel Dummer opened the Juvenile Psychopathic Institute. Although psycho-analysis had not been entirely unnoticed before, in that year G. Stanley Hall sponsored Freud's visit to the United States and helped to publicize the Freudian stance. During his American lectures Freud held out that children were sexual creatures, and that repression of sexual conflicts led to adult emotional traumas and behavioral problems. His views on the significance of the sex instinct and his psychoanalytic method by which subconscious mental conflicts could be uncovered and resolved drew scattered adherents after the 1909 lectures. They also aroused much antagonism in the psychi-atric community. Healy stood somewhere in the middle, interested but not entirely committed to the Viennese school of psychology.[44]

Although he would have preferred a term that "savored less of highly technical considerations and . . . acrid disputations," Healy included psy-choanalysis in his list of "working methods." Particularly appealing was the notion that delinquent behavior could be driven by unconscious motivations or, as he wrote in *The Individual Delinquent*, forces that did "not appear above the surface." All sorts of wrongdoing could be accounted for by subconscious or repressed emotions; "there is little in the way of misbehavior," Healy asserted two years later, "to which mental conflict may not lead."[45] While Meyerian notions of maladjustment were pervasive in Healy's diagnoses, Freudian "mental conflict" appeared in only 7 percent of the young people sent for study at the JPI. Healy found that proportion significant, and the facts of the cases fascinating. In 1917 he consolidated the findings about mental mechanisms into a separate volume, *Mental Conflicts and Misconduct.* The new ideas about sexual repression suggested to Healy possibilities for understanding many aspects of human behavior, far beyond their application to delinquency. He proposed a sexual origin "for social self-assertions, for the pettier unpleasant attitudes and frames of mind, for undefined dissatisfactions and social dislikes." "Even many impulses to good behavior," Healy thought, could be accounted for by "mechanisms active in subconscious mental life."[46]

Despite his belief that "repression" caused some acts of delinquency, Healy cautioned that the study of "*mental mechanisms . . .* in their relation to misconduct" should "proceed with full conservatism."[47] When Healy considered psychoanalysis as a method of treatment, he further distanced his stance from that of Freud. Psychoanalysis worked only with delinquents of average intelligence, he found; dream analysis was useless; and psychoanalytic symbolism did not explain delinquency. But Healy could be maddeningly inconsistent. In *Mental Conflicts and Misconduct* he also wrote, "All of these mechanisms [of mental conflict] depend for their existence upon feelings or emotions, and what is there to compare to various phases of sex life and to sex ideas as producers of emotion?"[48]

The limits of Healy's attraction to psychoanalysis are evident in a comparison of his writings and *The Mental Hygiene of Childhood,* published by William A. White in 1919, four years after *The Individual Delinquent.* White, an early Freudian convert, bluntly borrowed the language of psychoanalysis to argue that the behavior of children displayed two primary instincts—the self-preservative or ego instinct and the race-preservative or sex instinct. Adult mental hygiene problems (White referred specifically to the dependent and criminal classes) were due to inadequate parental handling of the two instincts, particularly the mismanagement by parents of a child's sexual curiosity. A parent who represented sex as "nasty," for example, was creating the mechanism for repression. So was the parent who petted and indulged her child, establishing an unhealthy "mother fixation." White's commitment to Freudian interpretations of human behavior was wholesale. Healy intended his book to absorb, then rise above, contending theories of human behavior by demonstrating the value of an eclectic approach when making an *individual* diagnosis.[49]

PUBLIC REACTION

Both popular and professional reception of Healy's work at the Juvenile Psychopathic Institute was overwhelmingly positive. Healy spoke regularly and with authority at national conferences of welfare and prison reformers.[50] Juvenile court personnel, physicians and psychiatrists, and the social welfare community praised his tabulation of the causes of juvenile crime and signaled its usefulness for their work with children.[51] *Mental Conflicts and Misconduct* was Healy's fourth book in three years. A specialized study of "pathological lying" and a volume about "honesty" written for parents appeared in 1915 along with *The Individual Delinquent.*[52] In a short time William Healy became a nationally recognized expert among the many experts searching for ways to alleviate public dependency and delinquency by focusing on the problems of youth.

Other courts followed the Chicago example and forged links with the sciences of human conduct. After visiting the JPI, Boston's first juvenile court judge, Harvey H. Baker, became an enthusiast, consulting about his most difficult cases with L. Eugene Emerson, a local Freudian psychologist. In 1913 the Hennepin County (Minnesota) Juvenile Court had a research department investigating the causes of delinquency. Financed by the Minneapolis Juvenile Protective League, it was staffed by a physician, a psychologist, and a nurse and worked mainly with delinquents considered "feebleminded." The city of Chicago acknowledged the institute's value to the juvenile court by assuming fiscal responsibility for the clinic when Dummer's five years of seed money ran out.[53]

Healy, however, found the Cook County administration a less congenial sponsor than the Progressive child savers. The number of court cases he was asked to diagnose grew too large to permit time for research. The local political machine threatened to replace Augusta Bronner, the staff psychologist, with a patronage appointee. When a group of public-spirited citizens offered Healy and Bronner the directorship of a similar institution in Boston (and guaranteed ten years of funding) the pair took their expertise to Massachusetts in 1917. At the Judge Baker Foundation, named as a memorial to Harvey H. Baker, who died in 1915, they duplicated the structure and procedures of Chicago's Juvenile Psychopathic Institute.[54] After only a few months experience with Healy and Bronner, Judge Frederick Pickering Cabot, Baker's replacement on the Boston court, was ready to sing the praises of the Judge Baker Foundation. "The advantage in Dr. Healy's diagnosis," he told a local conference on probation, "is that he tells us something about the child's personality (leanings) . . . We often know more nearly in what way to experiment in making our contacts [for the child]."[55]

Healy had once promised Ethel Dummer that "if . . . would-be reformers are good for anything at all we can give them material on which to work."[56] Dummer and her associates, and a nationwide audience, certainly seemed pleased with both the investigative results and the practical applications of the project. Yet the evidence Healy collected and the clinics he directed represented a fundamental change in the Progressive code of delinquency prevention. The choice of a medical professional as chief researcher tilted the balance away from the environmental interpretations for delinquency that supported community-based solutions sponsored by child savers and maternalists. When Healy pictured the delinquent as an individual mind at risk he made the Progressives' recommendations for community intervention and welfare legislation as inappropriate in delinquency work as the "general theories" of causation roundly condemned in *The Individual Delinquent*. The clinic promised that intervention based on a model of the doctor-patient relationship rather than the passage of broad welfare measures or the restructuring of the economic environment could alleviate the problems of a maladjusted delinquent who was, after all, the unique product of a mind interacting with the circumstances of life. A reformer at heart, Healy helped to sound the death knell of Progressive environmentalism and community intervention even as Ethel Dummer's institution and Healy's research and diagnostic work in Chicago and Boston provided the inspiration for a national "child guidance movement" to create more court-affiliated clinics.

THE CHILD GUIDANCE MOVEMENT

As he watched from a hospital window while Boston crowds celebrated the World War I armistice, William Healy reflected on the popular energy in the streets below. Progressives had hoped that the war would provide an opportunity to extend the reaches of social reform; while the actions of the Wilson administration disillusioned some, Healy remained an optimist. In a letter to his friend and patron Ethel Dummer he ruminated, "I was lying here and thinking last night that if some tremendously forceful man or group could come along and say, 'Now' & say it & say it until he had the people aroused to the fact that this is one of the most wonderful periods of possibility with the national consciousness new born [such a person would have the opportunity] to lastingly & progressively change conditions of general human nurture." Healy did not see himself as that leader; his part in the effort to create a more "general well being" would be "to continue to accumulate undeniable evidences of the benefits and sometimes entirely therapeutic efforts of better nurture and better education."[57] Although eschewing the role of organizer in his correspondence with Dummer, Healy soon began to work closely with a small group of professional psychiatrists and a large private philanthropy to spread the promise of delinquency prevention through court-affiliated clinics.

Media reports about crime and criminals created a receptive atmosphere for a nationwide delinquency prevention program. In 1917 Bernard Glueck, director of the psychiatric clinic at New York's Sing Sing penitentiary, published research revealing the early manifestations of delinquent behavior among prison inmates.[58] Glueck's findings took on added meaning when, in the aftermath of World War I, the American press discovered and publicized a national "crime wave." Robberies and murders seemed to be on the rise as the country returned to peace. Editorials cast blame widely, calling attention to the criminal consequences of prohibition, drug addiction, radical propaganda, the dimming of street lights due to a coal shortage, and even the ease with which thugs now could escape in automobiles. Some used the opportunity to criticize inefficient law enforcement and a parole system that turned criminals loose after short sentences; these critics usually demanded harsher sentences and more police. Others turned with a new urgency to prevention and made plans for early interventions into the lives of juvenile delinquents.[59]

In 1921 at Lakewood, New Jersey, the Commonwealth Fund brought together an exclusive group of delinquency specialists to consider solutions to the crime problem. The fund was one of a relatively new breed of private philanthropies that financed a broad range of programs aimed at solving social problems. The Rockefeller Foundation was, perhaps, the best known of these organizations. During the early twentieth century the Rockefeller

Fund and its offshoot, the Laura Spelman Rockefeller Memorial (LSRM), funded medical research and social welfare projects that included social hygiene, child development, and parent education. The Harkness family, whose wealth came from investments in Standard Oil, established the Commonwealth Fund in 1918; its administrators selected juvenile delinquency as one of the fund's first target areas. Both Healy and Bronner were among those invited to help the fund's directors plan a prevention program.[60]

At the Lakewood, New Jersey, meeting Healy did not have to sell the value of individual psychological study of delinquents; he was among colleagues who dismissed social factors (the conference report specifically mentioned "poverty, variations in employment, migration to cities with consequent exposure to bad housing and other similar conditions") as beyond the scope of their discussion. In addition to Healy and Bronner, those participating in the Lakewood conference included the psychiatrist Bernard Glueck, Martha P. Falconer of the American Social Hygiene Association, Charles W. Hoffman, judge of the Cincinnati Juvenile Court, J. P. Murphy, of the Philadelphia Children's Bureau, Thomas W. Salmon, medical director of the National Committee for Mental Hygiene, and Henry W. Thurston of the New York School of Social Work.[61] As late as March 2, Ethel Dummer appealed for the inclusion of Julia Lathrop. "She is, to me, the wisest woman we have," Dummer wrote to Healy. But only Edith Abbott was there to protest the psychiatric consensus among the participants, noting that the Illinois Child Labor Law of 1917 had done more to prevent delinquency than all Healy's "excellent" psychological work at the Juvenile Psychopathic Institute.[62]

Even before the Lakewood meeting Healy and Bronner had been in contact with the Commonwealth Fund to discuss direct support for the Judge Baker Foundation. They asked for aid to publish their findings, to fund treatment and follow-up studies of the children examined at the clinic, and to provide specialized training in the techniques of delinquency evaluation.[63] Participants at Lakewood favored Healy's requests and recommended that Boston's Judge Baker Foundation and a similar clinic to be created in New York City become training centers for the psychological approach to delinquency. However, when the fund's new director, Barry Smith, announced its "delinquency prevention program" in November 1921, the plans were much more ambitious than the proposals of the Lakewood conferees.

Instead of funnelling so much support to the Judge Baker Foundation, the initiative called for two new undertakings, a new Bureau of Children's Guidance in New York City to operate as a psychiatric clinic for children and training institute, and a program of demonstration clinics to tempt the many juvenile courts not yet using psychological services. "Flying clinics," Healy described them to Ethel Dummer, "doing the same sort of work that we inaugurated in Chicago." The NCMH directed the demonstrations and selected St. Louis as the site for the first clinic. In all, one rural and seven urban demonstrations were conducted between 1922 and 1927. The Commonwealth Fund provided seed money only. Following a demonstration, courts had to find local funding to continue operation of their child guidance clinics.[64]

The Commonwealth Fund transferred its attention to other philanthropic child welfare endeavors within a decade, but its delinquency prevention program left behind a network of psychological institutions for children. All but one of the demonstration clinics achieved permanency, and many communities developed their own programs without Commonwealth Fund financing. In 1936 a count of local clinics recorded 235 nationwide, most, like Healy's original institutes, in the larger urban centers.[65] The new clinics made available therapy as well as diagnostic services, and the focus of clinic work moved beyond delinquency to include troublesome "nondelinquents," changes described in later chapters. Signaling these changes, the delinquency prevention program adopted a new name in 1922. Ethel Dummer's psychopathic institute became a "child guidance" clinic. The name change also indicated the program's close adherence to the individual, psychological paradigm of troublesome behavior.

Both the ideological framework and the institutional structure for child guidance were in place when the Commonwealth Fund initiated its delinquency prevention program. Chicago Progressives led by Ethel Dummer and William Healy made a space in child saving for the sciences of human conduct. The child savers' space had a physical dimension. They created a research institute as an addendum to the juvenile justice system and housed there the application of new ideas from psychology and psychiatry. The founders of the JPI expected that by examining individual delinquents, their clinician would help the juvenile court judge understand difficult cases by fixing points for intervention. As a researcher the JPI director was supposed to uncover common threads of causation; in turn, his discoveries would improve community efforts to solve a troubling urban problem.

Instead, William Healy created the "individual delinquent," a character whose misbehavior represented a unique response to a specific environment. Healy's space was intellectual. In *The Individual Delinquent* Healy absorbed and reproduced the many interpretations of troublesome children swirling about in the child-saving arena, then ordered those explanations with new ideas from psychology and psychiatry. It was Healy's eclectic structure of causation that solidified his stature with the child savers —the multiplicity of explanations was a virtue because it legitimated many community and legislative approaches to delinquency prevention. But it was the individualizing of the problem of juvenile crime and the normalization of the individual delinquent that earned Healy his role as a father of child guidance. First at the JPI and then at the Judge Baker Foundation, Healy fashioned a professional model for delinquency work.

Having made space in the child-saving arena for psychiatry and psychology, child savers found themselves with less and less control over how the space was used. Although the professional model did not immediately replace the Progressive child-saving agenda, the relative authority of the environmentalists and those who spoke for a new psychological paradigm of child behavior had begun to shift. The causes of Healy's delinquent had little to do with the social structure or economic order of the community in which the delinquent lived. Rather, the individual delinquent could be, indeed should be, reclaimed through individualized or therapeutic intervention. The site for this reclamation was the child guidance clinic.

3

Building the
Child Guidance Team

William Healy and Augusta Bronner went to Boston in 1917 as both researchers and clinicians. With comparative evidence from two cities, they continued publishing careers that eventually totaled fifteen books, including six co-authored volumes about crime, delinquency, rehabilitation, foster parenting, and psychoanalysis. Healy's last study (*Criminal Youth and the Borstal System,* written with Benedict Alper) appeared in 1941. As clinicians the Judge Baker Foundation co-directors soon established an active practice supervising evaluations for local courts and child welfare agencies, and occasionally seeing children referred by a school principal or brought in by a distraught parent. Practitioners from three different professions participated in the diagnostic process used in Boston. Medicine, psychology, and social work joined forces to create a multidisciplinary team evaluation that distinguished child guidance from other psychological services for children.

In 1917 the team approach employed at the Judge Baker Foundation was a novel professional structure. Healy and Bronner undoubtedly knew of the cooperative effort of psychiatrists and social workers at some of the psychiatric institutions. The practice they created at the Judge Baker clinic (which became the model for the Commonwealth Fund's demonstration clinics), however, appeared to be far more egalitarian than the hierarchical order of, for example, their neighbors at the Boston Psychopathic Hospital. Although the three professions of child guidance conducted individual examinations, they worked together to construct a program or recommendation for each child's rehabilitation. This teamwork—the professional relationships that lay behind the authority of child guidance—can be reconstructed by examining the clinic's daily practice. In the 595 cases opened during 1920 we can observe the rituals of diagnosis and recommendation that framed work at the Judge Baker Foundation. The rituals protected the separate professional identities of each of the team's participants while they enabled child guidance to speak to its public with one voice.[1]

Ritual—the formalized ceremonies or patterned social acts of a culture—is a concept not usually applied to rational or scientific behavior. Rather, the term brings to mind the shared celebrations of holidays or the unwritten but commonly accepted rules of etiquette. It has often been associated with religious and political behavior. Building from the pioneering work of Victor Turner and Clifford Geertz, anthropologists have explored the many functions of ritual in the creation of community and the maintenance of social order. In particular, they have shown that rituals can mask social conflicts by providing an expression of shared cultural values.[2]

This interpretation of rituals is also a useful tool for examining the professional culture of the child guidance team. Rituals associated with the process of evaluation in the clinic sustained the separate professional identities of child psychiatrists, psychologists, and social workers. The formalized evaluation processes defined the terms of professional cooperation and the boundaries of responsibility in the child guidance workplace. At the same time the rituals allowed two relatively new professions, applied psychology and social work, and the new medical specialty of child psychiatry to speak to the local child-saving community with the voice of "child guidance," a more authoritative voice than any one of the professions could claim by itself. When the Commonwealth Fund began to finance child guidance demonstrations, planners adopted the Judge Baker Foundation's team as the model for staff relations in the new clinics.[3]

Representatives of these three professions constructed the rituals of practice as they interacted with the *clients* and *patients* of the Judge Baker clinic. The two terms, laden with implications about the authority of the professional expert and the dependency of the supplicant for help, require explanation. "Client" is the current term of choice in the social service sector—psychologists and social workers see "clients," in part because those seeking help are ostensibly encouraged to devise their own plans for action. Social workers employed the word as early as the 1920s; in the helping professions it is more often associated with the "client-centered" therapy of the psychologist Carl Rogers.[4] Rogers contended that in a therapeutic situation, the potential for change resides within the individual; the therapist's role is to create a supportive environment, in which the change can take place. As it is presently employed, use of "client" connotes respect for (and even a bit of professional dependence on) the help seeker's point of view. Before 1931, when therapy was not yet a regular part of the Judge Baker Foundation's services, I reserve the use of client for an independent referral agency—the person or organization who requested help from the child guidance clinic. In 1920 the juvenile court was the clinic's primary client, but private child welfare agencies also sought the clinic's advice about troublesome children. The influence and independence of these agencies are readily apparent in their dealings with the clinic. Indeed, I argue that the administrative needs of the clients in many ways shaped the practice of child guidance at the Judge Baker Foundation.

Healy and Bronner introduced themselves to the Boston community not as competitors but as "specialized consultant[s]" for the many agencies working with troublesome young people.[5] For the co-directors, part of the appeal of the Boston clinic was the opportunity to work with local child savers who complemented the work of the juvenile court. To satisfy the needs of these clients, the clinic staff offered a range of diagnostic services in one location. They fine-tuned evaluations to correspond to the resources of the agencies and, for a short time, made follow-up consultations a part of their routine. With their clients the child guidance clinic worked to achieve a cooperative professional relationship.

Throughout the book I use the word "patient" to designate the parents and children seen at the clinic. In this chapter the word usually signifies an involuntary participant in the clinic's operations, and most often indicates the families and children referred by courts, schools, and other welfare agencies. Required to accept the clinic's services or offend the judicial system or the charity workers, these patients did not make the choice to seek out psychological help. Progressive ideals of social service "helpfulness" structured the treatment of the clinic's patients; the staff expected families to engage willingly in diagnostic procedures that were often time consuming and usually intruded on family privacy. Though their influence on the clinic's rituals is more difficult to gauge, these patients, too, like the clients who represented them, shaped the daily life of the child guidance professionals. Nonetheless, the authority of the clinic depended at first on how successfully the staff convinced the Boston child welfare community of the usefulness of its services. The rituals of diagnosis enabled the child guidance team to make its case.[6]

PATIENTS AND CLIENTS IN 1920

The Boston to which William Healy and Augusta Bronner relocated was similar in many respects to the familiar urban landscape of Chicago. Like Chicago, Boston in 1920 was a city teeming with immigrants. More were of Italian and Irish background than in Chicago, where the largest groups were the Slavs and the Germans. Both cities had small African American populations, although Chicago's was a bit larger, showing the beginnings of the great migration from the South. Boston was a much smaller urban area than Chicago, with a total population of 392,000, only about two-thirds that of Healy's first home.[7] In both towns child savers considered juvenile delinquency one of the worst of the many social problems exacerbated by rapid urban growth.

As they had in the nineteenth century, charitable Bostonians continued to devote their time and resources to the welfare of the troublesome child, although by 1920 many of the child-saving agencies were staffed by paid workers. The Massachusetts Society for the Prevention of Cruelty to Children, the Children's Aid Society, and agencies identified with the city's separate ethnic and religious groups took under their wings the destitute, the neglected, and the orphaned. Truant officers scoured the neighborhoods, visiting nurses combed the tenements, settlement house workers offered recreational clubs as enticements to leave the streets, and the juvenile court's probation staff busily collected reams of information about young offenders. If the child savers had their way the dependent and delinquent children of Boston would never be left to the mercy of harsh, dangerous, and unsupervised city life.[8]

Juvenile offenders and their families were the new clinic's first patients, involuntary participants in the development of a new field of research and treatment. The state's only juvenile court operated out of Boston in 1920.[9] Harvey H. Baker's rule had given way to the management of Frederick Pickering Cabot, who, in addition to sitting as the children's judge was also a trustee of the new Judge Baker Foundation. Boston officials recorded about three thousand delinquencies a year when the Judge Baker Foundation opened. Only half of these offenders were tried in the juvenile court, and the judge did not send all of them to the Judge Baker Foundation before sentencing.[10] In 1920 Healy and Bronner saw 315 of Judge Cabot's delinquents, over 50 percent of their cases.[11] Who these delinquents were and the range of troublesome behavior they brought to the attention of the clinic constrained the world of child guidance in the 1920s.

The great majority of delinquents at the Judge Baker Foundation in 1920 were either immigrants themselves or the children of immigrants, and the numbers reflected the ethnic mix in Boston. Children of Italian heritage represented the largest immigrant group seen at the clinic, followed by Irish, Jewish, and both English- and French-speaking Canadians. The clinic saw only fourteen African Americans (.02 percent of the cases) during the entire year. When the staff made note of a "race" case, in 1920 or in 1935, usually the reference was to the child of a Jewish family, not one who was "colored." [12] Whatever the ethnic background, most of the clinic's young patients were adolescent boys; in Boston, the juvenile court processed nine times as many males as females.[13]

Whether boy or girl, immigrant or native-born, most of the young people shared one characteristic; they were economically disadvantaged youngsters, children of Boston's lower classes. The precise economic status of these families was often difficult to ascertain from the case records. Social workers did not always record family incomes. More useful were the rich evaluative phrases from the clinic's files that typically described lives of poverty and marginality: a widow who worked as a cigar stripper, poor though "sensible" and "neat" (1601); a large family that received nine dollars a week from the city and made do with the wages of the older children (1609); a laborer working sporadically, whose home was "dirty, barely furnished" (1700); and the illiterate wife of an immigrant shoemaker, who suffered from goiter (1809). Again and again in the Judge Baker records appear the stories of widows receiving mothers' pensions or trying to eke out a living as waitresses or factory workers, families living on "aid" or (because Boston had a central register for charities) identified as previous recipients of charity, and fathers working on the wharves or as a nonunion carpenter or a laborer on the elevated railroad.

Although Healy and Bronner preached relentlessly that juvenile delinquency could not be predicted solely from a life of "dire poverty," a majority of the clinic's patients lived with some degree of economic insecurity. Day in and day out, the Judge Baker staff listened to the stories told by parents and children too poor to afford a modestly furnished house or an occasional outing. Physical examinations showed that these children were not necessarily malnourished; most ranked as normal on pediatric age-weight charts.[14] But even if they had enough to eat, most had little else of material ease. When the clinic's co-directors tallied their first Boston cases by economic background, they found that only a few families lived in "comfort," able to give children some spending money, or in "luxury," with frequent cultural opportunities and even some extravagances."[15] The principles and procedures of child guidance were tried out and refined first in the context of urban poverty.

The clinic's patients shared similar backgrounds; they also engaged in similar delinquencies. Tales from the patient files showed the narrow scope of troublesome behavior that occupied the clinic and the court in 1920. An eleven-year-old Catholic youth was arrested with two companions for entering an unoccupied house and stealing small articles (1902); the ten-year-old son of Italian immigrants was caught selling fruit without a license (1997); and a fourteen-year-old African American was brought to court by his foster parents as a stubborn child because he refused to go to school, and this "excellent foster family" found him bad tempered and very stupid (1823).[16] Playing ball on Sunday landed one Jewish youth in court, and a second offense, petty stealing from his brother, gave rise to a "stubborn complaint" against the boy (1847).[17] Stealing cigars from a fruit stand (1598), stealing clothing from a foster family before running away (1599), stealing a $15 ring (1600), stealing shoes from the workplace (1611 and 1617), stealing cuff buttons and baseballs from a neighborhood store (1615): the list of complaints was repetitious and formed a pattern of petty annoyance.[18] Boys stole from neighborhood merchants, truanted from school, and ran away from home to spend time "bunking out."

The girls also shoplifted, truanted, and bunked out, but the most common delinquency charge against a young girl in the early twentieth century was "immorality with the opposite sex." Healy and Bronner reported that about 50 percent of the girls in a sample of their first Boston cases had committed acts of "immorality." The charge covered a range of actions. A fourteen-year-old Roslindale girl, in her first year of high school, was sent to the Judge Baker Foundation by the school visitor, not the court, but her "delinquencies" were typical: lying, truancy, and "an abnormal interest in boys" (1680). In another case the Bethesda Society, a private charity for white girls, wanted Healy and Bronner to investigate Alice's sexual delinquencies. Her parents had sought the agency's help when, in a final act of defiance, Alice had not returned home from a Girl Scout party one evening, only to be found later with a boy and accused of "sex immorality" (1594). "Immorality" also covered the behavior of Mary Beeler, twelve years old and on probation from the Cambridge Court for staying out late and taking money for her "sex affairs with men" (1688).[19]

It is not surprising that child welfare agencies referred two of these three cases of "sex immorality," since workers from these services frequently took charge before the trials of the girls arrested for delinquencies. Charity workers were quick to make use of the Judge Baker Foundation's services. During the clinic's first ten years of work, welfare and child-placing agencies referred at least a third of the clinic's patients.[20] Like the delinquents, these children did not belong to the wealthiest classes of Boston society. Some had been removed from their birth families by the local Society for the Prevention of Cruelty to Children and were now living with foster parents. Others came from the Boston Children's Aid Society or from one of Boston's many church-sponsored child saving agencies, or they were the sons or daughters of parents supported by the Federated Jewish Charities.

Which particular children the clinic saw depended on the judgment of Boston's child-saving community. Judge Cabot recalled that in the early days of court-clinic cooperation, he had no clear guidelines to follow when choosing which delinquent needed a psychological examination.[21] The "rather dull looking" appearance of a seventeen-year-old Roxbury youth in court for evading a streetcar fare suggested the need for an examination (1948). The fifteen-year-old son of a plumber was directed to the clinic because the judge found it "hard to understand" why a boy who did not need money had stolen $40 from his employer (1659). Cabot sent boys to the clinic when he was unable to make sense of their behavior or when he observed a conspicuous physical or mental handicap. Repeat offenders alarmed the Boston juvenile justice community, as they had the women reformers in Chicago. The lad brought to court in 1917 for stealing a ride, in 1918 for begging, and again in 1920 for selling lemons without a license was an obvious candidate for a diagnostic evaluation (1818).[22]

Charity's use of the Judge Baker facilities was often as haphazard as was the court's, although gender often seemed the subtext in decisions to seek a psychological evaluation. For instance, a Social Service agent from South Boston, when tackling the case of a blind widow whose family lived on twelve dollars a week brought home by one daughter, asked the clinic to find out why the woman's seventeen-year-old son would not work steadily

(1623). The "immorality" of agency girls matched the "sex delinquencies" of young women from the juvenile court; agency boys, in contrast, often appeared to be entirely lazy, without even the initiative to steal. To the charity agents in 1920, both boys and girls threatened to become permanent dependency problems just as they had in the nineteenth century. Some Boston charities had begun to look to the Judge Baker Foundation for recommendations to ward off further trouble.

In sum, Healy and Bronner did not choose the children they evaluated in 1920. The concerns of the clinic's clients dictated which children became child guidance patients and the subjects of future child guidance research. In 1920 adolescents from the lower classes who defied the reformers' interpretation of social, moral, and mental norms found themselves before the court or in the clutches of a caring social service agency bent on changing their behavior. Healy and Bronner promised to make child-saving efforts more rational and efficient by individualizing each child and recommending from the many different solutions available the appropriate path to rehabilitation. Some children were "feebleminded," a few were psychopathological or showed signs of somatic illness, but by the available standards of physical and mental measurement most were normal, except for their delinquencies. How then could these apparently normal delinquents be sorted into functional categories for the agencies charged with reforming troublesome children? The Judge Baker consultation subdivided the normal by both social and psychological characteristics. The evaluation consisted of a complex diagnostic process performed by three separate professions working together as "child guidance."

RITUALS OF DIAGNOSIS: THE CHILD GUIDANCE TEAM

Evaluations at the clinic involved patients in four different examinations by experts in three distinct fields, a process that consumed most of a morning or afternoon.[23] A physician, a psychologist, and a social worker took the child and the family apart, analyzed the pieces separately, then put them back together again to form an "individual delinquent." As they participated in the professionals' rituals of diagnosis, the patients provided members of the child guidance team with an opportunity to highlight the separate clinical identities of the three professions and to fortify the boundaries separating their work.

There was never much question of the administrative hierarchy in child guidance during the 1920s. Male representatives of the medical profession usually served as directors of the clinics.[24] The Judge Baker Foundation, with a shared directorship that represented both genders and two professions, was unique in this respect. Establishment of a hierarchy in clinical practice was a different matter. During these pioneering years the boundaries of responsibility sometimes blurred in the crush of daily work, with social workers and psychologists called on to fill the role of the psychiatrist. The literature from each discipline bristled with discussions of status distinctions and functional differences as each profession offered ways to understand and redirect human behavior.[25] In child guidance practice the tools with which each profession approached the patient, the distinct analytic tasks assigned as the profession's contribution to the puzzle of diagnosis, and the specific patient (child or parent) evaluated by each profession reinforced each practitioner's separate professional identity.

The Psychologist

A child who passed through the clinic's evaluation procedure in 1920 encountered only two of the three team members—the physician and the psychologist. Although each was assigned the same patient, the tools and tasks sharply differentiated the identities of the disciplines. In child guidance work psychology made two contributions to the definition of a child's individuality—an assessment of his or her mental ability and a determination of the child's personality. One of the psychologist's first responsibilities was to create a cooperative atmosphere in which the child would agree to complete a battery of IQ and aptitude tests. These tests were the tools, and the interpretation of their results the task of the practitioner of applied psychology.

Standardized tests for sorting and labeling groups of children and adults were a relatively new addition to educational technology in 1920. In 1909 Henry H. Goddard reported his use of the Binet test with students at the Training School for Backward and Feeble-Minded Children at Vineland, New Jersey, and in 1916 Lewis Terman published his Stanford revision, the Americanized version of the test that became standard in the 1920s. From Terman too came the idea of an "intelligence quotient," an individual measure of intellect most psychologists believed a valid way to compare mental abilities. Testing was so much a part of professional identity that the applied psychologist was sometimes called a psychometrist.[26]

A few in this field had begun by 1920 to think of themselves more precisely as "clinical" psychologists and, drawing on the example of Lightner Witmer of Philadelphia, called attention to their interest in diagnostic examinations of individuals, not the large groups usually tested and categorized by applied or educational psychologists. To some the "clinical" label allied psychology with the practice of medicine or psychiatry. It implied that the psychologists used their tests to work with the psychotic or the mentally backward. At a meeting in 1918 of the newly formed American Association of Clinical Psychologists, Arnold Gesell, a pediatrician and psychologist, spoke of the "many problems common to psychiatry and to clinical psychology," but warned his colleagues of the need to respect the "cleavage" between the two fields. The cleavage took on increasing importance by 1920, as clinical psychologists could be found working alongside physicians in psychopathic hospitals, institutions for people diagnosed with epilepsy and with mental retardation, the public schools, and child guidance clinics.[27]

At the Judge Baker Foundation, the distinctions Gesell applauded were more blurry than in many clinics because of the particular psychiatrist and psychologist in residence. Bronner, with a Ph.D. in psychology from Columbia University, was quite at home administering tests to the delinquents or working in the capacity of psychiatrist with the girls. Girls (and often the very young boys) always talked with a woman acting as the psychiatrist, and before Anna Skinner joined the psychiatric staff part-time at the end of the decade, Augusta Bronner and occasionally the other psychologists (all women) performed this role.[28] Moreover, Healy, while in Chicago, had devised several aptitude tests that contributed to his reputation as a "psychologist." In 1927 the two worked together to produce a comprehensive handbook of mental tests.[29] Despite the anomalous leadership role of the chief psychologist at the Judge Baker Foundation, the staff psychologists, in Boston and at other demonstration clinics, maintained their discrete professional purpose through the ritual practice of administering and interpreting standardized tests.

The case files of the Judge Baker patients contain accounts of the psychologists' efforts to engage their subjects in the test-taking task and the reports of test results. The IQs recorded at the clinic in 1920 ranged from the 54 of a "low grade moron" who "can't be expected to make progress in regular grades" (1968) to the "markedly supernormal" 135 of a boy from Russia whose family was being partially supported by Jewish charities

(1805). Most were like the sixteen-year-old girl from Chelsea who showed a normal IQ of 90 with "good ability" (1889). When Healy and Bronner reported on the results of four thousand cases from both Chicago and Boston, they found that close to 75 percent of both boys and girls tested in the mentally "normal" range. The co-directors often deprecated the use of IQ alone to sort and label children, and they used other test results to shape clinic discussions.[30] The research publications from the Judge Baker Foundation, however, often represented "mental status" solely in terms of the intelligence quotient. "The decade of the 1920s was the heyday of the testing movement," recalled Florence Goodenough, a psychologist who participated in the development of tests for children, "the age of innocence when an IQ was an IQ and few ventured to doubt its omnipotence."[31]

Successful completion of these tests presented quite a challenge to both the psychologist and her subjects. She had to coax the best possible performances from children who were at the clinic precisely because they had already failed to cooperate with adult expectations of behavior. Bronner, in one of her first publications, described the various types of attitude problems encountered by the clinical psychologist: deliberate deception, recalcitrance, sportiveness (treating the test as a joke), anger, resentfulness, and fear. A successful clinical psychologist had to be not only a master of the variety of tests then on the market but also a master at enticing an unwilling patient to participate in the evaluation. These displays of "attitude" by the test takers allowed the clinical psychologist to contribute more to the diagnosis than a simple IQ score or standardized test result. The psychologist's report on the child was one step in the evaluation of the child's personality.[32]

"We are primarily students of personality," Healy had written in *The Individual Delinquent*, as he described the tests administered to young recidivists in Chicago.[33] "Personality" began to take on new connotations in the early twentieth century. Before the turn of the century, self-help authors who offered plans for personal success were concerned with building "character," an ascetic, self-sacrificing quality demanding respect and admiration, a quality that made one stand out from the crowd. This "character," as Warren Susman has argued, was appropriate to the abstemious culture of the age of industrial expansion; it shaped the ground rules of child-rearing advice in the nineteenth century. In the twentieth-century society of mass living and mass consumption, happiness came from the ability to get along with and be pleasing to others, qualities of one's "personality."[34] Edmund Conklin, author of an adolescent psychology text-book, defined personality in 1935 as the "most inclusive term available to the psychologist for the designation of an individual. Personality means the sum total of what an individual human being is. It includes all that is native and all that has been acquired."[35] A wholesome personality signified characteristics that enabled a child to interact successfully with other children or with family members, and predicted the child's prospects for success in adult life. Collectively these qualities indicated the level of a child's personal "adjustment," or fit with the environment. An emotionally demonstrative, cooperative, and gregarious child was, by the clinic's values, well adjusted; a timid, unresponsive, or weak-willed one was a maladjusted "personality failure." Delinquents typically showed signs of maladjusted personalities.

During the test period a psychologist recorded her "impressions" of the child's personality for her final report. The Dorchester youth whose probation officer was concerned by his loafing, gambling, and inability to stay with a job for any length of time showed "good ability" on the tests. Bronner also observed that he was emotionally "superficial," "weak," "easy-going," "pleasure loving," "irresponsible," a "glib talker," and "not at all manly" (1637). Especially important was the child's ability or inability to relate to the examiner. Qualities of timidity, arrogance, or self-assurance were duly noted in the description of the child's mental ability, as was the child's willingness to cooperate or make an effort during the test period. All were grist for the psychologist's evaluation of a child's degree of adjustment.[36]

After a child completed the battery of tests, the psychologist constructed an interpretative report (sometimes called a "psychograph" by Healy and Bronner) that was typed for the patient's file on pink sheets of paper. Each profession had its own color. Although a minor point of administration, the ritual of color coding the different narratives acknowledged the separate identity of each team member even in the files. A psychiatrist, too, was a "student of personality" who also observed the child-patient and recorded interpretations of the child's degree of adjustment. The psychiatrists, however, always recorded their accounts on white so they could be quickly distinguished from the psychologist's "impressions." The psychologist's tools—her standardized tests—legitimated her impressions, but they were, nonetheless, mere descriptions of the child that left unanswered the question of personality formation and the causes of personality failure. These tasks fell to the mental analysis of the psychiatrist.

The Physician/the Psychiatrist

The physician had a dual role to play in the evaluation process. As a student of somatic illness, the doctor relied on medical technology to examine the child's health, to uncover or rule out physical causes of misconduct. As a student of personality, the psychiatrist used tools of the "talking cure" to explore the hidden meanings of a child's troublesome behavior. Both tools and technique differentiated the psychiatrist's narrative of the child's mental state from that of the clinical psychologist.

As the Judge Baker Foundation's physician in 1920, William Healy performed the medical exams, noting on a preprinted form such items as weight and nutrition, age of first menstruation, and the state of tonsils, teeth, and eyes. "Needs glasses," "teeth badly in need of attention," and "boy needs building up physically," were a few of the comments that helped the team identify potential sources of trouble for judges and agency workers. For some of the girls, and especially for African American children of both sexes, Healy requested Wassermann tests to detect syphilis.[37] The purpose of the medical exam was more complex, however, than the simple evaluation of physical condition; with the child stripped naked, the doctor also began in the examining room, through conversation with the child, the search for clues to the patient's personality.

After the physical evaluation the psychiatrist continued the unearthing of personality by eliciting, in child guidance parlance, the child's "own story." Listening to and recording the child's account represented to Healy a significant departure from the techniques of examination used in the psychological clinics. He sprinkled case descriptions in *The Individual Delinquent* with phrases such as "as the girl told us" and "from the boy's own story," elevating the words of the troublesome child to a status nearly equivalent to those of the accusatory adults. In child guidance, the professional identity of the psychiatrist was pinned to an ability to gain a child's confidence and record a child's words. In the field of child welfare this technique made Healy one of the innovators. Whereas William Osler, dean of clinical medicine in the early twentieth century, advised doctors to listen carefully to their patients, and Freud and his followers made the patient's story a prelude to diagnosis and treatment, in child welfare work only the juvenile court proceedings were infused with this personalism. Even Freud, in his famous work with Little Hans, did not treat the boy directly, and Anna Freud's important work with children still lay in the future.[38]

Although they invited the child-patients to talk freely about their troublesome behavior, Healy and those who followed his technique did not permit the child to speak without direction or interpretation. In 1926 the National Committee for Mental Hygiene published a set of guidelines to direct efforts to learn the child's "point of view, to understand his attitude." Psychiatrists were advised to raise questions about the child's family relationships and attitudes toward school as well as play interests, fears, dream life, companions, habits, and emotional conflicts.[39] The patient records showed a clear pattern in the questions asked in 1920. Psychiatric interviewers wanted to know about a child's companions, the things they did together, and, especially, the extent of their sexual activities.

This line of questioning often confounded the children. Six years after her visit to the clinic Bessie was still upset because the welfare worker had told her the visit was for vocational guidance, and instead, the psychiatric interviewer asked questions mainly about sex interests (1660). From the case record, it is clear that the staff asked Bessie for other types of information, but the preponderance of material on the sexual experiences of Boston's youths in this and other files suggests that Bessie's recollection of her experience was not completely without foundation. With young children, interviewers asked about dirty words, dirty pictures, and "touching," both self and others. With adolescents, the issues were much the same: how much and what kind of sexual activity had the child engaged in; masturbation or fornication; and with which sex. These psychiatric interviewers did not frame questions to elicit stories of incest, although they did seek evidence of "sex play" (the clinic's term) between siblings.[40]

Healy reported in 1915 that 13 percent of the recidivists in his Chicago study had "encountered some early sex experience sufficiently serious to be accounted by the student a causative factor of delinquency."[41] By 1920 the psychiatric interviewer was inclined to anticipate a sexual component in most of the cases, and in many instances the tales told by the patients supported the original hypothesis. In the clinic's records children who were early introduced to sexual experiences also engaged in delinquent behavior.

The findings applied to both genders, and this, perhaps, was one of Healy's more understated discoveries. For decades reformers had been trying to rein in the sexuality of working-class adolescent girls, going so far as to label their actions delinquent. Through his clinical practice, Healy pointed out that the delinquencies of young boys and adolescent males might also be connected to sexual experiences. He did not propose that the sexual acts of the boys were delinquencies. Rather, Healy believed that if the mental images of these experiences festered in a boy's mind, he might find an outlet in criminal behavior.

The story of nine-year-old Nathan Meyer (2029) showed how Healy and Bronner constructed the connections between unruly behavior and sexual experiences. The boy stole from his family, sucked his thumb, and frequented a dump with a group of older youths. His mother had also caught him masturbating and "playing with" his sister and other little girls. The Children's Aid Society agent wanted a consultation because Nathan's mother hoped to place him with another family. Nathan told his story to Dr. Bronner "in a very straightforward manner with very little need for suggestive questions." There were both "bad boys and bad girls" in his neighborhood. They stole from trucks on the streets and from stores. "Who is the worst boy you ever knew about stealing?" Bronner asked. "Nick is . . . Because he does the baddest in other ways . . . He talks bad[;] he's the worst one. He does bad with boys and with girls." Nick was also the first to tell Nathan about "bad words." With Bronner, however, Nathan was too embarrassed to repeat Nick's phrases. Although he described what some of the boys did with girls, Nathan denied having taken an active role, saying that he had only watched. "Again and again [Nathan] tells us that it was Nick who first of all told him about both stealing and bad words, etc." Nathan indicated to Bronner that he "[had] never told his father or mother or anyone just what these boys . . . said." "In response to a direct question as to whether he thinks that if he could stop thinking about these bad words he could stop stealing," Bronner reported, "he says he thinks he could."

For Healy and Bronner the mechanism that explained the relationship between Nathan's "sex play" and his delinquent behavior was the "mental conflict," defined by Healy as "a conflict between elements of mental life, [that] occurs when two elements, or systems of elements, are out of harmony with each other." It was a term "not at all difficult to understand," he assured readers of *Mental Conflicts and Misconduct*. A "constellation" of ideas and memories formed a mental element, and around such a constellation, a "complex" might develop. A "complex" has "energy producing powers," and hence could cause misbehavior. But more important, "portions of an active complex [were] left in the mental background as subconscious"; they were "repressed." It was the repressed portion of the delinquent's mental life that Healy and his associates hoped to expose.[42] "Since nothing," Healy believed, ". . . so stirs emotions as the affairs of sex life," the child guidance psychiatric interviewers went exploring for "hidden sex thoughts or imageries, and inner or environmental sex experiences."[43] Exposure, Healy and Bronner assumed, would eliminate the source of the misconduct. "Now for the first time," they recorded about another young thief referred by the Children's Aid Society, "this boy's inner mental life and his sex habits are known [and] there should be a change in his behavior if re-educative measures are carried out" (1877).

The psychiatrist provided the team with a mechanism to explain the delinquent with an average IQ, an interpretation that retold the child's "own story" in the language of personality maladjustment. Psychiatric examiners made their unique contribution by exposing the evidence of mental conflicts or the far less frequent signs of incipient mental illnesses. At the Judge Baker Foundation in 1920, the psychiatric examinations of troublesome children uncovered enough examples of mental conflict, usually related to sexual experiences, to provide the psychiatrist with a professional identity separate from that of the clinical psychologist. The psychiatric examiner at the Judge Baker was not always a trained physician, but the connection between mental conflicts and misconduct differentiated "child psychiatry" from other aspects of the clinic's evaluative work.

The psychiatric examination concluded the child's experience at the Judge Baker clinic in 1920. As the child met with the psychologist and the psychiatric interviewer, the clinic social worker completed a study of the child's environment. Children might reveal feelings about their misbehavior, or they might describe neighborhood bad boys and bad girls, but it was the social worker's job to document these "own stories" through discussions with the child's parents (or possibly with records from the referral agency). The "mental analysis" of the child's personality was confirmed or denied or modified by the rituals of social work.

The Social Worker

When Healy and Bronner took charge of the Judge Baker Foundation they employed a full-time social worker as the third member of their clinic's team. Her task was to investigate the family's background and the social setting. Her presence also offered a familiar point of reference at the Judge Baker clinic for social work agents from child welfare societies, and she helped to legitimate the clinic's services by forming a bridge between the clinic's psychological interpretation of delinquency and the agency's options for helping a child. A similar staff structure was imposed at the Commonwealth Fund's first demonstration clinic in St. Louis, and succeeding clinics maintained a ratio of three social workers for each psychiatrist and psychologist.[44] The social worker's tools, tasks, and patients were more amorphous than those of the other two professions, but here too the rituals of diagnosis provided a separate identity for child guidance social work.

Although social work drew on a long and lively tradition of individual evaluation and assistance, the child guidance social worker belonged to a new breed, with intellectual ties to dynamic psychiatry as well as roots in nineteenth-century altruism. "In the past," Mary C. Jarrett, a social worker at the Boston Psychopathic Hospital and an outspoken representative of these new specialists, advised her mental hygiene colleagues in 1918, "the economic interest has been paramount in social case-work, and is still dominant; but there are indications that the dominant interest is becoming psychological."[45] Jarrett and others who specialized in the field of mental hygiene had begun to think of themselves as "psychiatric" social workers. They were students of personality and individual adjustment rather than simple purveyors of relief.

As the new generation of social workers redefined casework, their investigations began to expose signs of individual maladjustment behind problems of social dislocation and economic inequality. Mary Richmond's influential texts on "social diagnosis" and "social casework" tried to change the old-fashioned, commonsense advice of the friendly visitor into a scientific formulation of adjustment issues. The question of professional training in the psychology of adjustment was answered when Smith College opened a psychiatric social work program in 1918, with other schools soon offering similar courses. Some psychiatric social workers, such as Jessie Taft of Philadelphia, even saw therapeutic potential in their investigations and claimed that the tools of casework could cure personality maladjustment as well as identify it.[46]

Particularly as social workers began to find employment in mental hygiene institutions, psychopathic hospitals, and child guidance clinics, their new claims to expertise generated friction and exacerbated the problem of establishing a working relationship with psychiatry. Questions about the professional status and scientific legitimacy of social work developed within the circles of both disciplines. Throughout the 1910s psychiatrists likened social work to nursing, thereby denigrating its "science" and attaching a subordinate status to the field. Mary Jarrett acknowledged in 1918 that medicine and psychiatry accorded equal ranking to social work "only by courtesy," then added that many disputed even the courtesy. Yet as social workers relied more and more on psychiatric interpretations of troublesome social problems, Jarrett and her colleagues expected greater acknowledgment of their professional expertise.[47]

During the 1920s psychiatrists advised one another to take social work seriously. Modern social work was no longer the "meddling influence of sentimental spinsters or volunteer society matrons," according to the director of the NCMH delinquency prevention division in 1926 as he called for an "alliance of forces" between the two fields.[48] Yet some who proclaimed the need for cooperation, like Lawson Lowrey, the director of the second demonstration clinic in Cleveland, continued to find the intricacies of social work elusive. "It is not easy," he reflected, "to obtain a clear understanding of what is usually meant by social case-work, to grasp the interrelationships of the processes employed in case-work technique and to see the field in its complicated professional relationships."[49] His solution was to recommend more training for social workers in the principles of dynamic psychiatry, and many in both fields agreed. Although both groups seemed to need an "alliance," the calls in psychiatric journals usually made clear that social workers could be granted more authority and collegial status only if they remained professionally subordinate to the psychiatrist.

When Healy and Bronner hired their first social worker they, too, had in mind an alliance of forces, but it was the social worker's investigatory and record-keeping skills, not her psychiatric acumen, that made her an essential part of the Judge Baker team. Despite a new model of psychiatric social work evident in the professional literature and present in Boston just across the way at the Boston Psychopathic Hospital, a Judge Baker social worker was charged with describing the setting in which a child became maladjusted or conflicted. Social work at the Judge Baker Foundation throughout the 1920s followed the pattern established at the beginning of the decade—the social worker used her casework investigatory skills to study the child's background and create a "social history" of the troublesome child.

The types of questions she asked and the people with whom she spoke distinguished the social worker's tasks from the psychologist and the psychiatrist. Social workers drew their information from members of the troublesome child's family—usually the mother, but the father too was occasionally drafted for an office interview. Social workers expected their sources to respond freely and honestly to an extensive list of questions inquiring about the parents' physical and mental health and hereditary background and the status of the troublesome child's siblings. Parents were supposed to provide developmental facts about their offspring along with descriptions of their habits and interests and especially any incidents of delinquency that had gone undetected by the courts.[50] Outside the clinic the social worker investigated the material condition of the home and the neighborhood and the "home influences," referring here to the method of discipline, the parents' physical presence in the home, and the degree of "immorality" (meaning principally alcohol or sexual relations outside of marriage).

The case of a fifteen-year-old boy (1609) charged in the Boston juvenile court with petty street stealing shows how the clinic's social worker, identified in the case file as Mrs. Barnes, defined her tasks. During the interview Barnes ascertained that Franco Perron's mother was a widow with many children. Her husband had been a tailor making $25 a week, but now the family survived on a little aid from the city and the incomes of some of the older children. The social worker always inquired about any family history of alcoholism or insanity, but no hereditary problems were noted in this report. When prompted, Mrs. Perron also recounted a birth history for Franco and a health history (both without incident). Then the social worker asked about habits and attitudes and Mrs. Perron told of her trials with a boy who was "lazy" and who would not hold a job (behavior clearly delinquent in this impoverished family). Franco's court record also listed loafing, bunking out, and excessive gambling in addition to the charge of stealing. "It is a case for thorough renovation," the final report summarized.

Her need to rely on Mrs. Perron for the detailed developmental and behavioral history meant that a vital part of Barnes's task was to assess the mother's character and truthfulness. Like the psychologists and psychiatrists, psychiatric social workers were becoming "students of personality," but in 1920 the clinic still relied on them to be judges of character. The character assessments determined the reliability of the social history she collected. Personal appearance and demeanor counted in assessing a parent's story. Mrs. Perron was "neat" and "intelligent" though "illiterate."

Equally important was the degree to which a parent took seriously the accusations against the child and was willing to cooperate with the clinic.

Mrs. Perron questioned her boy's guilt, usually indicative of an unreliable witness, but this mother was also observed to be "much worried about the boy" and "cooperative" with the social worker, points in her favor. In another case Barnes found the woman's story "unreliable" when the mother of a fifteen-year-old charged with larceny denied that her son was also troublesome at home. Barnes believed the mother wanted to protect her son from incarceration in a state reformatory (1600). This mother's response was a self-protective stance common among families that depended on their children for financial assistance—guilt might mean the institutionalization of the boy and the loss of his income. Mrs. Perron was also surely conscious of her possible loss when she protested Franco's guilt. Nonetheless Mrs. Perron earned high marks at the clinic because, despite her poverty, she did not leave her children in order to work herself. The discovery of a mother's employment required the social worker to question a woman's commitment to her children and to look closely at how much supervision she offered.

The social worker's assessment of character often hinged on her appraisal of a parent's potential for overseeing her children's activities. Parental control might be deduced from the types of habits children exhibited. Alcohol, coffee, and tobacco were thought to stimulate misbehavior, and their use by a child indicated a parent who was a poor family manager. Franco, unfortunately, was a heavy smoker. Sleep patterns—irregular or late bedtimes—indicated lax control. The presence of bad habits such as persistent bedwetting or masturbation provided comment on the parents as well as the child in the social history.

A parent's character was also evident in the family's choice of home and neighborhood. Was the home rented or owned? How many rooms did the family occupy? Did the child have a separate bedroom? How was it furnished? Did the children have recreational facilities in the home or was the home so inadequate that fun had to be sought in the street? Mothers earned a social worker's good will if their homes were "neat" and "tidy" despite lives of poverty, but "dirt" stained a mother's clinic record as well as her living quarters. External appearances and material possessions shaped the social worker's evaluation of the Perron family in 1920. Mrs. Perron apparently met some of these standards for cleanliness, but the area in which she lived was a different story. Franco had grown up in a neighborhood of "exceedingly bad conditions," where he was able to come into contact with "bad companions" and "immoral girls."

While she may have commented on the parent's feelings about the child—was the mother protective, kindly, bitter?—the social worker at the Judge Baker Foundation was not concerned in 1920 with the internal dynamics of family relationships. Hers was a surface perception of child rearing. Their overall competency as parents, their willingness to cooperate with the clinic, the level of intelligence in the home, and the material assets of the family were the most important elements of the social worker's report. When neither mental conflict nor intellectual defect could be found, it was the social worker's description of the child's environment that often swayed the final determination of the child's personality and the clinic's recommendations. Charged with determining a plan for the troublesome child, the clinic staff regarded its investigation of the family as a crucial step in deciding whether or not a child could return to the home. In Franco Perron's case the report recommended first that the family should move from the neighborhood. Acknowledging that relocation would be "difficult" for this family, the clinic next recommended "placing," and the court interpreted this as a sentence to the state reformatory.

With no scales or standardized test scores to guide them, social workers relied on the authority of detail to make their case for or against a family and prove their value to the clinic's team. White pages from the psychiatrist were marked by their brevity; the green pages of the social history, in contrast, were a thorough jumble of carefully recorded facts laced with middle-class value judgments. The presentation of this minutia in a narrative history of the child and family constituted the social worker's specific contribution to the "scientific" child guidance analysis of each individual troublesome child. In 1920 the social worker's meticulous commentary defined the social context of troublesome juvenile behavior and often determined the clinic's recommendations.

Far from being the least important member of the professional team in 1920, the social worker was probably the most influential in the cases of the great majority of troublesome children who did not show signs of "feeblemindedness" or mental conflict.[51] Despite the acrimonious debates among the professions, in practice social workers, because they were women, had a far more grounded claim to authority in the child guidance clinic of 1920 than did psychiatrists. As women they had worked with and spoken for children and the needy, the patients who were expected now to fill child guidance rolls. As women of "sentiment" their presence gave legitimacy and public recognition to the whole undertaking of child guidance at a time when neither psychiatry nor psychology could quite provide such an acceptance grounded in science. Assigning to the social worker the role of intermediary between the clinic and the agency clients made the clinic's public face a familiar one. Speaking the same language, working on the same turf, usually of the same gender, social workers from the clinic could convey new psychiatric recommendations in a familiar discourse. Both psychiatry and psychology needed the female social workers and the feminine values they represented in 1920.

The workplace provided clinical psychology, child psychiatry, and social work with frequent and repeated opportunities to construct professional relationships and test professional boundaries. The lines of demarcation evident in 1920 would not remain static in the next two decades as clinics looked to families and schools for direct referrals and as the workplace became a center of treatment as well as diagnosis. In print and at meetings tension among the team's three professions ran high during these years. As the clients and services changed, however, the diagnostic rituals established in the first child guidance programs masked conflicts over workplace boundaries by emphasizing the unique and essential contribution of each profession, a contribution defined by the use of different techniques of analysis and consultation with different patients. The rituals did more, however, than gloss over the issues of status hierarchy and the functional boundaries of the three professions. In addition to enabling cooperation in the workplace, the team's rituals of diagnosis also constructed a single voice of "child guidance," a voice with more authority to speak about the troublesome child than any individual profession. In the clinic this voice took the form of a summary statement with recommendations generated at a team conference.

THE SUMMARY AND RECOMMENDATIONS: THE AUTHORITY OF CHILD GUIDANCE

After their separate evaluations the staff met in conference to produce the yellow sheets of case summaries and recommendations. This was the final ritual; clients were invited to take part in the proceedings as the team members pooled their knowledge to construct the unique route to delinquency taken by the individual patient.[52] The route—termed the "direct causation"—was never simple; five or six "direct causations" were not uncommon in the average summary. Recommendations, also known in 1920 as a case "outlook," presented plans for rehabilitation and sometimes predicted a dire future if no changes were made. Through these summaries and recommendations, presented to clients by the social worker, the team communicated their unified message of child guidance.

The summary statements from the 1920 case files contained three messages that enabled courts and welfare agencies to justify a decision to seek help from the Judge Baker clinic. First, the format of the summary statement with its complex list of causative factors pointed out just how difficult it was (surely too difficult for one individual or agency) to explain the troublesome child's conduct. In addition, the summary statements narrowed the meaning of social environment, and designated family deficiencies—and especially evidence of family neglect—as the clinic's more refined definition of environmental influences. Family intervention was a service child welfare agents were prepared to offer. Both the complex presentation and the restricted use of environment drew clients toward the clinic's primary conclusion—that the troublesome children described in these case reports were to be seen as victims, caught up in dynamics beyond their control. This blamelessness, in turn, justified the therapeutic response to misconduct. Complex causes, some of them hidden in the recesses of the child's mind, unsuccessfully mediated by the family of a child not responsible for the behavior or personality problem—this was the voice of child guidance in 1920. These shared precepts empowered all members of the child guidance team.

The use of these precepts was clearly evident in the clinic's handling of delinquency cases in which the psychologist diagnosed "mental defect." For many professional behavioral scientists in 1920 mental incapacity, as defined by performance on IQ tests, precluded other explanations of delinquency and virtually dictated incarceration to protect society from the "menace of the feebleminded." Henry H. Goddard, the leading proponent of these views, estimated that "25% to 50% of the people in our prisons are mentally defective and incapable of managing their affairs with ordinary prudence."[53] The views of Goddard and his supporters were simple— "feeblemindedness" meant crime and criminal behavior suggested "feeblemindedness." Little could be done by way of rehabilitation, which made identification and institutionalization of the mentally deficient criminal a matter of efficiency and economy.

Agents from the juvenile court and child welfare societies found the team's cognizance of the popular alarm and extensive intelligence testing an appealing part of a clinic evaluation. This was especially true for agencies that sponsored children in private homes or paid to educate them. When the Children's Aid Society received temporary guardianship of four siblings, its agent asked the Judge Baker Foundation to assess the eight-year-old's suitability for a rural placement. Finding the boy's IQ to be 74, with no special abilities, the clinic recommended institutionalization and the Children's Aid agent dropped the idea of foster care (1751). For the court, too, evidence of "feeblemindedness" could save time and money by reducing the number of delinquents seemingly misplaced in state reformatories. The ability to categorize and label by mental age proved to be one of the clinic's most attractive functions in the early 1920s.

While the diagnosis may have been straightforward, the clinic's recommendations for children with low IQs were far more complicated. Even at the Juvenile Psychopathic Institute Healy had given mixed signals about the relationship between "feeblemindedness" and delinquency. He often pointed to the significant number of delinquents who demonstrated subnormal ability. At the same time, however, Healy was one of the first to challenge the singlemindedness of Goddard and his supporters, earning him credit for helping to deflate fears about the public "menace."[54] The individual biographies in the case files showed how very complex the issue had become for the child guidance team. In these records "poor mental gifts," to quote a Philadelphia physician, seemed to cause delinquency only when coupled with "poor mental training."[55] Bad companions, mishandling, and an unsupervised environment turned the "defective" child into a "defective" delinquent.

The significance of "mental training" was particularly evident in cases of female adolescents with limited intellectual ability. Presumably the unrestrained sexual activity of these young women would lead to pregnancy and the reproduction of both defective mentality and delinquency. Child savers often preferred institutionalization, and even sterilization, of these young women.[56] The Judge Baker Foundation summaries and recommendations, in contrast, reflected Healy's concern with individual assessment.

The Judge Baker staff carefully screened girls charged with sexual misbehavior for signs of mental incapacity. Likewise, nondelinquent girls who tested poorly were scrutinized for evidence of sexual activity. Yet despite the fear of sexual misconduct, the team did not regard "feeblemindedness" as a sufficient explanation for the sex delinquencies seen at the clinic in 1920, nor was institutionalization the only recourse. The cases of sixteen-year-old Alice (1594) and fifteen-year-old Josephine (1683) captured the clinic's nuanced response to sex delinquency. Alice, mentioned previously as a case of sexual immorality, performed poorly on the aptitude tests, but with her IQ of 84 the team did not feel comfortable labeling her "feebleminded," despite evidence of many instances of "sex immoralities" with neighborhood boys and the temptation of a nearby cheap dance hall. What to do with Alice? The social worker's study of the family suggested that if Alice were set to work at routine domestic tasks, her parents could supply adequate supervision to prevent future sexual misbehavior.

Josephine's IQ of 63 clearly labeled her subnormal. Yet even in this case, evidence of the girl's sex delinquencies and her defective mentality were together not sufficient reason to class this as an "institutional case." Josephine required institutionalization only because "nothing can be hoped in the way of good family protection." The clinic concluded that, with a mother who appeared to be mentally defective yet who also worked and refused to stop working even after the girl's immorality was explained, Josephine could expect no proper guidance during this period of adolescent sexual development. Alice, on the other hand, might be returned home because her family, which was financially stable, promised more supervision.

When the team did not find evidence of sexual immorality in a girl who fared poorly on the psychologist's tests, the Judge Baker staff looked to personality and the environment for explanations. Anne Manville (whose case Healy and Bronner published as part of a training manual for child guidance workers) was a fifteen-year-old brought to the clinic for vocational guidance by a family relief agency. Anne tested as a "high grade moron" (IQ, 71), but she was certainly not a sex delinquent. It was not because she was unattractive, nor was it because she had an especially good home situation. "Much has surrounded her that ordinarily would tend to drag a girl down, and indeed, did induct her sisters into vicious ways," Healy and Bronner noted. Instead, Anne's personality traits had saved her from degradation. She was neither "socially suggestible," nor "gregarious," nor "as restless as girls of her age frequently are." In Anne's case, personality had prevented delinquency, but the team went on to recommend that she be placed in a family who could maintain her unblemished record.[57]

The cases of Anne, Alice, and Josephine underscored for the clinic's clients the futility of relying on a simple explanation of delinquency. Other cases in which children had been misdiagnosed as "feebleminded" also registered the child guidance aversion to a single cause for troublesome behavior. Eleven-year-old David had been in court several times before he came to the clinic for an evaluation. Team research discovered that David was enrolled in one of Boston's "special" classes for the "mentally defective," but his performance on the psychologist's tests was clearly "average." The final report recommended that David be removed from the class for slow learners. He needed instead "discipline and hard work," and a Big Brother to supply "mental interests and recreation" (1818). The team suggested that with David's mental ability correctly identified, his chronic delinquent tendencies could be readily stifled.

Similar incidents of mislabeling and misdiagnosis provided child guidance with one of its most important discoveries. Not only were most of the children found to be intellectually normal, but a few of the delinquents or agency troublemakers could be classified as "supernormal." From evidence in their cases child guiders concluded that children with above-average ability, kept in school classes that failed to provide challenges, might turn to delinquency for intellectual stimulation, or they might withdraw from classroom activity and give every appearance of poor mental ability. Clearly a high IQ did not always prevent the development of delinquent behavior, and a simple equation of delinquency with low intellectual ability was inadequate. In the clinic's interpretations of the children, factors of personality and environment determined whether or not the child's intellectual ability or inability was used for delinquent or socially acceptable purposes.

Most of these children grew up in working-class immigrant neighborhoods, with a community spirit built around multifamily housing and lots of street life. Summary statements routinely listed the environment of urban poverty investigated by the social worker as a "direct causation" of delinquency. This was an explanation easily understood by the child welfare agents who moved through these streets. The evaluation of nine-year-old Anthony points out the complex relationship the team drew between poverty and crime. Anthony appeared to be a quiet, shy boy, but this son of Italian immigrants was accused of breaking and entering along with two companions. Anthony's father had died two years earlier during the influenza epidemic, and his mother now worked in a candy factory to support the family. Living in an unsavory neighborhood ("where all the boys and some of the girls are bad") with a working mother, Anthony suffered, according to the clinic, from "excessive lack of supervision," "excessive street life," and "bad companions." Even the boy's rather questionable mental ability did not overrule these environmental factors in the clinic's diagnosis. To save Anthony from a life of crime, the clinic recommended (as it did in many of these cases) that the family should move from this neighborhood and his mother should receive aid so that she could stay home to care for her children (1598).

Anthony's story was one of poverty, but the clinic's records presented it more directly as one of family management. Anthony's mother did not provide a buffer between the boy and the neighborhood. This story was one of myriad tales in which "lack of supervision" appeared in the summary statement. Mildred's was another. Ten-year-old Mildred stayed out late at night and hung around Boston's North Station; her mother, a Children's Mission agent, and the juvenile court judge (who was reviewing a stubborn complaint against the girl) were troubled by the girl's brash behavior. Mildred and her mother could be counted among the truly destitute in Boston even though the woman worked long hours for a local charity to try to support her family. Bronner's examination of Mildred was straightforward, and this "friendly," "alert" little girl showed no evidence of "repression." Mildred spoke freely about bad words and dirty pictures that circulated among her friends. Nor did the psychological tests support the school's placement of Mildred in a special class; the child was not "feeble-minded." Instead the staff concluded that Mildred was "growing up in street life." Left to her own devices while her mother worked, Mildred had developed an independent, insubordinate attitude. Bad companions, bad neighborhood conditions, and unwholesome recreation were all exacerbated by the "extreme lack of parental supervision" that allowed Mildred to roam the city at night (1835). Mildred's "delinquencies" appeared to be more suspicion than fact, but the "causative factors" were the realities of her life among the Boston poor and, most important, the perception that her family would not stand between Mildred and the streets. By making the family's ability to supervise a causal factor in troublesome behavior the child guidance team generated more evidence of the complexity of delinquency diagnosis and treatment.

A spider's web of complexity ruled these child guidance summaries. Social environment and mental ability were certainly critical elements of "direct causation," and fundamental considerations in the clinic's recommendations. Yet family supervision and individual personality modified both the poor environment and the weak intellect. The child guidance message was clear—clients had been right to seek an evaluation, because the conditions that created delinquency, evidenced by the findings in most of the cases, were too complicated for any one worker to diagnose. As child guidance clients were urged to believe, only the combined expertise of a team of professionals could supply an accurate representation of the problem, one that would point to the most direct and efficient changes needed to eliminate the delinquency.

These child guidance summaries also conveyed clearly the message that though troublesome, the children were not responsible for their plight. In part their poverty and the frequent lack of supervision shielded them from blame. But so did the very concept of personality. Created by the complex interaction of the child, the family, and the situation, personality did not mark a child permanently; it was malleable and could be changed. Moreover, it was more easily changed than a social structure that dictated poverty for some and wealth for others. And therein lay the confidence of the child guidance movement and its promise to the child savers. By first identifying the complex nature of the problem, child guidance could then simplify the process of reform. On the basis of their list of causes, the team designed recommendations for the individual child and family. Child savers could move the family, provide aid, find role models for the children, send them to camp for healthy recreation, change their schooling, or institutionalize them.

With the extensive commentary on the "menace of the feebleminded" and the evident "crime wave" among juveniles, a burning question of both humanitarian and economic concern to the child savers was when to institutionalize. Child guidance promised to sort out the hard cases who needed firm discipline and structure from the more easily modified cases who could be handled in the community or by the family. Did the team succeed? In evaluating the Judge Baker recommendations years later, judges complained that the proposals were often impractical. Healy, however, found that the child savers frequently sought evaluations but ignored the findings. Children that could have been saved by timely intervention were, he believed, left to drift into adult criminal careers. In 1920, however, without benefit of follow-up studies, the message from the three child guidance professions was one of untempered optimism. The single voice of child guidance would diagnose the problems of the troublesome child.

Creation of the child guidance team was an adroit stroke of profession building. Through the rituals of diagnosis—the routine practices of evaluation and recommendation—professionals from new areas of clinical work with children constructed separate identities in the workplace and created the boundaries that permitted interdisciplinary study of the troublesome child. The rituals of teamwork also created boundaries between the child guidance team and its clients, some of whom belonged to the same professions as the team members. The team spoke with an authority that no single profession had yet earned. Clinical psychology was a new area with practitioners who wanted to practice their skills on more than the "feeble-minded." Social workers faced gender barriers as well as questions about their training and expertise. Psychiatry was a field in flux, with some who would call themselves "social psychiatrists" trying to extend the application of the field to ordinary problems, including the troublesome child. The alliance formed through child guidance in the 1920s gave this eclectic combination of clinicians a powerful voice in the child-saving community. The alliance was formalized in 1926 when the American Orthopsychiatric Association, a group formed by some of the preeminent child guidance psychiatrists, reorganized to include psychologists and psychiatric social workers as members.[58] Orthopsychiatry, psychiatry to straighten crooked personalities, to rectify the problems of troublesome children, was a voice more powerful than that of the psychiatrists alone.

4

Popularizing Child Guidance

Child guidance did not stay in the clinic during the 1920s and 1930s; nor did it remain a method simply for steadying the life course of juvenile delinquents and unruly dependents. During these decades child guidance advice about emotional conflict, personality maladjustment, and the determining role of the family environment spread beyond the confines of social reform to become the discourse of private child rearing as well as the language of delinquency policy. Even the very medical world of Dr. Spock had a psychological tinge by 1945, and pediatricians, the nineteenth-century harbingers of professional child-rearing advice, acquiesced to the comprehensive explanations of troublesome behavior provided by child guidance. Practitioners from all three of the team's disciplines promoted the message in public forums, but they were not alone. Help with the popularization of child guidance came from many sources. In this chapter and the next, I look first at the efforts to popularize and advertise child guidance and then at the audience for the child guidance message.

Two new constructs entered child guidance discourse in the 1920s to facilitate the process of popularization. The first was the concept of "predelinquency," predicated on the belief that troublesome children of any sort were on the road to delinquency and should be identified and helped before they were labeled by the juvenile justice system. The second and more important concept was that of the "everyday child" (from families of any social class) showing ordinary signs of misbehavior any parent might anticipate. To the child guiders this form of trouble did not indicate psychopathic personality, "feeblemindedness," or delinquency, but it was to be reckoned a serious problem nonetheless. According to the child guidance script, it presaged a lifetime of maladjustment and unhappiness. Fortunately, the message continued, the troublesome behavior was correctable if its causes were properly identified and eradicated by applying child guidance principles.

Since Progressive child-saving agencies did not claim responsibility for these predelinquent and "everyday" problem children, the task of recognizing symptoms fell to others who came face-to-face with the young—pediatricians and general practitioners, teachers, and especially parents. To grow as a community service, child guiders would have to teach their clients to think about troublesome children in the language of personality and individual family environment rather than delinquency, class, and heredity. Ester Loring Richards, a psychiatrist from the Johns Hopkins School of Medicine, reminded her colleagues in 1926 that child guidance had not yet accomplished this educational task. "To the mothers you are a false pastor of the infant flock; to the teachers you are a pilgrim stranger in the land of pedagogy; to organized business you are a suspicious candidate for philanthropy; and to formal medicine you are more or less of an outcast, complacently classified with spinal adjustments and physiotherapy."[1] Others had strong claims to the "everyday child." Professional survival as well as professional authority depended on the popularization of child guidance.[2]

Many historians have hinted that successful professionalization of science and medicine depended on the public's mastery of new messages and incorporation of new services into everyday routine. Yet the process of popularization, or the means by which discoveries in the medical sciences make their way into public consciousness, remains elusive.[3] Child guidance provides a rich case study of medical popularization. How did this self-conscious community of professionals saturate the culture with notions of child mental hygiene? And who were their assistants in this task? The popularization of medicine in the twentieth century cannot easily be divorced from the emergence of a consumer culture and the power of advertising. To popularize child guidance was to advertise, to display a service and generate a need for professional assistance with troublesome children. Members of the child guidance community deliberately set out to suffuse the child-rearing market with their psychological explanations and prescriptions for problems, and they did so as a way to legitimate their professional authority and thereby expand the clientele for their services. Professional (and personal) aggrandizement, however, has to be balanced against the many popularizers of child guidance who were humanitarian activists, hoping to engineer a more perfect society by placing their faith in the promise of science.[4] Modern parents, they believed, had to trust in child guidance, or the modern child was doomed. This chapter identifies four situations in which child guiders publicly displayed their wares.

Child guidance specialists frequently gained assistance from individuals and groups outside the professions, and popularization took place in many forums. The child guidance popularizers drew strength from the publicity work of the National Committee for Mental Hygiene, and often found funding from the large philanthropies—the Commonwealth Fund and the Laura Spelman Rockefeller Memorial.[5] Although this support cannot be discounted, the direct points of contact between child guidance and the public determined the popular understanding and acceptance of psychiatric authority. Advice literature was one of the most popular forms of communication, published by commercial presses in magazines and books, or printed and distributed by government agencies, including the federal Children's Bureau and state divisions of mental hygiene. Face-to-face contact, through public lectures, clinic fund-raising events, and parent education programs was a second. The courtroom demonstration of the principles of child guidance during the nationally publicized Leopold and Loeb trial was a third path to public awareness. And efforts to engage the attention and support of pediatricians and general practitioners offered a fourth opportunity to promote child guidance and the clinics. The child guidance community and its allies used these key sites to try to convince modern parents of the need for psychotherapeutic help with the new troublesome child.

THE PREDELINQUENT AND THE EVERYDAY CHILD

By the time the Commonwealth Fund delinquency prevention program opened its third demonstration clinic in Dallas in 1923, the troublesome "predelinquent," rather than Healy's "early delinquent," had begun to claim the attention of the child guidance community.[6] Signs of predelinquency might include disobedience at home, negativism, stubbornness, rebelliousness, temper displays, stealing from parents, truancy, failure to get along with other children, school failure, sleep disturbances, fears, excessive fantasy, and many more unlovable juvenile traits. Child guiders such as George Stevenson, director of the Institute for Child Guidance in New York City, threatened that left uncorrected, these "more subtle evidences of non-adjustment [seen] in the home and the school" could lead children first to the juvenile court and possibly to a lifetime of crime.[7]

Because the behavioral characteristics could apply to many children, the threat of predelinquency might attract to the clinic families from social classes that did not usually think of their children as delinquent. "Predelinquency" expanded the clinic's catchment area, but the association with illegal activity and the courts made it less successful as an imperialist construct than the new image of the "everyday child."

The "everyday child" eliminated the stigma of delinquency and degeneracy (and lower-class welfare dependency) from the work of child guidance. When child guiders popularized the "everyday problems of the everyday child," they divorced the consequences of troublesome juvenile conduct from adult criminality and related it instead to a lifetime of emotional unhappiness and personal failure. In 1927 the psychiatrist Douglas Thom used the phrase as a title for his widely recommended book of advice for American parents, and the words soon became synonymous with child guidance work. "Most children are normal," Thom observed. "Few if any are perfect. It is with this normal group, which represents the great mass of children found in every social group, that we are primarily concerned."[8] These otherwise normal children were not immune to a host of annoying behaviors and emotions, from feeding and sleep problems to anger, fear, and jealousy, as well as the worrisome traits of the predelinquent. A colleague of Thom's went so far as to call the characteristics "absolutely unavoidable problems."[9] No parent could escape—the normal "everyday child" was trouble just waiting to be recognized. By identifying everyday behavior as problematic, child guidance knocked on the door of every family in the country regardless of class affiliation.

With the "everyday child" the popularizers of child guidance drew into their sights children of all ages as well as all social classes. Thom's book took middle childhood as its focus, but much of his clinical experience had been as director of the Boston Habit Clinic, a specialized mental hygiene institution for preschoolers opened in 1921. Habit clinics relied more directly than child guidance on the tactics of behaviorism to treat the very young, although thinking about the need for intervention was much the same as in child guidance for older children.[10] Left untreated, temper tantrums or refusals to eat promised more serious trouble as the child grew older. "Take care of the first five years and the rest will take care of themselves," cautioned the Massachusetts Society for Mental Hygiene as it offered parents a list of rules for keeping children "sound in body, mind and character."[11]

In another publicity pamphlet the Massachusetts Society for Mental Hygiene dramatized the everyday problems of the everyday preschool child through "The Story of Mother Wise." After following Mr. and Mrs. Want-To-Do-Right and their toddler through a day of temper tantrums about food and bedtime, a reader could empathize when Mrs. Want-To-Do-Right "leaned wearily against the living room door, her head in her hands," and asked aloud, "Whatever shall I do about Jane?" The child guidance campaigns usually portrayed parents, of both preschoolers and adolescents, in just such an exasperated state. "Whatever shall I do?" from a parent summoned the psychiatric community to action. Smilo, the health sprite, leaped to the rescue, introducing the Do-Rights to Mother Wise and her methods for raising six healthy and cooperative children. Jane's parents were quick learners and as they put out the cat for the night, Mr. and Mrs. Want-To-Do-Right "determined to do differently."[12]

"The Story of Mother Wise" contained a powerful lesson about wisdom and authority repeated in many guises by the popularizers. Plans for correcting Jane's behavior seemed to come from a straightforward sharing of knowledge by an older, wiser mother. Yet this "Mother Wise" was a fitting teacher for the young parents only because her advice mirrored child guidance precepts. Untutored maternal experience alone would not be effective, and modern parents of troublesome Janes and annoying older children required the assistance of professional guides. The pamphlet concluded, "When measures commonly used in child training fail, parents are advised to have their children examined at one of the following [child guidance and habit] clinics." Boston and the surrounding areas offered parents sixteen consultation sites.

Popularizers often used real life dramas and personalized stories to acquaint parents with the construct of the everyday problem, present in any household and in need of psychological attention before it grew to unmanageable, socially stigmatizing proportions. Douglas Thom, for example, sprinkled his advice books with "cases," presumably true accounts of his clinical work with children. "An effort has been made," he told parents of adolescents in the preface to Normal Youth and Its Everyday Problems (1932), "to illustrate many of these problems with brief descriptive stories of actual cases, without, however, including those in which the boy or girl was brought before the juvenile court, sent to a correctional school or reformatory, or otherwise institutionalized because of delinquent conduct, parental neglect, mental deficiency, or other serious handicaps." Parents could read of young Morton, whose "schoolmaster was fast losing patience with the continuous reports of this boy's smutty stories," and Felicia, whose mother complained that "her young daughter seems to 'hate' her."[13] "A little girl, aged three and one-half years," treated by Thom at the Habit Clinic because of "terrifying dreams, an intense fear of dogs, and extreme shyness," embodied the message about fear in Thom's discussion of younger children.[14] To personify the problems related to sex, Thom told the case of "*Alice,* a nine-year-old, [who] was brought to the clinic for two definite reasons; first because of hysterical convulsions, and secondly, because of her precocious sex interest and sex delinquencies, which had begun when the child was between five and six years of age."[15] The fear of dogs and terrifying nightmares were soon banished "by instructing the mother and giving the child a proper attitude toward animals." Alice, who had traveled the slippery slope to delinquency, could have been rescued earlier if her parents had known of the need for sex education. Thom did not overtly tell parents with everyday problems to go to a clinic for help, and yet in presenting the "cases" and their solutions he requested readers to acknowledge the wisdom he had "gleaned from a large experience with children and parents" and the "information we have gathered in the course of our efforts to meet actual needs in child training."[16]

Child guidance popularizers wrote to re-create the intimacy of the doctor-patient consultation. In format, the narratives in Thom's books duplicated the narratives of the child guidance clinic summary statement: the psychological work-up, the child's discussion with the doctor, and the social worker's description of the situation, followed by the successful outcome. These personal stories also replicated the methods of modern copywriters who turned the personal story ad, or the sociodrama, into an art form in the 1920s. Roland Marchand has called this advertising trend "'dramatic realism'—a style derived from the romantic novel and soon institutionalized in the radio soap opera." It was a style that "intensified everyday problems and triumphs by tearing them out of humdrum routine, spotlighting them as crucial to immediate life decisions, or fantasizing them within enhanced, luxurious social settings."[17] The ads told a commonplace tale of woe, with a happy ending that could be had through the purchase of a product. Listerine was one of the first to use this device successfully, with its "Always a Bridesmaid" ad warning of the dire consequences of halitosis.[18] To be sure, child guidance popularizers rarely fantasized luxurious social settings in their tales of troublesome children, yet for problematizing the "everyday" child's behavior an ordinary middle-class home served the same purpose. Only a sense of déjà vu had to be created: any mother could have found herself in a similar situation.

In sum, the child guidance community set about popularizing the clinics and their professional staff by psychologizing all child-rearing issues, from toddler to adolescent and from minor transgression to major delinquency or unhappiness. As they did so, they subordinated the problems of delinquency and dependency and the taint of mental retardation, although they certainly did not discard these issues. Rather, the troublesome child acquired an "everyday" face in the popularized versions of child guidance, one that looked remarkably like the reader's daughter or son. As the catchy phrase demonstrated that no child was immune to problem behavior, the personal style of presentation showed that incompetent parents (or, rather, those not educated in the principles of child guidance) from any social class could be responsible for creating a troublesome child. The stories helped to make the clinic a refuge for those with economic resources as well as for those who had to do without.

PRINTING THE MESSAGE

The personalized stories appeared as part of the printed record of child guidance popularization. Publishers of books, magazines, and newspapers provided the premier site through which parents learned about the significance they should attribute to everyday problems and the help professionally staffed clinics could provide. Douglas Thom was only one of many authors who took on the task of educating parents through print. *Mental Hygiene*, the primary journal for child guidance professionals, reviewed more than seventy-five books with child guidance themes published for parents between 1917 (when the journal began publication) and 1945.[19] Articles about children in mass-circulation women's magazines came from the pens of child guidance professionals and popularizers. Editors of *Parents' Magazine*, first published in 1926 as a popular journal devoted to all aspects of child rearing, deliberately adopted a child guidance perspective. Authors of books and magazine articles were joined by the syndicated newspaper columnist Angelo Patri, who offered up child guidance advice in answers to questions posed by parents. Government too contributed to the printed word as the federal Children's Bureau sponsored pamphlets for parents written by child guidance popularizers. The troublesome possibilities of normal childhood behavior became such a ubiquitous theme in the women's press that advertisers borrowed the message to create copy for consumer products. In all these printed venues, child guidance populariz-ers rewrote the relationship between parents and advisors as they planted troublesome children in families of all social classes.

Professional reviews of popularized advice books for parents, published in the journal *Mental Hygiene,* offer one window onto the expectations child guiders had for the process of popularization. Most important, and not unexpectedly, the process had a class bias. Reviewers often observed that the intended audience for the books was "parents of the so-called mid-dle classes," "average" but nonetheless "intelligent" or "educated" mothers and fathers.[20] In no case did a reviewer suggest the need to broaden this audience. Popularizers planned to reach the family in which a concerned, full-time mother rather than a nurse or nanny was the primary child rearer. Only one book, Eleanor Saltzman's *Learning to Be Good Parents* (1937), was reviewed as a text deliberately designed for "simple folk of limited financial means and probably limited education."[21]

Child guidance literature continued the flow of parenting manuals for middle-class families begun during the nineteenth century. For antebellum women from this class, motherhood had become the foundation of self-identity. They kept informed of the latest advances in medicine and used their knowledge and common sense to rear healthy children. At the turn of the new century, this class of women, the same ones who formed the early child study clubs or joined the National Congress of Mothers (precursor of the Parent-Teacher Association), would be called practitioners of "scientific motherhood." They conceded little to the experts. Books were guides, to choose from or ignore as common sense deemed appropriate. The respect they commanded contributed to the authority of the Progressive maternal-ists. Pediatric and psychiatric advice written for this class of women pro-moted careful child rearing as a way to avoid coming into contact with doctors or asylums. *Infant Care* (1914), the first pamphlet available to families from the federal Children's Bureau (and one written by a mother), never doubted the average mother's common sense or her ability to locate, and reject, expert wisdom when necessary.[22]

Dismantling maternal autonomy and establishing a new relationship between mothers and experts was an essential component of the popu-larization process, accomplished in part by appropriating and redefining "common sense."[23] The first step was to delegitimate maternal self-reliance.

In child guidance popularizations what mothers called common sense was belittled as "folk wisdom" or "maternal instinct," set in contrast to the superior evidence of scientific expertise. Common sense was also branded as old-fashioned, sometimes referred to as the "problem of the grandmothers," definitely not synonymous with progress. Having relegated maternal common sense to the ash heap, popularizers then commandeered the phrase for their professional therapeutic culture. For example, a reviewer praised author Anna Wolf, who, while urging that parents should trust their own common sense, also encouraged them to "supplement their own ingenuity by the knowledge of persons who have studied child development in a mental-hygiene sense."[24] Trust in the nebulous, intuitive common sense of maternal self-reliance frequently led mothers astray and prevented them from seeing signs of serious trouble in a child's misbehavior; real common sense led mothers to rely on the practitioners of child guidance.

Popularizers wrote to convince women of the need for consultation with experts, but during the 1920s and 1930s, not every family had access to a clinic. Popularizers also wrote to supply a substitute for face-to-face consultation. Writers and reviewers alike regarded the books as substitutes for trips to the clinic. Smiley Blanton, director of the Minneapolis Child Guidance Clinic, and Dorothy Gray Blanton wrote in *Child Guidance* (1927) that their book filled a niche between studies of the "problem child" and the "normal child." It was meant for "that single phase in which the normal child is the problem." Moreover, the book was specifically promoted as a "supplement to the guidance clinic and in an effort to meet the need where no clinics exist."[25] Similarly, the reviewer of Miriam Finn Scott's *Meeting Your Child's Problems* (1922) noted that few parents could "betake themselves and their child to the New York Child-Garden [the habit clinic conducted by the book's author] . . . Until habit clinics become general, most parents will have to depend upon the literature of a more enlightened parenthood for suggestions concerning the behavior problems of children. Does Mrs. Scott's book . . . make it possible for parents better to understand their children and then to retrain wherever retraining is indicated? It does."[26]

Reviewers judged manuals successful depending on how well the authors turned technical, scientific material into friendly advice. When Ester Loring Richards reviewed *Living with Our Children: A Book of Little Essays for Mothers* written by "a mother and teacher," she heartily approved of the absence of technical language in its pages. "The words 'psychology,' 'complex,' and 'repression' do not appear throughout the text, and yet its pages deal most helpfully with concrete problems of behavior adjustment involving instinct, habit formation, emotional states, and reasoning processes." Perhaps, Richards went on to suggest, this was precisely what "the laity" wanted; child guidance "theories" were useless unless "accompanied by corrective exercises and sensible suggestions." This "mother" had apparently succeeded where some of the more sophisticated child guidance popularizers had failed.[27] In addition to assessing readability reviewers also scrutinized texts for signs of conformity to the new psychological paradigm of child behavior, acting as an unofficial "police force" for the process of popularization.[28] For example, in an otherwise favorable critique, the reviewer of *Good Manners for Children* (1926) upbraided the authors for a "flagrant violation" of mental hygiene principles—suggesting that a well-mannered child speaks at table only when spoken to.[29]

Popularizers believed they had to walk a fine line between faithfulness to the child guidance creed and the need to share professional expertise with an untutored public. The separate professional language was a community-building strategy for child guiders. The complex vocabulary not only attested to their expertise; it distinguished child guidance from the common-sense and everyday language of motherhood. Yet, as Richards perceived, the laity had to be brought into the fold if child guidance was to succeed. The need to balance readability with expertise raised questions about who should popularize child guidance and the clinics.

Manuals written by mothers (without professional credentials) highlighted, for the reviewers, a tension between a desire to popularize and the determination to speak with one professional voice and delegitimate maternal authority. Although not "experts," these women, for example, Dorothy Canfield Fisher, the popular novelist and author of several child rearing books, were often professional writers whose skill with language made them valuable resources for the child guidance movement. Yet only if properly attuned to modern practices could they be considered effective substitutes for the clinic. Even an expert could be soundly cuffed for producing a book about "nervous, mischievous, precocious, and backward children" if the bad advice "must tend to fix the layman's belief that nothing is known scientifically of the problems discussed."[30]

Reviewers were particularly careful to inspect the works of medical and psychological faddists for adherence to child guidance principles. If not totally committed to the tenets of Freud, child guidance popularizers were expected to pay homage to the importance of the emotional content of a child's mind and the possibility of repression or hidden mental conflicts. William A. White's *The Mental Hygiene of Childhood*, with its "frankly psychoanalytic exposition" was nonetheless found to be an "invaluable" book for "intelligent parents."[31] In contrast *Auto-suggestion for Mothers*, written by a follower of the popular French psychotherapist Emile Coué, threatened the professionalism of child guidance[32] as did *The Child and the Home*, whose author was dismissed as "a vegetarian, a pacifist, and apparently a believer in drugless therapy."[33]

Psychological Care of Infant and Child (1928), by the behavioral psychologist John B. Watson, was less easily disowned. Watson had been a respected researcher before leaving his university position in 1920 and turning to the world of advertising. The habit clinics in particular relied on behaviorist techniques to treat the very young. The reviewer could certainly agree with Watson's claim that "no one to-day knows enough to raise a child"; every child guidance popularizer took that stance. Then, too, she found that "many of his specific suggestions" were "very excellent indeed." On the whole, however, Watson's views were too extreme for child guidance tastes (particularly his disapproval of demonstrations of parental affection), or they were merely hypotheses without proof. Watson, after all, denied any role to heredity and emotional instincts in personality formation. Child guidance took a more tempered view of the nature-nurture controversy.[34] Nonetheless, Watson's voice carried the same scientific authority child guidance writers wanted to project. The reviewer trod gently as she raised questions about his theoretical framework. Other writers, lacking Watson's scientific credentials, were more vulnerable. The few religious texts evaluated in *Mental Hygiene* met the reviewers' rigorous standards because the religious writers combined a notion of spiritual hygiene with sound child guidance principles.[35]

The *Mental Hygiene* reviewers encouraged and praised those who took up the task of popularization and sanctioned those who failed to meet the standards of simplicity, common sense, and psychological correctness. To the professional reviewers, manuals by those well known in the profession—Douglas Thom, Smiley Blanton, William A. White, and Ester Loring Richards—promised to become classics. But these same reviewers bestowed their blessing on any book that could teach parents how to identify an everyday problem, how to examine it from a psychological perspective, and how to seek help when common sense failed—in other words, how to rely on the common sense of child guidance. The books approved in *Mental Hygiene* found their way onto the recommended reading lists in *Parents' Magazine* and the bibliographies of child study clubs.

Mass-circulation women's magazines offered another print forum for popularization. Child management articles, promoting the themes endorsed by *Mental Hygiene* reviewers, appeared as regular reading fare in *Women's Home Companion, Ladies' Home Journal, Good Housekeeping, Better Homes and Gardens, The Delineator, Hygeia,* and *Saturday Evening Post.* Since the authors of many of the books directed their works to the attention of teachers and doctors as well as parents, these weekly and monthly publications were perhaps more effective in reaching a broad audience of fathers and especially mothers. Although never attaining quite the distribution of *Women's Home Companion, Ladies' Home Journal,* or (the most popular of all) *True Story Magazine, Parents' Magazine* was the most aggressive child guidance popularizer. "Our aim," the editors enthused in the first issue in 1926, "is to bring to you who are out on the firing-line, the scientific findings of the specialists concerning the child's needs of mind, body and spirit from birth to the twenty-first year."[36]

The child guidance view of trouble appeared in magazine advertisements as well as feature articles. This form of popularization, however, dispensed with the therapeutic solution. Commonsense consumption by the average mother replaced the common sense of child guidance intervention. Ads for Fletcher's Castoria, a children's laxative, frequently exploited the new definition of the troublesome child. "But—maybe she *isn't* 'Crying over nothing,'" the ad from the January 1935 issue of *Parent's Magazine* admonished a stern-faced mother confronting a sobbing child. "When a mild reproof brings a flood of tears," the text cautioned, parents should "take heed!" Both advertisers and child guidance authors problematized the expressions of a child's emotional life; crying, grouchy disposition, and nervousness rightly puzzled parents. The parallels stopped at this point, however, for in the advertising world the cause was not to be sought in psychology and the solution was a "mild, effective" laxative.[37]

In his history of the ad industry Roland Marchand has observed that advertisers "reflect" society to the extent that they depict the technology and material artifacts available at a given time. In this sense, child guidance popularizers made a newly democratized troublesome child available to the advertisers. The didactic advertisements popular in the 1920s and

1930s (selling, in addition to Fletcher's Castoria, Campbell's Soups, Wheetena, Quaker Oats, and scores of other products) drew moral lessons about product consumption from the same incidents popularizers used to sell the therapeutic culture of child guidance.[38] The story ad was an unintentional site for child guidance popularization. Yet, as did the child guiders, ad writers too promoted the belief that a child's everyday problems could no longer be resolved simply by the application of old-fashioned common sense.

Newspaper readers would have come into contact with the child guidance message through "Our Children," the nationally circulated advice column written by Angelo Patri, a New York City school principal. In the column Patri responded to parents' questions about everyday problems, inviting them to write him directly about their concerns. The replies often counseled the importance of a child's emotional life and the need to consult professional psychological help. Patri's allegiance to child guidance was not always as complete as loyalists in the field deemed necessary; one *Mental Hygiene* review accused the popular writer of a "happy dalliance on the outskirts of science."[39] Parents, however, apparently made the connection. Case files show that some families were drawn to the Judge Baker Foundation by advice in Patri's column.[40]

Through publications authorized by the Children's Bureau, the federal government also assisted in popularizing and legitimizing the messages of child guidance to an audience probably not reached by advice books or *Parents' Magazine*. Parents from all walks of life wrote to the federal Children's Bureau. Their letters suggest that many mothers regarded the bureau as an inexpensive substitute for medical advice they could not afford or could not access because they lived in rural areas. In reply to the queries, the Children's Bureau staff often mailed copies of its short, readable publications. This agency, established in 1912, was a bastion of Progressive maternalist concern for the welfare of women and children. The women of the Children's Bureau did not, however, write the messages about child guidance. In a move that marked the realignment of power between Progressive women and the rising generation of professional child experts, the Children's Bureau turned to recognized psychiatrists to promote child mental hygiene.[41]

William Healy was one of the first to advance child guidance through the Children's Bureau, with a pamphlet urging communities to undertake the "scientific study" of individual delinquents.[42] Douglas Thom's pamphlet

"Child Management" (1925) was aimed at parents, and raised the specter of the predelinquent. "Stealing is a harsh word to apply to the acts of children," Thom wrote, "[because] it is associated so closely with a criminal career." If parents excused petty thieving and deceived themselves with the belief that it was just "pilfering," or even "unselfish" if a child gave away what he or she stole, they established patterns early in life that could be "rarely overcome."[43]

"Child Management" made no attempt to simplify the ideas of child guidance. Thom wrote the pamphlet for the sophisticated reader, and did not include the simple and practical advice that *Mental Hygiene* reviewers were beginning to demand from child guidance popularizers. "Are You Training Your Child to Be Happy?" (1930) toned down the psychological jargon. The sentences were short, the words, easily understood. From Lesson 1, for example:

> *Do you want your child to form good habits?*
>   The first time you do something new it is hard.
>   Next time it is easier.
>   Next time it is very easy.
>   Soon you can do it and not think about it at all.
>   Then we call it a *habit*.[44]

Designed for the parents of preschoolers, the pamphlet did not have a unit on stealing, but the section entitled "Does Your Child Tell You the Truth?" asked parents to think about different kinds of lies and, without using the word, the motives behind the lies, before confronting a child with punishment.[45]

In the literate culture of the early twentieth century, popularizers looked to the written word as a fast and direct way to reach the public with the message of child guidance. Some combination of prestige, monetary reward, and community service no doubt motivated those who wrote the texts for public consumption. With not enough clinics to serve the whole nation, the child guidance community used the presses to engage the reading public. The resulting printed documents made the opportunity for consultation with specialized child mental health practitioners appear to be a necessary part of successful child rearing. By making "normal" and "ordinary" misbehavior a symptom of trouble, the child guidance popularizers set advice in a therapeutic rather than a preventive context. In doing so, they redefined the relationship between parents and advisors, usurping for child guidance practitioners the authority inherent in the control of "treat-ment." Rather than being seen as manuals for self-help, these texts are better read as prescriptions telling parents to invite child guidance inter-vention into their family relationships.

Whatever the personal motives of the authors, the sheer numbers of publications suggest that others outside the community of professional clinicians also stood to gain from the popularization of child guidance. For the Children's Bureau, presentation of "modern" scientific child-rearing advice helped to legitimize a novel federal department, unpopular with the Public Health Service, the American Medical Association, and conser-vative politicos who thought the agency part of a Bolshevik plot to destroy American democracy.[46] To continue mass producing child guidance advice, as they did throughout these decades, book and magazine publishers and advertisers must have been able to count on substantial sales from the motif of the troublesome child. Sales of books and magazines did not, of course, indicate parental practices. In purchasing a manual or requesting a Children's Bureau publication, however, parents showed that they agreed with the basic premise of popularized child guidance—"everyday" child rearing, as I will show in Chapter 5, had become a difficult and worrisome endeavor for many mothers and fathers. Printed forms of popularization fed a market for advice and constructed it at the same time. During the 1920s and 1930s if parents looked for help with bothersome children, most of the writings they might have found repeated some version of the child guidance message.

PUBLIC DISPLAYS OF CHILD GUIDANCE

Although a pen in the hands of child guiders was surely a powerful tool, popularization involved more than publication of the principles in a for-mat simple enough to be read by the average parent. Despite authors' efforts to create an intimate relationship with the reader, the books and pamphlets could still be distant, faceless artifacts. In contrast, the national parent education movement and the publicity department of a local clinic engaged parents directly. Their activities point to the role of public display and face-to-face contact in the process of popularization.[47] In each case, popularization performed functions for the publicists beyond the stated goal of transmitting modern principles of child rearing, and these alterna-tive functions were sometimes at odds with the message of child guidance—the identification and treatment of the "everyday problems of the everyday child" by trained professionals. Nonetheless, the Child Study Association of America (CSAA) and the Judge Baker Foundation publicity committee proved to be valuable public displays of child guidance.

Parent education programs were so widespread by the end of the 1920s that a team of investigators called them "one of our major industries." Extension services, PTAs, and the American Association of University Women participated in the parent education movement. The movement had, from its beginning, close ties to child guidance, and the Child Study Association of America, the largest and best known of the parent education groups, became a major conduit for the transference of child guidance and mental hygiene ideas from professionals to parents. "Parent" education referred to the voluntary formation of study clubs, usually led by lay leaders trained to conduct group discussions of child rearing. Both mothers and fathers could attend; women, however, were the major supporters, both as participants and as group leaders. Support from the Laura Spelman Rockefeller Memorial ensured that plans to expand parent education were well funded during these years of child guidance growth and development.[48]

The CSAA began in 1890 when a group of New York City mothers, financially secure and interested in G. Stanley Hall's child study work, formed the Society for the Study of Child Nature. Under the leadership of Bird Stein Gans, the women developed an active interest in mental hygiene and the psychological paradigm of child behavior. In 1912 the psychoanalyst A. A. Brill introduced the women to the teachings of Freud, and the club began the study of sex education from a psychoanalytic point of view. During the 1920s, with Sidonie Matsner Gruenberg as director, the renamed Child Study Association of America became the premiere parent education organization, establishing chapters in and around New York City, and nationwide. With funding from the LSRM, the group moved aggressively to provide up-to-date information to its group leaders and to publish material specifically for parents. When the CSAA adopted the principles of child guidance as part of its parent education program, the organization provided a forum for direct contact with parents outside the offices of the clinic.[49]

Local chapters functioned as both study clubs and self-help sessions for parents. Parents often gathered just to discuss readings, but a meeting also offered individual mothers and fathers a place to air personal child-rearing problems. If a family's trouble proved beyond the scope of other parents and the chapter leader, the CSAA headquarters provided a Consultation Service in New York City for the psychological evaluation of parent and child. As the CSAA "Yearbook" for 1930–31 reported, the service was a "clearing house," not a clinic, through which families were "directed to the best available source of help in the fields of psychology, psychiatry, vocational guidance, special school and the like."[50]

"Clearinghouse" is an apt description for the CSAA as well as its Consultation Service. CSAA group leaders saw themselves as the distributors of modern knowledge about child rearing, conduits channeling information between ordinary parents and the researchers in child psychiatry, psychology, and pediatrics. Group leaders who trained at CSAA headquarters in New York learned strategies from local child guidance experts well known within their professional circles. Individual chapters sometimes devoted an entire year of meetings to discussions of mental hygiene; all worked from a bibliography heavily loaded with publications approved in the pages of *Mental Hygiene*. Parents who could not join local chapters could write to CSAA headquarters for advice. Nor was the CSAA loathe to use new technology to promote its message; the organization produced a weekly radio program about child rearing, first broadcast over the NBC network in 1925.[51] Curious and questioning parents who attended child study meetings during the 1920s and 1930s would have found the content saturated with the messages of child guidance.

To say that the parent education movement was a site for child guidance popularization is not, however, to suggest that lay leaders and professionals shared identical perspectives on the process of popularization. The CSAA leaders agreed with child guidance practitioners that common sense had to be infused with scientific knowledge.[52] They differed over the persona of the infuser. When the CSAA leaders adopted the principles of child guidance as the central part of the group's educational mission in the 1920s, they also created a new identity for middle-class women volunteers as mediators between the world of science and the world of average parents. Having taught themselves the tenets of modern child rearing, CSAA volunteers and group leaders set out in the 1920s to educate other parents from all stations of life.

Increasingly, however, the child guidance community doubted the effectiveness of mere education and distrusted the laypeople who occupied the middle ground. Professionals expressed misgivings about the quasi-professional mediator role that parent educators had devised. The National Council of Parent Education, a group representing professional interests, began to question the ability of the movement's lay leaders to present child guidance accurately. Parent educators relied on direct personal contact in their efforts to popularize the message of child guidance; professionals worried that the mediators would overstep their bounds by unwisely contributing to or falsely interpreting the child guidance messages they transmitted.[53] Some professionals, as an internal LSRM report from 1927 noted skeptically, were "quite convinced that nothing can be done except by a trained psychiatrist who will spend months in reorganizing the emotional and mental life of the parents."[54] Nonetheless, as a site of popularization, the parent education movement provided child guidance with an audience of self-identified concerned parents who welcomed the personal contact writers of child guidance texts tried to achieve in print.[55]

Only two CSAA groups seemed to be operating in the Boston area in 1924, and in 1930 the number reporting to the national organization was down to one.[56] For this community, the Judge Baker Foundation publicity department provided an alternative site for public display and direct contact with child guidance. Created in 1928 by the institution's board of trustees and headed at first by a volunteer, Mrs. T. Grafton Abbott, the publicity department made sure that the clinic's name and staff appeared regularly in society news columns of local papers. Clippings pasted into publicity department scrapbooks told the story of a seemingly endless round of talks before parent groups not affiliated with the CSAA and luncheons with civic organizations from Boston and the suburbs. The publicity director took on many of the assignments, along with William Healy, Augusta Bronner, and one of the clinic's first paid psychiatrists, Anna Skinner.[57] Radio broadcasts by the staff gave the clinic local recognition, as did the annual lecture series that brought into town well-known child guidance personalities to talk to parents who could afford the $5.00 tickets.

These local displays not only popularized the message of child guidance but also advertised the financial needs of the local clinic. One of Abbott's first projects, the production of a silent film and accompanying phonograph record, was designed both to entertain civic groups and to loosen their purse strings. With the Judge Baker staff acting as themselves, the fifty-minute film, "Four Neighbors," presented the study and resolution of four "typical" child guidance cases. The *Boston Globe* critic said the film was "really excellently handled"; the *Boston Post* called the actors "really not at all amateurish"; and the *Boston Traveler* reported, "The audience loved it. We heard people murmuring, 'Wasn't it convincing?'"[58] The Publicity Department certainly hoped it was "convincing," since each showing of "Four Neighbors" was followed by a direct appeal for monetary contributions to support the operations of the clinic.

Individual clinics used different methods to finance their operations. Some received city or state money, others were attached to universities or hospitals, and quite a few drew on contributions to local Community Chest drives.[59] The Judge Baker Foundation relied on direct contributions and endowments through these years, although when its treatment department opened in 1931 the clinic began to use a sliding payment scale for its self-referred clients. Popularization and the publicity it generated were economic necessities for this clinic, and the local presses obliged by reporting on the dances, dinners, and lectures held on behalf of child guidance.

Public displays of child guidance functioned on several levels and, like the various published forms of popularized material, served purposes in addition to the transmission of new psychological knowledge from professional experts to the laity. In the form of parent education, popularization established a public role for some quasi-professional middle-class women volunteers. Their function as popularizers suggests the shifting balance of authority between credentialed professionals and mothers with common sense on their side. Of all the parent education organizations, the CSAA was most identified with psychological professionalism, yet the maternal culture of the organization was what made possible the group's assistance in the popularization of child guidance. Mothers, CSAA leaders believed, who understood other mothers and identified with their problems, could more easily communicate the new ideas than could the professionals. At the same time, the parent educators, by adopting so unquestioningly the child guidance messages, helped to legitimate the authority of the new experts and put stresses on the maternal culture that had given rise to the parent educator.

The publicity campaigns of the Judge Baker Foundation drew on the apparently voracious public demand for entertainment in the form of child-rearing advice in order to advertise the clinic's fund-raising schemes. In its enthusiasm to sustain services and even promote growth the publicity department invoked the "everyday child" and invited a financially secure class of parents to attend lectures about child-rearing concerns. The promise of work with the troublesome "other," Boston's dependents and delinquents, made, perhaps, a better claim to Boston's charity than the "modern" psychodynamic message of a declassed troublesome child. In the unsettled economic times of the 1930s the publicity department of the Judge Baker Foundation used both images of the troublesome child to help prevent this particular charity from disappearing.

Public display of child guidance took a different turn during the summer of 1924 when mental hygiene experts testified at the "trial of the century." As journalists wrote about the sentencing hearing for two Chicago youths guilty of kidnapping and murder, they made heady copy out of the mental conflicts and troubled lives of children. Through this news forum the courtroom, too, became a site for popularization of the psychologized interpretation of child behavior.

THE TRIAL OF THE CENTURY

On August 4, 1924, William Healy took the stand as an expert witness for the defense in the sentencing hearing of Nathan Leopold and Richard Loeb, two Chicago teenagers who had kidnapped and brutally murdered their young neighbor, Bobbie Franks. Healy was the second of three psychiatric notables—called in the press "the three wise men of the east"—who testified about the personalities of the two defendants. Along with Healy, William A. White, superintendent at St. Elizabeths Hospital in Washington, D.C., author of *The Mental Hygiene of Childhood* and in 1924 president of the American Psychiatric Association, and Bernard Glueck, former director of New York state prison at Sing Sing who had researched the relationship between juvenile conduct and adult criminality, made this trial a showplace of the principles of child guidance.

Chicago newspapers covered the case in lurid detail, from the initial report of the kidnapping through the courtroom scenes and the final sentencing. Associated Press stories, posted daily, turned the event into a long-distance learning experience. The *Boston Globe*, with the widest circulation of that city's papers, carried the articles with banner headlines. As the press reported the expert testimony of the defense team and the prosecution's disputatious response, coverage of the Leopold and Loeb hearing demonstrated that economic class did not immunize a child against psychological distress. Instead, the lives of the defendants showed in horrific fashion the consequences of untreated "everyday" problems.[60]

The Associated Press accounts told a tale of methodically planned violence. On May 21, 1924, fourteen-year-old Bobbie Franks was kidnapped and murdered by his two neighbors. What had led these wealthy and exceptional youths (the two had already graduated from the University of Michigan at an age when most youths were only beginning to think about going to college) to commit such a heinous act? It was a crime that neither the age nor the class of the perpetrators would have predicted. When confronted by the police, the two quickly confessed to the murder and faced the death penalty. The strategy of the defense team, led by the nationally known attorney Clarence Darrow, pled the boys guilty of the crime and requested a sentencing hearing to present mitigating circumstances. In preparation for the hearing, the defense arranged for psychiatric examinations of the two youths and for testimony from three figures who personified the child guidance paradigm of child behavior.

Psychiatric testimony to prove insanity was not unusual in murder trials of the day. Darrow, however, did not choose to apply an insanity defense.[61] Instead he attempted to use a "personality" defense that would allow the judge to exercise leniency. The testimony in the summer of 1924 showed the public how psychiatrists transformed the carefully planned violence of the two youths into the child guidance discourse of hidden motives, personality maladjustment, and distorted family relationships. Part of the magnetism of this event lay in the way the abnormal and abominable behavior of Leopold and Loeb was tamed and made normal through the analyses of the expert witnesses.

William A. White testified first for the defense. Prompted by Darrow, he created a picture of two troubled adolescents with intricate fantasy lives. Newspapers reported that Leopold liked to imagine king-slave scenarios (in which his friend Loeb also figured prominently); Loeb envisioned himself as the perfect criminal. Although strange, these fantasy worlds were, the psychiatrist argued, more closely tied to the realm of normal boyish daydreams than to insanity. Using the boys' childhood nicknames, White testified that Dickie talked to his teddy bear, and Babe showed both feelings of superiority (his superman complex) and feelings of inferiority about his size, indicating to White evidence of split personalities. Both had been raised by governesses. White thought Loeb's a particularly severe disciplinarian with no understanding of a boy's need for unfettered play with his peers. The reporters frequently included verbatim testimony to add spice to their commentaries. White, for example, was reported comparing his study of the "inner mental life" of boys to an X-ray's disclosure of a person's physical state. The importance White attached to Loeb's motives, his fantasies, his "somewhat prudish, austere and rigid" governess appeared under a page one, eye-catching lead.[62]

William Healy, who identified himself to the court as a physician and psychologist, had responsibility for assessing the intellectual abilities of the two youths. As he did with the delinquents at his clinic, Healy gave the boys a battery of psychological tests and used the results to reinforce White's conclusions. Babe and Dickie may have applied their "intellect" to plan and carry out the murder, but the entire incident suggested to Healy hidden emotional disturbances that had originated in childhood. Despite the boys' obvious intelligence, they displayed the judgment skills of much younger children, and Healy testified that each had an emotional age of about five. The director of the Judge Baker Foundation held his own against an aggressive prosecutor, repeating again and again the difference between "abnormality" and "insanity." Insanity was a legal definition and its application belonged to the courts. Abnormality, Healy contended, was a more proper label for the personalities of these boys.

Yet even as Healy spoke of abnormality, his testimony, like White's, created links between these abnormal boys and commonplace boyish or childish behavior. When the prosecution described Leopold and Loeb as cold-hearted killers, Healy and the defense experts countered with images of troubled youths. Early experiences had set in motion a chain of developmental problems that culminated in this particular crime. Even the "secret compact" between the youths (exposed in Healy's testimony as a homosexual relationship but not reported as such in the press) became a sign of the inherent normality of these boys. To the utter disbelief of the prosecutor, who contended that the compact was a symptom of depravity, Healy maintained that he knew "many children, very innocent children of fine people who get into many things of that sort" and still grew up in "very nice ways." As with so many of the actions and emotions of the boys, this behavior was childish rather than perverted.[63]

Those who followed the Associated Press accounts read that "Dr Healy and Mr Crowe fenced craftily," when the prosecutor wanted to pinpoint the expert's view of Loeb's mental state, but the doctor "retained his equanimity under a hot fire of cross-examination."[64] The prosecution called rebuttal witnesses more than two weeks after White had first taken the stand. By then, however, the story had been relegated to inside pages. Child guidance and the "alienists" had captured the big headlines.

The "trial of the century" offered a most unusual site for popularization. Three practitioners were paid to demonstrate expert knowledge on the witness stand. The defense used the principles of child guidance to fracture the prosecutor's airtight "hanging case" and win life imprisonment for two boys. The press drew sensationalist copy from the psychiatric testimony and used it to sell papers. This was the constellation of factors that expanded public awareness of child guidance in the summer of 1924. The prosecution tried valiantly to prove that this murder was fundamentally different from the acts of juvenile delinquency Healy routinely diagnosed in Boston. An Associated Press story quoted the state's attorney directly when he quipped that Healy had little experience "with criminals springing from millionaire families . . . who are college graduates."[65] In presenting the objections of the prosecution, the news accounts obliquely pointed out deficiencies in the psychological interpretation of child behavior. Yet the class issues were largely overlooked. When the "hanging judge" chose to mitigate the death sentence, his decision gave legitimacy to the defense strategy and by extension to the clinics' claim to represent troublesome children from all social strata.[66] Although "abnormal" and even "pathological" at some points in the trial, Leopold and Loeb were ordinary children whose families had done nothing to address the "everyday" problems. If ever there was a case with which to threaten the equanimity of everyday parents (and add legitimacy to child guidance), it was this "trial of the century."

WINNING OVER THE MEDICAL PROFESSION

Press reporting transmitted the defense team's use of child guidance principles to a wide audience, but what transpired in the Chicago courtroom was an exercise in popularization within professional circles. Defense testimony had to educate just one judge. This particular jurist, who sat on the board of trustees of Healy's first clinic, seemed predisposed to listen sympathetically to the "three wise men." The usefulness of a relationship between juvenile courts and child guidance was accepted by 1924. Despite efforts to woo their medical colleagues, the links child guiders had forged with other branches of medicine were much more tenuous during the 1920s and 1930s than the ties to the legal professions. Only a few medical schools included psychiatry as part of physician training programs, and Morris Fishbein of the American Medical Association was not alone in regarding psychoanalysis as medical quackery.[67] Child psychiatrists who made overtures to general practitioners and pediatricians were often confronted with open displays of skepticism. The creation of a working relationship between child psychiatry and general medicine shows popularization in the guise of creating a hierarchy of professional authority for the mental health of children. In this process, child guiders got help from some pediatric allies.

The two child medical fields developed in relative isolation in the early twentieth century. Pediatrics emerged as a medical specialty just as the late nineteenth-century discoveries in bacteriology revolutionized thinking about disease and treatment. Pediatricians were kept busy addressing high infant mortality rates from gastrointestinal diseases and, before the advent of vaccines and antibiotics, the ordinary childhood illnesses. This is not to say that the psychological aspects of child health were ignored entirely, but articles on behavioral problems were few and far between in the field's major journals. Pediatrics was a discipline of the body, not the mind.[68] Child psychiatry, in contrast, developed alongside and as part of adult mental hygiene and not as part of a broad field of child medicine. Child guidance practitioners confined their scholarly presentations largely to social welfare, mental hygiene, and psychiatry and psychology journals not restricted by an age specialization. During a meeting of the American Medical Association in 1930 Ester Loring Richards voiced a question that seemed to trouble practitioners in both fields. "To whom," she asked, "does the health of childhood belong?"[69]

Responding to her own query, Richards urged cooperation between the two fields. If doctors remained unaware of the "misfittings" (the emotional and behavioral problems) of children, then, Richards charged, their therapeutics would be incomplete. She called for the incorporation of psychiatry and psychobiology into training programs to graduate "psychiatrically intelligent" physicians. Bronson Crothers, a Boston pediatrician and neurologist, supported Richards's appeal. If doctors did not take up the challenge to become psychiatrically intelligent, Crothers predicted that "the work of handling the child will be taken up by someone not pediatrically intelligent."[70]

Not all pediatricians were so sanguine. In 1931 Joseph Brennemann, a pediatrician from Chicago, fumed that mothers were "unquestionably becoming psychiatrically minded," even if pediatricians were not. This knowledge was altogether a bad thing, for it interfered with a doctor's authority and a mother's common sense about child behavior. A little knowledge, Brennemann argued, inevitably led to self-diagnosis, but a mother, untrained in the complexity of psychological theory had "no way, no matter how intelligent she may be, of separating the chaff from the wheat, the half-baked theorist from the genuine authority." And Brennemann wanted his audience of pediatricians to recognize that much of what the psychiatrists and child guiders talked about was the basest chaff. Drawn from the world of abnormal personalities and largely untested, psychiatry hindered the pediatrician who wanted maternal respect. In his address to the New England Pediatric Society, Brennemann hurled his greatest contempt at the parent educators, but for this pediatrician, the overpopularization of child guidance in all its forms had become a "menace."[71]

Although Brennemann urged skepticism and most physicians still trained without benefit of child guidance insights, there were some signs of cooperation between the two fields of child medicine during the 1920s and 1930s. Several pediatric training programs developed liaisons with psychiatry and child guidance. The University of California established a part-time psychological service at its pediatric training center in 1921. Yale and Stanford medical schools created similar programs in 1927.[72] Then in 1931 the pediatrician Edwards A. Park, director of the Harriet Lane Home, the pediatric unit of Johns Hopkins Hospital, and Adolf Meyer, then head of the hospital's Henry Phipps Psychiatric Clinic, established a psychiatric consultation service for pediatricians that became a model for pediatric-psychiatric cooperation. They chose Leo Kanner, a student and friend of Meyer, to act as the liaison. Kanner shared Brennemann's wariness of some of the more speculative schools of psychiatry, but as a disciple of Meyer he wanted to teach pediatricians working at the Harriet Lane Home to "view the individual child as a psychobiological and sociological unit, instead of centering [their] attention exclusively on the bladder of the enuretic patient or on the larynx of the stammering child."[73]

Training a "psychiatrically intelligent" pediatrician was for child guiders a part of the popularization process. They approached pediatricians with two goals: education of pediatricians to the point where they conceptualized problems in psychological terms, and education so that pediatricians could recognize and treat "mild" behavior problems while knowing when referral to a psychiatric specialist was necessary. These were, of course, the same goals child guidance popularizers had for their work with mothers. To aid the process of popularization with the pediatricians, Kanner turned his experiences at the Harriet Lane Home into the first American textbook on child psychiatry. *Child Psychiatry* (1935) was promoted as a "guide and a reference book" for busy pediatricians, to "make them acquainted with the principles of unbiased and practical common-sense work with the personality problems of their little patients."[74] To be sure, Adolf Meyer's psychobiology was called "commonsense psychiatry," and Kanner built the pediatric-psychiatric consultations on a Meyerian foundation. There was more to the use of "common sense," however, than Kanner's relationship with Meyer.

JoAnne Brown, in a study of professional language, has suggested that legitimacy is often accomplished through appropriation of the metaphors of a competing profession.[75] Common sense was just such a metaphor. Mothers, as well as pediatricians, competed with child guiders for control over the well-being of the child. A crucial part of the popularization process was appropriation of "common sense," the code for maternal authority. The child guidance community debunked untrained, instinctual common sense, the stuff conferred through femininity and maternity. Although child guiders denigrated maternal instinct as decidedly antimodern, they also claimed that their modern ideas represented a new common sense, the common sense of psychiatric authority. Modern mothers who hoped to display maternal skills would no longer rely on one another. Instead they would turn for guidance to psychological and medical personnel who infused common sense with science. Child psychiatrists made a similar appeal to the pediatricians and general practitioners. Pediatricians, like mothers, represented unguided medical common sense; they, too, were not psychiatrically intelligent. Child guidance popularizers hoped to transform pediatrics as they were transforming motherhood. Like mothers, pediatricians would assimilate the new common sense, treat the simple problems, and know when to defer to the specialists.

The publication in 1945 of Dr. Spock's *Common Sense Book of Baby and Child Care* symbolized both the successful appropriation of words and the merger of pediatrics and child guidance. Sales of the book soared in the postwar baby boom. *Baby and Child Care* became the new mother's bible, a compendium of reassurance based on professional wisdom. Much of the book, of course, reflected the pediatrician's interest in ordinary childhood illnesses. But though trained as a pediatrician, Benjamin Spock had also studied child psychiatry during the 1930s, and psychiatric principles framed his advice to mothers. Chapters on physical health were complemented by discussions of the standard child guidance troublesome behaviors—fears, stealing and lying, contrariness and discipline, masturbation and puberty.[76]

Following the pattern of earlier successful popularizers, Spock's book was not laced with professional jargon. Instead of discussing the repressed mental activity of children, he talked simply of subconscious fears or anxiety. Although the libido, Oedipus and Electra complexes, and oral and anal stages of development were not addressed directly in the first edition of the book, still Spock acquainted parents with topics such as infantile sexuality and the romantic attachment of little boys or girls to the parent of the opposite sex. In his introductory "Letter to the Mother and Father," Spock told parents his book would give them "sensible present-day ideas of the care of a child, taking into account his physical *and* emotional needs" [emphasis added].[77]

Parents did not have to search far to find the meaning Spock gave to common sense. "Don't take too seriously all that the neighbors say," Spock wrote in a section entitled "Trust Yourself." "Don't be overawed by what the experts say. Don't be afraid to trust your own common sense." In his autobiography, Spock says he "wrote *Baby and Child Care* to tell parents about children, to give them confidence, and to keep them from being intimidated by relatives and professionals." Yet in the manual his pep-talk continued: "Bringing up your child won't be a complicated job if you take it easy, trust your own instincts, *and follow the directions that your doctor gives you*" [emphasis added]. Spock collapsed into one volume twenty-five years of child guidance popularization. Common sense and the medical professional had become one and the same; the emotional needs of children ranked on par with their physical needs; parents shaped the destiny of their offspring; and troublesome behavior was the norm.[78]

The success of *Baby and Child Care* attested to the popularity of the child guidance and mental hygiene movements and the success of the popularizers in reshaping the discourse of troublesome childhood. Once a product of financial poverty or genetic degeneration whose trouble was identified by the legal system, the troublesome child could in 1945 be found in any home from families of every social class. In democratizing the troublesome child the child guidance movement also redefined trouble. To be sure, some children were still labeled troublesome because they disrupted adult systems of education or law. More important, the child guiders charged, were those "everyday children" whose behavior threatened only the equanimity of family relations. Popularization relied on two very necessary constructs: "common sense" and "everyday problems." Both used the vocabulary of parenting and fitted the words with new meanings dependent on a professional understanding of hidden emotional conflicts.

Popularization took place in many different locations throughout these decades. The variety of sites was significant, for it proved the capacity of child guidance to saturate a broad middle-class culture with modern—read psychological and scientific—ideas of child behavior. This was a literate culture, and the child guidance movement relied heavily on the printed word to spread its message. Through texts, magazines, and newspapers, the popularizers told stories of parents who met trouble and conquered it with the help of child guidance. The personalism of the child guidance writings was a necessary ingredient in the popularization campaign. The "case" accounts and questions from "real" parents enabled child guiders to create the aura of a therapeutic relationship between readers and experts. The personal stories also allowed child guidance advice to adapt through these decades of prosperity, economic depression, and finally world war. Child guidance stories kept current, and promised to help parents do likewise.

Other sites of popularization furthered this style of personal contact. Radio broadcasts, for example, brought outside messages directly into the home. Parents could choose to listen, but they did not have to leave the intimacy of the living room to hear a discussion of the latest child-rearing advice. Public lectures about child guidance followed a venerable American tradition, combining adult education and entertainment. The parent education movement took the public lecture a step further; parent educators encouraged personal revelations of child-rearing troubles as a form of educational development. The publicity of the Leopold and Loeb trial also personalized child guidance, giving names and faces to both troublesome children and the child guidance messengers.

Popularization was a complex process through which individuals learned to identify with the message and speak the language of child guidance. The agents of popularization often came from outside the three child guidance professions, with agendas sometimes at odds with the knowledge and the professionals they represented. Yet collectively the child guidance popularizers endorsed the personal style of presentation, the appropriation and redefinition of commonly understood constructs, and the therapeutic stance. Along with advice, the popularizers relayed a tacit message about

the ownership of child-rearing wisdom. Professional child guiders were the true conveyors of the common sense required by parents. The personal style helped to mask the power relationship implicit in the appropriation of common sense and in the therapeutic content of child guidance advice. Popularization, in the end, demanded that parents acknowledge their dependency on the new child guiders.

However many the sites of popularization, the process of popularization succeeds or fails because of its audience. Pediatricians conformed quickly and appended the emotional welfare of the child to their list of concern even while denying any interest in becoming child psychiatrists. It seeme to fit a professional agenda, enabling pediatricians to maintain a primar connection with patients. Indeed, some thought pediatrics had an advar tage, for as the author of *Psychiatry for the Pediatrician* put it in 1948, "t pediatrician and pediatric clinic are free of the stigma which so often attached to the concept of psychiatry and even to child guidance, a which prevents so many parents from seeking the help which they ob ously need."[79] But, as the next chapter will argue, it was the very concerns of the "everyday parent" that enabled child guidance to const a successful public discourse about the ordinary troublesome child.

The Problem Behavior
of the Everyday Child

Mrs. Black sought advice from the Judge Baker Guidance Center in October 1935. She had read numerous "articles and books on child training" and recognized in her son the signs of a "problem type" adolescent (9439). Mrs. Alberti attended one of the JBGC publicity lectures, then took her six-year-old to the clinic to stop his nail biting and occasional stomach upsets (9423). When Melanie Grayson failed several language courses in high school her father asked the clinic for an evaluation (9237). After the child guidance team had helped Mrs. Evans with her son's problem, she recommended the clinic to an acquaintance with a similarly troubled child (9415); another mother turned to the Judge Baker staff despite friends who were "making her feel uncertain about the value of the contact" (9453).

The message of the child guidance popularizers resonated with these five Boston parents and many like them. By law, their children were not delinquent. About half of the new files opened in 1935 contained the stories of parents who, like the Blacks, Albertis, and Graysons, came to the Judge Baker clinic voluntarily for help with baffling, annoying, and disturbing children. Although the country was in the middle of the Depression, their family incomes were reasonably secure, unlike the family impoverishment that framed the clinic's work in 1920. The percentage of self-referred cases was lower at the JBGC than at other clinics (Philadelphia, for example), however, the Boston record was especially significant. When Boston's middle-class parents discovered troublesome children in their midst they turned to local child guidance experts even though the Judge Baker clinic and its directors were closely identified with delinquency and dependency.

Two sets of questions must be asked about this transition to a new class of clients. What made child rearing so "bewildering" for these parents? To

many parents, bewilderment captured the essence of child rearing during the 1920s and 1930s.[1] Why did they find themselves uncomfortable with the tasks of parenting and ready to seek the assistance promised by the popularizers? In other words, one question must address the social and familial context into which child guiders sent the popularizations. However, equally important for the development of psychological authority was the clinic's response to these voluntary, or self-referred, clients. While child guiders argued that troublesome children lived in all social classes, the middle-class parents of these children were certainly conscious of social differences and often talked about child-rearing problems in a language of class distinctiveness. The second question asks how the clinic staff honed child guidance diagnoses drawn from studies of the poor to speak to this new class of families.

Critics of twentieth-century child-rearing experts have often charged that just trying to follow the guidelines popularized by the psychological professionals created conflict between parents and children and caused parental ambivalence about their abilities. The advice was the culprit and parents were the victims of "intruders" into family life. This has been the perspective of Christopher Lasch and of Barbara Ehrenreich and Deirdre English, for example, historians and social critics who have attempted to gauge the impact of expert authority on families and especially on women.[2] The advice, no doubt, did sometimes cause confusion and consternation. Such a possibility was acknowledged even by a few of the advice givers. Leo Kanner, author of the first American child psychiatry textbook, also wrote *In Defense of Mothers* (1941) to castigate the eccentricities of "zealous psychologists" who established rigorous and unrealistic parenting regimes. Because of the advice, parents were discovering problems where, Kanner believed, none really existed.[3]

When we look at child guidance from the perspective of the bewildered child rearers, rather than the pushy psychological experts who promoted new parenting guidelines, we find a generation of mothers, fathers, and children trying to come to terms with the consequences of unprecedented cultural changes and economic development. Raising a child was surely difficult in the nineteenth century, and every other century, but for many families in the 1920s and 1930s, parenting seemed to offer new sets of trials.[4] The slow accumulation of lifestyle changes, apparent as early as the 1890s, reached a climax after World War I. The 1920s were defiantly "modern" and self-consciously "different," and commentators from the contemporary journalist Frederick Lewis Allen to the historians Peter Stearns and Ann Douglas have reaffirmed this transformation of culture after the Great War.[5] Children pursued modernity no less than their elders, and they did so in ways threatening to parents with conventional views of proper juvenile behavior. Mothers and fathers who expected juvenile subservience to parental authority found their commands challenged in too many new situations by too many new ideas. In this setting children and parents fought to create a new boundary between acceptable and unacceptable conduct, and child guidance became, for some families, a way to negotiate the conflict and define the expectations and responsibilities of modern parenthood.

The bewilderment caused by the behavior of children aged ten to seventeen, the years of puberty and adolescence (and the ages of the vast majority of child guidance clinic patients), is the focus of this chapter. The unconventional behavior of the era's prototypical young adults, the flapper and her boyfriend, usually suffices to demonstrate the new leisure activities and individual freedom of the post–World War I youth culture.[6] Although the younger children were no less a part of the generational conflict of the 1920s and 1930s, they have not received the same attention. Unlike the college students, these school-age children were still living in the family home, but they were old enough to emulate the behavior of their more self-reliant siblings. While parents recognized that experts had complicated the tasks of rearing infants and toddlers, it was these older youths who seemed to throw down the gauntlet and demand a duel between generations over the meaning of teenage independence and adult authority. Child guiders imposed themselves as referees or arbitrators of the new and bewildering generational conflict.

The question of how to be a parent in this environment of new challenges to adult authority often led child rearers to the sites of child guidance popularization and drew some, like the Albertis, the Blacks, and the Graysons, to a child guidance clinic. Many of these new clients were accustomed to using expert medical advice for childhood illnesses. The success of child guidance popularization can be measured by the willingness of families to entertain the possibility that experts could help with behavioral problems too. At the clinic, families found confirmation of their problems, a modified diagnosis of delinquency that restricted authoritarian parental control and a new doctrine of parenting that stressed the primacy of a child's emotional "needs." It was a conceptualization of the troublesome child that turned parental feelings of impotency and loss of authority into a virtue, even as it highlighted new parental responsibilities for the emotional welfare of their children.

THE PROBLEMS THEY CAUSE US

"What ails our youth?" George Coe, of Columbia Teachers College, asked in frustration for a generation of parents. In 1924 Coe accused the young of demonstrating a "craze for excitement; immersion in the external and superficial; lack of reverence and of respect; disregard for reasonable restraints in conduct and for reasonable reticence in speech; conformity to mass sentiment—'going with the crowd'; lack of individuality; living merely in the present and general purposelessness."[7] In short, the young seemed to disregard old-fashioned virtues of character, control, and individualism as they adopted new values of personality, playfulness, and social conformity. Many parents echoed Coe's unflattering description, although relentless daily contact with the faults drove child rearers to present their complaints in more prosaic terms. In conversation with the sociologists Robert Lynd and Helen Lynd during the 1920s, "Middletown" parents told of their worries about the conduct of children who spent less and less time in the family home and more hours in clubs, with peers, and especially with the opposite sex. Parents complained of uncensored scenes from movies and the unchaperoned freedom of automobiles as causes of unflattering sophistication in their offspring. The youths concurred about the points of contention, ranking use of the car and time away from home as major sources of disagreement with adults.[8] When the Lynds returned to Muncie, Indiana, in 1935, they noted that "the gap between the purposes and mutual understanding of parents and children observed in 1925 has apparently widened still further."[9] The change from prosperity to economic depression had not weakened the perception that modern life bred an abnormal conflict between parents and their young.

Parents who attended child study meetings or told stories at the child guidance clinics expressed the same confusion reported to the Lynds by the parents of this "average" American town.[10] Through the minutes of these mothers' meetings and the case files of the Judge Baker Guidance Center the parents can tell their side of the story.[11] On a scale of problem behavior, we would judge many of the Judge Baker children as severe behavioral problems. Stealing, running away, sexual misconduct, and failure at school were common complaints heard at the clinic but not necessarily at the child study meetings. Yet even at the clinic, parents often embedded these serious infractions in stories of aggravating problems framed as generational conflict and challenges to parental authority.

Child guiders were first introduced to the problem of generational conflict by stories about poor immigrant parents whose children had been charged as delinquents. Often born in the United States and subjected to American education and American entertainment, these youths rapidly adopted values contrary to the family standards brought from their native countries. Reformers studied and reported on children like Stella, one of the early cases at the Judge Baker Foundation. In the summary account, sixteen-year-old Stella was called "altogether [a] typical immigrant problem," who had run away from her family four times in the preceding eighteen months. To Stella's mother, the girl was "stubborn" and "headstrong," wanting to go to the movies two or three times a week, spend time at Revere Beach, and keep all her earnings for herself. Stella's mother had tried many methods to keep the girl "straight," and told her daughter, "if you will not obey me and if you will not always walk alone on the streets, then we will force you to get married to a good man who will look after you" (1889). In spite of the warnings Stella, and many like her, often gave vent to the desire for independence and for unrestrained play.[12]

In the early twentieth century social scientists began to analyze the rebellion of children like Stella not as a product of inherent badness but in the context of the immigrant family culture. In doing so these researchers, of whom the Chicago sociologist W. I. Thomas was among the most influential, discovered a new source for delinquent behavior in the conflict of values between parents with "old world" standards and their modern, Americanized children. In *The Polish Peasant in Europe and America* (1918–1920), Thomas and his collaborator, Florian Znaniecki, examined the family disorganization that followed the transplantation of peasant cultures into an American urban setting. Traditional values were of little consequence in the new environment, and parents lost the ability to control their children through cohesive family and community standards. Reduced, as in the case of Stella's mother, to forceful imposition of standards contrary to those the younger generation experienced in the larger world of school and work, immigrant parents found themselves with less and less influence over the behavior of their adolescents.[13]

Middle-class parents also perceived the conflicts dividing their families as tests of authority. Parents often described their complaints as a contest over expressions of compliance in family relationships, or over standards of comportment—sloppiness, untidiness, abuse of free time, or slavish concern about appearance. In 1931 Ralph Stodgill, a researcher at Ohio State University, sampled concerns about juvenile behavior among a large number of Columbus parents only to discover that defiance (disobedience, unreliability, and impertinence) ranked just slightly below overt delinquency and "direct conflict with the conventional code," such as masturbation. In this group of mothers (and a few fathers), most of whom were "slightly above average as to intelligence and educational advantages" and living in areas that suggested no sign of economic distress, Stodgill found that "parents regard *transgressions against morality and opposition to parental control* as more undesirable than *disrupting the quiet and routine of the household and breaches of family etiquette . . . [or] introvert, withdrawing behavior*" (emphasis in original).[14] Stodgill, who was trying to determine which behavior would lead a parent to the child guidance clinic, was dissatisfied with the outcome, citing parental ignorance of the psychological significance of introversion. At the JBGC, however, parents replicated Stodgill's findings. Children were troublesome when they were sullen, stubborn, ruthless, disobedient, defiant, demanding, and oblivious to the feelings of others in the family, especially their mothers.[15] Parents interpreted these personality characteristics as disregard for adult authority.[16]

Although never the sole factor in an adult's account of the child's misconduct, complaints about clothes and make-up appeared with some regularity in descriptions of youthful misbehavior. The social worker recorded in case no. 9455 that the mother "thinks it is wrong the way so much value is placed on clothes. [Worker] says that sometimes clothes are very important to a girl of [Sarah's] age. M. agrees but again says it should not be this way. Some girls want everything they see in the windows and still will not go out bec. of their lack of clothes." Girls who rouged their cheeks, painted their lips, and polished their nails presented visual reminders that a new code of conduct for adult women was seeping into adolescent self-images.[17] In a Child Study Association group whose leader wanted to discuss the need for adolescent independence, mothers took control of the prearranged program and instead debated the pros and cons of make-up for the young. Personal appearance was one of the primary arenas in which the girls of these child study parents contested the meaning of modernity. While the group leader urged that parents allow their children a degree of experimentation, the mothers remained skeptics. They distrusted the leader's belief that encouraging adolescents to "make their own decisions" outweighed the need to enforce adult standards for the young. Yet parents often hesitated to exert control at home. Instead they chose to debate the subject with other adults and look for reassurance from other parents.[18]

The ready availability of commercial entertainment also sparked conflict between parents and their adolescents. Douglas Thom observed in a Children's Bureau pamphlet that many parents complained of their adolescents' unwise use of free time. Children seemed no longer satisfied with the leisure activities of their parents' generation, and instead preferred "entertainment offered by commercial places of amusement to anything they might provide for themselves."[19] Among the middle classes, the threat to adult authority from commercial entertainment was represented by the movies. The picture shows, or nickelodeons, were routine and inexpensive entertainment even in the Progressive era, popular among the urban masses, and an activity reformers believed corrupted morals.[20] In New York City a local mothers' group devoted a meeting in 1916 to the reasons their more pampered children should avoid movies "depicting the dangers [of] some phases of city life,—the social evil, etc." While such films were detrimental to the morals of young girls who lived "in congested quarters and go out to work at a comparatively early age," even their own "more protected children" were not safe from the negative lessons taught in certain films.[21] With magazine articles already proclaiming "Sex O'Clock" in America, the child study group of 1916 anticipated the intensified concern about movies and sexual misconduct in the following decades.[22]

Movie viewing was a much utilized form of entertainment among Middletown adults in the middle of the Depression decade, although audiences were still, as they had been in the 1920s, often largely children. The perception among parents and professionals that movies interfered with "normal" childhood development remained unchanged.[23] *Our Movie Made Children* (1933), by Henry James Forman, summarized professional fears that motion pictures caused misbehavior. Provoking a range of responses—from truanting school to watch the films to explicitly imitating the sexual behavior of film stars—the movies appeared to threaten the behavior of young viewers of all classes.[24] Middle-class parents who raised the issue at the JBGC in the mid-1930s agreed with these doomsday evaluations.

When the parents of thirteen-year-old Phoebe Campbell (9247) talked with the JBGC team, they gave vent to their anxieties about the new expressions of fashion and entertainment. In 1935 the Campbells were as non-plussed by modern adolescent behavior as George Coe had been eleven years earlier. Although Phoebe was brought to the clinic ostensibly because of persistent bad dreams, the Campbell parents used this opportunity to raise questions about other facets of Phoebe's conduct. Forbidden to wear nail polish and make-up, Phoebe was also not allowed to go skating with a boy unless the "date" was chaperoned. Yet Phoebe resolutely defied the strictures of a father she considered puritanical and a mother she described as "old-fashioned." Another source of conflict was Phoebe's insistence that the choice of movies be hers alone. Phoebe demanded no parental interference in her Saturday afternoon entertainment, a privilege the mother of this child barely past puberty was unwilling to grant. Although films served as a focus for dispute, clearly the conflict between this daughter and her parents involved more than the quality of the movies she attended. Standards for adolescent behavior seemed so different from those of her youth, Mrs. Campbell told the Judge Baker social worker. How was she to know what was appropriate for Phoebe? If Phoebe was right about this issue, what other restrictions on her behavior might be called into question?

As the experience of the Campbells suggested, movie viewing emerged for both parents and children as one element in a shifting balance between adult authority and adolescent independence. "Is there or is there not such a thing as parental authority?" college professor Elliott Marshall demanded heatedly of his wife in Dorothy Canfield's novel *The Bent Twig* (1915), when their daughter disregarded his advice. Twenty years later Phoebe's parents echoed Marshall's question. Parents in both fiction and real life felt that adults could not claim as much control over their adolescents as they thought necessary for proper parenting. For the fictional Mrs. Marshall in the Canfield novel, adolescent independence was to be encouraged; she urged her husband to trust that their daughter would act responsibly.[25] The Campbells were less certain just how far an adolescent should be trusted. Parenting to the Campbells still signified a relationship of power and control, although they were unsure about what rules to enforce.

Other forces, in addition to commercial fashion and entertainment, also conspired to lure adolescents away from the standards of home and family, causing parents to despair over their ability to play out the supervisory role. A mother wrote to the Judge Baker staff five years after an impulsive shoplifting incident had first brought her daughter Eleanor (1604) to the clinic in 1920. "Is it right," the mother asked in her letter to Dr. Healy, "for my husband to allow [Eleanor] . . . to go out with Tom, Dick, and Harry automobiling going out to roadhouses and getting home at two to three o'clock in the morning? I begged him not to allow her to go. He will tell her, 'You mustn't come home so late, honey,' and perhaps two nights later she will come home later or not at all and nothing is said." Late nights and automobiling signaled to this mother that her child had crossed into behavior unfamiliar and unacceptable in a well-bred daughter. Yet the letter was a query. Eleanor's mother wanted confirmation that her standards of adolescent conduct were still appropriate; in 1925 she was unsure of her right to question her daughter's recreational choices.[26]

Child Study Association mothers in an "adolescent" study group from 1930 to 1931 also pointed out the problem of inappropriate friendships with "Tom, Dick, and Harry." What was a mother to do when children brought home friends of either sex who did not pass parental scrutiny, friends who were "vulgar, common people" on a level "below" that of the family? These child study mothers debated with the group leader the degree of independence and the level of trust a parent could assume appropriate for a teenage son or daughter. The leader urged the mothers to see in such choices a possible reaction to pressures at home, but, as the meeting drew to a close, a still-perplexed mother asked, "Do you mean we should not share in the choosing of our child's friends?"[27]

The choice of particular companions was important to these mothers because adolescent friendships assumed a new prominence in the 1920s. Age grading in large urban schools and the expansion of high school education provided the time and space in which the self-regulated values of the peer group could emerge as an alternative source of authority.[28] The importance of the peer group and its conflict with parental authority was often voiced as a battle over the time children spent away from home. In Middletown, 45 percent of the high school boys and 48 percent of the girls questioned reported "the number of times you go out on school nights" as a source of conflict with parents. An equally high percentage acknowledged spending fewer than four evenings at home during the week.[29] Parents at the clinic who complained that their children "stayed out late at night" or, like Eleanor's mother, worried about a daughter's automobiling escapades identified the predominant role of their children's choice of companions in family disharmony. Whether children in the 1920s and 1930s spent less time within the family circle than had previous generations was not as important as the legitimacy now given this separation by the new forms of entertainment.

Who the children were with took on greater importance when parents feared the consequences of unregulated movies and "automobiling," yet also found themselves part of a social setting that valued these same recreations. Make-up and fashion livened the appearance of adult women during these years. Men and women enjoyed outings at movies or in automobiles. What the children did was often mere imitation of their elders. Where, parents seemed to be asking as their children exerted more independence, was the line between adolescent play and adult privilege to be drawn?

The conflicts over friendships and recreation also frequently camouflaged a far more threatening challenge to the standards parents set for adolescent behavior. Parents of the postwar era detected signs of a new sexual freedom in these relatively inconsequential issues. "Adolescence is the development of sex," Bird T. Gans, group leader, informed the members of Child Study Association Chapter 13 in 1916.[30] These comfortably situated New York City mothers intended to investigate both cause and consequence of the sexual revolution among their youngsters. Over the next seven years, the group studied G. Stanley Hall's views on adolescent sexuality (a time of storm and stress), perused Freudian literature (emphasizing openness and honesty rather than secrecy), and read several fictional accounts of adolescent difficulties with sex urges, hoping to arrive at a practical understanding of sexuality.[31] In choosing adolescent sexuality as their research topic the members of Chapter 13 had singled out the issue that lurked behind many parent-child conflicts. While the parents of "Tom, Dick, and Harry" did worry about the leisure activities of their sons, it was the daughters of the middle class whose behavior raised special qualms.

What were the girls doing to arouse such anxiety? Apparently quite as much as their elders feared. John Modell's study of the dating behavior of high school students in the 1920s found a marked "sexualization of noncoital (or precoital) relations" among post–World War I adolescents.[32] "Mother, how far shall I go?" a Middletown daughter asked her mother, and researchers in the town found this mother's feelings of inadequacy representative of parental reaction to unfamiliar adolescent sexuality.[33] Parents and youth alike acknowledged that courtship might contain a sexual element beyond parental control.[34] Sexuality in service of imminent marriage and family, however, was scarcely the issue troubling urban middleclass parents in the interwar decades. Their consternation arose from the dating and petting rituals developed by high school students after World War I, behavior that both flaunted the sexuality of their daughters and showed in sharp relief the diminished authority of parents.

The "date" was an event controlled by high school students. It took place without parental supervision, and it excluded a parent's right to intervene or veto the choice of partner or activity.[35] These characteristics distinguished dating from previous carefully supervised forms of adolescent mixing. Moreover, a date was assumed to contain a certain amount of sexual experimentation, an amount carefully regulated by the teens themselves. Petting, Modell suggests, was "almost universal, in the sense that all daters petted at some time, [although] not in the sense that all couples petted."[36] Articles in magazines for parents that asked pointedly, "Must a Girl Pet to Be Popular?" confirmed for parents the equation of sexual experience and peer acceptance.[37] Nearly 50 percent of the Middletown high school's juniors and seniors agreed to a researcher's statement that "nine out of every ten boys and girls of high school age have 'petting parties.'" This particular ratio may have been prompted by statements from Denver's juvenile court judge Ben Lindsey, who recorded the extent of sexual activity among the city's young, including the sons and daughters of Denver's most respectable citizens, to be near 90 percent of all adolescents.[38]

Lindsey believed that the immoral and illegal behavior of middle-class youths occurred because parents failed to take time to understand their offspring, but the lament of a Dorchester woman whose daughter was seen by the Judge Baker staff in 1935 suggested that more was at work than passive or ineffectual parents. Marilyn's mother had tried to create a better, more trusting relationship with her daughter than her own experience as a youth. Yet at sixteen the girl deceived her about dates and pastimes. This mother wanted to know how far her daughter could be trusted with boys (9253). How far, however, now depended more on the standards of the adolescent group than the adolescent's father and mother, and attitudes toward petting formed a gaping divide between the generation of the parent and that of the child during the 1920s and 1930s.

The source of the conflict over the adolescents' "sexual revolution" lay as much in parental uneasiness about new adult sexual values as it did with diminished parental authority over their offspring. The disintegration of Victorian constraints on sexual expression began well before World War I. The reasons were manifold and have been discussed in detail elsewhere.[39] Here it is important to recognize that not all urban parents were comfortable with the sophisticated standards of adult feminine behavior aggressively displayed in films and magazines.[40] "Sex is one of the things Middletown has long been taught to fear," the Lynds observed in 1937.[41] Within their own marriages, ordinary parents remained unsure about the new sex roles and uneasy about new ideas of conjugal relations. Although the "flapper" was a popular female image, the public mood seemed more ambivalent than accepting during the 1920s. Marilyn's mother, for example, tried to adapt to her daughter's freer behavior, but, caught between her Victorian mother and her modern daughter, this mother found herself unable to do more than ask for guidance (9253). Other women expressed discomfort with open discussions of human sexuality; some told of their dislike of intercourse. The activities of their offspring, however, forced parents to confront new ideas about female sexuality. One response was to draw rigid lines of appropriate age behavior and to reserve for adults the prerogatives of the "modern" emotional and sexual standards. When lines were drawn, parents and their rebellious daughters sometimes found themselves looking to child guidance for mediation.

This is not to suggest that during these years boys presented no problems for middle-class parents. Ironically, a survey of high school seniors in a small Nebraska town found that boys recorded more hours per week spent on dates or at the movies than did girls.[42] Parental expressions about adolescent male sexuality, however, followed the nineteenth-century pattern. Masturbation rather than fornication led parents of boys to the clinic for help.[43] Delinquency, of course, continued to be an adolescent male phenomenon. With boys, however, middle-class parents often complained about poor performance in school.

During these decades most American children spent nearly as much time in the classroom as they did with their parents. Compulsory education laws passed in most states by World War I made primary schooling mandatory, but high school attendance also soared in the early twentieth century. By 1930, nearly 75 percent of youths aged fourteen to seventeen were in school, and 29 percent of those went on to graduate.[44] The social life of middle-class adolescents originated in school corridors, where, as the Lynds noted, "'dates' [were] exchanged" between lessons, and "all the urgent business of living" took place.[45] Such "socialization" was, perhaps, not what Progressive educators had in mind when they sought to reform the school into a socializing agency as well as an instrument for imparting knowledge. Both educators and adolescents agreed, however, that in the schools of the 1920s and 1930s one learned valuable lessons in personality development and socially acceptable deportment.[46]

If the activities of adolescents failed to arouse their parents' attention, teachers served as surrogates, in position to point out behavior unbecoming the younger generation. Both the compulsory education and the child labor laws enacted by Progressive reformers ensured that urban teachers would have under their control a growing number of students who wished to be elsewhere.[47] Education-related problems frequently arose among children in the lower grades, but high school students were not immune. Skipping school and lack of respect for the rules of the classroom formed one component of complaints, academic performance and vocational planning another. In addition to deliberate delinquencies such as stealing or lying, teachers found truancy and classroom disruption the most annoying misbehaviors; they frequently advised the parents of a troublemaker that steps were necessary to ensure the child's continuation in school.[48]

Parents facing a teacher's complaints or a truant officer's summons must have believed the misbehavior in school also represented defiance of parental authority. Sometimes the complaints about school merged with other sources of conflict. The parents of a fifteen-year-old Worcester truant, who appealed to the Judge Baker clinic for help, were "baffled" by their son's failure to attend school, and could explain it only in terms of the bad influence of his "crowd" (2105). Another mother was "at her wit's end" with her fifteen-year-old daughter. Not only was the girl defiant at home, but this mother had received a note from the girl's principal reporting her stubborn refusal to remove rouge and lipstick, the use of which was against school rules (9274). These children who vexed their parents in the family home also brought their parents to the attention of outside observers.

For those from comfortable circumstances unaccustomed to the attention frequently paid to families among the poor, a child with a blemished school record signified a failure to uphold class values as well as an intellectual weakness. In the middle-class work world of the 1920s and 1930s school performance and career choice were crucial to middle-class success in later life. Children who failed to measure up academically posed problems for parents concerned to establish their offspring in a financially secure adulthood. Teachers increasingly acted as the "gatekeepers to opportunity"; the training and certification provided by public education fulfilled a task once discharged by parents.[49]

A social worker at the Judge Baker clinic recorded Mrs. Montgomery's "disappointment" with her son John. His low grades and lack of persistence led the high school counselor to declare the boy an unlikely candidate for college. The Montgomery family, whose economic status came from a manufacturing concern, further feared that John's "nervousness, carelessness and tendency to dawdle" did not bode well for success in business. They asked the clinic for advice about a future course for John. John, for his part, was uninterested—he had no particular ambition and his low grades caused him no distress (9252). This battle in the Montgomery family exemplified the anxiety of myriad Judge Baker parents. Parents expected boys like John to do well in school; his casual disregard for his parents' expectations of adolescent purposefulness was another sign of adolescent defiance as well as a portent of future financial failure. Why, they wanted to know, was John such a failure when he had so many opportunities for success?

Records from the clinic showed that parents expected their daughters as well as their sons to succeed in school and looked for help when the girls truanted, earned poor grades, or caused classroom disturbances. When a tenth grader from a fashionable Boston suburb appeared to have trouble with Latin and French, her father, a chemical engineer, questioned whether she had the mental ability needed to attend college and what her plans for adult life should include. He sought advice because in his social milieu a college education was part of a girl's proper upbringing. As important for the girl, however, was a good marriage and when, a few years later, this daughter chose an unsuitable partner from a lower social class, her parents wanted to prevent the union (9237). Class and gender conflicts intertwined in the decisions to resort to the clinic. Both the parents and their daughter thought they found in the child guidance practitioners a group of impartial professionals who could mediate the family tensions, and in the case of the parents, help preserve the symbols of middle-class identity.

Educational issues were certainly bound up with broader issues about social status and class identity for many of these parents. In this rapidly developing economy parents recognized the connection between a secure social status and education even if their daughters and more frequently their sons would not. Parents like the Montgomerys no doubt understood the growing importance of professional and technological expertise in both business and government and assumed their sons would move into that world. For the poor, education had provided one way up the social ladder; for members of the middle class, academic success was imperative for the child to merely remain in good social standing. In the modern mobile society of corporate America, status was fragile and depended a great deal on educational credentials. School-related problems of middle-class parents were not as flamboyantly described in novels and magazines as were the questions of sex and popular entertainment. Nevertheless, these issues too drove mothers and fathers to search for help at the sites of child guidance popularization.

The economic dislocations of the Depression presented families with unique problems and accentuated generational tensions in novel ways. Glen Elder, in a study of Depression-era children from Oakland, California, found that while the income and occupational status of fathers could decline in hard times, education was a form of prestige that remained constant. For the parents of these West Coast youths, education was a tangible signifier of well-being in an era of great uncertainty.[50] When boys turned away from schooling, parents were troubled. The Elliotts (9297) came to the Judge Baker clinic in 1935 worried about their son, who was a frequent truant from high school. Even though the boy was sixteen, Mrs. Elliott knew there was "very little he could do if he did not go to sch., as there is so much unemployment."

Deportment and choice of recreational activities also continued to trouble parents in the 1930s. Pleasure-loving youths seemed out of place during a time of widespread destitution. Yet young people in Boston continued to give evidence of "wild behavior" and rebelliousness, staying out late at night and making unreasonable requests for material things a family could no longer afford. Sarah's mother talked to the Judge Baker social worker about a daughter who "never understands that she can not have everything." "M. gives several examples of how [Sarah] wants so many things and wants to go everywhere," the social worker reported, "and when M. explains that they can not afford it, [Sarah] does not understand." Money was only the tip of the problem, however. "People never used to have so much trouble with chn. as they do now," this woman told the social worker. "They just seemed to grow up." The worker added that this mother talked for the next forty-five minutes about "her anxiety over [Sarah's] lack of interest in her studies, her unreasonableness, her extravagance, and her lack of understanding of why she can not have everything she wants" (9455).

"Conditions in the Depression," Elder has concluded, "denied some young people the protected, nonresponsible experience of adolescence by extending adultlike [household and breadwinner] tasks downward into childhood."[51] The responsibilities devolving to teenagers further challenged notions of parental authority during adolescence. Some young people simply escaped parental control, joining the ranks of tramps and hobos. Other teenagers used the added responsibilities to claim greater independence while at home or in school. No doubt the otherwise "normal" defiance and rebellion of even their ten- and twelve-year-olds assumed added significance when parents already felt so much of their world beyond their control.

To be sure, not all American parents suffered because their children misbehaved, and some families drew strength from unaccustomed economic hardship. Moreover, the problems parents identified—both in the clinic and among themselves in study clubs—were wide ranging. At the clinic they included the forms of serious mental and emotional disorientation psychiatrists were long accustomed to treating; sometimes the problems reflected new child guidance constructs—sibling rivalry, for example, or concerns about a child's feelings of inferiority. Nonetheless, the youth problem that haunted many middle-class families after World War I, making them a ready audience for child guidance popularization, often translated into conflicts over deportment and education.

Both sets of problems raised fears for parents that they lacked the authority to discipline, an authority they believed necessary to provide their children with the equipment needed to succeed as middle-class adult men and women.

The mothers and fathers who participated in child study clubs, wrote for advice to magazine or newspaper columnists, or looked for help from child guidance professionals shared feelings of confusion and helplessness. Old strictures no longer seemed appropriate to the task of parenting this new generation. Instead, parents and children were caught in a vortex of changes—in gender relationships and the structure of the modern family, and in expectations about work and definitions of class and status. The forces reshaping the bond between parent and child had begun more than a century before; yet the confluence of technology, urban growth, commercial recreation, and economic dislocation made the period after World War I one of acute parental anxiety. Parents in Middletown were "wont to speak of many of their 'problems' as new to this generation, situations for which the formulae of their parents [were] inadequate."[52] Parents in Boston concurred. This was, indeed, a generation of mothers and fathers forced by their children to reconsider class and gender identities and to create new guidelines for the parent-child relationship. For many of these parents, the popularizers of child guidance provided a library of new ideas that helped to make sense of their thoroughly modern children, and encouraged them to see that "letting go" was not an affront to middle-class identity.

TRANSFERRING DELINQUENCY EVALUATIONS
TO MODERN ADOLESCENTS

In the clinic child guidance practitioners took the diagnoses designed for the poor and the delinquent and reshaped them to fit middle-class parental sensibilities. Yet as they did so, child guidance professionals allied with the children in the generational war over cultural standards. "After all," Douglas Thom wrote for the Children's Bureau, "the adolescents of today are merely accepting life as they find it when they make use of commercial amusements." [53] The adolescents intuited, and the professionals agreed, that punitive and authoritarian parental control was outmoded in a society that valued leisure, conformity, and the ability to get along with the group. These qualities, espoused so successfully in Dale Carnegie's *How to Win Friends and Influence People* (1936), were common to corporate America and undoubtedly shared by the professionals of child guidance. Carnegie offered adults "training in the fine art of getting along with people in everyday business and social contacts."[54] Child guidance set out to provide mothers and fathers with the language needed to accommodate parenting to the pulls of Carnegie's urban corporate culture, and offered parents the reassurance that their children already understood the qualities needed to succeed. Two redesigned constructs in particular, "social suggestibility" and "adolescent self-assertion," each part of William Healy's original formulation of delinquency causation, show how child guiders adapted their work to the problems of the everyday (middle-class) child.

In *The Individual Delinquent* Healy applied "social suggestibility" to weak-willed individuals, sometimes but not always "feebleminded," who were prone to follow the lead of "bad companions" and get into trouble with the law. The socially suggestible youngster engaged in delinquent behavior to earn the recognition of a strong leader. In these instances, following the leader was the sign of an antisocial personality.[55] Healy's interpretation did not survive the transformation of the clinic's clientele. When treating the everyday child's generational conflicts, child guidance practitioners also encountered evidence of social suggestibility—of young people who wanted to follow the crowd. With these adolescents, however, susceptibility to "social suggestion" indicated a sensitivity to peers and a willingness to be molded by the values of the group. Parents were admonished that a child who lacked such sensitivity risked the emotional trauma that came from being a social outcast. The subtext of this message condemned parents who, in an effort to uphold antiquated conceptions of family as the primary unit of socialization, tried to interfere with the norms of the adolescent subculture. Phoebe Campbell's parents disapproved of their thirteen-year-old daughter's efforts to conform to the social practices of her friends, including unchaperoned dating, but the clinic staff in 1935 encouraged the Campbells to allow Phoebe more freedom to participate in group-approved activities (9247). As Winifred Richmond warned readers of her guide to raising the adolescent female, the girl who would consciously be different should be regarded as the problem child. "Normal" adolescent development required that children begin to regard the peer group as a source of social standards.[56] By extension, normal parent behavior required a recognition that children were attuned to the modern social lifestyle in ways their (troublesome) parents were not.

In Leo Kanner's textbook of child psychiatry, social suggestibility was replaced by a discussion of "communal socialization," a healthy process of adjusting to the demands of the social order.[57] At the clinic, unpopularity with the group represented a potential cause of misconduct, as in the case of a young truant whose tendency to skip classes the staff psychiatrist attributed to the girl's failure to be accepted by her peers (9253). Difference and the inability to fit in, not efforts to conform and follow group standards, generated problems for modern adolescents. Peer influence, seen to cause lower-class delinquency, reinforced the values of leisure, of personality, and of corporate modernity among middle-class children, values shared by the professionals of child guidance. Adherence to peer standards was, therefore, something to be encouraged, often at the expense of parental authority. This is not to say that peer standards were always deemed appropriate, but when the modern values of the peer group conflicted with stodgy parental claims, child guidance privileged the peers.

With "adolescent self-assertion" child guidance professionals also manipulated the language of delinquency diagnosis to match the exigencies of middle-class parenting. In doing so, child guiders pursued a tack that enabled the professional experts to mediate between adolescent demands to engage in tantalizing leisure activities and a parental concern about standards and authority. When applied to the behavior problems of middle-class youth, adolescent self-assertion ceased altogether to be a category of misbehavior. It represented instead the healthy (and emotionally necessary) process of emancipation, or "psychological weaning," from family bonds.[58]

"In our own study of the causative factors of delinquency we have time and again seen every reason to put down adolescent instability as a cause of misconduct," Healy wrote in *The Individual Delinquent*.[59] Cases from the records for 1920 suggested the Judge Baker team did indeed attribute some delinquencies to the simple fact of age, especially when the experts lacked glaring evidence for a more specific cause.[60] Adolescence, however, meant more than mental instability stemming from physical changes. Among the qualities of adolescence identified as a factor in delinquency was the teenager's desire for self-expression, often expressed through "contrary suggestibility," or doing the opposite of what was expected by those in authority.[61] Juvenile delinquency could be, therefore, the consequence of a characteristic inherent in a stage of development. Although self-assertion was a trait of this period of life, in the delinquent it was not to be left unguided. Delinquency due to self-assertion required reeducation in training centers. In 1920 a rebellious girl of "supernormal intelligence" was first placed in a foster family and subsequently sent to the Lancaster Industrial School for Girls to provide her with missing parental direction and self-control (1641).

When child guidance experts began to encounter the parents of defiant but not delinquent youths, "adolescent rebellion" supplied a language through which they could explore the problem. It was, after all, an apt description of generational warfare within these families. As applied to the nondelinquents, however, expressions of adolescent self-assertion required of parents more understanding and generally less authority and fewer restrictions. Once again Phoebe Campbell's file revealed the clinic's efforts to mediate between parents and an assertive child with modern ideas. At the staff conference the team described Phoebe (whose parents were both mystified and outraged by her defiant behavior) as a normal adolescent girl, "feeling the desire for emancipation." For the clinic team, Phoebe's adolescent unruliness was a normal part of the growth process.[62] Phoebe's reactions to her parents' "over-restriction is about to be much more dangerous than anything she would get into if they allowed her more liberty," the team concluded. When Phoebe asked the staff psychiatrist to talk to her parents about giving her more responsibility for some of her behavior, the psychiatrist obliged and encouraged the Campbells to allow Phoebe to choose her own movies. The solution eventually presented to the Campbells was a compromise—if the parents developed more forms of entertainment for Phoebe in her own home she would demand fewer of the social privileges she seemed to crave. Although the clinic intervened to insist that Phoebe attend the camp chosen by her parents, the staff also warned that Phoebe's parents had to recognize the adolescent's need to free herself from parental control (9247).[63]

In the case of Phoebe Campbell, the clinic served as the arbitrator between the standards of parental authority and the norms of a new adolescent culture. As Douglas Thom proposed in his guide to raising adolescents, "The desire for personal independence and more control over one's own activities or thoughts is so normal an aspect of adolescence that the boy or girl who clings to his parents and fears to take any step that might possibly lead him further away from the security and protection of childhood is considered overdependent or immature."[64]

The clinic staff wanted Phoebe to continue to develop a sense of "personal independence," and to accomplish this, found it necessary to instruct her parents about the emotional needs of the adolescent.[65] A year later, the clinic reported this case "successfully closed." Phoebe told the visiting social worker that her parents had taken a different, presumably more lenient, attitude toward her since their meetings with the Judge Baker staff, and Mrs. Campbell continued to gain insight by participating in a mothers' club sponsored by the JBGC in 1936.

"It is a difficult and bewildering time for parents," an author in *Parents' Magazine* wrote to comfort the mothers and fathers of adolescents. "The only people who can help us are the children themselves. We have no choice but to ask them—and after all, the more honestly we admit our weaknesses to them, the more readily, I am convinced, will they admit and be guided by our strength."[66] Child guiders took sides as they mediated the conflicts between parents and children, and they appropriated and recast the language of delinquency diagnosis to do so.[67] Using constructs such as communal socialization and adolescent rebellion, they argued that children were often more aware of the qualities needed for success in modern society than were tradition-bound parents. Adult standards of decorum were not appropriate for young people who had to fit into a peer group and meld into a corporate culture. Victorian ideas about sex created mental conflict and rigid educational demands did more harm than good to the growing personality. Words like authority and control were not suited to the vocabulary of modern parenting. Conditions of modern life made parents "less dominant factors in the lives of their children," Douglas Thom advised in "Guiding the Adolescent" (1933). Parents had to "grasp the idea that their children are less dependent upon them than they were upon their parents." With the voice of expert common sense Thom concluded that "the most important contribution which the parent can make to the child is that of preparing him to assume the obligations and responsibilities which are associated with independence."[68] Overcontrol, not excessive freedom, created the rebellious behavior symptomatic of personality maladjustment. Judging from their behavior the children already understood. Child guidance practitioners and popularizers set out to inform their parents.

THE EMOTIONAL NEEDS OF MODERN ADOLESCENTS

Given the child guidance admonitions, a parent picking up Katherine Whiteside Taylor's book, *Do Adolescents Need Parents?* (1938), might well have expected the answer to be "no." By allying with the children, however, child guidance practitioners and popularizers did not dismiss the importance of parents, nor did they empower teenagers at the expense of parents. To continue to be a dominant influence in the lives of their children, parents heard from child guidance that they had to learn new ways to gain respect.[69] If child guidance delegitimated words like parental control and authority, at the same time its proponents created a new vocabulary for the parenting role through the concept of "emotional needs."

In child guidance theory, particularly as both practitioners and popularizers adopted ideas from psychoanalysis, emotional reactions were the cornerstone of a child's personality development.[70] Although modern children were attuned to the world around them, these same children were psychologically fragile and emotionally vulnerable. They did not understand their own emotions, nor the role those emotions played in personality adjustment and future happiness. Moreover, the scientific study of adolescence, beginning with G. Stanley Hall in the early twentieth century, pointed to the years surrounding puberty as ones of particularly intense emotions. Perceptive responses from adults, the child guidance experts agreed, would help teenagers learn to rein in emotional extremes and develop a healthy,

wholesome personality; ill-conceived adult reactions perpetuated emotional immaturity and maladjustment, and caused the generational warfare
parents found so bewildering.[71]

Child guidance urged parents to recognize that young people had three
dominant emotional needs. If children were to achieve an emotionally
healthy adulthood, they had to be given the opportunity for emancipation
while being surrounded by understanding and security.[72] Growing up, or
liberation from the family, had to occur at a steady pace, each step attuned
to the age of the child, if the child was to learn control of behavior and
emotions. Both too restrictive treatment and too rapid acquisition of freedom promised troublesome child behavior—rebellion or exaggerated dependency—and prohibited the development of a happy adult personality.
Remember the clinic's concern that the Campbells' restrictions on Phoebe's
social life would be more harmful than the degree of freedom she craved.
Understanding parents empathized with their adolescent and interpreted
situations as the child perceived them. Children also needed nonjudgmental parenting because this alone encouraged them to confide in adults,
prevented the appearance of mental conflicts, and helped to create a sense
of security.

For child guidance writers emotional security was a necessary prerequisite for personality adjustment. In infancy parents created a sense of
security by providing a safe physical environment and supplying the child's
physical wants. For the growing child or adolescent, an environment that
provided emotional security, freedom from doubts, worries, and anxieties,
was no less important. A sense of security, according to Douglas Thom,
gave children "a feeling of confidence, independence, and self-reliance,"
the necessary emotional equipment for adult life.[73] Security came through
healthy emotional attachments in the family. "Love for the child on the
part of both his parents" was the "first condition" of security. "Harmony
between the parents" was second. Parental rejection and family discord,
rather than family financial distress, were usually found to be responsible
for the feelings of insecurity so readily identified in clinic cases.

"Purely external causes of insecurity, such as irregular and inadequate
income and frequent changes of abode, with all that is involved in the way
of new adaptations to school and comrades, are of course also harmful to
many children," concluded Mary Sayles, a child guidance researcher and
author of *The Problem Child at Home* (1932), "though when the inner
harmonies of the home are preserved, such outer conditions need not be

wholly destructive."[74] In clinic records from the 1930s, child guidance workers used "environment" to register the emotional content of family relationships, not material goods or the physical space inhabited by the child. A "poor" environment signified not impoverishment, but a situation in which a child's emotional needs went unfulfilled.[75] Parents of modern adolescents had to become the caretakers of emotions; child guidance charged them with creating an environment in which a youth's emotional needs could be satisfied.

In the case of eleven-year-old Adam Forrest (9258) the JBGC staff worked backward from the child's troublemaking to uncover emotional conflict. Adam was a neighborhood hellion who started a fire in a barn, stole tools, and broke the windshield of a neighbor's automobile. He also ran away from home, took money from the family's maid, and generally made his stepmother's life miserable. None of these actions brought him to the juvenile court, but nevertheless this family with a "moderate" income turned to the Judge Baker clinic for help. After the usual round of tests and interviews with both parents, the team concluded that Adam was a normal lad showing all the signs of insecurity in his family situation. With a "careful and probably nagging" stepmother and a stepfather who seemed to reject Adam and threatened to "put him away," the clinic identified in the behavioral symptoms evidence of parental failure to meet Adam's emotional need for security. Adam's biological father was unknown; his stepfather remarried after his biological mother died. Adam probably suffered "internal conflicts about his parentage," and his newly constructed stepfamily did not provide an understanding environment. Security and parentage were a long way from the fire setting, stealing, and upsetting behavior Adam's parents had seen as their son's problems. In fact, the problem ceased to be Adam's at all as the clinic explored his parents' failure to meet his emotional needs and examined ways to change the parents.

The clinic's focus on family harmony and emotional conflict was, to be sure, partially theory driven. Child guidance clinicians cited the work of J. C. Flügel, a Freudian whose study, *The Psycho-Analytic Study of the Family* (1921), blamed family disorganization for the emotional and behavioral problems of children. Then, too, by 1935, when Adam's family brought him to the JBGC, David Levy had begun his studies of sibling rivalry and maternal overprotection in the United States, and in Europe Anna Freud and Melanie Klein were beginning to fashion the psychoanalytic interpretation of childhood behavioral disorders. In the works of both women, the family's emotional structure shaped the emotional and behavioral problems of its children. These theorists influenced mental hygiene literature and psychiatric casework discussions in the JBGC records. The Boston clinicians, however, often found the ideas of Alfred Adler, European architect of the "inferiority complex," a particularly useful framework for exploring the relationship between misbehavior and unsatisfied emotional needs.

An unmet need for security frequently led to feelings of inferiority, child guidance practitioners postulated. And while Douglas Thom called the "inferiority complex" a "much abused term," he nonetheless attributed "much of the unhappiness and inefficiency of life" to "feelings of inadequacy that children develop at a very early age."[76] According to Thom, feelings of inferiority were manifested in many forms of troublesome activity, though most frequently as careless indifference, illness, daydreaming, or delinquency. Both neurotic and delinquent behavior, either passive or aggressive, signaled signs of inferiority masking the unfilled need for security.[77]

Child guidance promoters such as Thom usually subscribed to a broader understanding of inferiority than that of Adler, who stressed the relationship between the emotions and a physical deficit such as a short stature or a physical deformity.[78] In the American mental hygiene movement, inferiority might be indicated by any perceived difference from the group to which a child had to adjust. Lawson Lowrey, of the Institute for Child Guidance in New York City, thought it best to define "inferiority complex" as the "conflicts that emerge over the differences that the individual finds between himself and the group or his ideals." Hence Lowrey identified not only physical constitution and intellectual ability but also race as factors in feelings of inferiority.[79]

At the Judge Baker clinic, diagnosticians also used the term with greater freedom than did committed Adlerians. Feelings of inferiority about physical stature or intellect sometimes surfaced as explanations of misbehavior. Such a label might also indicate misunderstandings between parents and children about adoption or illegitimacy, rivalries among children for a parent's attention, or a general sense of being unappreciated. Adam, the neighborhood troublemaker, had many symptoms of an "inferiority complex," although the term itself did not appear in his file. William, however, seen several months earlier, showed "marked feelings of inferiority," because of the birth of a new sister, the boy's small stature, and the family's poverty (9171).

The intensity of the clinic's commitment to diagnoses of unmet emotional needs was surely aroused by the swirl of theoretical discussion about emotion in the psychological literature. Other factors, however, in addition to considerations of theory, contributed to the reign of emotional needs in the clinic's repertoire of diagnoses. "Unmet needs," like the "everyday" problem child, was a useful category for the professional group of child guidance practitioners. Psychosocial explanations of troublesome children, posited on economic deprivation and few middle-class amenities, grew out of Progressive efforts to reconstruct delinquents in a middle-class image. The psychological environment that failed to gratify emotional needs rubbed out economic factors as explanatory principles for emotional disturbances. Indeed, feelings of inferiority could be found in any problem child, rich or poor, male or female, delinquent or not.

Emotional needs explained both the sex delinquencies of the working-class girl and the "wild," "pleasure-loving" behavior of one from the middle class, just as emotional needs accounted for the school problems of a middle-class boy and the truancy of a immigrant youngster. Failure to provide children with these elementary keys to happiness excused the infrequent cases of middle-class juvenile delinquency. The stories of Nathan Leopold and Richard Loeb, the era's notorious examples of juvenile crime, confirmed the "unmet emotional needs" diagnosis and provided evidence of the insidious role of unprotected emotions in the delinquencies of children from wealthy neighborhoods. Although emotional needs could generate delinquency among sons and daughters of the well-to-do, child guidance personnel found it far more likely that this class of children expressed unmet needs as rebellion, nervousness, childish behavior, or withdrawal, symptoms these professionals wished more parents would recognize as troublesome and to which they addressed much of the popularization literature. Of course, children of the poor could also be neurotic; but child guiders found outgoing, extroverted, personalities to be more common in the lower classes. Child guidance experts believed these boys and girls more often signaled unmet needs through delinquencies.[80] With "unmet needs" as its favored etiology for troublesome behavior, the clinic was in a position to service clients of all social classes.

As he had in 1915, once again William Healy helped his colleagues visualize the new explanatory framework of child guidance. In *The Individual Delinquent* Healy drew a "web of causation" to depict delinquency explanations; in 1936 Healy and Bronner replaced the web with the "life stream of feelings and activities" in which "unsatisfying human relationships" clog "the flow of normal urges, desires and wishes in the channels of socially acceptable activities" and result in delinquency (see Figure 5.1).[81] Although environment remained an important part of the "social histories," for only a few practitioners did it refer primarily to the neighborhood or the family's financial situation. James Plant, director of the Essex County Juvenile Clinic in Newark, New Jersey, still urged his colleagues to pursue the effects of poverty on child guidance cases. Influenced by the field of anthropology, Plant drew connections between culture and the economy, and the formation of personality. But during the 1930s child guidance publications in this vein were anomalous.[82] At the Judge Baker clinic notes on the family's economic status played a role in determining the clinic's fees, but rarely in diagnosing the nature of a child's problems. Instead, all three team members combined to calculate a family's emotional capital and propose ways to boost its assets to satisfy the unmet emotional needs of children.

"What ails our youth?" George Coe asked for a generation of parents, and child guidance answered, "If they are troublesome, they are simply exhibit-

THE GENERAL LIFE STREAM OF FEELINGS AND ACTIVITIES

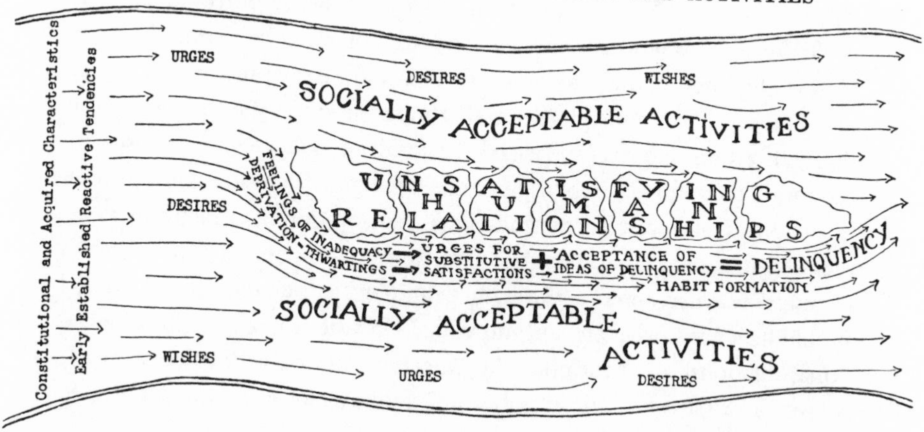

Figure 5.1 In 1936 Healy and Bronner depicted delinquency causation as a large blockage in the flow of human behavior caused by "Unsatisfying Human Relationships." William Healy and Augusta Bronner, *New Light on Delinquency and Its Treatment* (New Haven: Yale University Press, ©1936 by Yale University Press), p. 4.

ing the symptoms of unmet emotional needs." As the clients of child guidance came more and more from families with some financial security and the children brought for treatment were not legally delinquent, child guidance practitioners and popularizers reconceptualized both the problem behavior and the responsibilities of parenting. The interpretations of troublesome behavior provided by child guidance privileged children at the expense of mothers and fathers. Child guidance allied with the young in the cultural war between the generations. Emancipation demanded a jettisoning of parental control; understanding presumed a companionable or democratic rather than authoritarian relationship with a parent; and security required love and acceptance within the family setting, not harsh rules that prevented a child's interaction with peers. In each case clinicians concluded that the "cause" of a child's neurotic dependency, rebellion, delinquency, or feelings of inferiority was most often the attitude of the adults in the family. Defining the youth problem as one of unmet emotional needs was a crucial step toward reconceptualizing child guidance as "parent guidance."

The consequences of this new interpretation of troublesome behavior were revolutionary. Not only were all children potentially troublesome and all families potential child guidance patients, surely an excellent position for the new professionals, but unmet emotional needs also put responsibility for reforming troublesome youth squarely on the resources of the family. To be sure, American reformers had been blaming the family for troublesome children in one way or another since the early nineteenth century. Here, however, was an explanation that minimized the effects of economic disorganization and deemphasized the need for policy changes based on economic inequities. As child guidance highlighted the singular nature of juvenile misbehavior and the individualized solution, its practitioners attempted to write class out of the evaluation. No public redistribution of resources was necessary to eliminate delinquency; each incident could and should be solved privately and individually by the rearrangement of emotional relationships. At a point in American history, in the midst of the country's worst economic catastrophe, child guidance provided a way to care for all children without any economic restructuring.

Although child guidance allied with the children and identified their emotional needs, this reconceptualization of parenting was no more empowering for young people than for their parents. Had its promoters talked of children's "rights," child guidance might have challenged the hierarchical assumptions about age that lay beneath the generational conflicts. Had they spoke of rights, they might have laid the foundation for a public examination of the absence of guarantees for those rights. But child guiders chose instead the language of needs when its practitioners stood up for the children. As Linda Gordon has argued about single mothers, the needy are pitiable and pitied, but they are not entitled to recompense.[83]

The next two chapters go inside the Judge Baker clinic to look in detail at the relationship between the experts and their patients. I use the term *patients*, now, because emotional needs theory clearly designated the status of all parents of troublesome children, poor or economically more secure, as problematic if not outright pathological, and in need of assistance. It is an appropriate term, however, only when looking at child guidance from the perspective of the clinicians. Both children and parents, of all economic classes, continued to regard themselves as *clients* who could and would decide how much authority to grant these self-proclaimed experts in troublesome behavior. Parents' willingness to search for help with child rearing did not signify acceptance of all that child guidance offered. Indeed, child guidance clinicians focused increasingly on psychotherapeutic work with the parents in part because children proved to be such fickle allies of the professional expansion of child guidance.

Children and Child Guidance

Dr. Malcolm Finley had been meeting with Charles every week for a month when, in November 1935, the psychiatrist wrote in his notes:

> At the end of the interview the Ex[aminer] put it up definitely to [Charles] himself as to whether he would like to come in again. [Charles] at first said he didn't care. Ex., however, would not take this indefinite answer and told him that it was a matter of either yes or no. If [Charles] really wanted some help, really wanted to work out his problems and grow up to be a real man, the Ex. would be able to help him. However, if he didn't want any help, it would be a waste of time for both him and the Ex. (9431).

Charles agreed, told Finley he wanted no more meetings, and the JBGC's contact with the boy ended. In principle, child guidance sided with the modernity of adolescents and their search for independence. In practice, the team hoped to rein in or control the troublesome behavior of young people like Charles, a twelve-year-old accused of stealing at school and bullying younger children. Charles's refusal to cooperate threatened to make him one of the clinic's "failures." Instead, he was counted as a success. Although Charles chose to end his therapy, the boy's mother continued to come into the clinic about once every three weeks throughout the spring of 1936, and in 1937 she brought her second son for a consultation. The file was closed finally in April 1938 and the clinic noted a "good" prognosis for both boys, based primarily on changes observed in their mother.

Charles's story and this particular therapeutic exchange between psychiatrist and patient highlight the need to examine more closely the part played by children in the development of clinical practice in child guidance. Popularizers had urged parents to turn to the clinic for help, and some parents, including Charles's mother, had seen the wisdom of this advice. But until the psychiatrist asked, after several weeks of meetings, no one had consulted Charles. Nor have historians questioned the role that children played in the creation of children's medicine and the "child sciences." Children have never been very visible in history, and if showcased, they have been portrayed by historians primarily as receptors of historical change, as subjects of parental ministrations, or, in the case of science and medicine, as the objects of professional interpretation and intervention.[1] Works from labor history and the history of popular culture have begun to describe a very different, more active, historical "child."[2] This approach, when applied to the historical discussion of age-specialized clinical medicine, complicates the story of professional development and popular authority.

It is relatively easy to track in the published literature the professional debates over medical theory and therapy; the children are more difficult to get at. Case files help to give voice to these most silent of historical actors. Because of the psychiatrist's interest in the child's "own story," the white pages of the Judge Baker records reveal how these young people explained the world they inhabited to powerful strangers. Although filtered through a professional lens, these accounts provide clues to the child's understanding of the process of diagnosis and treatment and hint at the impact of child culture on practice in the clinic. The interpretations offered by the children of who they were and where they were going dictated the focus of child guidance work as surely as did the needs and wants of parents and professionals. In the clinics Charles and his peers were active, if unwitting, participants who helped to shape services and the child guidance approach to therapy.

In the previous chapters I have presented child guidance as a psychological paradigm that individualized and democratized (or disassociated from a class identity) the troublesome child, that turned common childhood behaviors into symptoms of psychiatric diagnoses, and that established the child's emotional vulnerability as the primary source of problems. I have also described child guidance as an interdisciplinary team, with each member part of a developing field in search of professional authority. In addition to the paradigm and the professions, child guidance was a specific set of services provided in clinical practice. By 1935 representatives of the three disciplines on the clinic's team furnished three specific services to children and parents. Sex education, provided by the child psychiatrist, and vocational counseling, often accomplished through tests administered by the psychologist, focused specifically on the young people. Therapy, however, was the primary service, for both children and parents. Child guiders at the Commonwealth Fund's demonstration clinics made individual therapy a part of the clinic's rituals when they accepted as patients the "predelinquents" referred by schools and parents. At the Judge Baker clinic the change from merely providing diagnoses to also offering treatment occurred a bit later, in 1931. Social workers, as they became more deeply enmeshed in the theories of psychoanalysis, began to function as therapists for parents, especially mothers, while psychiatrists continued to serve the child in a therapeutic capacity. Looking at these three services—sex education, vocational guidance, and individual therapy for parents and children—from the child's perspective helps to explain how these activities served to solidify the authority of child guidance.

The services and the children's stories that surround them can be better understood if gender differences, along with age, are brought to the foreground of the discussion. Finley's promise to help Charles become a "real man" was not simply a colloquial reference. As the child's IQ and the family's class identity receded in the clinic's lexicon of explanations for troublesome behavior, partly in response to the self-referred clients present in significant numbers by the 1930s, child guiders gave greater emphasis to gender differences. Sorting children into diagnostic categories remained one of the clinic's chief social responsibilities, and the shift from class to gender was a subtle one. Economic status continued to be duly noted in the social histories; parents labeled the problems of their offspring as threats to class identity. Nor do I mean to suggest that in William Healy's version of child guidance cultural expectations of adult gender roles played no part in deliberations about poor troublesome children. Progressive child savers gendered their solutions to delinquency and dependency, forcing the diagnostic clinics to incorporate gender considerations into their recommendations. Nevertheless, in the discussions and deliberations of 1935, child guiders understood and interpreted children less as rich or poor and more as masculine or feminine, a change related in large measure to the needs of growing numbers of voluntary clients.

Boys formed more than two-thirds of the clinic's caseload in 1935, and finding answers to questions of how to be a "real boy" and how to become a "real man" lay beneath both the clinic's explanations of misbehavior and the treatment goals for adolescent males.[3] The need to outline a complementary meaning for femininity was implicit in discussions of boyhood, yet the attributes of a "real girl" received less direct exploration. The staff and the boys shared an understanding of the demands of masculinity, and this common bond guided the clinic's array of services.

This chapter, however, belongs to all the children, male and female, poor and living in comfort, delinquent and troubled. Only by examining the bond between the child and the clinic can we map fully the contours of child guidance and measure the sources of its popularity in the 1930s. Since children worked mainly with the staff psychiatrists, how each viewed the other sets the stage for the discussion of gender and services in the clinic.

"THE CHILD AS THE THERAPIST SEES HIM": PROFESSIONAL EXPECTATIONS AND CLINIC REALITIES

Child psychiatry was a maturing discipline in the 1930s; practitioners were secure enough in their professional identities to raise questions about the success of their clinics, the techniques they used, and the nature of the relationship between psychiatrist and child.[4] In professional symposia psychiatrists debated the merits of using toys, or dream analysis, or "relationship therapy" that stressed working with both parent and child.[5] The biases of local psychiatrists determined which therapeutic approaches dominated in the clinics, but the point on which all in the field could agree was put by Lawson Lowrey in 1934. "No matter what treatment techniques are adopted or who is being treated," he told members of the American Orthopsychiatric Association, "the child remains the center of the treatment effort."[6]

How to create a successful relationship between the therapist and the young patient formed a common denominator in the discussions of therapeutic philosophies.[7] In the professional literature, all child guidance work with children depended on faith that in a very short time, often only one interview, the therapist could generate trust and acceptance in the child, enabling the child to talk about thoughts, feelings, and experiences that could not be mentioned without guilt or shame. During the 1930s psychiatrists used the word "rapport" to designate this special nature of a child's relationship with the psychiatrist. For some therapists rapport implied the specifically psychoanalytic meaning of transference; for others, like Samuel Hartwell, director of the Worcester (Massachusetts) Child Guidance Clinic, the term meant friendship.[8] "We were able to talk frankly of his behaviour,"

Hartwell reported on his rapport with one young delinquent met while practicing at the Judge Baker Foundation, "and he finally came to the point where he accepted the ideas I wanted him to, not because he believed them, nor because he felt that they were true, nor because he wanted to give up his bad habits, but because they came from me and because he believed that I was his understanding friend, who wanted to help him and probably knew best."[9] Therapists believed they needed a good rapport whether they chose to engage in traditional psychotherapy with the child, to assume the role of a "pal" giving good advice (a technique the JBGC psychiatrists called "bucking up"), or to apply indirect manipulation of the environment. Without rapport the therapist had no authority; with a good rapport child guidance therapists believed they could help the troublesome child adjust to adult expectations.

Discussions about therapy and rapport grew numerous in the 1930s in part because, despite the positive predictions about everyday children in the advice literature, the value of child guidance—its ability to change behavior and prevent criminal careers—was called into question by some investigators. In *One Thousand Juvenile Delinquents* (1934), one of many studies of delinquency made during their careers as mental hygiene researchers, Sheldon Glueck and Eleanor T. Glueck exposed the ineffectiveness of the Boston juvenile court system and its clinical adjunct, the Judge Baker Guidance Center. Perhaps more discomforting for clinic practitioners, especially in light of child guidance popularization efforts, were the studies of "successes" and "failures" with nondelinquents. A comprehensive survey of these studies found a 25 percent failure rate, along with only a modest amount of "adjustment" in the cases counted as successes.[10] No wonder then that David Levy, a New York psychiatrist, exhorted his colleagues to use "all the clinical tools that can be operated on behalf of the child."[11]

HOW THE CHILD SAW THE THERAPIST

Failure rates revealed the many individual examples of boys and girls who did not seem to benefit from the clinic's efforts at rapport. In practice, being a child-centered medical specialty held out unique challenges for the clinic psychiatrists. "One of the great difficulties confronting many physicians who deal with children . . . ," mused a conference discussant in 1931, "is that the child does not come to the physician as the adult does, but is brought. One cannot depend on the child for [the] spontaneous coopera-tion that the adult brings."[12] Not only were they not spontaneously coop-erative, the children were not attuned to the process and the goals of the practitioners and frequently made a shambles of the idealized practice described in the professional literature. What these children thought about their visits to the clinic—how they interpreted the work of child guid-ance—often contrasted with their parents' experiences and put the clinic's child-centeredness to the test.

Because the children were reluctant participants, they had far fewer options than their parents to determine the terms of their contact with child guidance. Parents, for example, could choose how much of the fam-ily's financial resources they were willing to commit to psychotherapy, and they could tie continued patronage to results. Although many parents con-fessed to being at their wit's end, they understood that the Judge Baker professionals provided a service, and they demanded a cost accounting, a reckoning of whether or not they had gotten their money's worth with a better-behaved child. Most wanted clear recommendations for changing the child's behavior and speedy turnaround time. When the clinic failed to meet their expectations, they withdrew. "We cannot work miracles," the staff noted in the summary of one instance of disgruntlement (9272). Miracles, however, were what child guidance promotions had been promis-ing, and cost-conscious parents set limits on how long they were willing to wait for miracles to happen.

Unlike the adults, the children could not so simply withdraw their pa-tronage to show their displeasure with the clinic experience. This is not to say they were any less effective than their parents in defining the limits of the child psychiatrist's authority. Children representing all referral agencies could and did withhold their cooperation, and they made clear to child psychiatrists that the decision to continue the clinic's model of treatment rested with themselves as well as their parents.

Just as the parents came with a set of expectations, so did the young people. In spite of the friendly attitude of the psychiatrist, the clinic was an adult institution representing the authority of the law or of medicine. Apprehension was probably the first reaction as, upon arrival, the children were led off to meet alone with the unknown doctor.[13] Added to the imme-diate anxiety about separation from familiar faces was the popular percep-tion of the clinic the children brought with them. A fourteen-year-old (taken to the clinic by an agent of the Church Home Society for Episcopal

Children) begged the doctor for a note to prove to his father that there was "nothing wrong with his head." The boy's family had been "ragging him," telling him the appointment meant that he was "crazy" (9263). Another boy, who called the process "silly," was probably echoing his father's disapproval of the study (9415); quite likely so was the juvenile delinquent who called the clinic a "louzy [sic] dump" (9298).

From the reactions of the children and the disappointment of the therapists, it seems clear that many of the young people failed to grasp the purpose of their visits to the clinic or what sort of participation was expected. Judge Baker therapists found particularly exasperating children such as case no. 9220, who was quite willing to play with the clinic's toys and art materials but was unwilling to initiate any serious discussion of his problems. In another case, an eleven-year-old said that he did not know why he was meeting with the psychiatrist and he did not "know that he had received any benefit at all . . . He was told that he should begin to think over in a little more serious manner some of the benefits he received. It would also be necessary for him to take a more active part in the visits or otherwise there would be no use in coming" (9212). Few were like the girl who described herself as having an "inferiority complex," a statement confirming that popularization had provided some adolescents as well as adults with a new language to describe life situations (9206).

Some children took to the friendly adults and confided their troubles; case no. 9242, for example, soon called the therapist his "pal."[14] Psychiatrists also identified quite a few who were less than "frank" in telling their stories. Dr. Finley called Frederick Smith "never really frank," even though they had met for fourteen sessions (9214). William Healy was similarly disturbed by a case he evaluated as a favor for a friend. The boy seemed "frank" at first, Healy wrote in the file; information from the youth's mother suggested, however, that "evidently [the] boy was playing up to me" (9221). Another adolescent seemed to make quite a good impression on Anna Skinner, the female psychiatrist who worked with the girls, but later she learned from the girl's older sister that the young patient thought she could "see through the old ladies" at the clinic (9215). The pretenses and deceptions disillusioned therapists. By not being "frank" children prevented rapport, that special bond which would allow for behavioral change.

The children, however, had legitimate worries about too much trust and too much frankness with their new-found friends. Some of the children were embarrassed by their troublesome behavior or by the questions the therapists asked; others were intent on making a good impression on another adult authority-figure, even if it involved stretching the truth. While telling their "own stories," children were invited to reveal private behavior and secret feelings about family members, revelations their parents might not sanction. One youth tried to protect his parents' income by lying to the psychiatrist. His mother's New Deal job would have been jeopardized if it were widely known that his father was also working (9202). Psychiatrists routinely asked the young people how their parents used discipline, who was the preferred parent, and what had been the child's sexual experiences. Conflict with family values particularly caused consternation for children when psychiatrists asked questions of a sexual nature. One young boy cried when Dr. Finley asked about his sex practices; his father had told him not to talk about "those things" (9242).

How easily a child could be caught in the middle between the demands of a powerful social agency and the family's values and standards. Loyalty to the family, usually regarded by the clinic team as an admirable trait, caused many children to be labeled "not frank," "not serious," or "uncooperative." Parents, demanding accountability from the clinic and faced with final responsibility for the child's behavior, felt within their rights to know what was going on in the closed-door sessions. At home, therefore, children might be questioned closely about what transpired during their appointments with the psychiatrist.[15] The interviewers promised children that the "own stories" were confidential. Many of the parents, much to their frustration, found that child guiders abided by the promise, but the children were not so easily convinced. One asked directly if the staff would divulge information to her mother (9275); another offered evidence from his foster home of the clinic's betrayal of confidence and questioned the security of his own revelations (9291).

Worried about tugs on their family loyalty, concerned about confidentiality, perhaps fearful of the whole process of the study, the young people took whatever openings they found to short-circuit the clinic's therapeutic approaches. They used forgetfulness as an excuse to avoid confronting a psychiatrist's questions; and they refused to be "frank," telling partial stories or outright lies. They bargained with the only capital they had, their time. They failed to show up for appointments.[16] They were late. Or they arrived whenever they wished, demanding to see the therapist immediately. Once at a session, they dallied with the examiner's time by declining to be "serious" and not working hard to reveal their feelings. Not all children, to be sure, made life so difficult for their therapists. Enough, however, showed up in the clinic's records to suggest that the glowing individual success stories often reported by the psychiatrists in their professional literature and popularizations have to be matched against the limits these children often imposed on the psychiatrists' authority to rehabilitate them.

In the final assessment, of course, the children had few rights and little power in their dealings with the child guidance movement. Their manipulations were minor compared with the efforts of the professionals to manipulate their behavior or coerce them into foster homes or state institutions. The extent of the child's agency in the clinical setting suggests that we need a separate term to describe relationships in children's medicine. *Client* is hardly adequate; all sides recognized that children had little choice about the decision to seek help from child guidance professionals. But the passivity of the *patient* role also scarcely describes the participation of the children in the formation of child guidance and clinical child psychiatry. It is more helpful to think of them as *juvenile negotiators,* or young people who negotiated around and through the burgeoning authority of the professionals to define the proper clinical and familial response to troublesome and troubled children, just as they also negotiated some of the terms of their therapy.

THE TURN TO GENDER, OR HOW TO BE A "REAL BOY"

The discourse of gender proved to be the common ground for negotiations between the children and their therapists. This was particularly true for the masculine identity shared by the boys and the male psychiatrists. Consider the assistance offered to Frederick Smith (9214). The boy had run away from home and spent several days with an older man—a stranger. A Children's Aid Society agent suspected the boy had been sexually abused, leading her to request the clinic's evaluation. The Judge Baker staff, she hoped, could discover what had happened during the runaway and then, in her terms, "set the boy straight." After several visits, Dr. Finley told his patient that he had "good stuff in him," that, indeed, Fred was a "real boy." By providing Fred with reassurance about his masculinity and accurate information about male and female sexuality and by acting as an appropriate male role model for Fred, the psychiatrist believed he could reaffirm the boy's gender identity and could, in fact, set straight even a child who had had such a tragic and identity-threatening experience.

The situation that brought Fred to the clinic was unusual, but the outcome of therapy promised by the staff psychiatrist was not. In the cases from 1935 the interpretation of gender differences provided a framework for rapprochement between the children, especially the boys, and their therapists. In highlighting gender, child guiders may have taken some of their cues from parents who often framed conflict with children as a battle over standards appropriate for males and females. Gender, along with social class and generational boundaries, guided the discussions of mothers and fathers seen in both child study clubs and the clinic's case files. Gender identity and the factors directing its (mal)formation also rode roughshod over the analytical tools of each of the child guidance professions. Finally, the boys themselves contributed to the clinic's emphasis on gender and gendered services.

In the field of social work, the "boy problem" had an honored place. The phrase was already an accepted part of child-saving parlance when the National Federation of Settlements began a special study by that name in 1915.[17] During the Progressive years, the Reverend William Forbush, author of *The Boy Problem* (1901) and founder of two special clubs or fraternities for boys, was just one of many who grew to believe that middle-class boys were as much in need of rescue and remasculinization as were the children of the poor.[18] Catholic social workers turned the boy problem into a specialized field of study during the 1920s when Brother Barnabas, director of the Boy Life Bureau of the Knights of Columbus, issued a call in 1924 for a "new profession." Boy guidance, a term he later changed to "boyology," aimed at preventing delinquency through "a program of directed activity for the boy's leisure time, and men trained professionally for his leisure-time leadership, just as teachers are trained to direct his mind, and doctors to care for his body."[19] "Give the boy a chance" served Brother Barnabas as the motto for boyology. The University of Notre Dame took up the project and established a separate department of "boy guidance" in the school's education program. The program bulletin listed sixty-two graduates as of 1931.[20]

The promotion of boyology at Notre Dame was indicative of the turn to gender among the professions that made up child guidance. In practice at the clinic, however, social workers claimed responsibility for the parents while male psychiatrists, whose belief in the need for a unique boy guidance drew on the preachings of psychoanalysis, took charge of the troublesome males. What Freud had to say about boys helped to justify the psychiatric professionals' interest in questions of gender identity and gender construction.

For Freudians the stages of personality development were clearly gendered. The most important period in Freud's developmental theory was the phallic stage, beginning at about age four and lasting until age seven, although children revisited the same issues, with great intensity, during adolescence. While in the phallic stage both boys and girls developed erotic feelings for the opposite-sex parent and a rivalry with the parent of the same sex. These uncomfortable feelings were resolved through a process of identification with or adoption of the sex role of the same-sex parent. Psychoanalysts used the terms Oedipus complex and family romance to describe the unconscious conflict that produced a child's sexual identity.

Freud believed the process was particularly torturous for boys. Love for his mother led the boy to resent his father. The desire to take his father's place with his mother resulted in ambivalence, psychic conflict, and a castration complex, or fear of mutilation. In the successful resolution of the boy's Oedipal conflict, the ego (the mental structure responsible for realistic satisfaction of libidinal or instinctual desires) renounced or sublimated these unconscious desires for the mother, relinquished the feelings of rivalry with the father, and intensely identified with the masculine role. Girls moved along a similar developmental path, coming, upon resolution of the conflict, to identify with their mothers. Freud theorized, however, that for females the experience was far simpler and less equivocal than it was for boys, and for girls it culminated in the wish for a child.

Normal resolution of the Oedipus complex created in individuals a superego or conscience, along with a strong ego ideal (the unconscious taking over of approved parental attitudes toward satisfaction of libidinal desires) expressed in appropriately gendered and socially approved forms of behavior. In sublimating their incestuous wishes for their mothers, boys developed the personalities of manly men, with heterosexual longings and the drive needed for business success. The path to manhood, however, was strewn with obstacles, particularly if the male and female figures in a boy's life were inadequate representatives of their genders. If not successfully navigated, these shoals could wreck a boy's personality and destroy his chance for happiness. The boy might lean toward homosexuality, engage in masturbation, or show signs of criminal tendencies, particularly when the psychological issues reappeared during the genital stage of psychosexual development reached at adolescence. At the very least, the ego's defense mechanisms—repression, fixation, regression, and reaction-formation—might become exaggerated and produce the signs of neurosis.[21] At the JBGC a diagnosis of "weak ego ideals" (often used as a synonym for lack of goals) figured prominently in the summary statements from 1935. For many child guidance psychiatrists the Oedipal theory justified efforts to develop rapport with the young patients and provide the boys with role models.[22]

While psychiatrists processed Freud's theories of psychosexual development and gender identity, psychologists too grew inordinately interested in "sex differences" research. In the 1910s female researchers in the field of psychology overturned the long-held belief that "mental traits" or cognitive ability separated the sexes. Far from putting to rest the question of difference, these findings only intensified the search for statistically verifiable distinctions between the sexes.[23] Beth L. Wellman, a developmental psychologist at the Iowa Child Welfare Research Station, cited 249 studies of sex differences in children when she reviewed recent literature in 1933. But Wellman added that "one must read almost every investigation in child psychology to gain a complete knowledge of the differences that have been found."[24]

When sex differences researchers explored the boundaries of the boys' world of the 1920s and 1930s, they found it remarkably distinct from that of their sisters. Boys matured physically much later than girls. In school, boys showed "reliably greater *interest* than girls in health, safety, money study, recreation and civil affairs"; girls were more interested in "etiquette, personal attractiveness and getting along with other people."[25] Boys were more skilled in math, less skilled in language. Their school grades, however, were not as high overall as were those of the girls; indeed, one researcher charged that girls wore a "sex halo" at school. In the classroom the conduct of the boys more often annoyed teachers—they were the troublemakers, the disturbers of class routine. In their leisure time boys and girls played with different toys and at different games. Boys formed "gangs," closely organized groups with specific leaders and genuine purpose; girls created gossipy "clubs," in which three or four close friends decided who could join and who was left out. The range of research during these decades demonstrated the creativity in this new field; developmental and educational psychologists set out to contrast motor skills, color preferences, sensitivity to light, parental preferences, introversion and extroversion, physical development, and even history retention.[26]

The sex differences research reached a crescendo in the work of Lewis Terman, known also for his interest in intelligence testing and his studies of gifted children. Terman and his co-workers produced two scales to measure personality differences—the "masculinity index" (a part of the studies of genius published in 1926 and 1930),[27] and the Aptitude-Interest Analysis Test, also called the M-F (masculinity-femininity) Test, published in 1936 as *Sex and Personality: Studies in Masculinity and Femininity*.[28] Similar to an IQ study, the M-F Test used interests and perceptions to determine an individual's degree of masculinity or femininity. In one word-association exercise, subjects chose from a list of five words the one that seemed "to go best or most naturally with the first." For the word "order," for example, the test takers were asked to choose from "buy," "command," "neat," and "quiet." Subjects selecting "command" were assigned a "+" sign for that question, which counted as one point toward masculinity. Those who chose "buy," "neat," or "quiet" earned a "−" sign, one femininity point.[29]

Although Terman foreswore the approach, many of the experiments appeared to be contests in which one sex came in first, the other last. The fires of gender competition crackled in the language of the debate; boys "excelled" at certain skills or were "superior," girls "surpassed" boys, or had "higher" scores. Terman and the other sex differences researchers showed little interest in sex similarities, although occasionally similarities were uncovered. Rather, their search for differences conveyed an uneasiness about the hierarchy of the sexes and a suspicion that meanings of masculine and feminine were coming undone. Gender definitions were in need of scientific verification so that masculine and feminine personality traits might be fixed permanently on a compass of gender identity.[30]

Taken together, the sex differences research, the interests of social workers, and the psychosexual developmentalism of the psychoanalysts offered child guiders a gendered framework for their categories of interpretation. The summary of case no. 9296 read in part: "We recognize in the family situation that this [boy] is entirely different from his [three] sibs., tho of course they are all girls." Staff members who wrote this report did not clarify the statement further. Professional research and theorizing in three different fields made the implications obvious to all on the child guidance team.

This interest in a gendered framework was sustained both by developments within the clinic and by a broadly shared understanding of the political and economic roles of men and women. Inside the clinic professional issues drew child guiders away from the language of poverty and neglect. Reasons for the change were rooted partly in the specific process of child guidance popularization. In the clinics the strong correlation made by Progressive child savers between class and delinquency overshadowed gender expectations during the 1910s and early 1920s. Interest in the problems of "everyday children" and voluntary family participation in child guidance helped to diminish the importance of the material environment in which troublesome children were raised. Thus the staff observed that Eddie's problem behavior had developed because Eddie had been "made feminine" by "unwise upbringing when little" (9183). They also recorded that Eddie's foster family (with whom he had lived since very young) was financially "very comfortable." The presence of both comments was not coincidental. As the new class of clients arrived at the clinic, gender moved to the foreground in the case discussions.

Questions of gender identity appeared, however, in cases from all economic groupings. The staff found that no matter what the class background, boys were often maladjusted because they had been "made feminine." Records showed that delinquents and nondelinquents alike suffered from weak ego ideals and poor role models. The need to appeal to a new class of clients helped to push the clinic in the direction of gender, but it did not fully account for the change. Rather, the clinic was a microcosm of cultural concerns about gender. During the 1920s and 1930s definitions of masculine and feminine were challenged on many fronts.

From the passage of woman suffrage to the presence of more women in the labor force, the equation of female and domesticity was under review in these years. With more women entering the work force in the 1920s than ever before, and particularly with the growing numbers of working mothers, feminine identification with home and family was becoming suspect. In his study of genius, Terman found, for example, that few of the gifted girls wanted to become housewives. Girls who went out automobiling and dancing compelled their parents to question standards for feminine behavior. George Chauncey has shown in his study of gay society in New York City how homosexuality, too, had become a powerful symbol of the cultural unease surrounding sexual differentiation. Flaunted in the nightclubs and bath houses of the 1920s and suppressed by the police in the 1930s, homosexual culture provided evidence that men and women were not always what they appeared to be.[31] The meanings of masculinity and femininity were under duress in popular culture; then came the Great Depression.

Economic necessity further blurred the lines of gender difference. Real men worked—at manly jobs, according to Terman and Miles, who asked M-F test-takers to indicate a liking or disliking for various occupations. "Farmer," "factory manager," and "plumber" earned masculinity points; "missionary," "poet," and "interior decorator" were scored as feminine. During the 1930s, however, when Terman and Miles perfected their test, many men did not work at all. The federal government responded to the masculinity crisis with laws intended to limit the work of females, but in many families, it was the woman's job that kept the family housed and fed. Constant reminders of the disruption evident in recently impoverished families might have been expected to move child guidance closer to its Progressive roots; instead, the failure of many men to perform as "good providers" for their families substantiated other concerns about masculinity.[32] The clinicians translated troublesome behavior that might have been interpreted as problems of material want into questions of personality adjustment, best understood in terms of ego ideals, sex roles, and gender identity.

THE BOYS AND THEIR WORRIES

Did boys, too, find masculinity a difficult identity to put into practice in the mid-1930s? What did a boy have to do to become a real man? How was a boy's interpretation of boyhood different from his parents' or the clinic's? Answers to these questions suggest another dimension to the functions of the gendered framework of child guidance.

The youths brought along to their meetings with the psychiatrists a commonly understood code of boyhood.[33] Most important, boys knew that the situation determined the characteristics of a "real boy"; following the code of boyhood in school, and often at home, got a boy into trouble, but being a school boy, or a family boy in the gang, made you a "sissy." The demands of the boys' culture often resulted in conflict with the values of parents, teachers, and the law. Yet, while appearing to ignore adult expectations and leaving many a mother out of patience, these boys, whose degree of misbehavior distinguished them from the general boy population, also shared popular expectations for masculine conduct. Their fears reflected worries about sexuality and sexual identity, their insecurities made masculinity something worth fighting for, and their vision of the future, though cloudy, was guided by a notion of the man as the family breadwinner.

Even if the clinic as an institution and child guidance as a process of evaluation scared the boys and made them reluctant participants, the boys and their psychiatrists could agree that it was tough to be a boy in the 1930s. The psychiatrist's task was complicated by the boys' code of conduct; but shared expectations about gender identity and a shared anticipation of the demands of manhood served to overcome some of the distrust and distaste evident in the youths' initial reaction to the clinic. Child guidance in Boston met the challenge of the juvenile negotiators with two types of services: sex education and vocational guidance. Neither activity was unique to the clinic, but both appeared with regularity in the records of the staff's activities in 1935. Each gave the children and their parents (and their surrogate parents, the child welfare agencies) a measure of accountability, and both provided a means through which the therapist could attempt to create a good rapport with the boys to help them develop into "real men."

For the boys, their parents, and the psychiatrists, evidence of what Healy had once called "abnormal sexualism"—homosexual behavior and masturbation—was more worrisome than problems with boy-girl relationships.[34] Parents did not tend to list their boys' heterosexual exploits as proof of troublesome conduct, and clinicians believed that homo- and autoerotic behavior caused greater mental conflict than sex play (the clinic's term) with girls. A boy might reveal that he played with girls on the street, but a qualification that the activity was not "dirty" signaled the psychiatrist to probe no further (9255).[35] At the same time, psychiatrists carefully elicited confidences about what a boy was doing with other boys, what went on in his gang, and what were the sleeping arrangements in his home (meaning did he sleep with his brothers).

Through direct questioning an examiner hoped to gather information about sexual knowledge and experiences, and evidence of guilt or repression. With considerable prodding, boys revealed their fears and their random sexual acts, behavior that became a focus of succeeding meetings with the psychiatrists. Donald (9203), for example, confessed to participation in the sexual activities of a group of older boys. While he "couldn't say exactly why fellatio was wrong," Donald told the interviewer that he knew "he didn't want to do it and felt ashamed." In 1935 the boys were expected to treat discussion of these shameful pleasures in a straightforward, "frank" manner. Psychiatrists assumed that such openness could reduce conflict about the behavior and, more important, channel it toward adult hetero-sexuality.

The sexually abused Frederick Smith (9214), whose story occasioned Dr. Finley's "real boy" comment, was one whose experiences provided the clinic with cause for concern about homosexuality, but more ordinary were accounts divulged by boys like sixteen-year-old Henry Franklin (9261). The staff psychiatrist told Henry that boys of his age usually confronted only three problems: family relationships, masturbation, and relations with others of the same sex. Henry had no record of homosexual acts, yet given this encouragement he confided his unsuccessful efforts to win both boy- and girlfriends and voiced his fear of homosexuality. The clinic offered reassurance to boys such as Henry and Frederick. Frederick's ordeal was described as another of "life's experiences." Henry's problem was some-thing that he could overcome; his fears were "common" among boys, a normal part of adolescent development. Without condoning homosexual-ity, the child psychiatrists diminished its significance for the boys and offered them guidance on the road to a heterosexual masculine identity.

Worries about overt acts of homosexuality were evident in only a few of the boys' stories. Far more pervasive was the fear of being tagged as un-manly by peers. In the boys' culture, a nickname gave a boy his status and identity. A study from 1937 reported the not-surprising fact that boys preferred "masculine" nicknames such as Spike or Machine Gun Butch.[36] To be called a "sissy," as many of these boys were, was to be ostracized by peers who understood childhood in gendered terms. In boy culture a "sissy" behaved like a girl, and it was a most humiliating sobriquet. "He had collected butterflies [at] one time, but was called a sissy by [his brother] and some of the other boys," the staff psychiatrist recorded during one interview with Jimmy (9300). "He was afraid of being a sissy and didn't like to be called one. Dan [a friend] played with dolls with his little sister and was a sissy." Along with butterfly collecting and playing with sisters, sissies went to the opera with their mothers (9314), took dancing lessons (9241), could not swim or hit a ball (9300), or just looked and sounded different. Boys called William (whose teacher wanted help from the Judge Baker because he "steals, lies, disobeys, annoys and is notoriously a nuisance at home, at school and at play") a sissy because he was shorter than others in the gang (9171). So William had to fight to protect his identity. When called a sissy, boys defended their boyhood even if doing so conflicted with adult definitions of good behavior.

The boys used other tags with effeminate connotations, on themselves and on others, to indicate the gendered meaning of physical imperfections. Case no. 9172, a seventeen-year-old, was defensive about his "girlish appearance." Another older boy who stuttered reported that he fought because other boys called him a "fairy" (9241). A partially paralyzed fourteen-year-old who also disliked his female teachers worried about becoming a "pansy" (9173). The relationship between appearance and masculinity had been internalized by the boys in these cases. Although physical prowess might help overcome the stigma of a physical disability, the appearance of difference still hinted at a lack of the stuff it took to be a real boy.[37]

The words "fairy," "pansy," and the like were a part of American vernacular by the 1930s, but how well the boys understood the implications of such taunts remains a question; the extent of their misinformation about reproduction, puberty, and adolescent sexual development was tremendous.[38] Many of the boys, especially the younger ones, came to the clinic with minimal knowledge of reproduction and gross misunderstanding of nocturnal emissions and masturbation. The clinic called this naiveté "unsophisticated."[39] Boys often denied masturbating. As mentioned earlier, one cried because his father told him never to "talk about those things" (9242); another was judged "frank as far as he goes but makes it obvious that he is avoiding certain questions, particularly in the matter of sex" (9297); most eventually confessed to the practice, and then admitted their fears. Frequently the boys had been cautioned by parents (and sometimes by medical professionals) about the dangerous consequences of masturbation. It was a "loss of life's blood," or a "loss of nourishment." It would cause physical illness, or make them insane, or cause warts to grow on their faces, and one boy had been told by another that if a white fluid came out he would have a baby.[40] Some of these warnings stemmed from nineteenth-century medicine; though ideas were changing, they still retained a hold on boy culture in the 1930s.

From Healy's study of the roots of delinquency to Freud's theories on the origins of adult neuroses, the framework of child guidance convinced clinic psychiatrists of the need to alleviate this guilt about masturbation with accurate information. Although the sex education movement certainly did not originate in the clinic, child guidance professionals became early advocates of sex instruction for the young. Its roots, as Allan Brandt and others have shown, lay in Progressive era concerns about family instability and venereal disease. The CSAA promoted open and honest discussions of human sexuality. During the 1920s and 1930s Rockefeller money funded social science research projects sponsored by the Bureau of Social Hygiene. Schools tackled the task of providing students with knowledge about reproduction; books appeared specifically for young people.[41] In the clinic, the staff hoped to correct other expressions of antisocial behavior by making sure boys knew the facts of life. Child guiders advocated frank discussions between father and son as a way to inculcate healthy ideas about the male body and reproduction. When parents reneged, the psychiatrists stepped up to take their place, frequently asking parents for permission to give boys "straight information."

Few boys left the clinic without some knowledge of reproduction and reassurance about the normality of their sexual impulses. Some asked specifically for information; the boy who said that he was "repulsed" by the "sex talk" among his group, had, according to the psychiatrist, "very sketchy sort of information and asks for information, so we spend a good part of the int. straightening his ideas out. Insists he has never been involved in any sex misconduct but has speculated more or less about it and felt particularly unsophisticated. Perhaps this was the reason he . . . tried to appear 'tough' " (9311). And one boy, at least, identified the doctor's sex talk as the only real benefit gained from his visits to the clinic. He had no idea how he had been helped with his "problems," but now understood how he could have a baby sister even though his mother had died in childbirth (9212).

Parents, too, profited from the clinic's commitment to sex education. Though child guiders thought sex education produced closer ties in the family, many parents seemed eager for the staff to undertake the task of instruction, and quite likely saw the clinic's willingness to discuss adolescent sex drives with rebellious teenagers as the ideal means to avoid just such confidences.[42] While supplying the social history of a ten-year-old with a reading difficulty, the boy's father indicated that he hoped the clinic would also give the boy some sex education (9268).[43] The social worker took this father's request for sex education as an opportunity to inquire about the man's attitudes. She reported that she engaged in a lengthy discussion with her client, disabusing him of the notion that masturbation caused insanity and dullness.[44] For some boys and their parents sex education was a tangible service, one with measurable results, much less subject to failure than a nebulous promise of changed behavior or the even more difficult task of building a masculine identity in those who found themselves labeled unmanly.

The clinic's sex education did not appeal to all parents, however. The case of a fifteen-year-old youth convicted of accosting women on the street and putting his hand under their dresses (9224) illustrates both the clinic's approach to the boy's sexual feelings and lingering parental doubts about the wisdom of child guidance. In his assessment of the case, Dr. Finley suggested that the boy

> had developed rather prematurely from a physical, sexual point of view and because of this he had probably been having a good many impulses, and drives that he has had difficulty controlling and learning how to handle. Masturbation is also a normal thing in all boys and should be really looked at from this point of view. Because of the attitude taken by [the] M. and F. in this respect, [the boy] had practically no outlet for these drives, which the average b[oy] had, and because of his early and probably excessive sexual impulses, he had used the touching experiences as an outlet. We felt that if [the boy] was allowed to come in here and talk over his feelings, attitudes, and tendencies along this line, we could help him to reorient himself and take a more normal outlet and point of view, also help him to find some other acceptable outlet.

The boy's father, a police officer, was eager to work with the clinic until told by the social worker to avoid making an issue of the problem and to take a more understanding attitude toward his son. The social worker tried to convince this father that the clinic "was not trying to force the practice of masturbation on the boy, but to make him feel that he was not abnormal or different from other boys because he had the impulse to practice it, or even if he had already done so." At the next clinic appointment this father explained that he had "decided to let the matter drop as far as the JBGC was concerned. Said he understood that the Dr. advised masturbation and he felt he could not stand for that." He had been "happy" after his first clinic visit, and told friends about the help he expected to get. " 'And now,' shaking his head sadly, 'I found out what you really want to do.' " Working as he did with criminals, this man knew the doctor was wrong to suggest that masturbation could do no harm.[45] To the contrary, the staff urged sublimation of sexual urges, not giving in to them, and not repression.

Guilt about masturbation, child guidance workers believed, made the boys unhappy and quite possibly led to delinquency. This case confirmed their thinking.

Sex education was a gendered activity in the clinic. Male doctors did most of the explaining, and boys were the recipients of this information. Anna Skinner provided one girl with "full sex information," when it became obvious that the mother had not done so (9283).[46] In another case, the psychiatrist, unsure of the girl's knowledge, read a sex education book to her (9433).[47] Parents occasionally asked the psychiatrist for help with their girls as well as their boys. "J. is beginning to develop but as yet has not started to menstr[uate]," the intake interviewer reported of a twelve-year-old. "M. thinks there may be some things on which J. is not clear, and she would like to have the doctor talk with her about them" (9442). But, for the most part, sex education played a lesser role in negotiations with the girls.[48] The quiescence may have been related to the fact that most of the girls had reached puberty. Few still thought that babies came from hospitals—as did one of the younger ones (9453), who was given more accurate information.

More likely, when psychiatrists went looking for evidence of sexual knowledge in the girls they, like the parents, were looking not for signs of ignorance but for signs of "sophistication," meaning too much knowledge, or experiences that might be the beginning of more serious sex delinquencies.[49] Knowledgeable girls were termed "cases for prevention," and some were institutionalized. In at least one instance the psychiatrist believed only ignorance would make happiness possible—the case of an adolescent who told of wanting an exciting career instead of marriage. The therapist, Eleanor Pavenstedt, decided to withhold aspects of sex education, particularly detailed descriptions of intercourse, "bec. I thot it very possible that if this g[irl] ever marries she may be somewhat frigid and may not adjust very easily to sex relations and that she might then become upset when she found that she did not respond as she had been led to believe women did respond" (9433). The files offer few clues to adolescent female concerns about sexual orientation. Although the clinic staff sometimes described mothers as "mannish women," and lesbian relationships in general aroused mental hygiene alarm, the girls did not reveal caustic nicknames and did not own up to homosexual feelings.[50] All around, sex education seemed a less pressing need for girls than for the clinic's boys.

Although psychiatrists generally claimed that accurate knowledge about human reproduction was essential for future happiness, when boys and

girls talked about the future it was more often in the context of employment. For some of the boys and their parents, vocational counseling was a
second tangible service offered at the clinic. For psychologists and psychiatrists, it was another technique that would encourage frank discussions in
the clinic as well as enable a child to find happiness in adult life. For social
welfare agencies working with the unemployed, it was a vital part of a
program to reduce the numbers dependent on public and private support.

Child guidance advice recommended that all boys and girls should be
taught the value of work, either through chores around the house or by
work outside the home. Work, like directed leisure, was a necessary part of
learning discipline; it provided children with controlled independence, and
it played a role in sublimating unwanted sexual urges.[51] Many of the boys
did odd jobs for pay, but in their culture, housework was not meant for
boys. Gordon, whose father had deserted the family, still refused to help
out at home because he felt he was being asked to do "girl's work" (9258).
School, the immediate path to a future career, filled time at the present, but
the boys, so many of whom represented problems for the educational
system, made few connections between today's activities and tomorrow's
job. Philip, at fifteen, had no particular ambition except to work at some
simple job and "earn money which would give him a sense of accomplishment in contrast to [the] feeling of wasting time in school" (9449).

For boys such as Philip employment was an attribute of manliness.
William, the short, feisty "sissy," had an unemployed father, but William,
like Philip, understood that in the American economy, support of the
family was a male parent's responsibility. When prodded to name three
wishes for himself, William asked to stop his stealing, to do better in school,
and then included a wish for a job for his dad (9171). William, however,
like most of the boys at the JBGC, did not have employment goals for
himself.

While the boys expected their fathers to bring home wages and they
knew that as men they would be expected to find employment, their aspirations for future careers were, like William's, quite hazy. One boy opted for
a traditional, stable job in agriculture, and hoped to quit school to get farm
work (9425). For him the future lay in the work of the past. Others spoke
of joining their fathers as skilled laborers or craftsmen, a pattern that
remained a part of urban ethnic tradition. More often the code of boyhood
especially valued the new and the heroic (and to the Judge Baker professionals, the apparently unrealistic), whether it was an uncle who went west

to seek his fortune or a Charles Lindbergh who flew the Atlantic.[52] Several cast their gazes on glamorous new careers in aviation.[53] The adolescent who wanted to try professional baseball and if he did not succeed in that career, move on to become a surgeon (9446) was surely representative of the child guidance advice literature that pointed out how difficult it was for boys to make a career choice in the modern work world. Ester Loring Richards reminded parents that choosing a career was complicated by rapid changes in industry and technology.[54] When Richards's book appeared in 1932, the Depression had intensified the problems of finding a career or even a job.

Vocational guidance, then, was a way to focus the attention of these boys on the future, by identifying their interests, and more important, their abilities. Just as they had appropriated sex education from other sources, child guidance clinicians also did not initiate the vocational counseling movement. Organized vocational guidance originated in Boston in 1908 when Frank Parsons, a law professor at Boston University, developed a program for young people at the Civic Service House, a local settlement house. By 1935 training in vocational counseling had a secure place in university departments of education. Schools assumed the task of providing vocational education and guiding youths to careers for which, presumably, they were suited intellectually. When the mental hygiene movement took up vocational guidance, it added emotional suitability to intellectual capacity and urged vocational counselors to consider a child's affective life and personality along with the IQ measurement.[55]

At the JBGC the staff tested for mental retardation to identify children suitable for institutionalization, since no one expected boys with low IQs to be self-supporting. Other measures of specific intellectual or mechanical abilities might suggest an appropriate college or trade school. The psychiatric assessment aimed to redirect boys who, though smart enough, were "thwarted" academically by psychologically damaging family relationships, or boys who were being pushed hard to succeed in college prep courses even though they were not "college material."

Specific requests for vocational guidance often came from agencies with guardianship of a child, although parents, too, took advantage of the clinic's service. Many of their questions concerned a child's suitability for secondary or postsecondary education. Should an agency, or a family, make a further investment in an individual child? The Boston Children's Friend Society, for example, asked for a psychometric examination and vocational guidance for a fifteen-year-old under their care. The boy wanted to go to a trade school and take mechanical and aviation courses, in preparation for joining the army air force. The agency thought perhaps a commercial course would be more suitable (9222).[56]

Both agencies and parents used the promise of vocational testing and advice as a ruse to lure children into the clinic for a diagnostic work-up. One adoptive father reported telling the boy they were coming to the clinic to "find out what [the boy] is fitted for"; the father's real goal was to discover if a neighbor's accusation about his overly strict discipline was "right" (9448). His successful use of this ploy is a hint that children, too, expected to benefit from access to vocational guidance. It is, however, just a suggestion, because the staff seemed to record fewer comments about reactions to vocational guidance than to other clinic services, and there is little evidence related to whether or not advice was followed.[57]

Girls, too, received vocational counseling at the JBGC.[58] Like the boys, many of these girls were referred by child-saving agencies, although a few parents sought employment advice about their daughters. Anita Ferris's mother, for example, was worried because the girl did not know what she wanted to do in the future; she asked the clinic for help. With her husband in "precarious" health, Mrs. Ferris knew that Anita could not depend on his support (9433). Vocational educators were taught to provide guidance to both sexes but to make allowances for gender differences.[59] At the Judge Baker clinic, staff often steered agency girls to commercial courses in school; a young girl with hazy ideas about the future talked of wanting to become a surgeon or a lawyer, but the clinic directed her to beauty school courses (9278). When Eleanor Pavenstedt discussed the future with sixteen-year-old Anita Ferris, the girl indicated an interest in journalism. She was guided to consider a two-year secretarial course because tests showed she lacked an aptitude for reporting. Anita told Pavenstedt she wanted a career because marriage was so "humble" and her parents' lives seemed so "futile." Pavenstedt urged her to consider marriage as well as a career, telling her that "if she looks around she will find that very few women who have only careers are really satisfied with them" (9433).

Anita, however, thought a career gave people a chance to grow and change (rather than stagnate as she saw her parents doing), and other girls at the clinic also saw work in their future. Case no. 9301 wanted career advice, although she rejected the clinic's suggestion of practical nursing because "it involves too much housework." As did the daughters, some mothers anticipated that their girls would be joining the paid work force. With her daughter failing in school, one woman was terribly worried that the girl would "not be able to do anything to take care of herself" (9455). While the clinic staff provided such girls with vocational guidance, the professionals also assumed that marriage should be the ultimate goal and that the girls would be taken care of by husbands who were good providers. The girls and their mothers were not so sure. Perhaps it was the result of freer employment opportunities of the 1920s, perhaps the effect of vocational education in the public schools, or perhaps, in the context of Depression economics, the women had begun to question the ability of husbands to provide for their support. Whatever the reason, the girls at the Judge Baker clinic seemed, on the whole, more focused on the search for careers than were their brothers, even though, as "real boys," the brothers expected to become breadwinners when they married.

In sum, vocational planning, like sex education, gave child guidance a practical mission in the community. Both were visible, comprehensible services with tangible results for both parents and children. Vocational counseling responded to the frequent parental complaints about laziness and lack of ambition. Sex education took on a task parents sometimes wanted to avoid. Equally important, the services created common ground for the clinicians and the juvenile negotiators. Sex education and vocational planning offered a way to establish the rapport needed to interpret and ultimately change troublesome behavior.

Child guidance personnel used these services in sex-specific ways. Girls gained less from the clinic's vocational guidance than did the boys, and the staff also put more restrictions on sex education for the girls. While the girls wanted help choosing a career, the clinic nudged them toward marriage and economic dependency as the proper feminine role. The two services worked far better to unite the concerns shared by the professional staff and the boys about the masculine role, and especially about adolescent male sexuality. Clinic staff drew on the study of adolescent sex differences and on the stories of the boys to create this gender-based system of practice. In doing so, however, they extended and amplified what the boys had to say. Boys defined themselves against other boys—who was strongest, who fought best, who was the leader, who looked normal. Child guidance defined them against a standard of gendered adult activity, and directed diagnoses and therapy toward the achievement of that goal. Questions surrounding the formation of masculine identity had become central to child guidance by the 1930s; the framework enabled the clinic to develop services that helped to solidify this field's hold on the child in trouble.

By the 1930s the child's primary relationship with the psychiatrist was built around individual therapy. For the clinic staff both sex education and vocational guidance created an opening to establish the rapport deemed necessary for a child's frank participation. Sometimes psychiatrists achieved the goal. A twelve-year-old told her mother that Dr. Skinner was "a wonderful person . . . it is so easy to talk with her" (9426). The juvenile negotiators, however, often confounded the best intentions of psychiatrists in the trenches at the JBGC. Boys and girls accepted the sex education, questioned the vocational guidance, and offered, at best, guarded participation in the interview process. In such a setting psychiatric work with children often became a holding action that focused on the practical services, while the clinic's social workers labored to modify the attitudes of more compliant, more articulate, and often more committed adults.[60] "Our treatment philosophy," Frederick H. Allen reported in 1930, "seems to be swinging away from the child in the direction of working out with parents and other adults their own problems, which cause them to adopt an attitude toward the child that produces a disturbance in the growing-up process."[61] Interpreting the child's problems as unsatisfied emotional needs was one step toward parent guidance. The difficulties presented by the children reinforced the emerging belief in child guidance circles that the best explanation for a troublesome child was a flawed parent, the proper function of child guidance was parent therapy, and the authority of the child psychiatrist rested on an ability to identify the parent factor. Even as they spoke of "parent guidance," the child guidance professionals took aim at one particular parent—the "pathological mother"—and here too the juvenile negotiators helped to shape the clinic's practice.

The Critique of Motherhood

If the clinic movement had a motto, child guidance researcher Helen Leland Witmer maintained in 1940, it would be "for every problem child a problem parent."[1] Ethel Sturges Dummer had written something similar in 1920. "Wrong environment and stupid parents are responsible for the unfortunate behavior of children," she instructed Ester Loring Richards.[2] The women used analogous language; the parent each referred to was more likely to be a mother than a father. Yet encoded in each adage were very different assumptions about the problems and "stupidities" exhibited by parents.

Dummer's problem mother was a poor one who mismanaged her children by failing to protect and control them. This mother's children became delinquents, adding further burden to already overtaxed social agencies. More fortunate mothers, epitomized by Dummer herself, were in a position to provide poorer mothers with guidance and to demand help for them from the state. Women of Dummer's class and experience were not averse to accepting advice, though they expected to form partnerships with the professionals. Theirs was a view of motherhood grounded in class distinctions.

Witmer's motto, written barely two decades later, declassed the problem mother. Witmer's problem mother signified any (and almost every) woman with emotional inadequacies that made her a controlling, overprotective, or rejecting parent. This mother's psychological maladjustment caused wounds to her child's personality that festered until they produced a rebellious, neurotic, unhappy, and socially dysfunctional youngster. No partnership was possible with such a mother; only professional intervention, largely through female social workers, could save both child and mother from the effects of morbid motherhood.

During the 1920s and 1930s child guidance professionals developed these ideas into a stinging critique of American motherhood. Researchers and clinicians blamed emotionally negligent mothering for what seemed to be an epidemic of emotional and behavioral problems among children of all classes. Support for the critique of motherhood came from every child guidance discipline, from behaviorists to psychoanalysts. The New York psychiatrist David M. Levy reported that child guidance workers saw the results of poor mothering "with monotonous regularity." John B. Watson dedicated his 1928 behaviorist manual, *Psychological Care of Infant and Child,* to the first mother capable of bringing up a happy son or daughter, but questioned the likelihood of finding such a person. The sociologist Ernest Groves called motherhood quite simply "pathological."[3] J. M. Flügel, whose book was translated as *The Psychoanalytic Study of the Family* (1921), reported that a "nagging or over anxious mother" would frequently produce a "rebellious son or daughter [who] may even become unfit for taking their place in any scheme of harmonious social life."[4] Having democratized the troublesome child and located evidence of "trouble" in homes of all classes, child guidance professionals also democratized the explanation for problem children. All children had emotional needs that only parents could meet; a new discourse of pathological motherhood explored the many ways mothers failed to provide their youngsters with understanding, independence, and security. A mother's power for harm, regardless of class background, seemed so pronounced that practitioners began to speak of the clinic's mission as the exercise of "family guidance."

The child guidance indictment of mothers has been read by historians as part of a broad devaluation of maternalism in the years after suffrage. Peter Stearns relates it to "American cool," a new emotional culture of distance and control suited to the requirements of a corporate bureaucratic economy. In such a climate, the mawkish celebration of "the dearest mother ever known" was best confined to Mother's Day. Ann Douglas has connected the attack on motherhood to the efforts of urban intellectuals to remasculinize a culture too long held in bondage by maternal sentiment. Others have found the locus of mother-blaming in the invasion of Freudian psychology. Finally, it has been tied loosely to the professionalization process, to misogynist male professionals hoping to reestablish patriarchal authority in the home and professional hegemony in the culture, or, more recently, to female professionals who took aim at ignorant motherhood in order to enhance the prestige of their work with children.[5]

I cannot dispute that the child guidance critique of motherhood resonated with many currents in American culture during the 1920s and 1930s. My questions, however, have less to do with these broad emblematic interpretations of mother-blaming than with the commitment made by child mental health workers to the critique of motherhood. To understand this commitment, we have to go inside the clinic, where the professionals designed the critique and practiced its message, and where the "pathological" mothers sought help. From this perspective we can highlight the routine practices that made the critique an available discourse for those troubled by social and cultural shifts, gave it scientific legitimacy, and bound this first generation of child guidance clinicians to its liberal application in so many circumstances. For the professionals a paradigm that removed responsibility from social structures and charged that the patient caused her own trouble divorced child guidance from the realm (and the taint) of social welfare; it structured workplace relations; and it established new lines of authority among the three team members, privileging the child psychiatrist even as social workers assumed more and more responsibility for producing a cure for the troublesome child.

The view from the clinic also allows us to begin to explore what this critique meant to mothers, if only those clinic mothers designated incompetent and psychologically dangerous by the child guidance team. Studies of maternal representations have been quick to assess the damage done to individual mothers by twentieth-century mother-blaming. The stories related by the clinic's mothers, however, tell a more complex, less conspiratorial tale of the effects of the pathological imagery. To be sure, these were mothers who wanted help; parenting a modern child was stressful and those parents who resorted to a child guidance clinic were quite truthfully, as many said, "at [their] wit's end." But they were not seduced by the clinic's new paradigm, did not always respect the authority of the experts, and perhaps most important, some of them used the critique to transcend the conflict of the parent-child relationship and address problems in other aspects of their lives as adult females. The mother's standpoint is often lost in historical scholarship about motherhood, and a goal of feminist research, as Ellen Ross explains, has been the "uncovering of hidden mothers and hearing their long silenced voices."[6] The clinic's records offer one way to approach that goal.

The critique of motherhood was integral to the development of child guidance authority. Although the frenzied studies of schizophrenogenic mothers, of cold rejecting mothers who allegedly caused autism, and of maternal deprivation lay in the future, the diagnoses of maternal pathology made during the 1920s and 1930s laid the groundwork for these later incriminating portraits of motherhood. In successive decades the problem mother constrained the parameters of child guidance research and clinical work, and surveys of clinical reports and popular parenting advice from the 1980s and 1990s have found that mother-blaming is still insidious.[7] By looking at the practitioners, parents, and children in the clinic we can begin to unravel the mundane reasons behind professional commitment to the critique of motherhood and explore further the extent of child guidance authority.

THE PATHOLOGY OF MOTHERHOOD

The facts in the case of Amelia Bush and her eleven-year-old son Richard were routine. In January 1935 Richard's teacher had proposed an evaluation of the boy, because Richard, despite an above-average IQ, was doing poorly in school. The evaluation turned up little about Richard to suggest a personality problem. Indeed to the psychiatrist he seemed like a quite normal youth. The social worker, however, found signs of emotional maladjustment in Richard's mother. The case conference recommended a grade change at school, an endocrine study, and therapy for both mother and son. Many of the cases from 1935 ended with similar recommendations. The social worker's next task was to inform Mrs. Bush of the findings and schedule appointments.

At this point, a routine case turned sour. Mrs. Bush was not convinced by the social worker's explanation. She continued to assert that Richard would outgrow his problems, though she acknowledged that a grade change might be appropriate. More distressing from the clinic's point of view, Mrs. Bush resisted the suggestion of therapy for herself and agreed to only a few sessions for her son. To ensure her patient's compliance, this staff member took the unusual step of calling on the psychiatrist, who forcefully and directly confronted the mother with the clinic's interpretation of Richard's school problems. "Quite frankly," he told the reluctant Mrs. Bush (according to the social worker's notes), "she was the basis of the whole problem." If Amelia "could work out her problem and past difficulties and see the relationship that they had with [Richard's] present difficulties, it might not even really be necessary to have [Richard] come in" (9201).

The harsh words from the psychiatrist caused this record to stand out among the 345 new cases opened during 1935. The sentiment, however, was not novel. By the mid-1930s maternal pathology was the core of child guidance; it supported the whole structure of professionals, institutions, and popularizations. Staff at the Judge Baker, though not themselves the authors of the studies that constituted the critique of motherhood, found its components handy diagnoses for the problems they were assessing in 1935. They used it lavishly, routinely labeling mothers "overprotective" or "overdirective," and less frequently "rejecting." With the diagnoses of maternal pathology, mothers, too, became child guidance patients, subject to prescriptions for therapy. It was so obvious to the clinic staff that Amelia Bush caused her son's laziness and lack of progress in school that, once this mother rejected a therapeutic relationship with the clinic, alternative recommendations for Richard were never carried out.

The child guidance critique of motherhood should not be confused with Progressive condemnations earlier in the century of the weak mothering skills of poor mothers. At the Judge Baker clinic in 1920, when Healy's patients generally represented Boston's working-class or dependent population and his Progressive-inspired eclecticism still dominated explanations of delinquency, mothers of delinquents routinely found themselves criticized for improper parenting. Occasionally the staff discovered a delinquent mother who incited her child to commit a minor crime.[8] More often the staff caricatured two types of mothers in the early files—irresponsible souls who failed to control their offspring, and women who lacked the information needed to act responsibly.

The first, while not herself a criminal, failed to supervise her children, giving them opportunities to engage in delinquencies. The staff reasoned that some weakness—a low IQ, an inherited propensity to alcoholism, or mental illness—or a life situation that necessitated employment prevented mothers from exercising the moral influence and discipline essential to keep children from the paths of crime.[9] The second group of mothers appeared in the cases from 1920 as "ignorant" or "unintelligent," or "poor manager[s]," words that indicated an absence of appreciation for the uniqueness of childhood and for the importance of the parent's role in sound child rearing.[10] A mother who lacked information also quite likely failed to supervise properly, yet in the clinic's discourse the two types of poor mothers were decidedly different. One mother did not care why her child misbehaved; the other simply did not know—about the significance of sexual experiences, about the seriousness of the offense, and about the importance of maternal supervision. The latter mother might learn skills from a social welfare agent; the former required the use of mother-substi-tutes, through institutionalization or foster placement of the children.[11] In both cases, however, an impoverished mother's inability to supervise her child was only one factor among many causes of juvenile delinquency in 1920, and poverty was as relevant to the clinic's characterization as mater-nity. The behavior of poor mothers, not a maternal attitude, accounted for a parent's role in delinquency causation.

During the 1920s and 1930s, as child guiders began to see more middle-class self-referred parents whose patronage child guidance actively sought and who often felt at sea when faced with challenges from a new adolescent culture, researchers and clinicians reframed their descriptions of problem mothers in terms of the emotional dynamics of parent-child relationships. Psychoanalysis provided the convenient theoretical framework to replace class-based interpretations of misbehavior. The accounts of pathological motherhood drew on the decisive role in personality formation attributed by psychoanalysts to the "family romance." Out of this Oedipal scenario Freudians constructed the origins of the universal feminine wish to bear a child. Unsuccessful completion of the Oedipal phase, however, might leave women emotionally scarred, unable to realize this wish. Their neuroses left them unhappy adults. On this belief about feminine psychology child guid-ance experts constructed the specific female pathologies that could derail personality development in the child.

Unlike the mothers of the delinquents the new breed of problem moth-ers usually supervised offspring very well. They were watchful and protec-tive, given to intervene when a child faced a risky situation. The mother discovered by the JBGC staff holding the hand of her ten-year-old son (as though he were no older than five, the staff observed) was one of them (9220). So was the mother who refused her son a bicycle because they lived near a street trafficked by automobiles (8122). These women mothered too conscientiously, personally dressed and fed children beyond the age of infancy, cajoled and nagged school-age youngsters about being on time and doing homework. They were overly possessive, speaking of their children as "my Lizzie" and "my Ralph" (9440). Yet they were also called "intelli-

gent" clients, women familiar with child guidance principles. Child guiders
indicted these mothers not for their behavior or their lack of knowledge
but for what clinicians saw as the skewed emotional content of the mother-
child bond; mother love itself, at least a badly distorted version of it,
seemed to be the culprit.

Pediatricians began telling middle-class mothers as early as the 1890s
that mother love was not enough, that instinct alone could not raise a
healthy child. The new message from child guidance called that same
mother love psychologically "dangerous." Mothers, John B. Watson believed, were way too affectionate, kissing their children when a handshake
would better foster independent personalities. The family sociologists Ernest Groves and Gladys Hoagland Groves, in more graphic commentary,
described the "octopus-mother," "unwilling to hand her child over to other
people, save to be admired as her creation." In a pamphlet for the Children's Bureau (1925) Douglas Thom warned against the "oversolicitous
mother," and Anna Wolf in *The Parents' Manual* (1941) urged that "children must have breathing space." Evidence from the clinics suggested to
researchers and clinicians that modern mothers were ruining their sons
and daughters by overmothering. The popular press called it "smother
love." [12]

David Levy gave the problem mother her clinical name in 1929. She was
"overprotective"; her sons and daughters suffered from the effects of "maternal overprotection." Levy practiced psychiatry at the Institute for Child
Guidance (the New York City training clinic sponsored by the Commonwealth Fund) during its brief five-year life. In that setting most of the cases
were chosen for their educational value and represented self-referred families whose offspring might have been called "predelinquent" or "everyday"
children. Levy's studies of mothers, substantiated by the research of Smith
College student social workers apprenticing at the clinic, appeared
throughout the 1930s; *Maternal Overprotection* (1943), for which he is best
known, compiled this earlier work into one volume. [13]

For Levy the figure of maternal overprotection was "well portrayed by a
mother who holds her child tightly with one hand and makes the gesture of
pushing away the rest of the world with the other." The description signified a woman's intense investment in the demands of mothering, often to
the exclusion of other important emotional relationships. Her involvement
might be communicated either as domineering, intrusive behavior or as
overindulgent, structureless child rearing that gave in to every childish
whim. In a 1931 report Levy identified four traits detectable in an over-

protective relationship: excessive contact between mother and child (the mother is always present, may even sleep with the child); infantilization (she dresses or bathes the child beyond the age when a child might take responsibility for those tasks); prevention of social maturity or independent behavior (she fights battles for her child, and will not allow risk taking); and inadequate maternal control (she is either excessively controlling or overindulgent).[14]

From Levy's vantage point these mothers "made maternity into a disease"; their "high degree of responsibility" resembled an "obsessional neurosis." The signs, though psychological, seemed to Levy as well defined as if the women suffered from an organic illness.[15] The result of overprotection was an unhappy, maladjusted child who could not develop proper ego strength, was not normally emancipated from the family, had poor work habits, suffered feelings of inferiority, withdrew from social contacts, compensated for that inferiority through acts of rebellion, and ended up at the child guidance clinic. As framed by the critique of motherhood, the troublesome child with unmet needs was merely a symptom of the mother's psychopathological condition.

Levy and his assistants often traced the cause of overprotection to a mother's relationship with her own parents. Through the death of a parent or poverty she had to meet early on the harsh realities of life, developing in the process a personality more responsible and more aggressive than a good mother should display. The personality maladjustments prevented these women from forming satisfactory marriages; unhappiness in the marriage aggravated the symptoms of maternal overprotection, causing the women to substitute the love and companionship of a child for that of a husband. Having been deprived of parental affection and childhood play, and now without fulfilling marital relationships, these mothers used their children to satisfy a hunger for affection and "thwarted ambitions."[16]

Overprotection was the most widely discussed form of maternal pathology during the 1930s, but it was by no means the only one. In her taxonomy of "mother types," Judith Silberpfennig, a physician at New York Hospital, pointed to the "openly aggressive" mother, the "anxious" mother, and the mother who shifted hostility toward other family members onto her children. These "types" she regarded as modifications of the more general "overprotection" diagnosis and not to be confused with the "*distant* mother."[17] The distant mother's pathology was more commonly known as "maternal rejection."

Rejection characterized a mother whose "behavior towards the child is such that she consciously or unconsciously has a desire to be free from the child and considers the child a burden."[18] It was a difficult diagnosis, wrote H. W. Newell, a Baltimore practitioner who had observed thirty-three cases, because rejection "is a matter of degree." All mothers might "reject" a child's demands at some point in child rearing, just as all mothers might occasionally overprotect without showing signs of morbidity.[19] The rejection the child guidance community worried about was more profound. Levy described its effects on the child as the creation of "affect hunger [meaning] an emotional hunger for maternal love and those other feelings of protection and care implied in the mother-child relationship," and he compared it to a "state of starvation." In the child, symptoms of rejection or affect hunger were similar to those of overprotection: too much aggression or too little initiative. This similarity further complicated the diagnosis, as did Levy's observation that overprotective behavior often masked feelings of maternal rejection. He found, for example, that mothers who had delayed maternity (a sign that indicated rejection of a woman's natural maternal destiny) and then jealously guarded an only child were compensating for guilt feelings by being overly solicitous.[20]

On the basis of his thirty-three cases, Newell concluded that the causes of maternal rejection were the same as the psychological factors lying behind overprotection and went on to suggest that "the most important single cause for a mother's rejection of her child is her own unhappy adjustment to her marriage."[21] Margaret Figge, a social work student at the Institute for Child Guidance, also found marital incompatibility to be a source of rejection. More important for Figge, however, was evidence of an "unhappy childhood" and a "lack of any emotional ties with their parents." A woman's flawed relationship with her own parents accounted for both her current marital unhappiness and her maternal rejection.[22]

The rejecting mother lingered on the fringes of child guidance discourse during the 1930s, never achieving quite the same popularity in the child guidance press as the overprotection diagnosis. In the clinic, too, overprotection was the diagnosis of choice. Staff usually saw the child's need for emancipation as more acute than the need for security. The similarities between overprotection and rejection made precise diagnosis a tricky task, and the subtleties of theory often eluded practitioners. At the JBGC, if a mother did not exhibit "overt rejection" her behavior was regarded as simple "overprotection" or "overdirection" and treated as such.[23] Making the distinction was significant for treatment, however. Practice led clinicians to believe it was far more difficult to alter the behavior of rejecting than overprotective mothers, since rejecting mothers lacked essential maternal feelings, which were present, if distorted, in the overprotectors.[24]

In the research literature the psychopathologies of motherhood appeared in all social classes. Cases from the Institute for Child Guidance provided the samples for most of the rejection and overprotection studies of the 1930s. The type of family seen at this clinic was "not usually seen by other social agencies," noted the institute's director, Lawson Lowrey, referring to the economic status of the clients. None of Levy's subjects was "dependent," though some were lower class. Figge recorded that the rejecting mothers in her study displayed a "slightly inferior economic status" in comparison with her control group of nonrejecting mothers; they "faced financial pressure and worry and the question of having to work outside the home." Newell, too, found that only 29 percent of his rejected patients came from "comfortable or well-to-do homes." Another of Levy's social workers, however, in reviewing overprotection cases from the Institute for Child Guidance, found that overprotecting mothers were "slightly richer on the average" than a nonoverprotecting control group, but concluded that economic status could "not be considered a factor of great importance in accounting for differences in the two groups' care of their children."[25] Instead the researchers removed the mother and child from a social context and pulled both mothers from "comfortable" homes and those who lived in poverty into the new child guidance critique of motherhood.

In JBGC cases, also, overprotection and rejection were to be found in every class grouping. Each troublesome child, of the delinquent or the "everyday" variety, was a probable symptom of a mother's failure, a sign of one of the maternal pathologies. The child guidance researchers and clinicians declassed the Progressives' criticism of mothers, just as they had democratized the Progressives' troublesome child. Any woman, no matter what her social class, was a potentially inadequate or inappropriate mother, likely to be the parent of a troublesome child.

Fathers did not escape entirely unscathed in this discourse, although child guidance discussions of fatherhood lacked the refinement, depth of support, and sheer gusto experts gave the critique of mothers. In the child guidance literature two types of fathers created pathological parent-child relationships—the authoritarian figure and the ineffectual male. The authoritarian type demanded strict obedience, often to outdated standards of conduct, and failed to provide children with understanding and independence. While this kind of father was frequently found in immigrant households, no class was immune to his presence. Such paternal attitudes often paralleled an overindulgent stance in the mothers, and planted the seeds of adolescent rebellion in the misunderstood youths. In contrast to the authoritarian was the spineless, frequently absent father. "One of the most pathetic situations in family relationships is the 'fatherless household,'" wrote Douglas Thom in *The Everyday Problems of the Everyday Child.* "By this I do not refer to the father who is dead nor the one who is separated from the family by sickness or divorce, but rather to the one who finds his business, his golf, or his club—in general, either his professional or social obligations—so engrossing that the family is denied his companionship."[26] These men who failed to participate in child rearing left their children to the mercy of a domineering mother or, by their absence, pushed mothers and children together, allowing overprotective attitudes to create an unhealthy bond between parent and child.[27]

A play, written and produced as a training exercise by psychiatry students at the University of Colorado, gave literary expression to the symptoms of paternal pathology. "Boy Trouble" is the tale of Ben Hicks, juvenile delinquent, and his upscale family, a nagging, overprotective mother and a distant, authoritarian father. "Children need masters," Mr. Hicks tells the psychiatrist, while criticizing his wife for "coddling" the boy. Father Hicks is the stereotypic authoritarian who does not demonstrate the child guidance understanding of the emotions that tie a child's behavior to parental attitudes. He thinks Ben's problem is the gang he runs with. The psychiatrist, consulted after Ben is caught stealing, carefully explains that the real issue is why Ben chose those bad companions. Mrs. Hicks tells the psychiatrist that she "tried so hard to be a good mother." "Am I to blame?" she asks. "Blame," the psychiatrist replies, "is not a good way to express it . . . Parents' attitudes toward their children are colored by their own emotional needs, some of which we must learn to suppress if we find they interfere with the satisfactory growth of the child."

A successful outcome is ensured when both mother and father, with the psychiatrist's help, are led to see the ways in which their emotional problems have resulted in bad parenting. Mr. Hicks is strict with Ben to "get even" with his own father, and throughout the play the psychiatrist seems inclined to fault Mr. Hicks. In the end, however, he is forced to apologize to Mr. Hicks for having thought him "almost wholly responsible for Ben's bad behavior." In child guidance stories Father (unlike Mother) rarely caused a child's problem by himself. More to blame (even though the psychiatrist shuns that word) is Mrs. Hicks, who overindulges Ben because she is seeking emotional satisfaction from her son.[28]

If we were to examine a clinic record for Ben Hicks we might find the psychiatrist explaining Mrs. Hicks's pathology as a consequence of an emotionally deprived childhood. Or the psychiatrist might have followed Levy's lead and diagnosed Mrs. Hicks as a case of "thwarted ambitions" for work or education. Child guiders sometimes explained overguiding, or attempts to dominate a child's school career or vocational plans, as the projection of a mother's unrealized goals onto her child.[29] Marriage had prevented Amelia Bush, for example, from attending a prestigious women's college, and her current quest for useful activity (she was attending secretarial school and preparing to enter the work force) was duly noted in clinic records. Had the client been more cooperative, this surely would have been a topic for the social worker to investigate (9201).

Child guiders might have considered breaking the intense, stifling relationship of overprotection by supporting a mother's efforts to find outlets for "thwarted ambitions." Might have, but did not. Feminist advocates of marriage and career received no support from child guidance. Although the occasional social worker pointed to the ameliorative prospects of work, more common was the opinion of the Judge Baker staff member who advised a mother, married to an employed husband, to quit her job to provide better care for her son (9286). Instead of encouraging mothers to work, child guidance professionals found that a mother's paid labor interfered with fulfillment of her child's need for security, understanding, and tempered independence. Constrained by the child-centered framework within which they operated, the engineers of maternal pathology recommended easing maternal overprotection by intensifying the relationship between husband and wife to create greater family harmony (for the child).[30]

"A wife devoted to her husband cannot be exclusively a mother," Levy advised when he and other psychiatrists and family sociologists recommended greater spousal companionship as a foil for overprotection. In his research Levy found that unsatisfactory sexual relations between husband and wife and a marriage without companionship prevented mothers and fathers from acting in the best interest of their children.[31] Incompatibility between spouses often erupted in family quarrels, and "disharmony" in the family spelled emotional insecurity for the child. "Every child has a right to a happy home," Ernest Groves and Gladys Hoagland Groves reminded readers of *Parents' Magazine*. To the child guidance community that happy home included a mother free from commitments—and the desire for commitments—beyond her family, but free also from a need to find emotional satisfaction solely in her relationship with her children.

As child guiders brought the pathological—overprotecting or rejecting—mother into focus, they also changed the lens through which to view good mothering. A good mother had to scrutinize the emotional aspects of the parent-child relationship as well as monitor a child's physical safety, and do both without overly constraining a child's emotional and physical development. It was a parenting stance difficult to achieve—supervising unobtrusively without dominating, guiding while allowing independence and individual expression, meeting emotional needs but looking elsewhere for emotional satisfaction. It was one that few, if any, mothers could sustain in all situations. Overprotection and rejection were the "everyday" mother's "everyday" diseases.

MOTHER-BLAMING AND THE CLINIC AS CONTEXT

To explain the claim that the pathological mother held on child guidance during the 1920s and 1930s we must go back inside the clinic, to the relationships that forged those interpretations. To be sure, broad changes in the political and economic roles of American women made gender relations problematic during the 1920s and 1930s and threw into confusion the values that sanctified motherhood. After states ratified the Nineteenth Amendment, wives (or at least those who were white) could vote alongside their husbands. Growing numbers of married women were entering the work force; most were poor, but long before the supermom debates of recent decades professional women, too, upset traditional patriarchal family structures by tackling the career versus family dilemmas. Mother's Day gift giving commercialized mother love, while the highly sexualized and materialistic image of the flapper contrasted with representations of maternal self-sacrifice. If we are to believe that a science is rarely independent of its social base, the pathologies of motherhood both drew strength from this dissonance and contributed to its power. Yet the critique of motherhood also has a professional history, the lines of which can be untangled only from within the work world of the child guiders. Mother-blaming came to dominate the field of child mental health because, along with its availability in the research literature, its appeal to psychoanalytically oriented practitioners, and its "fit" with larger cultural concerns, it seemed to work in the clinic.

The critique of motherhood was a most practical paradigm, reaffirmed daily by the clinic's routines. In the day-to-day dynamics of clinic process, child guidance professionals encountered the mothers of their cases far more frequently than the fathers. Simple procedural elements, like the hours during which the clinic provided services, dictated that mothers rather than working fathers brought troublesome children for evaluation. Mothers dominated the intake interviews, the initial meeting to determine the suitability of a case for the clinic's services.

During treatment social workers liked to talk to fathers, too, but fathers were often reluctant clients. A visit to the clinic required time off from work and that usually meant loss of income. More than one father complained of the wages lost when he visited the clinic. Fathers were too busy, too preoccupied, too engaged in the tasks of breadwinning. Moreover, some fathers saw recourse to the clinic as the mark of a mother's failure to fulfill her part of the family bargain. He worked, she raised the kids, and now she wanted costly help with that task. In a cost-benefit analysis the clinic seemed to have no value, and fathers found ways to shun its overtures. Even the fathers who concurred with the decision to seek child guidance counsel usually turned responsibility for regular appointments over to their spouses. The clinic respected this male position of distance or disinterest and chose, even in cases determined to be due to a paternal malady, to work through the more easily accessible mother. Clinicians thus met with and learned about the foibles of mothers, while the fathers in these files could elude the clinic's scrutiny. The explanation for this critique, however, involves more than simple familiarity, or familiarity breeding contempt.

The clinic's adherence to maternal pathology and commitment to parent guidance can also be traced to the practice of allowing juvenile negotiators to tell their "own stories." Use of the "own story" sensitized the team to nuances in the child's rendition of family dynamics, and children had ample reasons to blame mothers for the situation in which they found themselves. Mother was the parent who most often publicized a child's problems by making arrangements for the child guidance evaluation. Even if teachers or juvenile justice officials mandated the evaluation, the mother was the parent who followed through, seemingly siding with outsiders against the child. Overt opposition to the clinic (which might be heard as covert support for the child) tended to come from fathers. Without having any knowledge of psychodynamic theories of family relations, children could easily connect their mothers, their problems, and their dislike, distrust, and disdain for the intrusions of the child guidance clinic. This is not to say that child guidance experts were taken in by juvenile con artists, but the clinic provided a context in which children might easily blame their mothers for their predicament and, in privileging the voices of the children, child guidance practitioners would not have been immune to the child's interpretation.

Furthermore, the children apportioned family responsibilities in ways that supported the mother-blaming framework of child guidance. In their discussions with the psychiatrists, the young patients gave evidence of very different expectations for each parent. Fathers represented proper disciplinarians to many of these children. Fathers punished, and what fathers did as punishment children often described as "deserved." The staff psychiatrist for case no. 9314, for instance, recorded that the "Boy . . . seems to admire and identify himself with this F . . . accepts F's discipline in pretty good spirit." Renditions of paternal punishment stories often contained references to specific social infractions—stealing, lying, and so on. Moreover, from the child's perspective, a father's principal duty to the family was to provide material comfort through his role as breadwinner. Children who described a father's unemployment or the reduced economic circumstances of the family in 1935 saw the individual consequences of the Great Depression as a form of family failure. When children talked about their fathers, they described distant, judgmental figures who filtered in and out of the house on a daily basis, but seemingly without the ability to elicit strong feelings of responsibility for a child's thoughts or emotions.

Mothers, in contrast, were the emotional providers. Despite the importance they attached to the father's breadwinner role, children usually reported, when asked to apportion their family loyalty, that they loved their mothers better. None of this is new or surprising—popular culture idealized a sentimental vision of mothers and the children may have been reflecting these values. Nonetheless, the children at the clinic seemed to be defining their emotional relationships in terms of mothers while their physical or material relationships were shaped by fathers. The psychologist H. Meltzer's research with a group of children in early adolescence (aged eleven to fourteen, also the average age of Judge Baker children) showed similar findings. To test psychoanalytic ideas about Oedipus and Electra complexes, Meltzer asked his subjects to "shout out" the first ten ideas they had about mother and father. Out of the din, Meltzer concluded that "mother outranks father in numbers of items which are emotional, manual and physical. Father outranks mother in reactions which are social, economic, and intellectual." Thus in both psychological research and clinical practice, children charged mothers with responsibility for their feelings.[32]

Conflicts with mothers, even if they involved physical punishment, were far more often couched in terms of relationship infractions than the sorts of social infractions associated with the father's strap—backtalk and defiance brought about a mother's wrath. The same boy who thought his father's punishments justified was "very outspoken in his antagonism for M . . . Feels that she nags continually. Is extremely over-protective. 'Probably means all right but can't stand her'" (9314). Children, especially the boys, regarded their fathers as figures of authority. From a father the occasional disciplinary action was righteous, while a mother's routine oversight was just a "nagging sort of thing" (9311).[33]

The stories told by the juvenile negotiators reinforced professional imperatives to find in parent-blaming, and especially in pathological motherhood, the key to the troublesome child. Reading the children's stories in such a fashion is conjectural, to be sure. Comments were transcribed by the psychiatrists conscious of the terms of maternal pathology, the research shaped by cultural expectations. Privileging the child's "own story" in cases of troublesome behavior was, however, not the only procedure providing soil in which mother-blaming could flourish. The pathologies of motherhood also fostered the clinic's "team" spirit. By instituting "family guidance," or therapy for both mother and child, two developing professions competing for space within the same psychoanalytic framework maintained their mutually profitable "alliance of forces" in the field of child guidance.

Social work was a profession in flux during the 1920s and 1930s. Graduate course work exposed students to both the latest psychoanalytic theories exploring the interrelationship of emotional handicaps and the social workers' traditional territory of dependency and delinquency. Even before the child guidance movement got under way in 1922, Jessie Taft and other social work leaders had begun to rethink the nature of social casework; a few had identified the therapeutic potential in the history-taking that formed so much of the practicing social worker's daily routine. Yet as they entered the work force, in places like the Judge Baker Guidance Center, these new-style social workers found themselves, to their dismay, confined to what some described as "errand girl" status. Instead of the therapeutic stance they had been taught, they still listened to parental complaints, collected background for the "social histories," and mediated between psychiatric professionals and the clinic's clients. Disgruntlement surfaced during the 1920s, as social workers in practice sought increasingly autonomous roles in their relationships with psychiatrists.[34]

In 1926 a group formed the American Association of Psychiatric Social Workers to distinguish their specialized work from others in the American Association of Hospital Social Workers. These women (all were women at the time; in 1941 the membership list still included only two males) used their annual meetings to discuss membership criteria, training requirements, and especially the relationship between psychiatrists and psychiatric social workers.[35] Maida Solomon, a social worker from the Boston Psychopathic Hospital, in her presidential address from 1926 tackled the question, "Should psychiatric social work always be practiced in association with a psychiatrist?" Since the techniques and theories of the psychiatric social worker resembled those of the psychiatrist, Solomon concluded that psychiatric social workers could take over some of the simpler functions of psychiatrists.[36]

These new-style social workers threatened to disrupt the harmonious "alliance of forces" that held together the mental hygiene professionals. Marion Kenworthy, a psychiatrist, and Porter Lee, a social worker, approved of the blurring of boundaries they perceived at the Bureau of Children's Guidance in New York City, but other psychiatrists were less sanguine about the changes.[37] Acrimonious debates about territoriality could be heard at the various professional meetings. When commenting on a particularly civil discussion at a symposium on the child guidance clinic professions held at the 1930 meeting of the American Orthopsychiatric Association, Lee was pleasantly surprised by the tenor of the debate. "Usually," he told the audience, "when I have participated in or listened to any such discussion, there has been a good deal of controversy."[38]

The critique of motherhood and "parent guidance" helped to establish the basis for continued cooperative teamwork in child guidance settings. While sharing the same theoretical framework, the two groups of professionals preserved occupational distinctions and a working relationship by identifying separate therapeutic spheres of interest. At the 1930 meeting

Samuel Hartwell, a psychiatrist from the Worcester Child Guidance Clinic, claimed for his profession the right to study and treat the mind of the child while Charlotte Towle, a Philadelphia social worker, presented a discussion of the mother as patient.[39] At one time mothers and child guiders were potential partners in the task of reforming a troublesome child; now the pathological mother had become a patient in the eyes of child guidance clinicians, culpable and equally in need of therapeutic intervention by the clinic's trained staff. At the Judge Baker clinic many children received only minimal therapeutic treatment or none at all, while their parents were scheduled for regular visits with a social worker.[40] Had she acquiesced, Amelia Bush might have become just such a client, to be treated by one of the therapeutic approaches to maternal pathology available in the social worker's armamentarium.

No one factor better explains the child guidance commitment to the pathologies of motherhood than the changing class of families making use of the clinic's services. Signs of economic struggle still appeared in JBGC cases, particularly within families referred by the juvenile court or by Boston's welfare agencies. More and more, however, child guiders treated families that could be described as comfortably working class or simply "comfortable," the professionals' term for the financially stable. The family drama of conflicting personalities provided a more functional paradigm that could encompass troublesome behavior from all socioeconomic classes.

The clinics' procedures, however, are an important and overlooked context for the growth of professional adherence to the pathologies of motherhood. Because of the gendered labor arrangements in most of these families, mothers, far more often than working fathers, mediated between family members and the clinic. Administrative arrangements led both clinicians and children to see the mother as the person who publicized the bad behavior. By giving parents and children equal voice in the diagnostic conversations, the team's inclination to find mothers at fault was bolstered by the perceptions of parenting roles espoused by the children. The everyday rituals of diagnosis had been designed to give child guidance one authoritative voice. The tenuous harmony grew discordant as child guidance began to offer therapeutic services. The psychoanalytic framework of both psychiatry and social work made provision of therapy a contested service. "Family guidance," coupling the pathological mother and the troublesome child, enabled two sets of professionals to share an intellectual framework, occupy one institutional context, and preserve the appearance of a harmonious child guidance team.[41] Procedures thus reinforced the ideas germinated from psychoanalytic theories and nurtured in the United States by the research of David Levy and the Smith College social work students.

THE DISAPPEARING PATIENT

An occasional commenter tried to remind workers in the field that treating only the mother was not always sufficient intervention to change a troublesome child's behavior.[42] Few appeared to heed the warning. Child guiders expected mothers who consulted the clinic to develop a therapeutic relationship with the clinic. Regularly scheduled meetings with a social worker cannot be read as a mother's willingness to admit culpability for a troublesome child. But by examining the mothers' stories and their responses to the promise of therapy, we can begin to explore the meaning of the pathological representations for the mothers caught in the clutches of a mother-blaming clinic and culture.

To begin with, not all mothers who sought help at the JBGC in 1935 were convinced by the staff's almost rote diagnosis of maternal maladjustment. When social workers tried to impose an interpretation that did not mesh with maternal understanding, some mothers turned against the clinicians. "I'm not on trial here," one castigated a zealous social worker (9274). As she discussed her son with the JGBC staff, Amelia Bush challenged the very foundation of psychoanalytic theory, that hidden feelings lay behind our actions and those feelings should be uncovered through therapeutic conversations. Bush thought it best to let problems lie buried.[43] Others employed more sociological explanations for troublesome behavior, as did the family who believed gangster movies and crime in the streets made it impossible to train children properly. These parents explained that it was a community as well as a family responsibility to raise children well (9286). Still others saw the problems as developmental, a passing stage (9298), or more directly argued that troublesome behavior belonged to the child alone. If the boy felt inferior, he should change (9284).

These were the clinic's difficult, "uncooperative" parents, women who came to the JBGC in search of specific solutions to behavioral problems and persisted in trusting their abilities as mothers despite the mother-blaming of the clinic staff. When the child guidance team reinterpreted the problem in "family guidance" terms and prepared to treat not just the child but the parent too, these patients left. Psychoanalysts, of course, saw this behavior as probable evidence of resistance, implying an unconscious hold on the ego that interfered with the course of treatment. There was the simple resistance staff saw at intake interviews when parents talked too much or too little. As therapy progressed a more complex resistance appeared to develop in many women, a response to the transference relationship with the therapist or, in the case of child guidance, the social worker. The disappearing clients, therefore, did not challenge child guiders to reexamine their theories. Reasons for the failure to continue therapy were not heavily researched during these years. Instead clinicians absorbed the rejection of therapy into their explanations of parent-child relations and turned their uncooperative patients into further evidence of maternal pathology.[44]

There are, however, alternative ways to read the disappearance of many of these families from the records—the unfinished cases, the broken appointments, the inquiries from social workers that went unanswered. Since the cases sampled came from a mid-Depression year, the disappearing patients might indicate budget limitations that made psychotherapy a luxury. If we read the resistance in political terms, the presence of difficult patients suggests that in the 1930s, and even into the 1950s, the blow to maternal competency struck by the child guiders had not deeply wounded maternal consciousness, even among that class of Boston women who deliberately sought out help from child guidance.

Tom Wesley's mother had purchased popularized versions of child guidance advice. Now she wanted the Judge Baker clinic to study her son and suggest specific steps she could take to change his behavior. When the clinic focused instead on her son's need for independence, Mrs. Wesley began to cancel her appointments. When contacted by the social worker, Mrs. Wesley offered several explanations: she had a tutoring job that prevented regular appointments; she could not afford to come into town so often; and, most important, she "had expected the clinic to be able to tell her more definitely what was wrong with [Tom]." "As it is," the social worker reported, "she feels that what we told her she had already known. She thought we would be able to say, 'This and that is [Tom's] difficulty, and if you do so and so, such will be the outcome'" (9415). Tom's mother was not about to shift the discussion away from Tom; nor was she prepared to question her philosophy of mothering.

In 1955 Betsy Mazur, a social work student from Boston University, studied mothers who consulted the Worcester Child Guidance Center but refused treatment after the initial intake interview. Her findings corroborate my impressions of Tom's mother and others like her at the JBGC. Mazur's notes from the Worcester clinic's files suggested that intake interviewers routinely initiated mothers into the child guidance view of maternal culpability and the need for maternal participation in treatment. The women in this study (some of whom had to wait as long as sixteen months before being called for an appointment) turned down the invitation to form a therapeutic relationship. One mother, named Mrs. C by Mazur, described her decision to do the "modern thing" and seek a child guidance evaluation for her demanding, rebellious middle daughter. Her explanation for refusing treatment: in the interim she had learned to accept each child as an individual, hence she no longer needed help. To the clinic and to the student social worker, Mrs. C appeared to accept her role in her daughter's rebellion. Mrs. C's decision to refuse treatment might also be read as the recognition of her own ability to solve a parenting problem. The author of this study described mothers who sought help elsewhere (with a minister), found that the problem disappeared as the child grew older, and, believing that the public school system should assume responsibility for a slow learner, turned a boy's lack of progress over to his special education classes.[45]

These stories, rendered about a quarter-century after Levy began to diagnose women with maternal overprotection, when added to the statements from the JBGC files, suggest that many mothers, though willing to ask the experts for help, retained for themselves the right to evaluate and, if it seemed appropriate, dismiss the child guiders' suggestions. Mothers attempted to structure interaction with the clinic in ways that reaffirmed their capabilities rather than their pathologies. There may have been no organized protest against the psychological assault on motherhood when David Levy proposed it and child guidance clinics began to carry it out, but individual mothers regularly voted against it with their feet.

THERAPY FOR MOTHERS

For those mothers who chose to continue, the clinic provided "family guidance" in the form of a therapeutic relationship with one of the staff social workers. Most women received superficial advice and practical suggestions from the social workers, along with encouragement for efforts to reform parenting skills. A smaller percentage of cases involved insight therapy, a more intensive effort to expose mothers to the role of their emotions in the child's misconduct. Attitude therapy, specially developed for child guidance work with mothers, was reserved for a very few candidates.[46]

At intake an interviewer made clear to prospective clients the clinic's mission of "family guidance," and rated cases based on impressions of maternal responsibility. "Because the prob. was felt to be in the mother rather than in the chd," the case of a six-year-old was accepted by the Judge Baker staff, even though children that young were routinely referred to the Boston Habit Clinic (9423). Another mother who "tends to blame herself for everything that has happened at home," was tagged as an "intelligent client" (9419) suitable for treatment. After initial interviews, still called a "social history" by the social workers but now with much greater emphasis on family relationships than family material circumstances, the team determined how extensive a mother's treatment should be.

Despite a growing aversion to didactic practice in some social work circles, staff at the JBGC routinely offered superficial advice and practical suggestions to their clients.[47] With overprotection as the primary diagnosis, mothers most often received tips directing them to give their children more responsibility and independence. To the mother of a lazy and thus frequently tardy fourteen-year-old, social workers recommended purchase of an alarm clock so that "all waking responsibilities" could be returned to her son (9187). Another overprotective mother of an adolescent girl was advised to give her daughter more responsibilities for housework as a way to increase the girl's independence (9253). Phoebe Campbell's parents were instructed to allow Phoebe to choose a few of the movies she would attend (9247). No matter what degree of treatment the team planned for mother and child, social workers might begin with specific prescriptions for modifying a child's behavior. Since deliberate proposals for action were what many parents wanted from their clinic contact, social worker didacticism helped to keep edgy parents satisfied.

Social workers accompanied their advice and suggestions with encouragement and support for a parent's efforts to follow the clinic's recommendations. Although officially rejected for lengthy intensive therapy, one mother was permitted to return to the clinic twenty-six times. The staff allowed this woman's "feeling of need" to dictate appointments because the mother often seemed "anxious to report" her successes and failures. This mother frequently expressed her gratitude to the clinic as the social worker encouraged her efforts to allow her son more independence (9173). "Reassurance" was the clinic's code for this type of treatment.[48]

Advice could be accompanied by chastisement if a mother failed to follow through; though encouraged in their professional literature to allow parents to set the pace, in practice JBGC social workers were far from neutral in their assessment of their clients. The mother who was advised to turn "waking responsibilities" over to her son agreed to try despite the practical difficulties she voiced about the plan. The social worker's exasperation flowed over into her case notes; this mother's claims to have behaved "just as you said" seemed to mean she had really done just "the opposite" (9187). The case records from 1935 also did not indicate enthusiastic social worker support for initiatives from the patients. The records rang with skepticism, as from the social worker who hoped the family's plans to send their child to relatives would alleviate the mother-daughter conflict, but doubted the efficacy of the proposal (9253).

When advice and reassurance proved inadequate, the clinic considered two forms of therapy directed toward more substantial changes in the mothers. As George S. Stevenson and Geddes Smith explained in a 1934 history of child guidance, a mother might "[accept] the advice intellectually, but was estopped from putting it into effect by emotional needs or conflicts of her own of which she might or might not be conscious. To free the child from deleterious pressures it became necessary to help the mother solve the problems in herself which led to them."[49] Both insight therapy and attitude therapy, the "help" to which Stevenson and Smith referred, emanated from the work of David Levy, the architect of maternal overprotection.

The JBGC staff often hoped their efforts with mothers would open the way to insight into the emotional mechanisms dictating unhealthy parent-child relationships. As pioneered by Levy, insight therapy was a more intense approach than advice giving, one designed to elicit the mother's understanding and acknowledgment of a connection between her child's behavior and her own attitudes. From the case records at the Judge Baker it is difficult to determine exactly how the practicing social workers interpreted insight therapy differently from advice giving. One example suggests that a worker's perception of the possibility for parental change was a determining factor. The stepmother of a sulky, disobedient eleven-year-old with violent temper tantrums was at first "encouraged . . . to express her own unhappiness and dissatisfactions," and in doing so to recognize the relationship between her emotions and her treatment of the boy. But the staff declined to pursue these issues, because "it might be better not to stir up conflict which can in no way be improved under the present situation . . . As long as her attitude does not seriously interfere with the boy's mental development, it would be wiser to leave her more or less alone" (9212). Insight therapy represented a midway point between a simple pro-gram to modify behavior and more complicated treatment to generate self-awareness. Levy compared the mother with new-found insight to "a person with a deformity who accepts the fact of the deformity, makes the best of it and learns how to minimize the handicap as much as possible."[50] Even more so than the behavioral modification sought through advice and encouragement, insight therapy aimed to solve the child's problem by changing the parent.

Far more intensive, and reserved for only a small portion of child guid-ance clients, was attitude therapy, a technique in which mother and social worker agreed that regular appointments would be used, according to Levy, for "free elaboration of [the mother's] feelings." With attitude therapy a social worker encouraged her client to explore the emotions that affected her relationship with her child. Although not to be confused with psycho-analysis, attitude therapy was intended to allow a mother to become "more conscious of her underlying motivations and especially of her attitudes towards her own parents and her immediate family."[51] Successful comple-tion required two or three sessions a week, over several years.

It is not surprising that the Judge Baker staff prescribed attitude therapy only occasionally. The distance some families lived from the clinic made it impractical (9223). So, quite likely, did the fees, given that JBGC mothers diagnosed as overprotective came from all walks of life. Cost may have led fathers to protest extended therapy sessions (9241, 9269, 9288). One study of treatment suggested that as mothers improved, fathers "got worse." Paternal protest may also have been related to maintaining the balance of power in the family.[52] Equally likely, since professionals at the Judge Baker believed they were designing treatment programs to expose a mother's contribution to her child's problems, the child-centeredness of the child guidance mission did not encourage attempts to individualize a mother's emotional needs. Social workers were rarely averse, however, to lengthy and intense discussions with patients that focused on issues apart from the child, even if these talks were not labeled attitude therapy. Attitude therapy may not appear often in the records, but many a mother and social worker established an attitude therapy–like relationship that went beyond the issues directly connected to the child's troublesome actions.

Family guidance implied that fathers too would be included in the clinic's therapeutic services. Healy and Bronner reported that in 400 treatment cases evaluated from 1931 to 1934, they found fathers participating in 178, a figure they termed "striking."[53] Their comment did not register the degree of participation, however, and in the cases from 1935 contact with fathers was quite limited, often consisting of only one interview that could scarcely be construed as therapy. Even in the infrequent cases in which the staff conference labeled a father the cause of the problem, social workers chose to work through the mother.[54] Gender differences created boundaries between social workers and fathers, and fathers appear to have been given more ready access to the (male) psychiatrists. Intake interviewers usually tried to ascertain the extent of a father's commitment to the Judge Baker mission. His objections, however, did not prevent the clinic from accepting a mother and child for treatment. The mother who indicated that her husband would not be very cooperative because he thought psychiatric tests were "the 'bunk' " was nonetheless assigned to a student social worker (9423).

Especially when treating troublesome boys the clinic wanted the fathers' cooperation, for, as one mother was bluntly told when instructed to resume living with her husband, a boy at this age needed a man's control (9251). In the clinic's view, a father's control offered boys the opportunity for "independence" to engage in the "struggle" for adulthood, whereas a mother's overcontrol stifled that same struggle. Fathers were expected to break up the overprotective relationships with mothers, provide children with an ego ideal/role model, and promote masculine recreational activities. If fathers proved uncooperative, the clinic might recommend a father-substitute for the child, in the form of a group leader, a camp counselor, or more directly, the therapist, who represented himself as the boy's "pal." By trading stamps with boys, helping them gain independence in restrictive families, or writing letters to them at camp, the psychiatrists attempted to become the missing male role models for their charges while social workers tried to alter maternal attitudes and behavior.[55]

To judge the effectiveness of these therapies, how much or how little a child was changed by family guidance, is difficult. Healy and Bronner reported, in their first follow-up study of treatment cases, that 81 percent of the children had "favorable" careers, a figure even these researchers found "surprising." Of course, Healy and Bronner worked with no control groups, and the relationship between the clinic's intervention and the favorable career was one based solely on faith.[56] What fathers took from their experiences with the clinic's family guidance is just as difficult to assess; their contacts were so infrequent, their comments often filtered through both a mother and a social worker.[57] The mothers, in contrast, often verbalized their sense of the clinic's accomplishments. Few matched the gratitude of a Kingston mother who sent the staff an invitation to her son's wedding, an announcement of the birth of a grandchild, and in 1944, during an impromptu visit to the clinic, mentioned plans to change her will and leave a bequest to the Judge Baker Guidance Center (9204). More common was the attitude of the woman who referred to the clinic as her "safety valve" (9202).

Follow-up reports on about half the cases from 1935, collected in 1940 and 1941 and stored with the original records, suggest that the parents traced by the clinic usually survived their children's adolescence satisfactorily. Despite the mother-blaming, some women found that the experience at the clinic allowed them to devise new standards of parental authority. For those mothers willing to accept the framework of maternal pathology, the clinic's range of therapies offered, at the least, a respite from the trials of parenting the modern child.

For the women of child guidance, however, both mothers and social workers, the clinic's mother-blaming stance was helpful with more than just the trials of parenting. If we are to understand fully why more women did not follow Amelia Bush out of the clinic when the "interpretation" of troublesome behavior challenged their common sense, we have to examine all the uses of the diagnoses of maternal overprotection or rejection. Each treatment plan, whether the limited advice giving or the intensive attitude therapy, assured women of frequent contact with a social worker. Although the interviews may have confirmed for child guidance experts the general incompetency of American motherhood, mothers who engaged in the clinic's brand of therapy often understood the process differently. The Judge Baker case files hold the stories of mothers who manipulated the structure of treatment—the regularly scheduled conversations for advice and insight—to focus attention away from children and on to their anxieties about modern marriage and family life. Moreover, social workers concurred with this shift, and encouraged it. Attitude therapy provided some justification for the shifting focus of treatment, but the many clients and social workers not destined for attitude therapy also found that the critique of motherhood permitted some mothers, and by default the social workers, to confront the problems they faced as modern women.

"It has been obvious from the very beginning," the social worker Katherine Moore reported in 1933 as she assessed the social worker–client relationship at the Institute for Child Guidance. "Mothers tended to use the interviews consciously or unconsciously for their own purposes aside from help with the child."[58] At the Judge Baker Guidance Center, husbands and sex formed the bulk of the complaints. Comments on men who failed to share responsibilities and provide companionship for their mates were matched by expressions of dislike for the sexual side of marriage. In January 1935, the mother of a high school junior observed to her Judge Baker social worker that she had been talking very little about her son in recent interviews, and much more about herself and her marriage. Reassured by the worker, this mother continued to describe her husband's immaturity and lack of ambition, her thoughts of a legal separation, and her rejection of his sexual attentions. "M[other] says she feels better after talking about things that are bothering her," the social worker wrote in her records. She felt she "could not do this with friends," but talk with the social worker was "different" (9271). Another thought it "safe" to reveal marital difficulties to the social worker, safer than doing so with friends.[59]

The mothers who modified the clinic's child-centered agenda measured their marriages against a "companionate" or "democratic" ideal, and found them wanting.[60] They did not question the gendered division of labor that made mothers the primary providers of child care, but they did expect their mates to participate in disciplining the children and wanted husbands to spend leisure time with both their children and their wives. Occasionally a woman complained of her husband's failure as a breadwinner (9202, 9419), but more women wanted to talk about the lack of emotional support. For families where fathers were not so ideal, the clinic's commitment to parent guidance gave at least some women an outlet for expressing their disappointment. The woman who complained of her financial dependence used the meetings at the clinic to examine her desire to separate from a husband the staff described as a "sweet but quite inadequate person" (9202). Janet Landis, whose relationship with the clinic was detailed in the Introduction, also met many times with staff social workers to discuss her desire to live with another man (2086). In one instance, a disgruntled wife was encouraged to dwell on her husband's good points. After more than a year of intermittent meetings with the social worker in which she continued to describe her "unhappy" life with her husband, this Brookline woman reported with some satisfaction that her husband had been more considerate recently, taking her to dinner and a play (9171).[61]

The same women who displayed annoyance with substandard husbands also sometimes confessed to social workers their dissatisfaction with sexual relations in the marriage. Two found intercourse uncomfortable or fear-provoking, and did not appreciate their husbands' "demanding" ways (9253, 9171). Another was afraid of pregnancy, but reported that her husband refused to "take any precautions, saying it was up to her." She told of several "self-induced miscarriages" and described herself as "not interested in intercourse" (9439). For these women sex with men was something to be endured rather than enjoyed. Despite messages from movies, advertisements, and marriage manuals that promised only pleasure in the marriage bed, they did not find their husbands' attentions pleasurable. "M. says that she herself hated having relations with F. although she thought a great deal of him," noted the social worker of a proudly independent mother of seven. This woman did not particularly want to have so many children, but, according to the social worker's notes, she believed, "it was her duty as a wife to do as he wished." After her husband died, this woman rejected an offer of marriage, presumably preferring to take care of her children herself, rather than risk repeating the experience (9215).

The clinic staff offered the women no innovative solutions to the problems they faced; children continued to be the focus of the therapy and motherhood continued to dominate the team's overall perspective on the adult female. Neither suggestions for medical studies in cases of sexual dysfunction nor recommendations for psychotherapy beyond that provided by the clinic, even for patients termed severely neurotic, can be found in the case records from 1935. Nor did the staff urge divorce in cases with clearly mismatched husbands and wives. The professional literature recommended instead a strengthening of the husband-wife bond as a cure for an overly intense mother-child relationship, and the Judge Baker social workers followed that direction. Nonetheless, social workers who encouraged their patients to vent their frustrations with husbands gave tacit recognition to the difficulties women faced in a culture with unstable gender lines.

For these mothers the clinic's critique of motherhood offered a chance to talk about their concerns and voice their misgivings in a conservative fashion that would rarely threaten a family's status quo or a woman's commitment to domesticity. This is not to suggest that the Judge Baker mothers were indeed the maladjusted personalities the clinic oftentimes diagnosed, but they were, some of them at least, unhappy in family settings that at times restricted outside activities, that demanded a difficult-to-attain companionship between husband and wife, and that created a perhaps unrealistic measure for sexual satisfaction. In most instances the clinic staff provided a sympathetic ear and recommended some form of accommodation. Yet it would be misleading to say that these women wanted more from the clinic. The minimal benefits enabled some of them to use the misbehavior of their children to take stock of their personal situations and to discover private, individual adjustments to the demands of married life.

The critique of motherhood held out a solution to the problems of two groups of child guidance women. Each group—the mothers who came voluntarily to the Judge Baker Guidance Center, and the psychiatric social workers who were stretching the boundaries of practice—found in the diagnosis and treatment of pathological motherhood the temporary means to resolve issues of power and authority in relationships with husbands and children or in alliance with other child guidance professionals. The uses to which these women put the critique of motherhood help to explain the prominence of the diagnosis in clinic practice and its continued hold on psychiatric interpretations of the troublesome child. But the critique of motherhood remained just that—a damning indictment of maternal emotions. Although functional on a superficial level, neither group of Judge Baker women emerged either unscathed or empowered by the critique of motherhood.

As the diagnosis of pathological motherhood grew more entrenched, social workers took on a greater share of the clinic's workload. Providing mothers with therapy did not resolve all issues of professional identity for the psychiatric social workers. While social workers conducted the insight or attitude therapy, psychiatrists planned to maintain careful direction of the treatment. David Levy was quite specific about the professional hierarchy. "The social worker must be trained . . . to recognize the limitations in her therapy and to have free recourse to the psychiatrist. As an independent method out of contact with a clinical group, [attitude therapy] may be used indiscriminately and destructively."[62] Social workers may have established their unique expertise with mothers, but this did not generate professional autonomy or equality in the workplace. Psychiatrists had earned a position of greater authority on the child guidance team.

For social workers the critique of motherhood dictated more than subordination to a psychiatrist's direction. Diagnoses of maternal pathologies accompanied by plans for social workers to treat the mothers left social workers accountable for the outcomes of child guidance cases. Attitude therapy, in particular, for use as Levy dictated, "where treatment of the child failed because of problems in the mother," limited the psychiatrists' responsibility for the continued misbehavior of their patients.[63] By the mid-1930s reforming a troublesome child depended on modifying the psychological make-up of the mother. Since mothers caused the emotional turmoil, and with social workers the designated therapists for parents, psychiatrists could not be held liable if a child's behavior remained unchanged. "Case closed" because of "uncooperative mother" leaving a "poor prognosis" for the child was a familiar refrain in the clinic's records. With the construction of the pathologies of motherhood, child psychiatrists had won authority to define the causes of the emotional and behavioral problems of youngsters, yet they had displaced onto others the blame for failure to produce cures.

For mothers the consequences of the critique of motherhood are harder to measure, the lines of authority connecting experts and patients less clearly defined than those between professions. Difficult and disappearing patients dramatized the limits of child guidance authority in the 1930s. These individual acts of resistance hint at the extent to which mother-blaming permeated maternal culture. The compliant patients appeared to accept responsibility as pathological mothers, but they adjusted the clinic's services to meet their needs as adult women. Accommodation rather than autonomy, independence, or self-awareness was quite likely the principal accomplishment of child guidance therapy. The clinic's services enabled some women to adapt to dysfunctional family situations, or at least to survive the parenting phase; their gratitude and their respect for the clinic's services, evident in the friends and relatives they sent to the Judge Baker clinic, suggest they may not have wanted more. While the clinic saw family harmony as the key to a happy child, these women too valued family harmony and through their children located the means to resolve some of the tensions of modern married life. Former, and presumably satisfied, patients helped to build the clinic's reputation in the Boston community.

There was something for everybody in the clinic's reliance on the critique of motherhood. Except, of course, for the mothers of the delinquents, most of them from Boston's lower classes. To Ethel Dummer, "stupid parents" in a "wrong environment" explained most of the cases of juvenile crime. Social inequality afforded Dummer's mother a degree of protection; she shared the blame for delinquency with an inhospitable social setting. The pathologies of motherhood eliminated the need to incorporate any form of social inequality into discussions of the causes and solutions to social problems and left mothers alone to shoulder the responsibility. Delinquency for the Progressive women had represented a problem of social welfare often caused by the burdens of lower-class life and remediable by community efforts. In the hands of child guidance specialists, the eradication of delinquency became a therapeutic responsibility outside the bounds of public policy.

Though bearing the same degree of responsibility, the mothers of delinquents rarely found in the clinic the "safety valve" or emotional release offered by the patient status accorded to the women who were self-referred. The "delinquent" mothers, caught as they were in folds of the juvenile justice system, did not receive family guidance. Without the opportunity for long-term therapeutic contact to monitor their patients, the staff often deemed it more important to keep poor, now pathological, mothers away from the children rather than attempt to reconstruct family relationships. Welfare agencies may have employed social workers who carried out the clinic's recommendations for psychiatric treatment, but the far simpler solution was foster or institutional placement, a solution with a long history among child savers, and one the JBGC team returned to frequently. In the critique of motherhood all mothers were potentially pathological, but the child guidance clinic did not provide equal opportunity for cures.

8

The Limits of
Psychiatric Authority

"Just as the twig is bent, the tree's inclined." Alexander Pope's quotable words from his *Essay on Man* (1733–34) served many writers in the early twentieth century as a metaphor for the care and concern needed to socialize young people in modern times. The reference was especially apt for the child guiders, with its allusion to the young sprout that could be trained into a straight tree or a deformed one. Whether the tree symbolized a solitary psychopathological adult or a twisted national identity, care of each twig was key to the prevention of a maladjusted character. When child guidance set out in the decades after World War I to straighten all the bent twigs, they found many children leading lives that needed redirection. There were the delinquents who worried Progressive child savers because their youthful misconduct threatened to lead to adult criminality. And there were the "everyday children," whose problems, though "normal," disturbed families and schools and promised to cripple personalities permanently. In using Pope's metaphor, the practitioners and popularizers of child guidance positioned themselves in the straightening process, creating the role of the wise arborist. Only through the expert cultivator's careful monitoring would the bent twigs grow into productive, efficient, and happy citizens.

The image of twigs, trees, and wise arborists was a conceit adopted by the Judge Baker Foundation; promoters of the clinic even used *Straightening the Twig* to title a pamphlet publicizing its work.[1] Established at the height of the Progressive era's child-saving endeavors, the Judge Baker Foundation—now the Judge Baker Children's Center—is still in the business of bending twigs. In 1943, with support from the Rockefeller Foundation, the directors added a unit for work with infants and preschool children with Marian Putnam as director. In 1957 a grant from the Johns-Manville Corporation enabled the JBGC to move from the house on Beacon Street to its current, larger quarters on Longwood Avenue, near Boston's Children's Hospital. At the same time a residential program was added to the treatment services. The new location, in the midst of Boston's medical district, signified the clinic's closer ties to medicine and its diminishing connections to William Healy's world of social reform and juvenile crime.

The move to a bigger structure also attested to the clinic's continuing popularity with Boston's parents as the city moved from the Depression, to war, to the years of the baby boom. William Healy and Augusta Bronner retired from the clinic in 1947. They had tried to leave once before, but the exigencies of war intervened. "Both our leading men, Dr. Rosenheim and Dr. Gardner, have been called for special duties in the service and here we are, Dr. Bronner and I, back on full-time schedule," Healy wrote in 1944 to his old friend and patron Ethel Sturges Dummer. "And the demands upon our organization have been greater than they ever were before . . . The problems of this unstable and excited period seem peculiarly great, as everybody recognizes. Our aim is to do as much preventive work as possible and a most interesting thing in our own development is the fact that so many problems are brought to us directly from families." "It is," Healy concluded, "all a good sign."[2]

A good sign indeed. The courts and some welfare agencies continued to send families to the Judge Baker Guidance Center, yet when Healy and Bronner relinquished the directorship, private referrals accounted for more than 60 percent of the clinic's patients. Moreover, Boston was by then home to a range of psychotherapeutic options for young people, including the habit clinics, the Boston Psychopathic Hospital, a psychiatric unit at the Massachusetts General Hospital, psychiatrists who saw children in private practice, and psychiatrists and psychiatric social workers employed by private agencies. And Bostonians were not unique. As Americans entered the postwar baby boom, psychological interpretations of behavior dominated discussions of the troublesome child. Both public agencies and private families permitted child guidance to define the parameters of troublesome conduct and set guidelines for redressing the problems.

This book has traced how child guidance experts achieved such a degree of credibility by examining the conflicts and alliances that propelled a psychologized interpretation of the troublesome child into public and private discourse. The stark outlines of those relationships emerged inside the clinic, in the day-to-day contacts of professionals, parents, and children. The clinic frame presents a view of professional development from the inside out. However, it is an internalist perspective which assumes that professional authority was granted, not stolen, not foisted on the unsuspecting, and not entirely dependent on intellectual currents. It is also an approach that does not allow for solitary heroes, despite the instrumental role of William Healy in this story.

Lawson Lowrey, a child psychiatrist and clinic director who saw himself as historian for the child guidance movement, once wrote that "a new era started in psychiatry in 1909 when Healy began his work at the Juvenile Psychopathic Institute."[3] It is now time to expand on Lowrey's acclamation. A new era began when a group of maternalists wished to see how the study of the mind could help them better understand economically disadvantaged children in trouble with the law. The new era continued when young people caught the winds of modernity and challenged their middle-class parents in ways that seemed unknown to previous generations. The new era flourished when these parents found in child guidance a set of useful services to help them through the trials of raising a modern child. The child guidance movement, backed by mental hygienists at the Commonwealth Fund, created a network of clinics, providing a space for the development of three professions. Healy's research and practice, along with the many clinical studies and popularized writings of his colleagues, constructed a new language for discussions of the troublesome child.

The creation of child guidance—the clinic, the team, and the message—was a collaborative process. The collaboration and the popularity of child guidance stemmed from shared concerns and convictions. The United States in the early twentieth century was a society that valued economic growth and development, but the social and cultural changes this progress entailed were fearsome. The behavior of young people was one lightning rod for the turmoil, a code through which Americans could debate the instability, disorder, and lack of control they were forced to accept in the name of progress. Both laity and professionals acknowledged that growing up was a difficult task, and both accepted that it was a task that could be, indeed, had to be, regulated. Child guidance promised to return a degree of control to adults while still giving credence to the protests of youth. It was a promise that also promoted the interests of practitioners who made study of the child a professional livelihood.

The message of child guidance fulfilled this promise in three ways. From child guidance, parents learned that they could no longer teach children skills for success. Rather, they had to provide the environment in which young people would develop successful personalities, and that environment was defined in emotional, not economic, terms. One's economic destiny might be subject to distant market forces; child guidance promised that emotional destiny could still be shaped in the family setting. Child guidance also told parents to exercise control by granting independence to their young people and acknowledging the wisdom of peer culture. Youths were, on the whole, more attuned to the needs of a modern bureaucratic economy and a less restrictive consumer culture, and from the child guidance perspective these were values their elders might well emulate. Child guidance was not, however, a prescription for social anarchy with young people in charge. Parents and professionals shared a recognition of class and gender divisions in American culture. A final part of the message held that maintaining the boundaries between men and women and upholding the qualities of middle-class identity were requirements for parenting a child in the modern era. When things went awry, parents and professionals shared a belief that the imperfections threatening a child's class and gender identities were reversible. The authority of experts, as the example of child guidance shows, is constructed from just such points of contact where audience and professionals find common ground.

Despite the points of agreement, public acceptance of child guidance expertise came with reservations. From the beginning of Healy's delinquency study in 1909 to the boast in 1940 that child guidance covered all aspects of child welfare, patterns of resistance and counterpoints of authority limited the prospects of child guidance. The self-referred mothers and fathers, even when at their wit's end, retained a sense of parental know-how that could thwart the recommendations of the clinic's team. Children from all classes confounded the intentions of the psychiatrists. The specific needs of juvenile justice and welfare officials circumscribed child guidance prescriptions and prevented child guiders from providing much therapy to the delinquents. To erase these limits and neutralize other approaches to the troublesome child, the practitioners and popularizers of child guidance created a multidisciplinary team of experts, developed a critique of modern motherhood based on theories of family dynamics, built a continuum between delinquency and "everyday" misbehavior, and equated use of an expert with reliance on parental common sense and efficient welfare practice.

What was child guidance? By 1940 child guidance was the limited authority granted child science experts to determine the needs of young people, to define the emotional equipment needed for child rearing, to interpret the causes of juvenile misconduct, and to prescribe an appropriate response to the troublesome child. A highly motile society and a population of young people with leisure time and new opportunities to fill the hours created the setting for child guidance. The psychiatry of Meyer and Freud provided a language. The professionals, welfare and court clients, parents, and children put together the boundaries of the child guidance response to the troublesome child.

If the success of child guidance is measured by the number of clinics that followed its precepts, then in 1940 child guiders were right to boast. Cities large and small across the nation had opened psychiatric services for children during the 1920s and 1930s. While a few clinics were forced to close because of economic circumstances, others flourished in spite of the nation's financial straits.

If the success of child guidance is measured by its adaptability to unique social contexts, then once again child guiders could be proud of their accomplishments. As Ellen Herman and others have shown, psychiatrists took advantage of the turmoil of World War II to enhance the public image of the behavioral sciences. Psychiatric treatment of veterans promised to restore lives scarred by combat; psychology and psychiatry explained the psyche of the enemy to help the home front construct defenses. The spokespersons for child guidance also addressed their expertise to the problems of families in wartime. From 1940 to 1945 child guiders provided advice on how to compensate for the absence of fathers in the home, on the consequences to child mental health of working mothers, and on concerns about a new outbreak of juvenile delinquency. The war setting gave child guidance advocates another opportunity to expose the practical value of a psychological interpretation of the troublesome child, and they did not let the opportunity pass by.[4]

In the postwar years the practitioners and popularizers of child guidance continued to accumulate authority to define the causes and cures of the problems children cause us. Today, in a cynical age when laypeople are often skeptical of the wisdom of experts, we are still willing to accept psychological explanations for young drug abusers, child murderers, children who do not sit still in classrooms, and youngsters who wet their beds. We listen to those who continue to tell us that the dynamics of individual family relationships are responsible for the emotional and behavioral disorders we believe epidemic among the nation's children. As we develop both community and private solutions, we are bound by the limits of child guidance. I conclude this study of the authority of experts by briefly sketching four directions taken by child guidance after World War II: the intensification of the critique of motherhood; the elevation of child psychiatry to a separate medical specialty distinct from the practice of child guidance; the further marginalization of social-structural concerns in delinquency work; and the institutionalization of child guidance through state and federal backing. These four areas mark out the postwar paths to the consolidation of professional power and the expansion of child guidance resources. They also point to the limitations that our reliance on the message of child guidance has imposed on our understanding of the troublesome child.

MAL DE MÈRE

During and after the war both practitioners and popularizers intensified their attacks on mothers and created new forms of maternal culpability. Was it true, an anxious mother asked Judge Baker social worker in 1946, that "all [children's] problems are the mother's fault?" The social worker's attempt to qualify an affirmative answer was feeble, for this beautician and wife of a World War II veteran had pegged the fundamental characteristic of postwar child guidance work (13548). In 1966, when Franz Alexander and Sheldon Selesnick chronicled psychiatric history "from prehistoric times to the present," they acclaimed "the mother-child relationship . . . so important for ensuing pathology that it has probably received more attention than any other aspect of child psychiatry."[5] Mother-blaming continued to provide child guidance experts with the framework to support the patient role for parents, while it narrowed research options and diminished the influence of competing structural or environmental explanations of troublesome behavior.

It was not precisely *mother's* fault, psychiatrist Edward Strecker would have replied to the beautician, but the fault of *mom*. Strecker had been a consultant to the secretary of war and the surgeons general of the army and navy during the war, a position that permitted him to study psychoneurotic individuals rejected from military service. The investigation revealed to him the devastating effects on masculinity of "momism," an exaggerated version of David Levy's maternal overprotection. "What constitutes a mom?" Strecker asked in a series of postwar lectures. "Fundamentally a mom is not a mother. Mom is a maternal parent who fails to prepare her offspring emotionally for living a productive adult life on an adult social plane." A mom might come in any shape or size, "however, she does have one thing in common—the emotional satisfaction, almost repletion, she derives from keeping her children paddling about in a kind of psychological amniotic fluid rather than letting them swim away with the bold and decisive strokes of maturity from the emotional maternal womb." Strecker held moms responsible for everything from alcoholism and homosexuality to public-spirited "movements" and fascism.[6]

Strecker sensationalized his account of the weaklings being raised by American moms; others in the profession were more sterile and scientific, but their condemnation of mothers was equally scathing. In 1943 Leo Kanner identified "early infantile autism" as a specific disease syndrome. Autism described a child who, from birth, appeared to withdraw from human contact. The behavior, Kanner claimed, was the result of a "cold," obsessional mother. Such a woman might be sophisticated and intelligent, but she would be emotionally distant and impersonal in her relationship with her child. Kanner also reported that the fathers could be bookish and humorless, leading him to speak of the "refrigerator" parent of either sex who "just happened to defrost long enough to produce a child." Yet others heard only his accusation against mothers. Kanner, who always mistrusted the extremes of psychoanalysis, was dismayed that his original observations had fostered a "nothing-but psychodynamic etiology" that, for the time being, "stifled" further curiosity about the causes of autism.[7]

He should not have been surprised, however, for his initial report came in the midst of studies correlating evidence of maternal pathology with schizophrenia. In 1934 a group of researchers from the State Hospital for Mental Diseases in Rhode Island uncovered evidence of overprotection in patients who later developed a "schizophrenic syndrome." Jacob Kasanin and his coauthors Elizabeth Knight and Priscilla Sage observed that "one usually speaks of the over-protection exercised by the mother, but the paternal over-protection is just as important."[8] Not so egalitarian was the work of the psychoanalyst Frieda Fromm-Reichmann, whose texts made maternal pathology responsible for one of the most intractable psychological disorders. An Austrian by birth who immigrated to the United States in 1936, Fromm-Reichmann described her new homeland as a matriarchal society, one in which an "imperious mother" could be found at the heart of most childhood emotional problems. Her interpretation of schizophrenia, reported in 1948, attributed its etiology to rejecting, restrictive "schizophrenogenic mothers."[9]

René Spitz, an American psychoanalyst, found further confirmation of the health consequences of inadequate mothering when he investigated the high death rate, despite good physical care, of infants placed in foundling homes. "Hospitalism," Spitz called the phenomenon. A slow decline of the child's spirit and physical well-being, which Spitz labeled "anaclitic depression," occurred when the child was separated from its mother. "Hospitalism" was a psychological disorder caused by the absence of maternal affection.[10] In England the psychoanalyst John Bowlby, working at the behest of the United Nations, conducted a study of war orphans with results similar to Spitz's. A child who lacked a continuous relationship with its mother would suffer from "maternal deprivation" and was likely to grow into an emotionally troubled adult.[11] The work of Spitz and Bowlby, when generalized to the larger population and popularized during the 1950s, added support to concerns raised during World War II about "latchkey children" who suffered emotional loss and possibly engaged in acts of juvenile delinquency when left alone by, for example, a working (therefore, rejecting) mother.[12]

There were, to be sure, other professional voices, researchers who tried to temper the condemnation of mothers. Stella Chess, a professor of child psychiatry at New York Medical College, hoped in 1964 to bring attention to the failure of the experts to look beyond mother-blaming for other sources of childhood behavior problems. Chess warned that maternal pathology, or "mal de mère," as she called it in an editorial for the *American Journal of Orthopsychiatry,* was not an explanation well designed to meet the needs of children. Her own research on temperament hearkened back to Healy's original effort to individualize each child, to understand each delinquent as the product of a constellation of factors, and to allow each child a privileged relationship with the psychiatrist. In *Maternal Deprivation Reassessed* (1972), the British psychologist Michael Rutter qualified the work of John Bowlby. Separation from mother was *a* factor that could cause troublesome behavior, Rutter acknowledged. But surely it was not the *only* factor. The Bellevue psychiatrist Lauretta Bender and other renegades challenged conventional wisdom about childhood schizophrenia; Bender thought the disease had a biological foundation, attempted drug treatment with her patients, and suggested that "the mother of the schizophrenic child . . . shows a specific mechanistic process [because of] her efforts to help the child."[13]

Despite the qualifications and renunciations, "mal de mère" became an ideé fixe in the corpus of child guidance, explaining both the misconduct of the younger generation and their serious mental illnesses. Chess revisited "mal de mère" in 1982 and found it surprisingly alive and well.[14] Once legitimated by its practical function in the clinic, the critique of motherhood had assumed an intellectual life independent of its place in defining the relationship between clinicians and their clients.

To be sure, some mothers act in ways hurtful to their children, as do some fathers and some other adults, related or not. When evaluating mothers, however, child guiders ignored William Healy's program: no "individual mother" was paired with her individualized troublesome child. Instead, motherhood itself was made suspect, and it continues to provide lawmakers and political pundits with a convenient scapegoat for problems that will not go away. Molly Ladd-Taylor and Lauri Umansky conclude, in an introduction to essays about America's "bad" mothers past and present, that we must not allow this solitary figure to divert us from "poverty, racism, the paucity of meaningful work at a living wage, the lack of access to day care, antifeminism, and a host of other problems."[15] Rooting out and stigmatizing "bad" mothers, rather than scrutinizing the inequities in our culture's class, race, and gender relations, does not meet the needs of the nation's children. As both Leo Kanner and Stella Chess predicted, mother-blaming has limited the discussion of alternative explanations of the troublesome child.

AT THE MID-CENTURY CLINIC

The records of the Judge Baker Guidance Center from 1945–46 allow us to evaluate, in the aftermath of the war, the extent to which child guidance accusations of faulty parenting and maternal pathology had lodged in public consciousness. Stories from the files suggest that postwar parents came to the Judge Baker clinic already anticipating the kinds of diagnoses child guidance would provide them. Some families now openly invited an explanation of a child's problems that focused on parental responsibility. "Both pars. talked intelligently [about] the youngster and seemed to take a responsible attitude [about] his difficulties," wrote the social worker about the case of a ten-year-old boy with enuresis, who was described also as "irresponsible," "scattered," and "never finish[ing] what he starts." "It was F. who mentioned a couple of times that pars. might be themselves at fault, and if so, they wanted to be told it" (13495). For this mechanic and his wife, and many others in the clinic's files, the parent-blaming discourse of child guidance had become a way to organize their thoughts about child rearing.

Fathers in particular seemed more ready to invite child guidance assistance in 1945 than had the fathers of a decade earlier. While not as frequently as mothers (and with some fathers still faulting mothers), fathers were now prepared to tell the clinic about their parenting worries. Child guidance commentary on the significance of a strong father figure might account for the change, but the separation of families during the war also might have been a factor in the new willingness of fathers to read from the clinic's script.[16]

This was an ironic development, to be sure, since a striking feature of the records from 1945–1946 was the persistent assumption that, even with a flawed father, it was a mother's duty to change. Again the mechanic in case no. 13945 is representative. "Maybe it's my fault," he admitted to the social worker during one interview. The description of this man in the clinicians' summary might be seen as confirmation of his assessment: "The father is a disappointed, frustrated, uncommunicative individual, a conscientious worker [who] has shown little affection to the boy and has done very little with him." However, the team then went on to recommend that the parents be worked with "a good deal" so that "M. in particular may see how her emotional life is involved."

As in this instance, mother-blaming dominated discussions of the troublesome children examined at the clinic after the war. Mothers were "rigid," "restricting," "stubborn," "nagging," "too methodical," "aggressive," "sharp," "cold," "undemonstrative," "controlling," and showing "no expression of any real maternal feelings." The clinicians demonstrated great sensitivity to hidden meanings in the maternal emotions they observed. David Levy had alerted the field to the rejection of motherhood that he found beneath signs of overprotection. In the records from 1945–1946 the staff frequently noted that the feminine qualities of a mother often concealed far less positive—masculine—personality attributes. The "passive" woman was actually "domineering"; the appearance of the "timid looking woman" belied "her rather forceful, dominating behavior"; the mother with a "warm outgoing personality" rejected her daughter's spontaneous play.[17] Other mothers appeared to spurn femininity without compunction. One was "a mannish sort of person" (13561), whose husband appeared as a "namby-pamby"; another displayed a "mannish walk" (13453); still another was "an extremely masculine woman who has been unable to accept her mother role, who has insisted on working" (13471). To the clinicians a woman's display of "masculine" personality traits could explain the misbehavior of her children.[18]

Although families may have anticipated that the clinic would hold parents responsible, they were driven to child guidance because of its promises. As a woman told a Judge Baker social worker, every mother wanted a "perfect child" (13491); fulfilling that desire was the allure of child guidance. Despite the attraction, not every mother was willing to pay the cost child guidance extracted. A mother's ability to converse in the language of child guidance did not mean that she accepted unconditionally the therapeutic programs offered by the postwar child guidance clinic.

The mother of a ten-year-old, when told of the clinic's long waiting list and advised to consult the Habit Clinic, said that, "knowing the quality of the J.B. work," she preferred to "wait indefinitely" for an appointment. Yet when meetings were finally arranged, many weeks later, she found the experience not up to her expectations. Only three months after her initial appointment this mother chose to end her sessions. The doctor should make clear to her son, she felt, that children had to respect their parents. "She now feels that the dr. and the pars. are pulling [the boy] in opposite directions and therefore [he] is unhappy" (13500). As had parents a decade earlier, postwar families expected specific diagnoses and specific suggestions from the clinic. "I pointed out," one social worker reported of her conversation with a recalcitrant mother, "that I had made definite suggestions about activities for [her daughter] and M. had not wanted to accept this advice. M. remarked then that she believes she is entitled to her opinion. I agreed w. this but said again that we could not help M. unless she worked w. us." After this exchange, the woman sent a letter terminating her contact with the clinic (13560). Another mother reportedly became "quite hostile" during one of her last sessions. "She made it quite clear that she had hoped in coming in to us to have us take over for her and clear up the problems . . . When M. found out that actually we couldn't do this . . . she [became] somewhat annoyed" (13504).

This mother admitted that she guessed "she needed help more than anybody else," but she also retained a clear idea of what that help should entail. Mothers placed on the waiting list reported solving the problems themselves; others had second thoughts about initiating a clinic consultation.[19] Still others, while acknowledging the possibility of parental responsibility, offered other explanations. The mother of the ten-year-old with enuresis thought that comic books might account for her son's problems and, with perhaps greater insight, suggested that the war might have "had something to do with it." "All the boys had difficulty in concentrating last yr . . . they were just interested in drawing airplanes, bombs, swastikas, etc." (13495).[20] As had their Depression-era counterparts, the postwar parents placed boundaries around child guidance, even as they accepted some of its premises and voluntarily sought its remedies.

As significant as the signs of resistance in the postwar cases was the willingness of these parents to identify such qualities as "scattered," "defiant," "untrustworthy," "quiet," and "girl crazy" as problems that made a child imperfect, and problems that merited consultation with professionals. Though many a mother still resented the child guidance assumption of parental guilt, all these self-referred parents had come to accept that raising a child was a difficult endeavor and that a child's "everyday" troublesome behavior could become more extreme. Most important, they had come to believe that experts in the child guidance movement had the "magic bullets" they needed to change the behavior of a troublesome child, just as doctors now had antibiotics to change the course of an infection. Parental goals were not so much to save a child from an emotionally handicapped adulthood; parents did not share the clinic's sense of preventive mental hygiene. Instead, they saw the clinic, and the promise of child guidance, as a way to ease the immediate tensions caused by behavior they could not tolerate. Mothers' understanding of child guidance left many of them willing to give the clinicians a try, until the procedures impinged on a deeply held sense of maternal authority.

Child guidance after a quarter of a century had earned a degree of credibility with the parents of some of Boston's troublesome children, but it cannot be maintained that the intense critique of motherhood had entirely undermined the confidence of mothers or quelled their determination to retain a competing perspective on the causes of the troublesome child. This maternal perspective often appeared more sociological than that of the child guiders, setting the troublesome child and the family's problems in a broader community context. While there was no profound political component to the resistance of the child guidance mothers, either in 1935 or in 1945, surely modern feminists who question the contemporary currents of mother-blaming, or reassert the benefits of maternal thinking and women's ways of knowing, owe a small debt to these individual resisters. When Hillary Rodham Clinton writes that "it takes a village" to raise a child, she is asserting a position intuitive to some of the mothers who confronted the proselytizing of the child experts at the Judge Baker clinic and denied their accusations of maternal pathology.[21]

For the child guidance theorists, however, the uncooperative mothers were added proof of the accuracy of their critique. Despite some cautious questioning from within the profession, mother-blaming—as rejection, domination, deprivation, or overprotection—structured the way child psychiatrists and child psychologists researched and treated the problems of both troubled children and children in trouble with the law. By expending so much intellectual capital on theories of maternal pathology, the popularizers, practitioners, and researchers of child guidance both legitimated and limited their authority for the troublesome child.

PROFESSIONAL SPECIALIZATION

It was appropriate that Alexander and Selesnick, the historians of psychiatry who in 1966 underscored the role of the mother in research on child psychopathology, connected the idea to child psychiatry, only one of the three fields of child guidance. In the postwar years, child psychiatrists began the process of medical specialization, identifying themselves professionally more as members of the medical community than as representatives of a "movement" asserting a claim to all aspects of child welfare. Research interest in infantile autism and childhood schizophrenia, two relatively rare and difficult to treat disorders, signaled the new medical allegiance. Child psychiatrists also proclaimed the medicalization of their field by adopting new organizational affiliations. The American Orthopsychiatric Association continued to express the multiprofessional approach to the problems of the troublesome child, but in 1952 a group of psychiatric separatists formed the American Academy of Child Psychiatry. They restricted membership in the new organization to medically trained practitioners who belonged to the American Psychiatric Association and had two years of specialized training in childhood disorders. In 1959 child psychiatry achieved formal recognition as a subspecialty of medicine; specialized practitioners would be certified by the American Board of Psychiatry and Neurology.[22]

The credentials of specialization offered child psychiatrists a degree of professional legitimacy distinct from that of the multiprofessional team at a time when, once again, the functions of team members were overlapping. The critique of motherhood still required treatment of both parent and child, but during and after the war the growing popularity of child guidance services created a shortage of medically trained personnel for therapy with children. Child guidance psychologists and social workers took this opportunity to extend the range of their therapeutic functions, with psychologists assuming more clinical responsibilities than in the early clinics and social workers seeing children as well as parents. Medical specialization allowed child psychiatrists to claim professional distinctiveness (and superiority) as others now conducted all aspects of the work of resolving troublesome behavior.

The medicalization of child psychiatry after mid-century opened opportunities for the development of interests and interpretations outside the rigid boundaries of family dynamics and the critique of motherhood. As already noted, Lauretta Bender and her co-workers assigned an important role to biological factors in the etiology of childhood schizophrenia. Even at the Judge Baker clinic diagnoses of neurological dysfunction occasionally cropped up in the postwar explanations of misbehavior and personality maladjustment. Yet physiological or biological determinants did not suppress maternal pathology and family dynamics as the premiere cause of emotional and behavioral disorders. Quite possibly the medicalization of child psychiatry further helped to legitimize the child guidance critique of motherhood by granting it more stature as medical theory.[23] During the 1940s and 1950s child guidance clinics basked in the prestige earned by association with medicine. With the availability of antibiotics and, after 1955, a vaccine to prevent the frightening childhood disease of polio, postwar developments in child medicine elevated the authority of the doctor's voice. Through new organizations and special licensure child psychiatrists made it known that they, too, belonged to the medical profession.

Medical specialization, whether raising new biological issues or extending psychodynamic theories, did not blunt entirely the social-structural concerns that once led the founders of child guidance to claim responsibility for all aspects of child welfare. Over the years some spokespersons in the field continued to point to the eclectic origins of mental health and, along with demands for more treatment facilities, they called for renewed commitment to the cause of social reform. In 1970, for example, the Joint Commission on Mental Health of Children issued a report castigating the nation as a whole for neglecting the social and economic factors responsible for the well-being of children. Created in 1965 through an amendment to the Social Security bill of that year, the commission was yet another consequence of the assassination of John F. Kennedy. Senator Abraham Ribicoff sponsored the commission after learning that Kennedy's assailant had received no treatment when diagnosed in childhood with a serious emotional disturbance. A study of the mental health needs of children in the United States would be one way, the senator thought, to "prevent more Oswalds."[24]

In its final report the commission admonished the nation for permitting a "crisis" to exist in child mental health. Reginald Lourie, child psychiatrist and president of the Joint Commission, claimed that the "most important principle" underlying the group's work was the connection made among mental health, physical health, and the cultural and social forces influencing the development of children. "Babies are not born racist, violent, and without respect for the law," the report's authors noted; children learn this behavior from the culture in which they are reared.[25] Yet the report backed away from recommending broad social changes, fearing that changes in cultural patterns responsible for poverty and racism "tend to come about slowly." Instead, the commission lauded the family-centered approach of child guidance clinics and other family welfare agencies. Having found that only a third of the children needing mental health care actually received it, the commission recommended state and federal commitment to increase the availability of professional services for children.[26]

Although all the fields of child guidance participated in the investigations of the Joint Commission, child psychiatry supplied the framework for discussions of troublesome behavior. Both the medicalized agenda of the commission and the number of directors with medical degrees (more than 40 percent) point to a realignment of the child guidance alliance. Child psychiatrists, who had always been administrators of the child guidance clinics, could by the 1960s be regarded as managers in the field of child mental health. The readjustment of the professional partnership is symbolized by the fading from use of the term "child guidance." The three professions that once boasted of a common concern for child welfare could no longer claim to work with such harmony.

CHILD GUIDANCE AND THE JUVENILE DELINQUENT

As specialization and medicalization continues in the field of child mental health it is the troublesome children and their families, particularly those

young people judged to be juvenile delinquents, who will suffer most because of the loss of child guidance eclecticism. That loss is quite evident in
recent legislative efforts to charge and punish some young offenders as
adults. Today we are facing another wave of fear about juvenile offenders.
Unlike the children and adolescents whose fate was determined by the early
juvenile court and child guidance clinic, these young people commit heinous crimes. In Richmond, California, for example, police and prosecutors
debate how to try a six-year-old accused of the attempted murder of an
infant, while national headlines scream about adolescents who kill their
parents or randomly gun down classmates in schoolyard shootings. One
response has been to rebel against the message of child guidance and
overthrow the separate standards of juvenile justice. Since the crimes are
no longer simple thefts and sex delinquencies, there is public outcry that
we are pampering young offenders, that they must be held to adult standards of accountability if they commit grown-up crimes. Juvenile crime
bills, at the state and national level, demand boot camps or other forms of
punishment, rejecting in principle the psychiatric treatment programs long
advocated by the child guiders. Another response has taken the message of
child guidance to the extreme, suggesting that we punish parents for the
crimes of their children. Officials in Roanoke, Virginia, have put forward
such a proposal, and they are not alone.[27] The anger and disillusionment
evident in these alternatives are part of the legacy of child guidance.

During the years of professional development child guidance maintained an ambivalent relationship with children who broke the law. With
the founding of the Juvenile Psychopathic Institute and the Commonwealth Fund's commitment to a mental hygiene program for delinquency
prevention, the authority of child guidance rested on its possession of the
solution to a worrisome social problem. As clinicians participated in delinquency prevention programs, they found the families of the delinquents
difficult to work with. The structure of juvenile justice limited opportunities to provide therapy in addition to diagnoses for the delinquents. With
the explanation that family-generated emotional conflict created young
people with maladjusted personalities, some of whom engaged in overt
criminal behavior, child guiders went on to claim all forms of problem
behavior—delinquent or "everyday"—from any social class. Environmental or social-structural factors receded, if they did not entirely disap-
pear from the original eclecticism. The self-referred clients added a special
cachet, and they were sought after and valued. Nonetheless, the clinics

continued to provide services for juvenile courts, and child guiders continued to argue for a psychotherapeutic approach to social problem solving. William Healy and Augusta Bronner represented the whole field when they made this case in one of their last publications, *New Light on Delinquency and Its Treatment* (1936), a book that urged delinquency experts to pursue child guidance therapy with individual lawbreakers.

New Light on Delinquency was in part a defensive reaction to an organized academic resistance to child guidance that flourished during the 1920s and 1930s even as clinics became more prominent national fixtures. A group of University of Chicago sociologists contested the psychodynamic theories of behavior, arguing that human nature was a product of social living, not inner psychic drives and not instinct. To understand the actions of individuals, including criminal behavior, the Chicago sociologists examined the communities and neighborhoods in which the individuals lived. Their work recalled the traditions of Jane Addams and the settlement house founders of child guidance.[28]

The city of Chicago served these sociologists as the laboratory for a theory that tied delinquency rates to urban decay caused by rapid commercialization and industrialization of the city core. Using records of the Chicago Board of Education and cases from the Juvenile Court and the Institute for Juvenile Research (formerly the Juvenile Psychopathic Institute), Clifford Shaw and Henry D. MacKay plotted maps of "delinquency areas," in which unusually high rates of juvenile crime persisted over long periods of time despite changes in the ethnic composition of the areas. Shaw and MacKay found these neighborhoods most often concentrated in areas adjacent to business and industrial districts. Psychological explanations of misbehavior could not account for the presence of so many delinquencies in the designated areas, Shaw and MacKay reasoned. Instead they argued that the shared social conditions constituted the source of delinquency; given the environment in which these youths lived, delinquency might be considered a normal life experience rather than a sign of a disturbed personality.[29]

Although much of the research relied on aggregate analyses, Clifford Shaw also borrowed the "case study" method of child guidance to undermine the psychological interpretation of delinquency. In *The Jack-Roller* Shaw told the story of Stanley, whose career in crime began at age six when he joined his brother's gang of thieves. With a touch of irony Shaw confirmed his theory (that the neighborhood caused Stanley's delinquency) with interviews made at the Juvenile Psychopathic Institute. "Stealing was a common practice among the children and approved by the parents. When-ever the boys got together they talked about robbing and made more plans for stealing," Stanley told Shaw. Whereas William Healy's studies stressed the uniqueness of each delinquent's experiences, Shaw suggested that Stan-ley and others like him were products of a shared environment. Stanley spent most of his life in areas close to the "dirt and odor of the stock yards and factories," areas of rapidly changing ethnic populations as individuals who prospered "escaped to more desirable communities." Stanley's neigh-borhood was marked by "considerable disorganization and confusion of moral standards." Shaw successfully treated Stanley not with psychother-apy but with a new set of friends in a new social setting.[30]

Casework with individuals was "only a partial approach" to delinquency, wrote Ernest Burgess, a founder of the Chicago school of sociology, in a discussion of Shaw's study. "The life-history of Stanley, taken in conjunc-tion with the facts on the concentration of delinquency presented in *De-linquency Areas* and the analyses of boy gang life and organization in Thrasher's *The Gang,* provide a foundation for new modes of attack upon the problem of the delinquent and the criminal." Burgess called for the development of "techniques of group and community treatment."[31] With the Chicago Area Project Shaw and his associates attempted to create these techniques.

Begun in 1934, the Chicago Area Project conducted a delinquency pre-vention program in the largely Polish community of South Chicago. The plan relied on recreational programs, community involvement, and "curb-side counselling" as ways of "making the neighborhood conscious of the problems of delinquency, collectively interested in the welfare of its chil-dren, and active in promoting programs for such improvements of the com-munity environment as will develop in the children interests and habits of a constructive and socially desirable character."[32] At the heart of the pro-gram was resident participation in long-range planning and in daily opera-tions. The sociologists in charge believed that democratic control would rebuild the lost community organization and community control of young people, the elements thought to be responsible for the high delinquency rates. Putting parents back in charge involved community activism, not the child guiders' efforts to modify personalities through individual therapy.[33]

Fear of a new juvenile crime wave gripped public attention during the 1940s and 1950s and tested the strength of the child guidance commitment to solving the delinquency problem.[34] The federal Children's Bureau tried to meet the challenge by calling both for more community programs and for more child guidance clinics. JBGC practitioners learned during the early 1940s that the Rockefeller Foundation, which financed so much of the child guidance and child development work, was intent on taking child guidance further from its social problem solving origins. A foundation proposal to support Judge Baker programs stipulated that delinquency cases be reduced to only 30 percent of the clinic's workload. Individual child guiders still equated delinquency with personality structure and promoted the therapeutic services of the clinics. Yet the National Institutes of Health reported that after apprenticeship in delinquency work at the JBGC, child psychiatrist trainees quickly switched to private practice, deserting the social policy origins of the field.[35]

Meanwhile more studies critical of the clinics issued from criminologists. *New Light on Delinquency* had been, in part, a response to charges that the Boston juvenile court and the Judge Baker clinic were ineffective against the problem of delinquency. Several decades later two longitudinal studies, *Origins of Crime* (1959) by William McCord and Joan McCord and *Deviant Children Grown Up* (1966) by Lee Robins, again found the child guidance response to delinquency wanting. The McCords followed the careers of children who participated in the Cambridge-Somerville (Massachusetts) Youth Project of the 1930s. Designed to "prevent delinquency and develop character by means of friendly guidance," the project's results were "discouraging," according to the McCords. Boys who had been treated displayed rates of recidivism similar to those of boys who belonged to a control group, and when rates of criminality declined in both groups during adulthood, the McCords could not show a connection to the project's friendly guidance, including direct counseling about personal problems and advice and help to families.[36] Lee Robins reached similar conclusions in a study of a St. Louis child guidance center, stating that "whatever criteria of adult adjustment were used, clinic children were more maladjusted and sicker adults than were control subjects," and "the difference was particularly striking in rates of antisocial behavior."[37]

Despite their criticisms of child guidance–like therapy, neither study advocated broad programs of social reform to replace the therapeutic approach. Rather, each study rejected the concept of delinquency areas and instead identified "neglect" of a child by its parents as a principle cause of "sociopathy," the contemporary term for delinquent behavior. The McCords singled out emotional neglect, particularly by mothers (in contrast with any form of maternal love, such as overprotection). Robins focused on behavioral qualities of neglect, such as shoddy housekeeping or illicit sex. Of course the research about juvenile crime in the decades after Healy and Bronner left the Judge Baker clinic was not limited to these two projects. Nonetheless, the widely cited studies by Robins and the McCords illustrate the extent to which the message of parental culpability provided a frame for much of the postwar criminology research, even as child guidance clinics marginalized the treatment of delinquents. The child guiders' ambivalence about working with individual delinquents did not translate into a loss of authority for their psychodynamic interpretation of juvenile delinquency.

Current dilemmas—to treat or punish young offenders, to view them as responsible agents or as the victims of a mutilated individual psyche or an inequitable social structure—represent the legacy of child guidance. According to the child guiders, all troublesome children—those who were troubled and those in trouble with the law—shared the same psychological needs even if they did not share the same social and economic disadvantages. On the one hand, this legacy frustrates liberal efforts to combat juvenile crime with programs of income redistribution to address economic inequities. On the other hand, the legacy of child guidance also delegitimizes punishment plans premised on individual responsibility, those that denounce emotional trauma as another bugaboo of modern victimology. Child guiders have told us that children can be independent agents capable of speaking on their own behalf in the clinic setting; a modern children's movement exaggerates this independence, advocating the recognition of each child as a citizen to be guaranteed the protection of fundamental individual rights.[38] Yet the legacy of child guidance tempers our willingness to grant rights to juvenile delinquents. Who can demand rights when responsibility is denied, when, as the child guiders argued, misbehavior is a consequence not of individual choice but of the failure of others to meet a child's emotional needs? A resolution of the current dilemmas surrounding juvenile crime will have to move beyond the ambiguities left by a psychologized child and the child guidance movement.

CHILD GUIDANCE AND THE STATE

Child guidance practitioners consolidated and expanded their authority during the 1940s and 1950s despite the reservations of parents and children, the softening alliance of the three professions, and the marginalization of delinquency work. A good part of the authority accruing to child guidance after mid-century can be attributed to support from many levels of government. Legislators, attaching the authority of government bureaucracy to the psychologized interpretation of the troublesome child, stipulated the circumstances in which child guidance services had to be used by child-saving officials. Federal agencies and federal money directly supported the expansion of child guidance services, both nationwide and abroad. Government support helped to ensure funding and usage of child guidance clinics, and government requirements fostered the growth of a community of professionals enmeshed in the clinic's protocol.

The informal connection between the Boston juvenile court and the Judge Baker clinic was formalized in 1931. After that year Massachusetts correctional policy obligated courts to request psychiatric evaluations for juvenile offenders before delinquents were sentenced to a state institution. Legislation designated that the clinic appointed to study the child would include a physician trained in psychiatry, a psychologist, and a social worker. As of 1939 seventeen states, in addition to Massachusetts, authorized mental and physical examinations in similar circumstances.[39] Currently all states include in their juvenile codes provisions for the psychological evaluation of young offenders.[40]

The early promotional work of the Children's Bureau helped to convince the state legislators who set up these stipulations of the value of child guidance diagnoses. Throughout its history this federal agency was a powerful ally of the child guidance movement, promoting the clinics as community-sponsored delinquency prevention programs and as resources for individual families. When the social disruptions of World War II raised new alarms about juvenile crime, the Children's Bureau once again endorsed the services of the clinics, calling them a "valuable resource" for local communities.[41] James Gilbert, in his history of postwar delinquency, has characterized the Children's Bureau during these years as an organization beleaguered by bureaucratic conflict over domain. In such a climate leaders at the Children's Bureau used their support for child guidance and for the child science professionals to distinguish the bureau's delinquency work from that of other federal agencies. If children were not truly criminals, then, according to the Children's Bureau, law enforcement agencies such as the FBI could not be expected to police the problem effectively. Children's Bureau personnel encouraged programs that relied on the juvenile court and the therapeutic intervention of experts.[42] During its long tenure, this federal agency championed the message of child guidance aggressively and successfully. After mid-century other government departments gradually took over the programs of the Children's Bureau. By this time, however, other areas of the federal bureaucracy had also heavily invested in child guidance.

The federal commitment came as part of the National Mental Health Act of 1946. This legislation capped the successful self-promotion of psychiatrists during World War II; it was not specifically directed toward promoting child welfare. Nonetheless, with passage of this act, states received matching federal funds to open community mental health clinics, including centers specializing in the treatment of children and adolescents. Under the provisions of this act, the federal government also took responsibility for increasing the number of trained mental health personnel through grants-in-aid for training centers and stipends to students specifically for the study of child psychiatry.[43] The recommendations in 1970 from the Joint Commission on the Mental Health of Children asked for even more support along these lines.

One further sign of mid-century government institutionalization of child guidance was the eagerness of the occupation forces to make over Japanese child welfare policies in the likeness of American child guidance. According to Tatara Toshio, a historian of Japanese social work, the Bureau of Public Health and Welfare, housed within the general headquarters of the Supreme Commander of the Allied Powers (SCAP, the organization created to execute the terms of surrender with Japan), profoundly influenced a comprehensive Child Welfare Law put into effect in 1948 by the Japanese Diet. The 1948 law was a wide-ranging piece of legislation that Tatara says "radically modernized" Japan's child welfare policies. Prewar policies made no mention of children's rights or needs and grounded the rehabilitation of troublesome children in the traditional Japanese family system. In contrast, the new Child Welfare Law authorized the establishment of community child guidance clinics and promoted the professionalization of child welfare workers. Also in 1948 SCAP approved entry into Japan of American social service workers who could demonstrate practices current in the United States. Among those admitted was Alice Carroll, a social worker trained at the University of Pittsburgh, who helped to supervise local child guidance personnel and produced the first textbook for Japanese child welfare agents. Her caution that professionals from other countries had to be mindful of cultural differences helped to secure her text a prominent place in the child welfare literature of postwar Japan.[44] Carroll's caution, however, did not undermine the significance of the decisions made by SCAP. In yet another way government structures added to the postwar authority of child guidance.

The ideas and services of child guidance were deeply enmeshed in the political, professional, and intellectual culture after mid-century, framing research and shaping policy. Today, as representatives of the separate and specialized professions, child guiders continue to speak passionately as guardians of the needs of all children, whether troublesome, troubled, and just the "everyday" variety. Elizabeth Costello and a group of psychiatric researchers estimated in 1988 that 20 percent of American children display psychological disturbances serious enough to warrant treatment.[45] This figure would have been seemed shocking in the nineteenth century. Now we take it as routine, and know that the 20 percent Costello identified reflects only the worst of a difficult situation. Whether we choose to valorize the professionals who rescued troubled children, created the clinics, and popularized the idioms, or damn them for their misrepresentations, we must acknowledge the transformation they brought about in the first half of the twentieth century—they, the parents, and the children of child guidance. But I turn to my mother for a more personal account of the authority of these experts. Here was a woman raising two daughters in the postwar atmosphere created by the child guidance movement. As I was beginning my research in the records of the Judge Baker clinic I asked about her experiences with the experts. What books had she read? To whom had she listened? What authorities had she consulted? At the time her reply surprised me. She could not recall checking the popularized child-rearing advice. "We took you to Dr. Gabriel [our family physician]," she remembered, adding as an afterthought, "—of course I had your grandmother."

Although my mother never sought counsel at a child guidance clinic, she had absorbed one of the child guiders' most important messages. A mother's common sense would take her to a professional if there were signs of trouble. My mother's afterthought, however, points to the limits of her reliance on the experts. Child rearing for my mother was a blend of medical authority and maternal wisdom. My grandmother offered her an alternative source of expertise and my mother accorded her equal status as a child-rearing authority. Raising children was a task women understood; if not instinct, then certainly tradition gave my mother the freedom to ignore the advice of the experts, just as it framed the responses of many of the families who applied to the Judge Baker clinic for direct services with their troublesome children.

At mid-century, public sector support for the child guidance movement provided the clinic's experts far greater opportunities to influence explanations of children's failings, to frame definitions of the needs of children, and to manipulate programs for reform. In this venue, however, the limits of psychiatric authority measure not how far that authority has seeped into our consciousness, but how much it has restricted our vision. The child guiders' paradigm—the psychological needs of children and the psychological flaws of parents—colors our approaches to poverty, crime, and family. It makes us leery of sociological models and structural interpretations; it tightens the purse strings of many when they are asked for tax dollars to mediate the effects of racial discrimination or economic inequities; it leads us to examine only the individual schoolyard shooter instead of the culture in which he lives. If we intend to tame the troublesome child of the twenty-first century we will have to look beyond the psychology of the family. We must reconsider the paradigm signaled by William Healy in 1915 when he introduced American child savers to an emotionally damaged, though entirely normal, individual delinquent in need of help from a team of mental hygiene experts.

Notes

Abbreviations

AJO	*American Journal of Orthopsychiatry*
AJP	*American Journal of Psychiatry*
CSAA Records	Child Study Association of America Records, Social Welfare History Archives, University of Minnesota, Minneapolis
Dummer Papers	Ethel Sturges Dummer Papers, Schlesinger Library, Radcliffe College, Cambridge, Mass.
Gardner Collection	George Gardner Collection, Francis A. Countway Library of Medicine, Harvard Medical School, Boston
JBGC	Judge Baker Guidance Center
JBGC case no.	Judge Baker Guidance Center Records, Case Files, Special Collections and Rare Books, Francis A. Countway Library of Medicine, Harvard Medical School, Boston
LSRM Archives	Laura Spelman Rockefeller Memorial Archives, Rockefeller Archive Center, Sleepy Hollow, N.Y.
MH	*Mental Hygiene*
NASW Records	National Association of Social Workers Records, Social Welfare History Archives, University of Minnesota, Minneapolis

Introduction

1. Hyman S. Lippman, comments made to the American Orthopsychiatric Association Section Meeting, printed as part of "What Is Child Guidance?" *AJO* 11 (1941): 42.
2. "Child guiders" was not a label widely used during these years, but it appeared often enough that I have felt comfortable adopting it as a collective term for all the professionals who practiced in the clinics and popularized the ideas.

3. Benjamin Spock, *The Common Sense Book of Baby and Child Care* (New York: Duell, Sloan and Pearce, 1945, 1946), p. 332.

4. For specific studies of child guidance and the clinic movement, see Theresa Richardson, *The Century of the Child: The Mental Hygiene Movement and Social Policy in the United States and Canada* (Albany: State University of New York Press, 1989); Margo Horn, *Before It's Too Late: The Child Guidance Movement in the United States, 1922–1945* (Philadelphia: Temple University Press, 1989); and Pamela A. Holcomb, *The Pittsburgh Child Guidance Center, 1931–1981: Fifty Years of Leadership in Children's Mental Health Services* (Pittsburgh: Pittsburgh Child Guidance Center, 1985). Others who discuss the clinics include: Murray Levine and Adeline Levine, *Helping Children: A Social History* (New York: Oxford University Press, 1992); David J. Rothman, *Conscience and Convenience: The Asylum and Its Alternatives in Progressive America* (Boston: Little, Brown and Co., 1980); Linda Gordon, *Heroes of Their Own Lives: The Politics and History of Family Violence, Boston, 1880–1960* (New York: Viking Penguin, 1988); Peter C. Holloran, *Boston's Wayward Children: Social Services for Homeless Children, 1830–1930* (Rutherford, N.J.: Fairleigh Dickinson University Press, 1989); Joseph M. Hawes, *Children between the Wars: American Childhood, 1920–1940* (New York: Twayne Publishers, 1997); Hamilton Cravens, "Child-Saving in the Age of Professionalism, 1915–1930," in Joseph M. Hawes and N. Ray Hiner, eds., *American Childhood: A Research Guide and Historical Handbook* (Westport, Conn.: Greenwood Press, 1985), pp. 415–488; and Eric C. Schneider, *In the Web of Class: Delinquents and Reformers in Boston, 1810s–1930s* (New York: New York University Press, 1992), pp. 170–188.

5. See, for example, Milton J. E. Senn, *Insights on the Child Development Movement in the United States* (Monograph of the Society for Research in Child Development, vol. 40, nos. 3–4, 1975). Senn, a second-generation participant in child guidance, based his work on extensive oral histories conducted in the 1970s. Transcripts of these interviews can be found in the Milton J. E. Senn Collection of Transcripts and Tapes of Interviews on the American Child Guidance and Child Psychiatry Movement, History of Medicine Division, National Library of Medicine, Bethesda, Md.

6. On the discipline of child psychology, see Hamilton Cravens, *Before Head Start: The Iowa Station and America's Children* (Chapel Hill: University of North Carolina Press, 1993); Elizabeth M. R. Lomax, Jerome Kagan, and Barbara G. Rosenkrantz, *Science and Patterns of Child Care* (San Francisco: W. H. Freeman and Co., 1978), pp. 150–212; Christine Shea, "The Ideology of Mental Health and the Emergence of the Therapeutic Liberal State: The American Mental Hygiene Movement, 1900–1930" (Ph.D. diss., University of Illinois at Urbana-Champaign, 1980); Alice Boardman Smuts, "Science Discovers the Child,

1893–1935: A History of the Early Scientific Study of Children" (Ph.D. diss., University of Michigan, 1995); and Robert B. Cairns, "The Emergence of Developmental Psychology," in William Kessen, ed., *History, Theory, and Methods*, vol. 1, *Handbook of Child Psychology*, ed. Paul H. Mussen (New York: John Wiley and Sons, 1983), pp. 41–102.

7. Charles Rosenberg questioned the relationship between context and knowledge in "Toward an Ecology of Knowledge: On Discipline, Context, and History," in Alexandra Oleson and John Voss, eds., *The Organization of Knowledge in Modern America, 1860–1920* (Baltimore: Johns Hopkins University Press, 1979), pp. 440–455; see also Stephen Cross, "Designs for Living: Lawrence K. Frank and the Progressive Legacy in American Social Science" (Ph.D. diss., Johns Hopkins University, 1994), pp. 162–235.

8. Gerald N. Grob's two volumes on the twentieth-century history of American psychiatry and the mental asylum fit this mold. See *Mental Illness and American Society, 1875–1940* (Princeton: Princeton University Press, 1983); and *From Asylum to Community: Mental Health Policy in Modern America* (Princeton: Princeton University Press, 1991). Roy Lubove's study of social work is another: *The Professional Altruist: The Emergence of Social Work as a Career, 1880–1930* (New York: Atheneum, 1969). Influential critiques of twentieth-century uses of psychological interpretations of child behavior include Rothman, *Conscience and Convenience;* Christopher Lasch, *Haven in a Heartless World: The Family Besieged* (New York: Basic Books, 1977); and Barbara Ehrenreich and Deirdre English, *For Her Own Good: 150 Years of the Experts' Advice to Women* (Garden City, N.Y.: Doubleday, 1979).

9. Linda Gordon, *Heroes of Their Own Lives;* Michael B. Katz, *Poverty and Policy in American History* (New York: Academic Press, 1983); Molly Ladd-Taylor, *Raising a Baby the Government Way: Mothers' Letters to the Children's Bureau, 1915–1932* (New Brunswick: Rutgers University Press, 1986); and Mary E. Odem, *Delinquent Daughters: Protecting and Policing Adolescent Female Sexuality in the United States, 1885–1920* (Chapel Hill: University of North Carolina Press, 1995).

10. Roy Porter, "The Patient's View: Doing Medical History from Below," *Theory and Society* 14 (1985): 175.

11. JoAnne Brown, *The Definitions of a Profession: The Authority of Metaphor in the History of Intelligence Testing, 1890–1930* (Princeton: Princeton University Press, 1992); Elizabeth Lunbeck, *The Psychiatric Persuasion: Knowledge, Gender, and Power in Modern America* (Princeton: Princeton University Press, 1994).

12. Lunbeck, too, makes the institution central to her study; as does Sydney A. Halpern, in *American Pediatrics: The Social Dynamics of Professionalism, 1880–1980* (Berkeley: University of California Press, 1988), p. 19. See also Charles

Rosenberg, "Inward Vision and Outward Glance: The Shaping of the American Hospital, 1880–1914," *Bulletin of the History of Medicine* 53 (1979): 346–390.

13. The term "child science" belongs to Hamilton Cravens, who in his essay, "Child-Saving in the Age of Professionalism," equates it with professional child saving directed by pediatricians, psychologists, psychiatrists, and child development specialists.

14. On the development of adolescent medicine, see Heather Munro Prescott, *A Doctor of Their Own: The History of Adolescent Medicine* (Cambridge: Harvard University Press, 1998); and Bertram Slaff, "History of Child and Adolescent Psychiatry Ideas and Organizations in the United States: A Twentieth-Century View," *Adolescent Psychiatry* 16 (1989): 31–52.

15. See Lunbeck, *The Psychiatric Persuasion,* for the gender dichotomy in early twentieth-century psychiatry. The same phenomenon has been described in general medicine; see Susan Reverby, *Ordered to Care: The Dilemma of American Nursing, 1850–1945* (New York: Cambridge University Press, 1987); Barbara Melosh, *"The Physician's Hand": Work Culture and Conflict in American Nursing* (Philadelphia: Temple University Press, 1982); and Charlotte G. Borst, *Catching Babies: The Professionalization of Childbirth, 1870–1920* (Cambridge: Harvard University Press, 1995).

16. Philip Wylie, *Generation of Vipers* (New York: Farrar and Rinehart, 1942), p. 185.

17. On the Philadelphia clinic, see Horn, *Before It's Too Late.* On the St. Louis clinic, see Mildred Marie Bardelmeyer, "History of the Psychiatric-Child Guidance Clinic of St. Louis, Missouri, 1922–1940" (M.S.W. diss., Washington University, 1943). On race in the Richmond clinic, see Carolyn Worthington, "The Negro Children Referred to the Richmond Child Guidance Clinic in 1934" (M.S. thesis, College of William and Mary, 1936).

18. The Judge Baker Guidance Center (JBGC) case records are housed in Special Collections and Rare Books at the Francis A. Countway Library of Medicine, Harvard Medical School, Boston. All references to case material refer to the Judge Baker collection. Total cases, 1065; 595 were from 1920 and 345 from 1935, representing all cases opened during the given year. For the epilogue I selected a smaller sample of 125 files pulled from what seemed to be a midpoint in the last year (1945–46) of available records. By that time the clinic was so busy that families seeking help often had a long wait between the initial interview and a formal assessment. Intake date, therefore, was no longer a reliable guide to the timing of a patient's therapy.

19. The story of Janet Landis can be found in JBGC case no. 2086. When quoting from the reports in the files I have retained the original abbreviations unless to do so would make the meaning unclear. "M." and "F." always refer to mother and father, a relationship with the child, not an individual's name.

1. Constructing the Troublesome Child

1. Ellen Key, *The Century of the Child* (New York: G. P. Putnam's Sons, 1909).
2. On childhood in America, see Bernard Wishy, *The Child and the Republic: The Dawn of Modern American Child Nurture* (Philadelphia: University of Pennsylvania Press, 1968); Richard Meckel, *Save the Babies: American Public Health and the Prevention of Infant Mortality, 1850–1929* (Baltimore: Johns Hopkins University Press, 1990); Karin Calvert, *Children in the House: The Material Culture of Early Childhood, 1600–1900* (Boston: Northeastern University Press, 1992); Harvey Graff, *Conflicting Paths: Growing Up in America* (Cambridge: Harvard University Press, 1995); and Patricia Ferguson Clement, *Growing Pains: Children in the Industrial Age, 1850–1890* (New York: Twayne Publishers, 1997). Ann Douglas, *The Feminization of Culture* (New York: Alfred A. Knopf, 1977), discusses Little Eva; on the "bad boy" subgenre of nineteenth-century novels, see Glenna Matthews, *"Just a Housewife": The Rise and Fall of Domesticity in America* (New York: Oxford University Press, 1987), pp. 81–85. I discuss G. Stanley Hall and child study in Chapter 2.
3. I use the term "feebleminded" in this study because it was the turn-of-the-century designation for people thought to display signs of mental incapacity. The term "mental retardation" did not become common until the 1950s.
4. Benjamin Rush, *Medical Inquiries and Observations upon the Diseases of the Mind* (1812; reprint, New York: Hafner Publishing Co., 1962), p. 57. Discussions of Rush's stature in early nineteenth-century psychiatric medicine can be found in Norman Dain, *Concepts of Insanity in the United States, 1789–1865* (New Brunswick: Rutgers University Press, 1964), pp. 14–24; and Carl Binger, *Revolutionary Doctor: Benjamin Rush, 1746–1813* (New York: W. W. Norton, 1966), pp. 248–280.
5. Gerald N. Grob, *Mental Institutions in America: Social Policy to 1875* (New York: Free Press, 1973); David Rothman, *The Discovery of the Asylum; Social Order and Disorder in the New Republic* (Boston: Little, Brown and Co., 1971).
6. S. V. Clevenger, "Insanity in Children," *American Journal of Neurology and Psychiatry* 2 (1883): 585–601.
7. Barbara G. Rosenkrantz and Maris A. Vinovskis, "Caring for the Insane in Antebellum Massachusetts: Family, Community, and State Participation," in Allan J. Lichtman and Joan R. Challinor, eds., *Kin and Communities: Families in America* (Washington, D.C.: Smithsonian Institution Press, 1979), pp. 187–218; Nancy Tomes, *A Generous Confidence: Thomas Story Kirkbride and the Art of Asylum-keeping, 1840–1883* (Cambridge: Cambridge University Press, 1984); Ellen Dwyer, *Homes for the Mad: Life inside Two Nineteenth-Century Asylums* (New Brunswick: Rutgers University Press, 1987).

8. Eli A. Rubinstein, "Childhood Mental Disease in America: A Review of the Literature before 1900," *AJO* 18 (1948): 314–321.

9. Joan Jacobs Brumberg, *Fasting Girls: The Emergence of Anorexia Nervosa as a Modern Disease* (Cambridge: Harvard University Press, 1988), pp. 105–110.

10. On nineteenth-century neurology, see Eric M. Caplan, "Medicalizing the Mind: the Invention of American Psychotherapy, 1800–1920" (Ph.D diss., University of Michigan, 1994); and Bonnie Ellen Blustein, "'A Hollow Square of Psychological Science': American Neurologists and Psychiatrists in Conflict," in Andrew Scull, ed., *Madhouses, Mad-Doctors, and Madmen* (Philadelphia: University of Pennsylvania Press, 1981), pp. 241–265. For a discussion of ideas about children in the mental health literature, see Barbara Sicherman, "The Quest for Mental Health in America, 1880–1917" (Ph.D. diss., Columbia University, 1967), pp. 101–123.

11. Clement, *Growing Pains,* pp. 36–80, provides a brief survey of child-rearing advice. See also Philip J. Greven, Jr., ed., *Childrearing Concepts, 1628–1861* (Itasca, Ill.: F. E. Peacock Publishers, 1973); Mary Ryan, *Empire of the Mother: American Writing about Domesticity, 1830–1860* (New York: Harrington Park Press, 1985); and Anne L. Kuhn, *The Mother's Role in Childhood Education: New England Concepts, 1830–1860* (New Haven: Yale University Press, 1947).

12. Noted in Ruth B. Caplan, *Psychiatry and Community in Nineteenth-Century America: The Recurring Concern with the Environment in the Prevention and Treatment of Mental Illness* (New York: Basic Books, 1969), pp. 12–17.

13. This discussion draws heavily on R. P. Neuman, "Masturbation, Madness, and the Modern Concepts of Childhood and Adolescence," *Journal of Social History* 8 (1975): 1–27. Material quoted from pp. 10–11. See also Charles Rosenberg, "Sexuality, Class, and Role in 19th Century America," *American Quarterly* 25 (1973): 131–153; E. H. Hare, "Masturbatory Insanity: The History of an Idea," *Journal of Mental Science* 108 (1962): 1–26; H. Tristram Engelhardt, Jr., "The Disease of Masturbation: Values and the Concept of Disease," *Bulletin of the History of Medicine* 48 (1974): 234–248; Joseph Kett, *Rites of Passage: Adolescence in America, 1790 to the Present* (New York: Basic Books, 1977), pp. 133–135; and Jayme A. Sokolow, *Eros and Modernization: Sylvester Graham, Health Reform, and the Origins of Victorian Sexuality in America* (Cranbury, N.J.: Associated University Press, 1983), pp. 77–99. For a concise summary by a contemporary neurologist, see Edward C. Spitzka, "Insanity," in John M. Keating, ed., *Cyclopaedia of the Diseases of Children, Medical and Surgical* (Philadelphia: J. B. Lippincott Co., 1891), pp. 1038–1053.

14. Engelhardt, "The Disease of Masturbation," describes treatments and cures.

15. Joseph F. Kett, "Curing the Disease of Precocity," in John Demos and Sarane Spence Boocock, eds., *Turning Points: Historical and Sociological Essays on the Family* (Chicago: University of Chicago Press, 1978), pp. 183–211. See also

Kett, *Rites of Passage*, pp. 135–143; and Sicherman, "The Quest for Mental Health in America," pp. 111–123.

16. Richard C. Rapson, "American Children as Seen by British Travellers, 1845–1935," *American Quarterly* 17 (1965): 520–534.

17. Isaac Ray, "The Proper Time for Going to School," *Common School Journal* 13 (1851): 271.

18. "Reports on American Asylums," *American Journal of Insanity* 14 (1857–58): 378.

19. George Cook, "Mental Hygiene," *American Journal of Insanity* 15 (1858–59): 275, 277.

20. See Kett, *Rites of Passage*, pp. 137–143, for a discussion of precocity and changes in nineteenth-century sex roles. "In boyhood or girlhood," the physician Charles Folsom wrote in 1881, "comes first the dangers of confinement in the bad air of school rooms, and then the hurry and worry and strain of six, seven, or eight branches of study . . . and, after a few years, the break-down with which so many of us are already too familiar." Quoted in Kett, "Curing the Disease of Precocity," p. 185.

21. A. O. Kellogg, "Considerations on the Reciprocal Influence of the Physical Organization and Mental Manifestations," *American Journal of Insanity* 11 (1854–55): 217–224.

22. Edward H. Clarke, *Sex in Education: or, A Fair Chance for the Girls* (Boston: J. R. Osgood and Co., 1873).

23. On hysteria and neurasthenia, see Carroll Smith-Rosenberg, "The Hysterical Woman: Sex Roles and Role Conflict in 19th-Century America," *Social Research* 39 (1972): 652–678; and Barbara Sicherman, "The Use of Diagnosis: Doctors, Patients, and Neurasthenia," *Journal of the History of Medicine and Allied Sciences* 32 (1977): 33–54. Also useful is Caplan, "Medicalizing the Mind," pp. 169–247. For a discussion of hysteria as a male condition, see Mark Micale, "Charcot and the Idea of Hysteria in the Male: Gender, Mental Science, and Medical Diagnostics in Late Nineteenth-Century France," *Medical History* 34 (1990): 363–411.

24. Charles K. Mills, "Hysteria," in Keating, ed., *Cyclopaedia of the Diseases of Children*, p. 958.

25. Ibid., p. 962.

26. Stuart M. Blumin, *The Emergence of the Middle Class: Social Experience in the American City, 1760–1900* (New York: Cambridge University Press, 1989), examines these values.

27. Edward C. Spitzka, *Insanity: Its Classification, Diagnosis, and Treatment* (1887; reprint, New York: Arno Press, 1973), p. 379.

28. Bernard Sachs, *A Treatise on the Nervous Diseases of Children, for Physicians and Students* (New York: William Wood and Co., 1895), pp. iii, 86–87.

29. Ibid., pp. 104–105.
30. David A. Stumpf, "Bernard Sachs," in Stephen Ashwal, ed., *The Founders of Child Neurology* (San Francisco: Norman Publishing, 1990), pp. 563–577.
31. L. Emmett Holt, *The Diseases of Infancy and Childhood* (New York: D. Appleton and Co., 1897), p. 31.
32. In addition to Richard Meckel's study, *Save the Babies*, other useful histories of pediatrics include Sydney A. Halpern, *American Pediatrics: The Social Dynamics of Professionalism, 1880–1980* (Berkeley: University of California Press, 1988); and Thomas E. Cone, Jr., *History of American Pediatrics* (Boston: Little, Brown and Co., 1979).
33. For a more detailed discussion of Holt and his role in the development of pediatrics, see my article, "Sentiment and Science: The Late Nineteenth-Century Pediatrician as Mother's Advisor," *Journal of Social History* 17 (1983): 79–96. On the subject of infant feeding, see Meckel, *Save the Babies*, pp. 40–91; Rima D. Apple, *Mothers and Medicine: A Social History of Infant Feeding, 1890–1950* (Madison: University of Wisconsin Press, 1987); and Manfred J. Waserman, "Henry L. Coit and the Certified Milk Movement in the Development of Modern Pediatrics," *Bulletin of the History of Medicine* 46 (1972): 359–390.
34. Informed or "scientific" motherhood is discussed in Chapter 4. On maternal attitudes to infant illness and death, see Nancy Schrom Dye and Daniel Blake Smith, "Mother Love and Infant Death, 1750–1920," *Journal of American History* 73 (1986): 329–353.
35. Holt, *The Diseases of Infancy and Childhood*, pp. 696–697, 757.
36. Ibid., pp. 652, 653, 685.
37. Ibid., p. 688.
38. Ibid.
39. Ibid., pp. 755–757.
40. Useful accounts include James W. Trent, Jr., *Inventing the Feeble Mind: A History of Mental Retardation in the United States* (Berkeley: University of California Press, 1994); and Peter L. Tyor and Leland V. Bell, *Caring for the Retarded in America: A History* (Westport, Conn.: Greenwood Press, 1984). On hereditarian thought, see Charles E. Rosenberg, "The Bitter Fruit: Heredity, Disease, and Social Thought," in Rosenberg, *No Other Gods: On Science and Social Thought* (Baltimore: Johns Hopkins University Press, 1976), pp. 25–53; Mark H. Haller, *Eugenics: Hereditarian Attitudes in American Thought* (New Brunswick: Rutgers University Press, 1963); and Daniel J. Kevles, *In the Name of Eugenics: Genetics and the Uses of Human Heredity* (Berkeley: University of California Press, 1985).
41. Kerlin's ideas are discussed in Trent, *Inventing the Feeble Mind*, pp. 86–88; and Tyor and Bell, *Caring for the Retarded*, pp. 80–84.
42. Isaac Kerlin, "Juvenile Insanity," *Transactions of the Medical Society of the State of Pennsylvania* 12 (1879): 611–620.

43. John M. O'Donnell, "The Clinical Psychology of Lightner Witmer: A Case Study of Institutional Innovations and Intellectual Change," *Journal of the History of the Behavioral Sciences* 15 (1979): 3–17.

44. On academic psychology, see John M. O'Donnell, *The Origins of Behaviorism: American Psychology, 1870–1920* (New York: New York University Press, 1985); and Donald S. Napoli, *Architects of Adjustment: The History of the Psychological Profession in the United States* (Port Washington, N.Y.: Kennikat Press, 1981).

45. Jacob A. Riis, *The Children of the Poor* (New York: Scribner's Sons, 1892); and Riis, *How the Other Half Lives; Studies among the Tenements of New York* (New York: Scribner's Sons, 1890).

46. The term child saving was in wide use in the 1890s; see, for example, the National Conference of Charities and Correction, *History of Child Saving in the United States: Report of the Committee on the History of Child-Saving Work to the Twentieth Conference, Chicago, June, 1893* (reprint, Anthony Platt, ed. [Montclair, N.J.: Patterson Smith, 1971]). For an understanding of nineteenth-century child welfare reformers, see Paul S. Boyer, *Urban Masses and Moral Order in America, 1820–1920* (Cambridge: Harvard University Press, 1978); Peter C. Holloran, *Boston's Wayward Children: Social Services for Homeless Children, 1830–1930* (London: Fairleigh Dickinson University Press, 1989); Joan Gittens, *Poor Relations: The Children of the State of Illinois, 1818–1990* (Urbana: University of Illinois Press, 1994); Linda Gordon, *Heroes of Their Own Lives: The Politics and History of Family Violence, Boston, 1880–1960* (New York: Viking Penguin, 1988); and Joseph M. Hawes, *The Children's Rights Movement: A History of Advocacy and Protection* (Boston: Twayne Publishers, 1991).

47. Studies of nineteenth-century juvenile delinquency and the institutions established to control this behavior include: Joseph M. Hawes, *Children in Urban Society: Juvenile Delinquency in Nineteenth-Century America* (New York: Oxford University Press, 1971); Robert M. Mennel, *Thorns and Thistles: Juvenile Delinquents in the United States, 1825–1940* (Hanover: University Press of New England, 1973); Steven Schlossman, *Love and the American Delinquent: The Theory and Practice of "Progressive" Juvenile Justice, 1825–1940* (Chicago: University of Chicago Press, 1977); Anthony M. Platt, *The Child Savers: The Invention of Delinquency,* 2d ed., enl. (Chicago: University of Chicago Press, 1977); Barbara Brenzel, *Daughters of the State: A Social Portrait of the First Reform School for Girls in North America, 1856–1905* (Cambridge: MIT Press, 1983); and Eric C. Schneider, *In the Web of Class: Delinquents and Reformers in Boston, 1810s–1930s* (New York: New York University Press, 1992).

48. Schneider, *In the Web of Class,* pp. 15–50.

49. Schneider, *In the Web of Class; Boyer, Urban Life and Moral Order;* and Gordon, *Heroes of Their Own Lives* discuss the Children's Aid Society and the Society for the Prevention of Cruelty to Children.

50. On women in the settlement houses and the Progressive movement, see Allan

F. Davis, *American Heroine: The Life and Legend of Jane Addams* (New York: Oxford University Press, 1973); Robyn Muncy, *Creating a Female Dominion in American Reform, 1890–1935* (New York: Oxford University Press, 1991); and Linda Gordon, *Pitied but Not Entitled: Single Mothers and the History of Welfare, 1890–1935* (New York: Free Press, 1994).

51. These reformers have been called "maternalists" by some historians; in Chapter 2, I discuss this term and the specific work of the Chicago maternalists.

52. Jane Addams, *Twenty Years at Hull House* (1910; reprint, New York: Macmillan Co., 1961), p. 181.

53. On Boston, see Schneider, *In the Web of Class*, p. 149; on Denver, D'Ann Campbell, "Judge Ben Lindsey and the Juvenile Court Movement, 1901–1904," in N. Ray Hiner and Joseph M. Hawes, eds., *Growing Up in America: Children in Historical Perspective* (Urbana: University of Illinois Press, 1985), pp. 149–160.

54. Secondary accounts are in Platt, *The Child Savers*, pp. 74–136; and Gittens, *Poor Relations*, pp. 105–120. Timothy D. Hurley, *Origins of the Illinois Juvenile Court Law* (1907; reprint, New York: AMS Press, 1977), is a contemporary perspective.

55. Quoted in Hurley, *Origins of the Illinois Juvenile Court Law*, pp. 119–120.

56. Gittens, *Poor Relations*, p. 109.

57. James Bennett, *Oral History and Delinquency: The Rhetoric of Criminology* (Chicago: University of Chicago Press, 1981), pp. 104–111.

58. Holloran, *Boston's Wayward Children*, pp. 207, 213; Addams, *Twenty Years at Hull House*, p. 181.

59. Schneider, *In the Web of Class*, p. 148.

60. A good contemporary assessment can be found in Bernard Flexner, "The Juvenile Court as a Social Institution," *Survey* 23 (February 5, 1910): 607–638. See also Ellen Ryerson, *The Best-Laid Plans: America's Juvenile Court Experiment* (New York: Hill and Wang, 1978).

61. The description "priceless" is borrowed from Viviana Zelizer, in *Pricing the Priceless Child: The Changing Social Value of Childhood* (New York: Basic Books, 1980). Zelizer uses the adjective to describe the willingness of families to devote monetary resources to children, rather than see children as producers of resources through early entry into the work force.

62. Joseph M. Hawes, in *Children in Urban Society*, pp. 3–9, tells the story of Jesse Pomeroy.

2. William Healy and the Progressive Child Savers

1. "Child Study Its Soul; Juvenile Psychopathic Institute Founded by Leading Sociologists," Chicago *Record Herald*, 20 April 1909. A copy is located in the Ethel Sturges Dummer Papers, Schlesinger Library, Radcliffe College, Cam-

bridge, Mass. On Progressivism and the social sciences, see Stephen J. Cross, "Designs for Living: Lawrence K. Frank and the Progressive Legacy in American Social Science" (Ph.D. diss., Johns Hopkins University, 1994), pp. 90–225; Ellen Fitzpatrick, *Endless Crusade: Women Social Scientists and Progressive Reform* (New York: Oxford University Press, 1990); and Rosalind Rosenberg, *Beyond Separate Spheres: The Intellectual Roots of Modern Feminism* (New Haven: Yale University Press, 1982).

2. The term child saving was in wide use in the 1890s; see for example, the National Conference of Charities and Correction, *History of Child Saving in the United States: Report of the Committee on the History of Child-Saving Work to the Twentieth Conference, Chicago, June, 1893* (reprint, Anthony Platt, ed. [Montclair, N.J.: Patterson Smith, 1971]). Among historians, the term assumed its negative connotation after the publication of Anthony M. Platt's *The Child Savers: The Invention of Delinquency* (Chicago: University of Chicago Press, 1969). Similar interpretations can be found in Susan Tiffin, *In Whose Best Interest?: Child Welfare Reform in the Progressive Era* (Westport, Conn.: Greenwood Press, 1982), and the "social control" interpreters of Progressivism, including David M. Rothman, *Conscience and Convenience: The Asylum and Its Alternatives in Progressive America* (Boston: Little, Brown and Co., 1980). See also Eric C. Schneider, *In the Web of Class: Delinquents and Reformers in Boston, 1810s–1930s* (New York: New York University Press, 1992).

3. Seth Koven and Sonya Michel, "Introduction: 'Mother Worlds,' " in *Mothers of a New World: Maternalist Politics and the Origins of Welfare States* (New York: Routledge, 1993), p. 2; Robyn Muncy, *Creating a Female Dominion in American Reform: 1890–1935* (New York: Oxford University Press, 1991), pp. xii–xiv (emphasis in original). See also Molly Ladd-Taylor, *Mother-Work: Women, Child Welfare, and the State, 1890–1930* (Urbana: University of Illinois Press, 1994); and Theda Skocpol, *Protecting Soldiers and Mothers: The Political Origins of Social Policy in the United States* (Cambridge: Belknap Press of Harvard University Press, 1992).

4. Hamilton Cravens lays out the Progressive/professional dichotomy in "Child-Saving in the Age of Professionalism, 1915–1930," in Joseph M. Hawes and N. Ray Hiner, eds., *American Childhood: A Research Guide and Historical Handbook* (Westport, Conn.: Greenwood Press, 1985), pp. 415–488. On the relationship between Progressivism and professionalism, see in addition to Cross, "Designs for Living," John Burnham, "Psychiatry, Psychology, and the Progressive Movement," *American Quarterly* 12 (1960): 457–463; Richard Meckel, *Save the Babies: American Public Health Reform and the Prevention of Infant Mortality, 1850–1929* (Baltimore: Johns Hopkins University Press, 1990); Mary Jo Deegan, *Jane Addams and the Men of the Chicago School, 1892–1918* (New Brunswick, N.J.: Transaction Books, 1988); Mary O. Furner, *Advocacy and*

Objectivity: A Crisis in the Professionalization of American Social Science, 1865–1905 (Lexington: University of Kentucky Press, 1984); Victoria L. Getis, "A Disciplined Society: The Juvenile Court, Reform, and the Social Sciences in Chicago, 1890–1930" (Ph.D. diss., University of Michigan, 1994); and Christine Shea, "The Ideology of Mental Health and the Emergence of the Therapeutic Liberal State" (Ph.D. diss., University of Illinois at Urbana-Champaign, 1980). Molly Ladd-Taylor, in *Mother-Work,* points out the irony of professionalization for the female reformers. Elizabeth Lunbeck, in *The Psychiatric Persuasion: Knowledge, Gender, and Power in Modern America* (Princeton: Princeton University Press, 1994), pp. 25–45, charges that this professional domain was also a masculine one.

5. After passage of the Illinois juvenile court act, the women of the Chicago Juvenile Court Committee reconstituted the group as the Juvenile Protective Association. The group carried out investigations of the environmental factors influencing delinquency and conducted child labor surveys. Robert M. Mennel, *Thorns and Thistles: Juvenile Delinquents in the United States, 1825–1940* (Hanover, N.H.: University Press of New England, 1973), p. 149.

6. On Ethel Sturges Dummer, see Robert M. Mennel, "Ethel Sturges Dummer," in Barbara Sicherman and Carol Hurd Green, eds., *Notable American Women: The Modern Period* (Cambridge: Belknap Press of Harvard University Press, 1980), pp. 207–210. Dummer tells her own story in "Life in Relation to Time," in Lawson Lowrey and Victoria Sloane, eds., *Orthopsychiatry, 1923–1948: Retrospect and Prospect* (New York: American Orthopsychiatric Association, 1948), pp. 3–13, quote p. 9. See also Dummer's autobiography, *Why I Think So: The Autobiography of a Hypothesis* (Chicago: Clarke-McElroy Publishing Co., 1937).

7. The recidivism statistics, collected by the Research Department of the Chicago School of Civics and Philanthropy, were cited by Henry W. Thurston in "Ten Years of the Juvenile Court of Chicago," *The Survey* 23 (February 5, 1910): 658.

Reports of the organizing activities of the research committee can be found in the Dummer Papers, Box 30. The correspondence in the Dummer Papers gives a far better account of the founding of the Juvenile Psychopathic Institute than do the recollections of William Healy in a 1960 interview with John Burnham. See "Oral History Interviews with William Healy and Augusta Bronner" (1960, 1961), transcript, Houghton Library, Harvard University. Healy's account of his role in the planning stages of the JPI can also be found in Healy and Augusta F. Bronner, "The Child Guidance Clinic: Birth and Growth of an Idea," in Lowrey and Sloane, eds., *Orthopsychiatry, 1923–1948*, pp. 14–16. See also Alice Boardman Smuts, "Science Discovers the Child, 1893–1935: A History of the Early Scientific Study of Children" (Ph.D. diss., University of Michigan, 1995), pp. 136–140.

8. Progressive era child-centered programs for urban youths are described in

Tiffin, *In Whose Best Interest?;* Joan Gittens, *Poor Relations: The Children of the State in Illinois, 1818–1990* (Urbana: University of Illinois Press, 1994); and Leroy Ashby, *Saving the Waifs: Reformers and Dependent Children, 1890–1917* (Philadelphia: Temple University Press, 1984). For the Hull House view see Jane Addams, *The Spirit of Youth and the City Streets* (1909; reprint, Urbana: University of Illinois Press, 1972).

9. Dummer, "Life in Relation to Time," p. 9.

10. "Constitutional inferiority" was a synonym for psychopathy, and the term often implied some physical abnormality as well as abnormal mental traits. See William Healy's definition in *The Individual Delinquent: A Text-Book of Diagnosis and Prognosis for All Concerned in Understanding Offenders* (Boston: Little, Brown and Co., 1915), pp. 575–576. Elizabeth Lunbeck discusses the various meanings of the term in *The Psychiatric Persuasion,* pp. 342–343, n. 74. See also her article " 'A New Generation of Women': Progressive Psychiatrists and the Hypersexual Female," *Feminist Studies* 13 (1987): 513–543.

11. Form letter signed by Ethel Dummer, 2 January 1909, Dummer Papers.

12. George Mead to Harry Linenthal, 28 January 1909, Dummer Papers. On early twentieth-century pediatrics, see Smuts, "Science Discovers the Child"; Meckel, *Saving the Babies;* and Sydney Halpern, *American Pediatrics: The Social Dynamics of Professionalism, 1880–1980* (Berkeley: University of California Press, 1988). On child development, see Hamilton Cravens, *Before Head Start: The Iowa Station and America's Children* (Chapel Hill: University of North Carolina Press, 1993). On the child study movement, see Amy Green, "Savage Childhood: The Scientific Construction of Girlhood and Boyhood in the Progressive Era" (Ph.D. diss., Yale University, 1995); and Leila Zenderland, "Education, Evangelism, and the Origins of Clinical Psychology: The Child-Study Legacy," *Journal of the History of the Behavioral Sciences* 24 (1988): 152–165. A contemporary account: Sara E. Wiltse, "A Preliminary Sketch of the History of Child Study in America," *Pedagogical Seminary* 3 (1895): 189–212.

13. Healy biographies include Grant Hulse Wagner, "William Healy, M.D., Father of the American Child Guidance Movement" (M.A. thesis, University of Maryland, 1981); and Jon Snodgrass, "William Healy (1869–1963): Pioneer Child Psychiatrist and Criminologist," *Journal of the History of the Behavioral Sciences* 20 (1984): 331–339. See also Healy's personal recollections in Burnham, "Oral History Interviews with William Healy and Augusta Bronner." On medical study in Europe, see Thomas Neville Bonner, *American Doctors and German Universities: A Chapter in International Intellectual Relations, 1870–1914* (Lincoln: University of Nebraska Press, 1963).

14. William Healy to Julia Lathrop, 4 April 1908, Dummer Papers.

15. "Child Study Its Soul," *Chicago Record Herald,* 20 April 1909. Clipping in Dummer Papers.

16. On the Progressives' support for applied research, see Getis "A Disciplined Society," pp. 1–50.
17. Healy, *The Individual Delinquent*, p. 4.
18. Edith R. Spaulding and William Healy, "Inheritance as a Factor in Criminality," *Bulletin of the American Academy of Medicine* 15 (1914): 27. For a more qualified statement, see Healy, *The Individual Delinquent*, p. 188. On eugenics, see Daniel J. Kevles, *In the Name of Eugenics: Genetics and the Uses of Human Heredity* (Berkeley: University of California Press, 1985); and Diane B. Paul, *Controlling Human Heredity, 1865 to the Present* (Atlantic Highlands, N.J.: Humanities Press, 1995).
19. Healy, *The Individual Delinquent*, p. 447. Goddard's views were also closely tied to the eugenics movement. See Leila Zenderland, *Measuring Minds: Henry Herbert Goddard and the Origins of American Intelligence Testing* (New York: Cambridge University Press, 1997).
20. Healy, *The Individual Delinquent*, p. 23.
21. Ibid., p. 183.
22. Ibid., p. 218.
23. "We show clearly, and others have shown, that in the majority of cases offenders are bred under bad home conditions," Healy wrote in *The Individual Delinquent*, p. 282. Other contemporary studies emphasizing environmental factors include: Edith Abbott and Sophonisba P. Breckinridge, *The Delinquent Child and the Home* (New York: Charities Publication Committee, Russell Sage Foundation, 1912); Thomas Travis, *The Young Malefactor: A Study in Juvenile Delinquency, Its Causes and Treatments* (New York: Thomas Y. Crowell and Co., 1908); and Hannah Kent Schoff, *The Wayward Child: A Study of the Causes of Crime* (Indianapolis: Bobbs-Merrill Co., 1915). Schoff was president of the National Congress of Mothers (PTA) and of the probation association affiliated with the Philadelphia Juvenile Court. On her interest in juvenile delinquency, see Elizabeth J. Clapp, "Welfare and the Role of Women: The Juvenile Court Movement," *Journal of American Studies* 28 (1994): 378–379.
24. Healy, *The Individual Delinquent*, pp. 282–315, quote p. 291.
25. See Lela B. Costin, *Two Sisters for Social Justice: A Biography of Grace and Edith Abbott* (Urbana: University of Illinois Press, 1983); and Muncy, *Creating a Female Dominion in American Reform*, pp. 66–91, for discussions of these women in the context of Progressive social reform. Neither book, however, specifically examines *The Delinquent Child and the Home*.
26. Abbott and Breckinridge, *The Delinquent Child and the Home*, pp. 6, 7, 10, 160.
27. Ibid., pp. 5, 10.
28. On the mothers' pensions movement, see Joanne L. Goodwin, "A Experiment in Paid Motherhood: The Implementation of Mothers' Pensions in Early Twentieth Century Chicago," *Gender and History* 4 (1992): 323–342; Ladd-Taylor,

Mother-Work, pp. 135–166; and Skocpol, *Protecting Soldiers and Mothers,* pp. 424–479.

29. William Healy, "Factors Other than Legal in Dealing with Criminal Cases," *Proceedings of the 39th National Conference of Charities and Corrections,* 1912, p. 188.

30. Healy, *The Individual Delinquent,* p. 22.

31. Ibid., p. 3, n. 1.

32. Ibid., pp. 3, 10–12.

33. Allan Brandt's study of social hygiene, *No Magic Bullet: A Social History of Venereal Disease in the United States since 1880* (New York: Oxford University Press, 1985), is another example of this phenomenon. See also John C. Burnham, "Medical Specialists and Movements toward Social Control in the Progressive Era: Three Examples," in Jerry Israel, ed., *Building the Organizational Society: Essays on Associational Activities in Modern America* (New York: Free Press, 1972), pp. 19–30.

34. G. Stanley Hall, "The Contents of Children's Minds upon Entering School," *Princeton Review* 2 (1883): 249–272. On Hall, see Dorothy Ross, *G. Stanley Hall: The Psychologist as Prophet* (Chicago: University of Chicago Press, 1972); Smuts, "Science Discovers the Child," pp. 45–87; and Green, "Savage Childhood," pp. 45–74.

35. Smuts, "Science Discovers the Child," p. 50. *The Biography of a Baby* (1900), the published version of Millicent Shinn's master's thesis from the University of California at Los Angeles, was probably the best-known popular account.

36. See Green, "Savage Childhood"; Roberta Wollons, "Educating Mothers: Sidonie Matsner Gruenberg and the Child Study Association of America, 1881–1929" (Ph.D. diss., University of Chicago, 1983); and Gail Bederman, *Manliness and Civilization: A Cultural History of Gender and Race in the United States, 1890–1917* (Chicago: University of Chicago Press, 1995), pp. 77–120.

37. The history of this dynamic new, "extra-mural" (Pols), "Progressive" (Lunbeck) psychiatry is related in Barbara Sicherman, "The Quest for Mental Health in America, 1880–1917" (Ph.D. diss., Columbia University, 1969); Gerald N. Grob, *Mental Illness and American Society, 1875–1940* (Princeton: Princeton University Press, 1983); Elizabeth Lunbeck, *The Psychiatric Persuasion;* and Johannes C. Pols, "Managing the Mind: The Culture of American Mental Hygiene, 1910–1950" (Ph.D. diss., University of Pennsylvania, 1997). On Meyer as a "major" contributor to child guidance, see Ethel Kawin, "The Contribution of Adolf Meyer and Psychobiology to Child Guidance," *MH* 29 (1945): 575–590.

38. On the psychobiology of Adolf Meyer, see Meyer, "The Role of the Mental Factors in Psychiatry," *American Journal of Insanity* 65 (1908): 39–56; and Alfred Lief, ed., *The Commonsense Psychiatry of Dr. Adolf Meyer: Fifty-Two Sel-*

ected Papers (New York: McGraw-Hill, 1948). See also Sicherman, "The Quest for Mental Health," pp. 208–222; David Tanner, "Symbols of Conduct: Psychiatry and American Culture, 1900–1935" (Ph.D. diss., University of Texas at Austin, 1981), pp. 81–160; and Grob, *Mental Illness and American Society,* pp. 112–118.

39. Adolf Meyer, "Modern Psychiatry: Its Possibilities and Responsibilities," in Lief, ed., *The Commonsense Psychiatry,* p. 293.

40. See Lunbeck, *The Psychiatric Persuasion.* On the origins of psychopathic hospitals, see Grob, *Mental Illness and American Society,* pp. 135–142; and Richard Wightman Fox, *So Far Disordered in Mind: Insanity in California, 1870–1930* (Berkeley: University of California Press, 1978), pp. 40–52. According to Grob, the two most important institutions were the Boston Psychopathic Hospital and the Phipps Psychiatric Clinic at Johns Hopkins Hospital.

41. Reports of children seen at these institutions can be found in James V. May, "The Functions of the Psychopathic Hospital," *American Journal of Insanity* 76 (1919–20): 28–29; C. Macfie Campbell, "The Role of the Psychiatric Dispensary: A Review of the First Year's Work of the Dispensary of the Phipps Psychiatric Clinic," *American Journal of Insanity* 71 (1915): 447–454; and Douglas Thom, "The Out-patient Department," in L. Vernon Briggs. ed., *History of the Psychopathic Hospital, Boston, Massachusetts* (Boston: Wright and Potter Printing Co., 1922), p. 158.

42. William A. White, "Childhood: The Golden Period for Mental Hygiene," *MH* 4 (1920): 259; 267. On the National Committee for Mental Hygiene, see Pols, "Managing the Mind," pp. 117–206; and Sicherman, "The Quest for Mental Health," pp. 281–410. See also Norman Dain, *Clifford Beers, Advocate for the Insane* (Pittsburgh: University of Pittsburgh Press, 1983). Healy was not a member of the organizing group, although, once in Boston, Healy participated in the activities of the Massachusetts Society for Mental Hygiene.

43. James Jackson Putnam, "Review of *The Individual Delinquent,*" *Psychoanalytic Review* 2 (1915): 470. On the transmission of Freudian ideas to the American psychiatric community before World War I, see John Chynoweth Burnham, *Psychoanalysis and American Medicine, 1894–1918: Medicine, Society, and Culture* (New York: International Universities Press, 1967); Nathan Hale, *Freud and the Americans: The Beginnings of Psychoanalysis in the United States, 1876–1917* (New York: Oxford University Press, 1971); and Fred Matthews, "The Americanization of Sigmund Freud: Adaptations of Psychoanalysis before 1917," *Journal of American Studies* 1 (1967): 39–62.

44. The standard reference on Freud's visit is Saul Rosenzweig, *Freud, Jung, and Hall the King-Maker: The Historic Expedition to America (1909)* (St. Louis: Rana House Press, 1992).

45. Healy, *The Individual Delinquent,* pp. 115, 119–120; William Healy, *Mental Conflicts and Misconduct* (Boston: Little, Brown and Co., 1917), pp. 11–12.

46. Healy, Mental Conflicts and Misconduct, pp. 13–14. See also the chapter on mental conflicts and repressions in Healy, *The Individual Delinquent,* pp. 352–399.

47. Healy, *Mental Conflicts and Misconduct,* p. 3.

48. Ibid., p. 29. See also Healy's chapter on mental conflicts and repressions in *The Individual Delinquent,* pp. 352–399.

49. William A. White, *The Mental Hygiene of Childhood* (Boston: Little, Brown and Co., 1919), p. xiv.

50. Healy's attendance at conferences is attested to by the wealth of his published work, many of the articles representing the substance of papers given to a wide variety of organizations, including the American Prison Association, the Physicians Club of Chicago, and the National Conference of Charities and Correction. Passing references in Healy's correspondence with Ethel Dummer (in the Dummer Papers) indicated Healy's willingness to speak about his work to both local and national groups. See also "Juvenile Delinquency," an editorial in the *Journal of the American Medical Association* 70 (1918): 388–389, recommending Healy to physicians as the authority on delinquency study.

51. In addition to the *Psychoanalytic Review* critique, cited above, positive reviews of *The Individual Delinquent* appeared in *Annals of the American Academy of Political and Social Science* 61 (1915): 293; *Survey* 34 (1915): 164; and *Journal of the American Institute of Criminal Law and Criminology* 6 (1915–1916): 849–859.

52. William Healy and Mary Tenney Healy, *Pathological Lying, Accusation, and Swindling: A Study in Forensic Psychology* (Boston: Little, Brown and Co., 1915); and William Healy, *Honesty: A Study of the Causes and Treatment of Dishonesty among Children* (Indianapolis: Bobbs-Merrill Co., 1915).

53. Roy M. Cushman, "Harvey Humphrey Baker: Man and Judge," in *Harvey Humphrey Baker: Upbuilder of the Juvenile Court* (Boston: Judge Baker Foundation, 1920), pp. 1–10; Mrs. Frederick W. Reed, "Research Work in the Minneapolis Juvenile Court," *American Review of Reviews* 48 (August 1913): 214–217.

54. See Burnham, "Oral History Interview with William Healy and Augusta Bronner," 25 January 1960. Bronner provided the account of the decision to leave Chicago; see also Healy and Bronner, "The Child Guidance Clinic: Birth and Growth of an Idea." Biographical material on Augusta Bronner can be found in Gwendolyn Stevens and Sheldon Gardner, *Pioneers and Innovators,* vol. 1, *The Women of Psychology* (Cambridge, Mass.: Schenkman Publishing Company, 1982), pp. 198–203. Healy was not alone in finding that juvenile court politics in Chicago were unsavory. Articles in national periodicals described the controversy over patronage appointments of probation officers. The conflict be-

tween "science" and politics flared frequently between the child savers and the local politicians. See, for example, "Probation and Politics," *The Survey* 27 (March 30, 1912): 2003–2014.

55. Quoted in M. A. DeWolfe Howe, *The Children's Judge: Frederick Pickering Cabot* (Boston: Houghton Mifflin Co., 1932), p. 69.

56. William Healy to Ethel Dummer, 26 July 1911, Dummer Papers.

57. William Healy to Ethel Dummer, 8 November 1918, Dummer Papers.

58. Bernard Glueck, "Types of Delinquent Careers," *MH* 1 (1917): 171–195; Bernard Glueck, "Study of Admissions to Sing Sing," *MH* 2 (1918): 85–151.

59. Examples of "crime wave" announcements in the national press include: "Causes of America's 'Crime Wave,' " *Literary Digest* 63 (27 December 1919): 14; "Crimes, 'Crime Waves,' Criminals, and the Police," *Literary Digest* 60 (8 March 1919): 62–62; "America's High Tide of Crime," *Literary Digest* 67 (11 December 1920): 11–13; Charles Frederick Carter, "The Carnival of Crime in the United States," *Current History Magazine of the New York Times* 15 (February 1922): 753–761; "The Crime Wave of 1935," *Survey* 46 (4 June 1921): 307–308; and "The 'Crime Wave,' " *Survey* 47 (21 January 1922): 622–623.

60. The Commonwealth Fund was a project of Stephen Harkness's widow Anna and son Edward. Information on Commonwealth Fund sponsorship of child guidance can be found in Margo Horn, *Before It's Too Late: The Child Guidance Movement in the United States, 1922–1945* (Philadelphia: Temple University Press, 1989); A. Harvey McGehee and Susan L. Abrams, *"For the Welfare of Mankind": The Commonwealth Fund and American Medicine* (Baltimore: Johns Hopkins University Press, 1986); and Judith Sealander, *Private Wealth and Public Life: Foundation Philanthropy and the Reshaping of American Social Policy from the Progressive Era to the New Deal* (Baltimore: Johns Hopkins University Press, 1997), pp. 138–146. A copy of Thomas Salmon's memorandum to the Commonwealth Fund proposing the Division on the Prevention of Delinquency is located in the Healy-Bronner Papers in the George Gardner Collection, Francis A. Countway Library of Medicine, Boston, Mass. Other studies of the role of the large philanthropies include Richard E. Brown, *Rockefeller Medicine Men: Medicine and Capitalism in America* (Berkeley: University of California Press, 1984); and John F. McClymer, *War and Welfare: Social Engineering in America, 1890–1925* (Westport, Conn.: Greenwood Press, 1980).

61. Quoted from the Commonwealth Fund report of the Lakewood conference. Cited in Horn, *Before It's Too Late,* p. 27. A description of the Lakewood Conference is contained in a lengthy letter from William Healy to Ethel Dummer, 16 March 1921, Dummer Papers. McGehee and Abrams, *"For the Welfare of Mankind,"* list the participants, p. 628, n. 27.

62. Ethel Dummer to William Healy, 2 March 1921, Dummer papers. Edith Abbott's comment is quoted in Horn, *Before It's Too Late,* p. 30.

63. Copy of a "Report of Dr. William Healy and Dr. Augusta Bronner" (to the Commonwealth Fund, not for publication) is located in the Dummer Papers.
64. William Healy to Ethel Dummer, 3 May 1922, Dummer Papers. The additional projects in the field of delinquency prevention sponsored by the Commonwealth Fund in 1922 and growing out of the Lakewood conference included funds for training psychiatric social workers and visiting teachers at the Bureau of Children's Guidance, and for the establishment of a Division on the Prevention of Delinquency within the NCMH to coordinate the demonstrations. A description of these programs and the eight clinics can be found in George Stevenson and Geddes Smith, *Child Guidance Clinics: A Quarter Century of Development* (New York: Commonwealth Fund, 1934), pp. 20–47.
65. Figures are from Helen Leland Witmer, *Psychiatric Clinics for Children* (New York: Commonwealth Fund, 1940), pp. 56–57.

3. Building the Child Guidance Team

1. Although the term "child guidance" was not employed until 1922 (to refer to the Commonwealth Fund's demonstration clinics) I will use "child guidance" to describe activities at the Judge Baker Foundation because Judge Baker's three-part process of evaluation identified this clinic's professional relationships more closely with these future entities than with existing psychiatric or psychopathic institutions. On professional relationships at the Boston Psychopathic Hospital, see Elizabeth Lunbeck, *The Psychiatric Persuasion: Knowledge, Gender, and Power in Modern America* (Princeton: Princeton University Press, 1994), pp. 25–45. Guenter B. Risse and John Harley Warner, "Reconstructing Clinical Activities: Patient Records in Medical History," *Social History of Medicine* 5 (1992): 183–205, suggest the different levels of historical data revealed in patient records.
2. Victor Turner, *The Ritual Process: Structure and Anti-structure* (Chicago: University of Chicago Press, 1969); and Clifford Geertz, *Local Knowledge: Further Essays in Interpretive Anthropology* (New York: Basic Books, 1983). On ritual and conflict, see Max Gluckman, ed., *Essays on the Ritual of Social Relations* (Manchester: Manchester University Press, 1962).
3. Pearl Katz, "Ritual in the Operating Room," *Ethnology* 20 (1981): 335–350. On interprofessional rivalry, see Andrew Abbott's study, *The System of Professions: An Essay on the Division of Expert Labor* (Chicago: University of Chicago Press, 1988).
4. The social worker Mary Richmond called on her colleagues to use the term "client" for their subjects, rather than the more clinical word "case" preferred by doctors and psychiatrists, or the older social work reference "applicant." But Richmond could not have had in mind the social workers in a clinic such as

Healy's. When the clinic was supplying diagnostic services, the child guidance social worker's "client" or "applicant" was rarely a family member. Mary Richmond, *What Is Social Case Work: An Introductory Description* (New York: Russell Sage Foundation, 1922), pp. 27–28. "Client-centered therapy" was promoted by Carl Rogers, who worked in the child guidance field during the 1930s. The first statement was Rogers, *Counseling and Psychotherapy* (Boston: Houghton Mifflin Co., 1942). The term client or customer also belongs to those, who, like Paul Starr in *The Social Transformation of American Medicine* (New York: Basic Books, 1982), view the practice of medicine from an economic perspective.

5. George S. Stevenson and Geddes Smith, *Child Guidance Clinics: A Quarter Century of Development* (New York: Commonwealth Fund, 1934), p. 80.

6. On the importance of the patient, see Roy Porter, "The Patient's View: Doing Medical History from Below," *Theory and Society* 14 (1985): 175–198. Edward Shorter, *Doctors and Patients in Historical Perspective* (New Brunswick: Transaction Press, 1991), and N. D. Jewson, "The Disappearance of the Sick-Man from Medical Cosmology 1770–1870," *Sociology* 10 (1976): 225–244 discuss the doctor-patient relationship.

7. Bureau of the Census, "Population, 1920," vol. 1, *Fourteenth Census of the United States taken in the Year 1920* (Washington, D.C.: Government Printing Office, 1921), p. 63. Stephan Thernstrom, *The Other Bostonians: Poverty and Progress in the American Metropolis, 1880–1970* (Cambridge: Harvard University Press, 1973), pp. 111–134, provides a description of the Boston population during the years of clinic growth.

8. Boston agencies are among the best studied in social welfare history. Peter C. Holloran, *Boston's Wayward Children: Social Services for Homeless Children, 1830–1930* (Rutherford, N.J.: Fairleigh Dickinson University Press, 1989), and Linda Gordon, *Heroes of Their Own Lives: The Politics and History of Family Violence, Boston, 1880–1960* (New York: Viking Penguin, 1988), are two of the most useful studies for this period. Eva Whiting White, "Social Agencies in Boston, 1880–1930," in Elizabeth Herlihy, ed., *Fifty Years of Boston: A Memorial Volume* (Boston: Boston Tercentenary Committee, 1932), pp. 528–559, describes the various public and private agencies. See Stephen Hardy, *How Boston Played: Sport, Recreation, and Community, 1865–1915* (Boston: Northeastern University Press, 1982), for a discussion of recreational opportunities in the city.

9. "Chap. 489: An Act to Establish the Boston Juvenile Court," *Acts and Resolves Passed by the General Court of Massachusetts, in the Year 1906* (Boston: Wright and Potter Printing Co., State Printers, 1906), pp. 658–659. "Chap. 413: An Act Relative to Delinquent Children," approved during the same session, defined a "delinquent child" as "any boy or girl between the ages of seven and seventeen

years, who violates any city ordinance or town by-law, or commits an offence not punishable by death or by imprisonment for life." Ibid., pp. 426–433.

10. Seven district or police courts handled the remainder. Elizabeth P. Putnam, "Boston's Juvenile Court System," *Survey* 44 (13 November 1920): 250–252.

11. During the first ten years of Healy's Boston work almost 55 percent of the roughly six thousand youths examined by the Judge Baker staff came only because the court demanded a clinic judgment. The figures were compiled by Sheldon Glueck and Eleanor T. Glueck as part of the Harvard Crime Survey begun in 1926, and were published as Glueck and Glueck, *One Thousand Juvenile Delinquents: Their Treatment by Court and Clinic* (Cambridge: Harvard University Press, 1934), p. 49. Margo Horn has found a significantly lower figure (one percent) for the Philadelphia Child Guidance Clinic during the years 1925 to 1945. See Horn, *Before It's Too Late: The Child Guidance Movement in the United States, 1922–1945* (Philadelphia: Temple University Press, 1989), p. 161. The Judge Baker Foundation figures are more in keeping with those of other demonstration clinics: Norfolk, Virginia reported that 32 percent of its first 247 cases came from the juvenile court; St. Louis reported 74 percent. Philadelphia, where the initial request for a clinic came from the Public Charities Association of Pennsylvania, was unusual in this respect. Cited in Stevenson and Smith, *Child Guidance Clinics*, pp. 27, 45–46.

12. Eric Schneider, "In the Web of Class: Youth, Class, and Culture in Boston, 1840–1940" (Ph.D. diss., Boston University, 1980), gives an ethnic breakdown of juvenile court cases for the years 1907–1937. Nearly three-quarters of the delinquents came from families with foreign-born fathers, mainly of Irish, Italian, or Jewish background (p. 350). Healy and Bronner found roughly the same proportions in their comparison of Boston and Chicago repeat offenders seen at the clinics. William Healy and Augusta F. Bronner, *Delinquents and Criminals, Their Making and Unmaking: Studies in Two American Cities* (1926; reprint, New York: Macmillan Co., 1969), pp. 107–109.

13. Healy and Bronner found that about 75 percent of a large sample of cases seen in the first three years after the clinic opened were young males. (The figure for cases opened in 1920 was closer to 66 percent.) For the same study they collected court statistics for the years 1909–1921. In contrast to Boston, the Chicago ratio of girls to boys appearing in the court was roughly 1:3. Healy and Bronner, *Delinquents and Criminals*, pp. 90–93, 255. Charity workers in Boston often interceded to rescue delinquent girls before they appeared in the court. In Judge Baker Foundation case nos. 1702 and 1727 girls were rescued from the juvenile court by charity workers who then asked for the clinic's evaluation. Only one-third of the girls seen at the clinic in 1920 were direct juvenile court referrals.

14. Healy and Bronner, *Delinquents and Criminals*, pp. 132–133.

15. Ibid., pp. 117–121.
16. The year 1920 was not unusual. African American youths were rarely seen at the Judge Baker Foundation. Except for requests for Wassermann tests for syphilis in the African American patients, I could detect no particularly stereotypical methods or diagnoses in Healy's work. In this case, for example, the boy was found to be "subnormal" mentally, yet in the case conference, the Judge Baker staff noted that his ability and personality characteristics, though they might be "partially racial," were also "peculiar to this individual." Apparently Healy applied his notions of individual assessment to blacks as well as whites. In another example, the only mention of African Americans in *The Individual Delinquent*, Healy wrote, "The overwhelming attraction which negro men occasionally have for white girls and women, directly leading in our social life to delinquency, is to be explained by the hypersexualism of the female attracted" (p. 403). Gender was a more significant explanatory category than race for this practitioner.
17. In Massachusetts, parents could file a "stubborn complaint" to declare a child unmanageable and unwilling to submit to family authority; such a charge could result in institutionalization in a juvenile correctional facility. An assessment of the first cases seen at the Judge Baker Foundation found this to be a factor in 10 percent of the boys sampled. Glueck and Glueck, *One Thousand Juvenile Delinquents*, p. 100.
18. Healy and Bronner (*Delinquents and Criminals*, p. 165) thought that the delinquencies in Boston were not as serious as those in Illinois, a fact they attributed to activities of the Boston child welfare agencies.
19. Ibid., pp. 170–174. On Progressive era interest in the sexual delinquencies of adolescent females, see Steven Schlossman and Stephanie Wallach, "The Crime of Precocious Sexuality: Female Juvenile Delinquency in the Progressive Era," *Harvard Educational Review* 48 (1978): 65–94; Elizabeth Lunbeck, " 'A New Generation of Women': Progressive Psychiatrists and the Hypersexual Female," *Feminist Studies* 13 (1987): 513–534; Kathy Peiss, *Cheap Amusements: Working Women and Leisure in Turn-of-the-Century New York* (Philadelphia: Temple University Press, 1986); Mary E. Odem, *Delinquent Daughters: Protecting and Policing Adolescent Female Sexuality in the United States, 1885–1920* (Chapel Hill: University of North Carolina Press, 1995); and Ruth M. Alexander, *The "Girl Problem": Female Sexual Delinquency in New York, 1900–1930* (Ithaca: Cornell University Press, 1995). Only the crimes of the girls have been so extensively examined in light of early twentieth-century gender expectations. The boys' crimes against property and rebellion against school authority, if discussed at all, are presented as an issue of class, as in Eric C. Schneider's study of the Boston juvenile court, *In the Web of Class: Delinquents and Reformers in Boston, 1810s–1930s* (New York: New York University Press, 1992).
20. Glueck and Glueck, *One Thousand Juvenile Delinquents*, p. 49. Healy and Bron-

ner actively pursued social service clients when they moved to Boston. William Healy and Augusta F. Bronner, "The Child Guidance Clinic: Birth and Growth of an Idea," in Lawson G. Lowrey and Victoria Sloane, eds., *Orthopsychiatry, 1923–1948: Retrospect and Prospect* (New York: American Orthopsychiatric Association, 1948), p. 34. In 1920 of the 280 cases not coming from the juvenile court, over 80 percent were agency referrals.

21. Sheldon Glueck and Eleanor T. Glueck cited conversations with Judge Cabot held while preparing the manuscript of their critique of the court and clinic. *One Thousand Juvenile Delinquents,* pp. 30–31.

22. Only an examination of the court records comparing referred and non-referred cases—a task beyond the scope of this project—might make more explicit the reasons for the decision to send child and parents to Healy's clinic. Practitioners at other clinics, particularly those less closely attached to the court system, were more fortunate. The Institute for Child Guidance, the training institute in New York City (in operation from 1928 to 1933), specifically chose patients based on their research and educational value. See Murray Levine and Adeline Levine, *Helping Children: A Social History* (New York: Oxford University Press, 1992), who argue that such criteria led psychiatry and child guidance in the 1930s to focus on the less serious cases involving neurotic behavior, rather than extreme psychological abnormalities.

23. A policy statement from 1931 warned parents to anticipate a first appointment of three hours. This may have been somewhat shorter in 1920, before the establishment of the clinic's treatment department. Policy guidelines dated September 1, 1931, Gardner Collection.

24. An exception was the rural New Jersey Monmouth County clinic, one of the Commonwealth Fund demonstrations. Here the clinic was directed by the psychiatrist Christine Leonard. More territorial conflict ensued in other types of institutions, where the two professions worked closely or competed for the same population. For example, at the Ohio Bureau for Juvenile Research (similar to the Judge Baker Foundation, although the identity of the Ohio clinic was much more closely tied to its director's interest in mental retardation), the physicians on staff helped to dethrone the administration of the psychologist Henry H. Goddard. See Hamilton Cravens, "Applied Science and Public Policy: The Ohio Bureau of Juvenile Research and the Problem of Juvenile Delinquency, 1913–1930," in Michael Sokal, ed., *Psychological Testing and American Society, 1890–1930* (New Brunswick: Rutgers University Press, 1987), pp. 181–182. Donald S. Napoli, *Architects of Adjustment: The History of the Psychological Profession in the United States* (Port Washington, N.Y.: National University Publications, 1981), pp. 53–54, describes a similar conflict between psychological and psychiatric administration in Missouri, this one also involving an institution for people with mental retardation.

25. During the 1920s this debate was most pronounced in the *American Journal of*

Psychiatry and in *Mental Hygiene*. Gerald N. Grob has concluded that the reconstructing of psychiatry along the lines of Adolf Meyer and the National Committee for Mental Hygiene helped to create an environment conducive to the emergence of other mental health professionals. See Grob, *Mental Illness and American Society, 1870–1940* (Princeton: Princeton University Press, 1983), p. 233. These other groups were initially allies, Grob states, and the alliance functioned harmoniously until the 1930s when conflict erupted, especially between the psychiatrists and psychiatric social workers. This study suggests a psychiatric profession with far less authority than Grob finds, but Grob's focus on custodial institutions precludes further comparison.

26. On the importance of testing to the development of the discipline of psychology, see Sokal, ed., *Psychological Testing and American Society, 1890–1930*. The popularity of these tests in the public schools is addressed by Paul Davis Chapman, *Schools as Sorters: Lewis M. Terman, Applied Psychology, and the Intelligence Testing Movement, 1890–1930* (New York: New York University Press, 1988).

27. The next year the American Association of Clinical Psychologists became a section of the American Psychological Association. Gesell's comments were made as part of "The Field of Clinical Psychology as an Applied Science: A Symposium," *Journal of Applied Psychology* 3 (1919): 82. For another discussion of the same issues, see J. E. W. Wallin, "The New Clinical Psychology and the Psycho-Clinicist," *Journal of Educational Psychology* 2 (1911): 121–132, 191–210.

28. In *The Individual Delinquent* Healy addressed the gender question, writing, "There is much room for the work of intelligent and well-trained women in this field. Especially the objective psychological work, namely, the giving of the tests, can be done successfully by them. Rather less well are they fitted for the other parts of the work. The reason for this is, of course, that men and boys are not going to reveal much of their inner troubles to women" (p. 37). Bronner played a major role in designing the tasks of the Judge Baker team.

29. William Healy, "A Pictorial Completion Test," *Psychological Review* 21 (1914): 189–203; Healy, "Pictorial Completion Test II," *Journal of Applied Psychology* 5 (1921): 225–239; Augusta Bronner, William Healy, Gladys M. Lowe, and Myra E. Shimberg, *A Manual of Individual Mental Tests and Testing* (Boston: Little, Brown, and Co., 1928).

30. Healy and Bronner, *Delinquents and Criminals*, pp. 150, 154. In *The Individual Delinquent* (pp. 79–103) Healy recommended using a range of tests for general intelligence, tests to determine the extent of formal education, and tests for special abilities (for example, memory, attention span, motor coordination, and ability to profit from experience). A minimum schedule listed by Bronner and Healy in their 1928 guide included the Stanford revision of the Binet-

Simon IQ test; reading, spelling, and arithmetic tests; an information test; a tapping test for motor coordination; a pictorial completion test and form boards; and a sentence completion test for language comprehension.

31. Florence Goodenough, *Mental Testing: Its History, Principles, and Applications* (New York: Rinehart, 1949), p. 68.

32. Augusta F. Bronner, "Attitude as It Affects Performance of Tests," *Psychological Review* 23 (1916): 303–331.

33. Healy, *The Individual Delinquent,* p. 51.

34. This discussion of personality relies on Warren Susman, " 'Personality' and the Making of Twentieth-Century Culture," in Susman, *Culture as History: The Transformation of American Society in the Twentieth Century* (New York: Pantheon Books, 1984), pp. 271–285.

35. Edmund S. Conklin, *Principles of Adolescent Psychology* (New York: Henry Holt and Co., 1935), p. 3. Other contemporary texts of personality include Ernest R. Groves, *Personality and Social Adjustment* (New York: Longmans, Green and Co., 1930), and William H. Burnham, *The Wholesome Personality: A Contribution to Mental Hygiene* (New York: D. Appleton and Co., 1932).

    On early personality and character tests, see Harold Rugg, "Is the Rating of Human Character Practicable?" *Journal of Educational Psychology* 11 (1921): 425–438, 485–501; and 12 (1922): 30–42, 81–93. See also Mark A. May and Hugh Hartshorne, "Objective Methods of Measuring Character," *Pedagogical Seminary* 32 (1925): 45–67; and F. L. Wells, *Mental Tests in Clinical Practice* (Yonkers-on-Hudson: World Book Company, 1927), pp. 263–288. Personality tests were not routinely used in child guidance clinics. Andrew W. Brown, speaking of work at the Illinois Institute for Juvenile Research, reported in 1935 that personality tests were not used as frequently as intelligence, educational, or vocational tests, "first, because they tend to overlap the psychiatric interview, and secondly, because we are not sure of the validity of the results, and thirdly, there are relatively few cases to whom the questionnaires apply." Andrew W. Brown, *The Practical Use of Tests in a Child Guidance Clinic* (Chicago: Illinois Institute for Juvenile Research, 1935), p. 24.

36. For a discussion of the descriptive, qualitative nature of personality assessment, see Floyd H. Allport and Gordon W. Allport, "Personality Traits: Their Classification and Measurement," *Journal of Abnormal Psychology and Social Psychology* 16 (1921): 6–40.

37. Healy's chapter on "Physical Conditions: Peculiarities and Ailments," in *The Individual Delinquent,* pp. 214–235, discusses these observations. Syphilis as a factor in juvenile delinquency was discussed in Thomas Haines, "Incidence of Syphilis among Juvenile Delinquents: Its Relation to Mental Status," *Journal of the American Medical Association* 66 (1916): 102–105. In *The Individual Delinquent* Healy proposed that "these harmless blood tests" be given to "all children

who come under public care" (p. 205). See James H. Jones, *Bad Blood: The Tuskegee Syphilis Experiment,* expanded ed. (New York: Free Press, 1993) for a discussion of contemporary medical beliefs about the extent of syphilis among African Americans.

38. A good statement of Healy's belief in the effectiveness of this approach can be found in "Report of the Director of the Juvenile Psychopathic Institute, 1914," p. 35, Gardner Collection. Healy's approach to the child was similar in some respects to that used by juvenile court judges like Ben Lindsey, whose Saturday morning "snitching bees" and ability to pull confessions from his charges were notorious. On the similarities of the methods used by judge and psychiatrist see chapter 5, "Snitching Bees and Talking Cures: the Early Juvenile Court," in James Bennett, *Oral History and Delinquency: The Rhetoric of Criminology* (Chicago: University of Chicago Press, 1981), pp. 104–122.

39. Division on Prevention of Delinquency of the National Committee for Mental Hygiene, "Psychiatric Examination of a Child," *MH* 10 (1926): 304–306.

40. Linda Gordon, "Incest and Resistance: Patterns of Father-Daughter Incest, 1880–1930," *Social Problems* 33 (1986): 254–267.

41. Healy, *The Individual Delinquent,* p. 410; comparative figures, males, 13 percent and females, 18 percent, were given in Healy and Bronner, *Delinquents and Criminals,* p. 180.

42. William Healy, *Mental Conflicts and Misconduct* (Boston: Little, Brown and Co., 1917), pp. 22–24; p. 315.

43. Healy, *The Individual Delinquent,* p. 353. See published cases in chapter 14, "Conflicts Resulting in Stealing," in Healy, *Mental Conflicts and Misconduct,* pp. 243–274; and Judge Baker Foundation, "Case Study No. Sixteen," in *Case Studies, Series I* (Boston: Judge Baker Foundation, 1922–23). Mental conflict was not always related to sex experiences; Healy also included conflicts over parentage "and other matters" in his discussion of these cases (*Mental Conflicts and Misconduct,* pp. 183–225).

44. Stevenson and Smith, *Child Guidance Clinics,* p. 25.

45. Mary C. Jarrett, "Psychiatric Social Work," *MH* 2 (1918): 283, 290.

46. Mary E. Richmond, *Social Diagnosis* (New York: Russell Sage Foundation, 1917); and Richmond, *What Is Social Case Work: An Introductory Description* (1922). Jessie Taft, *Jessie Taft: Therapist and Social Educator, A Professional Biography,* ed. Virginia P. Robinson (Philadelphia: University of Pennsylvania Press, 1962). On the history of social work, see Lunbeck, *The Psychiatric Persuasion;* Roy Lubove, *The Professional Altruist: The Emergence of Social Work as a Career, 1880–1930* (Cambridge: Harvard University Press, 1965); John H. Ehrenreich, *The Altruistic Imagination: A History of Social Work and Social Policy in the United States* (Ithaca: Cornell University Press, 1985); and Daniel J. Walkowitz, "The Making of a Feminine Professional Identity: Social Workers in the 1920s," *American Historical Review* 95 (1990): 1051–1075.

47. Jarrett, "Psychiatric Social Work," p. 286. Jarrett was somewhat sympathetic to the psychiatrists' complaints, and she used this opportunity to call for a more scientific approach in social work and more training. Jessie Taft, "What the Social Worker Learns from the Psychiatrist about Her Problem Children," *Modern Medicine* 1 (July 1919): 240–245; and Mary C. Jarrett, *The Psychiatric Thread Running through All Social Case-Work* (New York: National Committee for Mental Hygiene, 1922). Elizabeth Lunbeck (*The Psychiatric Persuasion*, pp. 25–45 and passim) traces the conflict back to issues of gender. Working with relationships at the Boston Psychopathic Hospital Lunbeck shows how interest in problems of everyday life forced psychiatrists into the domain of the social worker at the same time that the new breed of social worker was appending the language of dynamic psychiatry to her casework.

48. Ralph P. Truitt, "Relation of Social Work to Psychiatry," *AJP* 82 (1925): 103–105; see also Herman Adler, "Relation between Psychiatry and the Social Sciences," *AJP* 83 (1927): 661–670.

49. Lawson Lowrey, "Some Trends in the Development of Relationships between Psychiatry and General Social Case-Work," *MH* 10 (1926): 277.

50. The staff expected family members to augment the formal accusations of delinquency, and many reports revealed long histories of general unruliness, petty pilfering, truancy, and running away, behavior not previously subject to the court's scrutiny.

51. Both Roy Lubove (*The Professional Altruist*) and Elizabeth Lunbeck (*The Psychiatric Persuasion*) address the question of the social worker's status. Lubove argues that psychiatry helped give social work legitimacy by providing the field with specialized skills and training, an interpretation that seems unwarranted in the early years of child guidance work. And, as I will argue in Chapter 7, a change in clients enabled clinic social workers to use the principles of dynamic psychiatry to lay claim to a new set of problems, thus generating a new form of professional legitimacy. Lunbeck claims that no amount of psychiatry could give social workers professional legitimacy because social work, defined as sentiment not science both within and beyond the field, was inherently feminine and consequently could not adapt to the masculinist professional ethos.

52. One observer's (somewhat jaded) appraisal of the summary conferences, completed for the Bureau of Social Hygiene (a privately funded social science research institution, founded in 1911), described the proceedings:

> Dr. Healy and Dr. Bronner sit side by side at a table facing a girl with a noiseless typewriter. Seated around the room are medical doctors, psychologists, mental testers and social workers. . . . Dr. Healy relates a case history, the typist taking it down as he talks, then he calls on the people who have interviewed and examined the child. The results are informally discussed by everybody who wants to say anything, and recommendations are made. Dr. Healy dictates from time to time as a significant point

is brought out. I believe that Dr. Healy sees all of the cases that are sent to him [from the juvenile court] but naturally he has to allocate the details of examination to his assistants . . .

The efficacy of this work seems to depend largely on how Dr. Healy is feeling and how successful the social worker and psychologist are in estimating the intangibles of the child's background . . .

Opinions of Dr. Healy's work which I heard expressed by people in Boston differed, although it was generally agreed that Dr. Bronner was the rudder of the combination.

Healy was in his sixties by this time; Bronner was considerably younger. The pair married in 1932 following the death of Mary Tenney Healy. "Boston Juvenile Court," typescript, no date (part of a series of evaluations conducted between 1930 and 1935), Bureau of Social Hygiene Collection, series 3, box 13, folder 235, Rockefeller Archive Center, Sleepy Hollow, N.Y.

53. Henry H. Goddard, *Feeblemindedness: Its Causes and Consequences* (New York: Macmillan Co., 1914), pp. 6–7. Peter L. Tyor and Leland V. Bell, *Caring for the Retarded in America: A History* (Westport, Conn.: Greenwood Press, 1984), 106–114, discuss the "menace of the feebleminded," as does James V. Trent, Jr., *Inventing the Feeble Mind: A History of Mental Retardation in the United States* (Berkeley: University of California Press, 1994). On Goddard, see Leila Zenderland, *Measuring Minds: Henry Herbert Goddard and the Origins of American Intelligence Testing* (New York: Cambridge University Press, 1998).

54. Mark H. Haller, *Eugenics: Hereditarian Attitudes in American Thought* (New Brunswick: Rutgers University Press, 1963), pp. 115–117. "We have had occasion to note immense variations in the ethical feelings of feeble-minded individuals," Healy told the American Association for the Study of the Feeble-minded in 1918. "This has been so marked that in certain instances we have found the accepted dictum which holds that the feeble-minded person is a potential delinquent to be utterly untrue." William Healy, "Normalities of the Feeble-Minded," reprinted from American Association for the Study of the Feeble-Minded, *Proceedings,* 1918. A copy is located in the Gardner Collection.

55. Quote is from John H. W. Rhein, "Mental Condition of Female Juvenile Delinquents," *New York Medical Journal* 106 (1917): 725. Rhein, a Philadelphia physician, read this paper to the Girls' Aid Society.

56. This topic is discussed in Tyor and Bell, *Caring for the Retarded in America;* Philip R. Reilly, *The Surgical Solution: A History of Involuntary Sterilization in the United States* (Baltimore: Johns Hopkins University Press, 1991); and Steven Noll, *Feeble-minded in Our Midst: Institutions for the Mentally Retarded in the South, 1900–1940* (Chapel Hill: University of North Carolina Press, 1995).

57. Judge Baker Foundation, "Case Study No. 18, Three Mentally Defective Girls," *Case Studies, Series I,* p. 5-a, 7-a.

58. Lawson G. Lowrey, "The Birth of Orthopsychiatry," in Lowrey and Sloane, eds., *Orthopsychiatry, 1923–1948*, pp. 190–208. The American Orthopsychiatric Association was established in 1924, with William Healy as the organization's first president.

4. Popularizing Child Guidance

1. Ester Loring Richards, "What Has Mental Hygiene to Offer Children at the End of 1926?" *MH* 11 (1927): 2–3.

2. Paul Starr, *The Transformation of Modern Medicine* (New York: Basic Books, 1982), p. 37, suggests that in the early nineteenth century domestic medicine books served a similar purpose. By creating a public conversant with medical issues the books prepared the way for public acceptance of medical authority. On the audience for modern self-help books, see Wendy Simonds, *Women and Self-Help Culture: Reading between the Lines* (New Brunswick: Rutgers University Press, 1992).

3. The process of popularization, or the means by which scientific and medical knowledge is transferred from a community of professional experts to the community at large, has not been a popular topic among historians of science and medicine. Within the history of science, in particular, the subject is, as Roger Cooter and Stephen Pumfrey have observed, "bereft of master narratives." Roger Cooter and Stephen Pumfrey, "Separate Spheres and Public Places: Reflections on the History of Science Popularization and Science in Popular Culture," *History of Science* 32 (1994): 253. Three exceptions are Nancy J. Tomes, *The Gospel of Germs: Men, Women, and the Microbe in American Life* (Cambridge: Harvard University Press, 1998); John Burnham, *How Superstition Won and Science Lost: Popularizing Science and Health in the United States* (New Brunswick: Rutgers University Press, 1987); and Roy Porter, ed., *The Popularization of Medicine, 1650–1850* (London: Routledge, 1992). See also Judith Walzer Leavitt, *Brought to Bed: Childbearing in America, 1750–1950* (New York: Oxford University Press, 1988); and Terra Ziporyn, *Disease in the Popular American Press: The Case of Diphtheria, Typhoid Fever, and Syphilis, 1870–1920* (Westport, Conn.: Greenwood Press, 1988), p. 3. JoAnne Brown, "Professional Language: Words that Succeed," *Radical History Review* 34 (1986): 33–51, has suggested that language, and in particular the use of metaphor, provides professionals with a recognizable façade (social workers who adopt the language of medicine, for example); experts form new professions by appropriating the language of existing professionals. See especially Emily Martin's use of the concept of "saturation" in *Flexible Bodies: The Role of Immunity in American Culture from the Days of Polio to the Age of AIDS* (New York: Beacon Press, 1994).

4. Stephen J. Cross, "Designs for Living: Lawrence K. Frank and the Progressive

Legacy in American Social Science" (Ph.D. diss., Johns Hopkins University, 1994), describes the continuing desire for social betterment promoted by professionals even as the Progressive reform impulse subsided. On the creation of a consumer culture, see William Leach, *Land of Desire: Merchants, Power, and the Rise of a New American Culture* (New York: Vintage Books, 1993); and T. J. Jackson Lears, *Fables of Abundance: A Cultural History of Advertising in America* (New York: Basic Books, 1994).

5. On the NCMH, see Johannes C. Pols, "Managing the Mind: The Culture of American Mental Hygiene, 1910–1950" (Ph.D. diss., University of Pennsylvania, 1997). On the contributions of the Commonwealth Fund, and the LSRM see A. Harvey McGhee and Susan Abrams, *"For the Welfare of Mankind": The Commonwealth Fund and American Medicine* (Baltimore: Johns Hopkins University Press, 1986); Christine Shea, "The Ideology of Mental Health and the Emergence of the Therapeutic Liberal State" (Ph.D. diss., University of Illinois at Urbana-Champaign, 1980); and Judith Sealander, *Private Wealth and Public Life: Foundation Philanthropy and the Reshaping of American Social Policy from the Progressive Era to the New Deal* (Baltimore: Johns Hopkins University Press, 1997).

6. George S. Stevenson and Geddes Smith, *Child Guidance Clinics: A Quarter Century of Development* (New York: Commonwealth Fund, 1934), p. 30.

7. Ibid., p. 47.

8. Douglas Thom, *The Everyday Problems of the Everyday Child* (New York: D. Appleton and Co., 1927), p. viii. Thom was applying a colloquial meaning to the word "normal," one that suggested "average" or "ordinary." This definition often competed in the literature with the "normal" used in professional discourse, which implied more often mental retardation or psychopathology. For example, Stevenson and Smith concluded in their review of the child guidance movement in 1934, "It is manifestly unfortunate for a clinic which is striving for the confidence of the parents of more normal children to be thought of as a center for the care of the feebleminded." Stevenson and Smith, *Child Guidance Clinics*, p. 72. See Elizabeth Lunbeck, *Psychiatric Persuasion: Knowledge, Gender, and Power in Modern America* (Princeton: Princeton University Press, 1994), pp. 46–77, for an account of early twentieth-century psychiatric interest in other aspects of "everyday life."

9. Harry M. Tiebout (of the Institute for Child Guidance in New York City), "Review of *Wholesome Parenthood* by Ernest R. Groves and Gladys Hoagland Groves," *MH* 14 (1930): 547.

10. Douglas A. Thom, "Habit Clinics for Children of the Pre-School Age," *MH* 6 (1922): 463–470; and U.S., Department of Labor, "Habit Clinics for the Preschool Child," by Douglas A. Thom, Children's Bureau publication no. 135 (Washington, D.C.: Government Printing Office, 1923). See also John G. Orme

and Paul Stuart, "Habit Clinics," *Social Service Review* 55 (1981): 242–256. Habit clinics relied extensively on techniques of behavior modification to establish new patterns of behavior (parents were often encouraged to institute a reward system—a star chart, for example, on which the child pasted stars for good behavior). I include them in this discussion of popularization because discussions of "child management" or the training of very young children contributed to the general atmosphere of concern about parenting, and also because child guidance practice was eclectic. Although clinicians searched for mental conflicts, they also relied on behaviorism for therapeutic intervention.

11. "How to Keep Our Children Sound in Body, Mind, and Character" (Boston: Massachusetts Society for Mental Hygiene, publication no. 35, n.d.).

12. "The Story of Mother Wise" (Boston: Massachusetts Society for Mental Hygiene, 1926).

13. Douglas Thom, *Normal Youth and Its Everyday Problems* (New York: D. Appleton and Co., 1932), pp. vii, 50–51, 128–130.

14. Thom, *Everyday Problems of the Everyday Child,* p. 155.

15. Ibid., p. 282.

16. Ibid., p. vii.

17. Roland Marchand, *Advertising the American Dream: Making Way for Modernity, 1920–1940* (Berkeley: University of California Press, 1985), p. 24.

18. Ibid., pp. 18–20.

19. This count is based on a survey of the reviews in *Mental Hygiene* from volume 1 (1917) to the year preceding the publication of Benjamin Spock's *Baby and Child Care* (1945, 1946). The total number of advice books published during these years was certainly much greater; even *MH* reviewed a few that were found to be inappropriate from a child guidance perspective.

20. Anni Weiss-Frankl, "Review of *The Parents' Manual: A Guide to the Emotional Development of Young Children* by Anna W. M. Wolf," *MH* 26 (1942): 654.

21. Meta L. Douglas, "Review of *Learning to be Good Parents* by Eleanor Saltzman," *MH* 22 (1938): 309.

22. See Rima D. Apple, "Constructing Mothers: Scientific Motherhood in the Nineteenth and Twentieth Centuries," *Social History of Medicine* 8 (August 1995): 161–178; and Nancy Pottishman Weiss, "The Mother-Child Dyad Revisited: Perceptions of Mothers and Children in Twentieth Century Child-Rearing Manuals," *Journal of Social Issues* 34 (1978): 29–45. This view is in contrast to that presented by Barbara Ehrenreich and Deirdre English, *For Her Own Good: 159 Years of the Experts' Advice to Women* (Garden City, N.Y.: Anchor Books, 1978). See Mary P. Ryan, *The Empire of the Mother: American Writing about Domesticity, 1830 to 1860* (New York: Institute for Research in History and the Haworth Press, 1982) on the nineteenth-century advice market.

23. See Clifford Geertz, "Common Sense as a Cultural System," in *Local Knowledge:*

Further Essays in Interpretive Anthropology (New York: Basic Books, 1983), pp. 73–93.

24. Weiss-Frankl, "Review of *The Parents' Manual.*"

25. Smiley Blanton and Dorothy Gray Blanton, *Child Guidance* (New York: Century Co., 1927), pp. v–vi.

26. Alma Binzel, "Review of *Meeting Your Child's Problems* by Miriam Finn Scott," *MH* 7 (1923): 640–641.

27. Ester Loring Richards, "Review of *Living with Our Children: A Book of Little Essays for Mothers* by Clara D. Pierson," *MH* 8 (1924): 360–362.

28. The idea of an institutionalized "police force detecting and sanctioning counterfeit claims" made by popularizers was suggested by Stephen Hilgartner, "The Dominant View of Popularization: Conceptual Problems, Political Uses," *Social Studies of Science* 20 (1990): p. 534, who argues that scientists do not have such a force to control public discourse about science.

29. Jessie C. Fenton, "Review of *Good Manners for Children* by Elsie C. Mead and Theodora Mead Abel," *MH* 12 (1928): 162.

30. John T. MacCurdy, M.D., "Review of *Abnormal Children (Nervous, Mischievous, Precocious and Backward): A Book for Parents, Teachers and Medical Officers of Schools* by Bernard Hollander, M.D.," *MH* 1 (1917): 319.

31. John T. MacCurdy, "Review of *The Mental Hygiene of Childhood* by William A. White," *MH* 3 (1919): 711–712.

32. Frederic J. Farnell, "Review of *Auto-suggestion for Mothers* by R. C. Waters," *MH* 11 (1927): 621.

33. Harry M. Tiebout, "Review of *The Child and the Home* by B. Liber," *MH* 12 (1928): 429.

34. Jessie Chase Fenton, "Review of *Psychological Care of Infant and Child* by John B. Watson," *MH* 12 (1928): 616–618. On Watson's influence, see Ben Harris, "'Give Me a Dozen Healthy Infants . . .': John B. Watson's Popular Advice on Childrearing, Women, and the Family," in Miriam Lewin, ed., *In the Shadow of the Past: Psychology Portrays the Sexes* (New York: Columbia University Press, 1984), pp. 126–154.

35. The reviewer of *A Study in Babyhood* complimented its author for taking on the "difficult task of presenting some of the modern tenets of child guidance and the mental hygiene of childhood—or, to be more exact, of babyhood— with a decidedly religious flavor." On the whole she found the book a sound effort to synthesize science and religion. Grace Corwin Rademacher, "Review of *A Study of Babyhood* by Mary S. Haviland," *MH* 15 (1931): 190–191. An earlier book by the same author received a much less favorable review because of its failure to examine the child's motives or the child's agenda, preferring to defer to the "perverse streak in human nature" as her explanatory principle. Thaddeus H. Ames, "Review of *Character Training in Childhood* by Mary S. Haviland," *MH* 5 (1921): 631–633. See also Helen Alden Klein, "Review of

Consider the Children—How They Grow by Elizabeth M. Manwell and Sophia L. Fahs," *MH* 25 (1941): 474–475.

36. "Parents, We Are Here!" *Children, the Magazine for Parents* 1 (October 1926): 1. Magazine production of child-rearing advice is discussed in Celia B. Stendler, "Sixty Years of Child Training Practices," *Journal of Pediatrics* 36 (1950): 122–134; Richard A. Meckel, *Save the Babies: American Public Health Reform and the Prevention of Infant Mortality, 1850–1929* (Baltimore: Johns Hopkins University Press, 1990), p. 149; and Emily R. Blumenfeld, "Childrearing Literature as an Object of Content Analysis," *Journal of Applied Communications Research* 4 (1976): 75–88. On women's magazines of this era, see Jennifer Scanlon, *Inarticulate Longings: The Ladies' Home Journal, Gender, and the Promises of Consumer Culture* (New York: Routledge, 1995); and John Tebbel and Mary Ellen Zuckerman, *The Magazine in America, 1741–1990* (New York: Oxford University Press, 1991), pp. 89–107. On *Parents' Magazine,* see Steven Schlossman, "Perils of Popularization: The Founding of *Parents' Magazine,*" in Alice Boardman Smuts and John W. Hagen, eds., *History and Research in Child Development* (Monograph of the Society for Research in Child Development, vol. 50, nos. 4–5, 1985), pp. 65–77.

37. This particular ad appeared in *Parents' Magazine* 10 (January 1935): 49. The Fletcher's Castoria stories appeared regularly during the 1930s in *Parents' Magazine* and in *Women's Home Companion.* To be sure, L. Emmett Holt and other first-generation pediatricians had proved that bowel problems, which caused such a high rate of infant mortality, were preventable—that care in feeding would help preserve the health of young children. Readers of women's magazines doubtlessly came from the same class of parents who regularly consulted physicians about physical health problems, and the Fletcher's ad may have been conceived from this perspective. Nonetheless, the image was intended to demonstrate that children were not "just bad" and that therapeutic intervention rather than punishment was the preferred solution. The baffled mother and emotional child were part of the repertoire of child guidance imagery.

38. For this discussion of advertising, I have borrowed heavily from Marchand, *Advertising the American Dream.* See particularly his discussion of "The Parable of the Captivated Child," pp. 228–232.

39. Gladys Hoagland Groves, "Review of *What Have You Got to Give?* by Angelo Patri," *MH* 12 (1928): 185–186. Robert L. Griswold, *Fatherhood in America: A History* (New York: Basic Books, 1993), pp. 108–115, 119–126, contains a discussion of parents' letters to Angelo Patri, as does Ralph LaRossa, *The Modernization of Fatherhood: A Social and Political History* (Chicago: University of Chicago Press, 1997), pp. 144–169. For biographical details, see "Angelo Patri, Educator, Dead; Pioneered in Liberal Teaching," *New York Times* (24 September 1965), p. 39.

40. References to Patri can be found in JBGC case nos. 9202, 9220, and 9275.

41. On the Children's Bureau, see Kriste Lindenmeyer, *"A Right to Childhood": The U.S. Children's Bureau and Child Welfare, 1912–1946* (Urbana: University of Illinois Press, 1997); Robyn Muncy, *Creating a Female Dominion in American Reform, 1890–1935* (New York: Oxford University Press, 1991); and Molly Ladd-Taylor, *Mother-Work: Women, Child Welfare, and the State, 1890–1930* (Urbana: University of Illinois Press, 1994). Ladd-Taylor, *Raising a Baby the Government Way: Mothers' Letters to the Children's Bureau, 1915–1932* (New Brunswick: Rutgers University Press, 1986), reprints samples of the correspondence. Initially, at least, women at the Children's Bureau sent personalized replies. The first Children's Bureau pamphlet, "Prenatal Care," appeared in 1913, followed the next year by "Infant Care."

42. U.S., Department of Labor, "The Practical Value of Scientific Study of Juvenile Delinquency," by William Healy, Children's Bureau Publication no. 96 (Washington, D.C.: Government Printing Office, 1922).

43. U.S., Department of Labor, "Child Management," by Douglas A. Thom, Children's Bureau Publication no. 143 (Washington, D.C.: Government Printing Office, 1925), pp. 28–29.

44. U.S., Department of Labor, "Are You Training Your Child to Be Happy?," Children's Bureau Publication no. 202 (Washington, D.C.: Government Printing Office, 1930), p. 1.

45. Ibid., pp. 33–34.

46. On opposition to the Children's Bureau, see Lindenmeyer, *"A Right to Childhood,"* pp. 83–87; and Ladd-Taylor, *Mother-Work,* pp. 169–177.

47. The private letters parents exchanged with Angelo Patri and with the Children's Bureau offered a degree of intimacy midway between the published manuals and a visit to the clinic. Although the opportunity to write was surely a form of popularization, the letters themselves are better viewed as a modification of the individual doctor-patient relationship achieved in the clinic and are not discussed here. On the content of these letters see Ladd-Taylor, *Raising a Baby the Government Way;* and LaRossa, *The Modernization of Fatherhood,* pp. 144–169.

48. William I. Thomas and Dorothy Swain Thomas, *The Child in America: Behavior Problems and Programs* (New York: Alfred A. Knopf, 1928), p. 295. On the history of parent education, see Julia Dent Grant, *Raising Baby by the Book: The Education of American Mothers* (New Haven: Yale University Press, 1998). On LSRM funding of parent education, see Steven Schlossman, "Before Home Start: Notes toward a History of Parent Education in America, 1897–1929," *Harvard Educational Review* 46(1976): 437–467, and Schlossman, "Philanthropy and the Gospel of Child Development," *History of Education Quarterly* 21 (1981): 275–299.

49. Roberta Wollons, "Educating Mothers: Sidonie Matsner Gruenberg and the Child Study Association of America, 1881–1929" (Ph.D. diss., University of

Chicago, 1983) discusses the transformation of this organization. I have also drawn from materials in the Child Study Association of America Records at the Social Welfare History Archives, University of Minnesota, Minneapolis, Minn.

50. Material on CSAA programs can be found in the Programs and Yearbooks published yearly by the organization. Copies can be found in the CSAA Records, box 1.

51. "The Child Study Association of America, 1888–1933: A Chronicle of Growth," typescript, CSAA Records, box 35, folder 357.

52. See the Laura Spelman Rockefeller Memorial (LSRM) Archives, Series 3.5, at the Rockefeller Archive Center, Sleepy Hollow, N.Y., for notes on the funding of parent education. The fund's efforts to reorient the child guidance movement to one of parent education began and ended with the plans developed for the Monmouth County (N.J.) demonstration clinic. The Memorial took over the work of the demonstration clinic in 1923 and reorganized the delinquency prevention services into a program specifically for community education. Administrators at LSRM stipulated that the clinic's directors were to "utilize its case material for teaching mothers, doctors, teachers and the various classes of social workers i.e. nurses, case workers etc. what are the intelligent and wholesome methods of dealing with children." The following year the Memorial directors changed their minds. See the "Memorandum of Interview" with Mrs. Louis B. Thompson and others, November 25 and 26, 1923, LSRM Archives, Series 3.5, box 34, folder 358; and Stevenson and Smith, *Child Guidance Clinics*, pp. 31–33.

53. Mary Shirley, *Can Parents Educate One Another? A Study of Lay Leadership in New York State* (New York: National Council of Parent Education, 1938).

54. "Child Study and the Education of Parents," typescript, LSRM Archives, Series 3.5, box 30, folder 316.

55. Julia Grant, "Caught between Common Sense and Science: The Cornell Child Study Clubs, 1925–1945," *History of Education Quarterly* 34 (Winter 1994): 433–452, shows that concerned parent participants also questioned the wisdom of group leaders. I will discuss parent responses further in Chapter 5.

56. Local chapters were listed in the CSAA Yearbooks. CSAA Records, box 1, folders 8 and 9.

57. The scrapbooks were discovered in a closet under a staircase at the current Judge Baker Children's Center, which retains possession of the scrapbooks.

58. Typescript of the " 'Four Neighbors' Explanatory Speech" and the description of the film contained in the newspaper reports are located in the Healy-Bronner Papers, Gardner Collection.

59. Stevenson and Smith, *Child Guidance Clinics*, pp. 138–140.

60. The following account is based on stories appearing from July 21, 1924, through August 15, 1924, in both the *Boston Daily Globe* and the *Boston Eve-*

ning Globe. The *Boston Transcript,* with a much smaller circulation, covered the trial only sporadically. My discussion draws from Paula Fass's study of the sentencing hearing and its place in American culture, "Making and Remaking an Event: The Leopold and Loeb Case in American Culture," *Journal of American History* 80 (1993): 919–951. See also Catherine L. Covert, "Freud on the Front Page: Transmission of Freudian Ideas in the American Newspaper of the 1920s" (Ph.D. diss., Syracuse University, 1975). Dorothy Nelkin, *Selling Science: How the Press Covers Science and Technology* (rev. ed., New York: W. H. Freeman and Company, 1995), discusses contemporary issues. In contrast to the argument here, Paul M. Dennis concludes that press coverage of psychological research during the 1930s contributed to a decline in the prestige of American psychology. See " 'Johnny's a Gentleman, but Jimmie's a Mug': Press Coverage during the 1930s of Myrtle McGraw's Study of Johnny and Jimmy Woods," *Journal of the History of the Behavioral Sciences* 25 (1989): 356–370.

61. Charles Rosenberg, *The Trial of the Assassin Guiteau: Psychiatry and the Law in the Gilded Age* (Chicago: University of Chicago Press, 1968), provides one account of the insanity defense. See also Janet Tighe, "A Question of Responsibility: The Development of American Forensic Psychiatry, 1838–1930" (Ph.D. diss., University of Pennsylvania, 1983).

62. "Loeb Aimed at Perfect Crime," *Boston Evening Globe* (1 August 1924), p. 1.

63. "'Childish Compact' Tied Slayers Together," *Boston Evening Globe* (4 August 1924), p. 1; in "Loeb Willing to Kill a Relative," *Boston Daily Globe* (5 August 1924), p. 1, the reporter summed up Healy's testimony as "a contrasting of the emotional and intellectual lives of Leopold and Loeb. With the indicated purpose of swaying the court's judgment toward mitigation in fixing punishment because the undeveloped emotional sides of their personalities had overshadowed their powerful intellects and had made them incapable of resisting putting into action the crimes as built up in their childish phantasies."

   People of the State of Illinois v. Nathan Leopold, Jr. and Richard Loeb, Criminal Court of Cook County (Illinois). Testimony of William A. White and William Healy, "Trial Transcript," pp. 978–1658 (Healy's words are found on pp. 1561–1562). Leopold-Loeb Collection, Charles Deering McCormick Library of Special Collections, Northwestern University Library, Evanston, Ill.

64. "Boy's Slayers Mentally Diseased, Says Boston Alienist," *Boston Evening Globe* (5 August 1924), p. 1.

65. Ibid.

66. Paula Fass questions the degree to which the press gave approval to the testimony of the witnesses. Fass, "Making and Remaking an Event," pp. 928–929. Healy, in a letter to Ethel Dummer, was enthusiastic about the trial's "educative" value. "Only a day or two ago I answered an inquiry from a *prosecuting attorney* [emphasis in original] in a large city in Ohio who wanted to know

where he could find the right man to join forces with him and study his cases. Think of this, from a prosecuting attorney! This is the farthest I have every [*sic*] known our work to go." Healy to Dummer, 20 November 1924, Dummer Papers.

67. Morris Fishbein, *The New Medical Follies: An Encyclopedia of Cultism and Quackery in These United States, with Essays on the Cult of Beauty, the Craze for Reduction, Rejuvenation, Eclecticism, Bread and Dietary Fads, Physical Therapy, and a Forecast as to the Physician of the Future* (1927; reprint, New York: AMS Press, 1977), pp. 181–204.

68. Burnham, *How Superstition Won and Science Lost*, also discusses how scientists became part of the audience for popularization (pp. 205–207). On the development of pediatrics during the early twentieth century, see Thomas E. Cone, *The History of American Pediatrics* (Boston: Little, Brown, 1979); Sydney A. Halpern, *American Pediatrics: The Social Dynamics of Professionalism, 1880–1980* (Berkeley: University of California Press, 1988); Rima D. Apple, *Mothers and Medicine: A Social History of Infant Feeding, 1890–1950* (Madison: University of Wisconsin Press, 1987); and Meckel, *Save the Babies*.

69. Ester L. Richards, "Special Psychiatric Problems in Childhood," *JAMA (Journal of the American Medical Association)* 95 (1930): 1011–1015; "Abstract of Discussion on Papers of Drs. Richards and Anderson," ibid., pp. 1018–1020.

70. Richards, "Special Psychiatric Problems in Childhood," pp. 1011–1015; and "Abstract of Discussion on Papers of Drs. Richards and Anderson," pp. 1018–1020. See also Crothers's book, *A Pediatrician in Search of Mental Hygiene* (New York: Commonwealth Fund, 1937).

71. Joseph Brennemann, "The Menace of Psychiatry," *American Journal of the Diseases of Children* 42 (1931): 376–402.

72. See, for example, Jessie Taft, "How Can We Safeguard the Child against Mental Disease?" *New York State Journal of Medicine* 17 (November 1917): 481–485; and Eleanor I. Keller, "Mental as Well as Physical Therapy for Children," *Archives of Pediatrics* 36 (1919): 277–283. Programs discussed in William S. Langford and Katharine M. Wickman, "Orthopsychiatry in Pediatrics," in Lawson G. Lowrey and Victoria Sloane, eds., *Orthopsychiatry, 1923–1948: Retrospect and Prospect* (New York: American Orthopsychiatric Association, 1948), p. 289. For a general account of the "pediatric-psychiatric alliance," see Leo Kanner, "The Development and Present Status of Psychiatry in Pediatrics," *Journal of Pediatrics* 11 (1937): 418–435.

73. Leo Kanner, "Introduction: Trends in Child Psychiatry," in John G. Howells, ed., *Modern Perspectives in International Child Psychiatry* (New York: Brunner/Mazel Publishers, 1971), p. 10. A good statement of Kanner's views can be found in his article "Work with Psychobiological Children's Personality Difficulties," *AJO* 4 (1934): 402–412.

74. Leo Kanner, *Child Psychiatry* (Springfield, Ill.: Charles C. Thomas, 1935), p. xvii.

75. JoAnne Brown, "Professional Language: Words That Succeed."

76. As the book went through many printings and editions, the title of Spock's manual also changed, though the message remained the same. *The Common Sense Book of Baby and Child Care* (New York: Duell, Sloan and Pearce, 1945, 1946) became *The Pocket Book of Baby and Child Care* (New York: Pocket Books, 1946), and in succeeding editions the title was shortened to *Baby and Child Care.*

77. Spock, *The Common Sense Book of Baby and Child Care,* p. 2.

78. Ibid., p. 3. Benjamin Spock and Mary Morgan, *Spock on Spock: A Memoir of Growing Up with the Century* (New York: Pantheon Books, 1989), p. 262. On Spock, see Lynn Z. Bloom, *Doctor Spock: Biography of a Conservative Radical* (Indianapolis: Bobbs-Merrill Co., 1972); A. Michael Sulman, "The Humanization of the American Child: Benjamin Spock as a Popularizer of Psychoanalytic Thought," *Journal of the History of the Behavioral Sciences* 9 (1973): 258–265; and William Graebner, "The Unstable World of Benjamin Spock: Social Engineering in a Democratic Society, 1917–1950," *Journal of American History* 67 (1980): 612–629.

79. Hale F. Shirley, *Psychiatry for the Pediatrician* (New York: Commonwealth Fund, 1948), pp. 427–428.

5. The Problem Behavior of the Everyday Child

1. The best-known community study from the period, Robert S. Lynd and Helen Merrell Lynd's *Middletown: A Study in American Culture* (New York: Harcourt, Brace and Co., 1929), reported that "a prevalent mood among Middletown parents was bewilderment, a feeling that their difficulties [outran] their best efforts to cope with them" (p. 51).

2. Christopher Lasch, *Haven in a Heartless World: The Family Besieged* (New York: Basic Books, 1977); Barbara Ehrenreich and Deirdre English, *For Her Own Good: 150 Years of the Experts' Advice to Women* (Garden City, N.Y.: Anchor Press/Doubleday, 1979); and Carole E. Joffe, *Friendly Intruders: Childcare Professionals and Family Life* (Berkeley: University of California Press, 1977).

3. Leo Kanner, *In Defense of Mothers: How to Bring Up Children in Spite of the More Zealous Psychologists* (Springfield, Ill.: Charles C. Thomas, 1941).

4. This was not the first time, of course, that parents found their children following different values. Years ago Philip J. Greven, Jr.'s study, *Four Generations: Population, Land, and Family in Colonial Andover, Massachusetts* (Ithaca: Cornell University Press, 1970), pointed out the effects of economic change on parent-child relations in one colonial New England town. During the 1920s the

subject of rebellious youth reached a crescendo in the popular press, and the parents I have studied concurred with the media's representations of adolescence. Judge Ben B. Lindsey captured this sense of change and conflict in the title of his book (coauthored with Wainwright Evans), *The Revolt of Modern Youth* (New York: Boni & Liveright, 1925).

5. Frederick Lewis Allen, *Only Yesterday: An Informal History of the 1920s* (New York: Harper & Row, 1931); Peter Stearns, *American Cool: Constructing a Twentieth-Century Emotional Style* (New York: New York University Press, 1994); and Ann Douglas, *Terrible Honesty: Mongrel Manhattan in the 1920s* (New York: Noonday Press, Farrar, Straus and Giroux, 1995). On women and modernity, see Nancy F. Cott, *The Grounding of Modern Feminism* (New Haven: Yale University Press, 1987).

6. Paula Fass, *The Damned and the Beautiful: American Youth in the 1920s* (New York: Oxford University Press, 1977); Elaine Showalter, *These Modern Women* (Old Westbury, N.Y.: Feminist Press, 1978); Kevin White, *The First Sexual Revolution: The Emergence of Male Heterosexuality in Modern America* (New York: New York University Press, 1993).

7. George A. Coe, *What Ails Our Youth?* (1924; reprint, New York: Charles Scribner's Sons, 1926), p. 2.

8. Lynd and Lynd, *Middletown,* pp. 131–142, 267.

9. This fact the Lynds found attributable only in part to the economic uncertainty caused by the Depression. Roberts S. Lynd and Helen Merrell Lynd, *Middletown in Transition: A Study in Cultural Conflicts* (New York: Harcourt, Brace and World, 1937), p. 168. In contrast, the sociologist Glen Elder's study of the effect of the Depression on family relationships reported parent-child conflicts in fewer that half the families in his sample who suffered economic deprivation during the 1930s. These same families reported increased incidents of marital discord, however. See Glen Elder, *Children of the Great Depression: Social Change in Life Experience* (Chicago: University of Chicago Press, 1974), pp. 93–94.

10. The Lynds' surveys have become a standard measure of the attitudes of "average" Americans during the 1920s and 1930s. Middletown did not, of course, represent more than a reflection of white Midwest values. While sensitive to class differences, the sociologists did not attempt to analyze diverse racial categories.

11. I have used the clinic records to identify the types of problems that children, coming from families in moderate or affluent circumstances, presented to their parents. This drastic measure of seeking psychiatric help was often a last resort for parents, suggesting that the "problems" identified from the clinic cases require corroboration from other sources. Thus I have used the minutes of local mothers' meetings of the Child Study Association to confirm the preva-

lence of these problems. The minutes are located in the CSAA Records. (These minutes were from clubs in New York City. A group operated for a short while in the Boston suburb of Brookline, but minutes from this club were not available. Nor were the records of a similar parents' group sponsored by the Judge Baker Guidance Clinic in 1936.) Parents, both at the clinic and in study clubs, unreservedly articulated their concern about the actions of their youngsters. The interpretations of the conduct, provided by group leaders or clinic staff members and evident in the questions asked to elicit information, and in diagnoses, did not obscure the qualities of the activities that troubled these parents. See also Robert L. Griswold's discussion of fathers' letters to Angelo Patri in *Fatherhood in America: A History* (New York: Basic Books, 1993), pp. 108–115.

12. These generational conflicts were ubiquitous in immigrant communities, and the literature is extensive. For a small sample, describing Italian immigrant mothers and daughters, see Sharon Harman Strom, "Italian-American Women and Their Daughters in Rhode Island: The Adolescence of Two Generations, 1900–1950," in *The Italian Immigrant Woman in North America,* ed. Betty Boyd Caroli, Robert F. Harney, and Lydio F. Tomasi (Toronto: Multicultural History Society of Ontario, 1978), pp. 191–204. Strom found less conflict than the story of Stella would suggest. See also Judith Smith, "Italian Mothers, American Daughters: Changes in Work and Family Roles," ibid., pp. 206–221. For other examples of conflict in immigrant families, see case nos. 1832, 1839, and 1847. Marjorie Roberts, "Italian Girls on American Soil," *MH* 13 (1929): 757–768; and John Levy, "Conflicts of Cultures and Children's Maladjustments," *MH* 17 (1933): 41–50, presented the views of child care workers and mental hygienists. Kathy Peiss, *Cheap Amusements: Working Women and Leisure in Turn-of-the-Century New York* (Philadelphia: Temple University Press, 1986), describes the situation from the girls' point of view.

13. William I. Thomas and Florian Znaniecki, *The Polish Peasant in Europe and America,* ed. and abr. Eli Zaretsky (Urbana: University of Illinois Press, 1984). Thomas's ideas about the influence of pulls from the larger society and the restrictions immigrant families attempted to impose on their daughters were developed in *The Unadjusted Girl* (Boston: Little, Brown and Co., 1923).

14. Ralph M. Stodgill, "Parental Attitudes and Mental Hygiene Standards," *MH* 15 (1931): 813–827, quotes pp. 819–820 (emphasis in original). Stodgill's questions were modeled on a study of teacher attitudes that uncovered similar discrepancies between the activities teachers saw as troublesome—that is, those that physically disrupted class—and those found worrisome by mental hygienists. See E. K. Wickman, *Children's Behavior and Teachers' Attitudes* (New York: Commonwealth Fund, 1928).

15. During a meeting of CSAA Chapter 375, the secretary recorded, "The question

was asked: What could have gone wrong with a girl who in childhood and pre-adolescence had been sweet and lovable now has become moody—temperamental—resentful of criticism." Chapter 375, "Minutes," 29 October 1930, CSAA Records, box 27, folder 276.

16. Contrary to this discussion Joseph F. Kett, *Rites of Passage: Adolescence in America, 1790 to the Present* (New York: Basic Books, 1977) suggests that generational conflict was never as intense as popular writers portrayed; he found youth in the 1920s poised between "conventionality and unconventionality," but suggests that surveys showed youth and adults sharing similar values. "Adults who were unsure of their own standards," Kett writes, "could neither impose them on youth nor sanction whatever youth did. In a society where the old was not yet dead nor the new strong enough to stand, to postulate a conflict of generations and then to disarm the conflict by calling for sympathy with the problems of youth gave adults a basis for savoring the new without giving up the old" (p. 264). Few parents in this study were willing to sympathize with their young as a way of disarming the conflict. Indeed Kett's analysis is based not on the parents who confronted the young but on those experts who proposed to analyze and explain what Kett calls a new self-consciousness, rather than new behavior, among the young.

17. JBGC case nos. 9215 and 9245 provide good evidence of this conflict; see Fass, *The Damned and the Beautiful*, p. 216. Fass also discusses the connection between dress and cosmetics and adolescent sexuality, pp. 279–288. Lois W. Banner, in *American Beauty* (New York: Alfred A. Knopf, 1983), points to the existence of substantial fashion and cosmetics industries by the 1920s, and to a clientele ready and willing to consume these products. Kathy Peiss, "Making Faces: The Cosmetics Industry and the Cultural Construction of Gender, 1890–1930," *Genders* (1990): 143–169, describes the mass marketing techniques that encouraged women to purchase, as Charles Revson of Revlon Cosmetics put it, "hope in a jar."

18. Chapter 375, "Minutes," 30 December 1930, CSAA Records, box 27, folder 276. William Leach, in *Land of Desire: Merchants, Power, and the Rise of a New American Culture* (New York: Vintage Books, 1993), relates much of this conflict to the "individualizing" of children as a separate market—for toys and "juvenile" products—by early twentieth-century department store merchandisers. The adolescent market is a phenomenon usually associated with teen culture of the baby boom generation. If not yet directly marketed to, adolescents surely saw themselves as part of the culture of consumption.

19. U.S., Department of Labor, "Guiding the Adolescent," by Douglas A. Thom, Children's Bureau Publication no. 225 (Washington, D.C.: Government Printing Office, 1933), p. 53.

20. William Healy included moving pictures among the environmental factors

that caused juvenile delinquency—the visual imagery depicting acts of crime stimulated thoughts of illegal activity while the numerous scenes of lovemaking encouraged sex delinquencies among older adolescents and younger children as well. See Healy, *The Individual Delinquent* (Boston: Little, Brown and Co., 1915), pp. 306–310, quote p. 308. "Crime and the Movies," *Literary Digest* 69 (7 May 1921): 19; and "How Motion Pictures Promote Crime," *American Review of Reviews* 63 (May 1921): 555, presented similar views in popular magazines.

21. Chapter 13, "Minutes," 23 March 1916, CSAA Records, box 1, folder 4.

22. "Sex O'Clock in America," *Current Opinion* 55 (August 1913): 113–114.

23. Lynd and Lynd, *Middletown*, pp. 263–265; and *Middletown in Transition*, pp. 260–262. On the popular reaction to films, see Lary May, *Screening Out the Past: The Birth of Mass Culture and the Motion Picture Industry* (New York: Oxford University Press, 1980). The American Youth Commission counted approximately 20,000 motion picture theaters at the beginning of the 1940s, and reported that young people aged sixteen to twenty-four formed about one-fourth of the viewing audience. A more important statistic, however, was the one finding that urban youth attended two shows each week. C. Gilbert Wrenn and D. L. Harley, *Time on Their Hands: A Report on Leisure, Recreation, and Young People* (Washington, D.C.: American Council on Education, 1941).

24. *Our Movie Made Children* (New York: Macmillan Co., 1933) represents James Henry Forman's summary of investigations undertaken from 1929 to 1933 at the request of the Motion Picture Research Council, the industry's self-policing agency.

25. Dorothy Canfield (Fisher), *The Bent Twig* (New York: Henry Holt and Co., 1915), p. 189. Members of Chapter 13 of the Child Study Association favorably reviewed Canfield's novel soon after it was published and the leaders of the national organization continued during the 1920s to recommend the author's fictional account of childrearing in the modern era. Chapter 13, "Minutes," 28 February 1917, CSAA Records, box 1, folder 4. See Benjamin C. Gruenberg, ed., *Outlines of Child Study: a Manual for Parents and Teachers,* rev. ed. (New York: Macmillan Co., 1927), for the reference to writings by Dorothy Canfield Fisher. These "Outlines" were prepared under the auspices of the Child Study Association of America for use by local chapters.

26. On women and the automobile, see Virginia Scharff, in *Taking the Wheel: Women and the Coming of the Motor Age* (New York: Free Press, 1991).

27. Chapter 375, "Minutes," 12 November 1930, CSAA Records, box 27, folder 276. Another example comes from JBGC file no. 9266. In this African American family, the daughter attacked her mother with a knife, frustrated by the mother's restrictions on the girl's socializing. The mother claimed that she wanted to protect her daughter from going around with youths in the neigh-

borhood whom the mother felt were not good enough for her daughter's company.

28. On the importance of the peer group see Fass, *The Damned and the Beautiful*, pp. 120–167. On the growth of education, see David B. Tyack, *The One Best System: A History of American Urban Education* (Cambridge: Harvard University Press, 1974). For a contemporary assessment, see Charles H. Judd, "Education," in *Recent Social Trends: Report of the President's Research Committee on Social Trends*, 2 vols. (New York: McGraw-Hill Book Co., 1933), pp. 325–349; and Lynd and Lynd, *Middletown*, pp. 181–187.

29. Lynd and Lynd, *Middletown*, pp. 134–135; Fass, *The Damned and the Beautiful*, pp. 88–89.

30. Chapter 13, "Minutes," 2 March 1916, CSAA Records, box 1, folder 4.

31. Chapter 13, "Minutes," 1916–1923, CSAA Records, box 1, folder 5. contains the reports of this group's study of adolescent sexuality.

32. John Modell, "Dating Becomes the Way of American Youth," in Leslie Page Moch and Gary D. Stark, eds., *Essays on the Family and Historical Change* (College Station: Texas A&M University Press, 1983), p. 98; see also Beth L. Bailey, *From Front Porch to Back Seat: Courtship in Twentieth-Century America* (Baltimore: Johns Hopkins University Press, 1989).

33. Lynd and Lynd, *Middletown in Transition*, p. 169.

34. Diaries and letters of courting couples in the decades before the 1920s revealed considerable independence in behavior once an engagement was announced. See Ellen Rothman, *Hands and Hearts: A History of Courtship in America* (New York: Basic Books, 1984), pp. 179–284.

35. I am using Modell's definition of "date," from "Dating Becomes the Way of American Youth."

36. Ibid., pp. 93, 95. See also the chapter "Modern Youth: the 1920s" in John Modell, *Into One's Own: From Youth to Adulthood in the United States, 1920–1975* (Berkeley: University of California Press, 1989), pp. 77–120.

37. Eugenie A. Leonard and Margaret Bond Brockway, "Must a Girl Pet to Be Popular?" *Parents' Magazine* 71 (June 1932), cited in Modell, "Dating Becomes the American Way of Youth," p. 94.

38. Lynd and Lynd, *Middletown*, pp. 139–140. For Lindsey's opinions, see Lindsey and Evans, *The Revolt of Modern Youth*. On petting parties, see Allen, *Only Yesterday*, pp. 95–96. Phyllis Blanchard, psychologist at the Philadelphia Child Guidance Clinic, surveyed 252 "new women" between the ages of eighteen and twenty-six, and confirmed that petting was a major source of family conflict in the 1920s. See Blanchard and Carlyn Manasses, *New Girls for Old* (New York: Macaulay Co., 1930), pp. 68–69, 264. Douglas A. Thom, "Guiding the Adolescent," pp. 84–85, provides another discussion by a child guidance expert.

39. According to Carl Degler, well-educated middle- and upper-class women ex-

pressed a "frank and sometimes enthusiastic acceptance of sexual relations." See in particular Carl Degler, "What Ought to Be and What Was: Women's Sexuality in the Nineteenth Century," *American Historical Review* 79 (1974): 1467–1490, quote p. 1486. A more recent statistical study of the same sample used by Degler has raised questions about the degree of acceptance these women expressed, suggesting that Victorian-era women were not as "modern" in their sexual behavior as portrayed by Degler; expressions of pleasure, moreover, did not necessarily result in increased frequency of coitus. Nancy S. Landale and Avery M. Guest, "Ideology and Sexuality among Victorian Women," *Social Science History* 10 (1986): 147–170. See also Carol Zizowitz Stearns and Peter N. Stearns, "Victorian Sexuality: Can Historians Do It Better?" *Journal of Social History* 18 (1985): 625–634; James R. McGovern, "The American Woman's Pre–World War I Freedom in Manners and Morals," *Journal of American History* 55 (1968): 315–333; and Peter Gay, *Education of the Senses,* vol. 1, *The Bourgeois Experience, Victoria to Freud* (New York: Oxford University Press, 1984). Those who discuss the sexual revolution of the 1920s among the young include Fass, *The Damned and the Beautiful;* Kevin White, *The First Sexual Revolution;* and Peter G. Filene, *Him/Her/Self: Sex Roles in Modern America,* 2nd ed. (Baltimore: Johns Hopkins University Press, 1986).

40. Elaine Tyler May, *Great Expectations: Marriage and Divorce in Post-Victorian America* (Chicago: University of Chicago Press, 1980), describes similar ambivalence about new sexual attitudes seen in divorce proceedings. Both May, and Modell, "Dating Becomes the American Way of Youth," point out that the behavioral changes did not affect the "double standard," and young women were forced to balance Victorian sensibilities and modern expectations.

41. Lynd and Lynd, *Middletown in Transition,* p. 169.

42. Girls, however, spent more time on "personal care," called "primping" by the authors. C. C. Crawford and Roy W. Mayer, "How High-School Seniors Spend Their Time," *School Review* 43 (October 1935): 598–602. Another survey, of two hundred New York City high school girls, suggested that girls used their free time to engage in "worth-while activities," and that critics of the way the young use their leisure time should be wary of unjustified accusations. Ada E. Orr and Francis J. Brown, "A Study of the Out-of-School Activities of High-School Girls," *Journal of Educational Sociology* 5 (1931–32): 266–277.

43. This subject is discussed more fully in Chapter 6.

44. Tyack, *The One Best System,* p. 183.

45. Lynd and Lynd, *Middletown,* pp. 188, 211–218.

46. See Marvin Lazerson, *Origins of the Urban School: Public Education in Massachusetts, 1870–1915* (Cambridge: Harvard University Press, 1971); Reed Ueda, *Avenues to Adulthood: The Origins of the High School and Social Mobility in an American Suburb* (New York: Cambridge University Press, 1987); and Sol Cohen, "The Mental Hygiene Movement, the Development of Personality and

the School: The Medicalization of American Education," *History of Education Quarterly* 23 (1983): 123–149 for discussions of the transformation of the purpose of education. For a contemporary summary of character education programs in the schools, see William I. Thomas and Dorothy Swaine Thomas, *The Child in America* (New York: Alfred A. Knopf, 1928), pp. 273–294.

47. Healy reported the truancy figure for Boston during one year, 1917–18, as 1.1 percent of the school population. Judge Baker Foundation, "Case No. Eleven," *Case Studies, Series I* (Boston: Judge Baker Foundation, 1922–23), p. 5-a. Attitudes of the helping professions toward truancy in Boston are described in David Tyack and Michael Berkowitz, "The Man Nobody Liked," *American Quarterly* 29 (1977): 31–54.

48. On teacher-identified problems, see E. K. Wickman, *Children's Behavior and Teachers' Attitudes*. Wickman concluded that teachers identified immoralities, dishonesties and transgressions against authority as the most serious problems they faced, followed by disorderliness in the classroom and aggressive personality and behavior traits. Of least importance were withdrawn, recessive personalities and behavior traits.

49. The phrase is borrowed from David Tyack, *The One Best System*, p. 199. To get an education was traditionally perceived as the American way out of poverty and the way to get ahead. Good grades in school signified to some immigrant families that a child might experience a better life than his or her parents, although not all immigrants encouraged education for the sake of later financial comfort. For many families, the trials of the moment made early entry into the work force imperative. See JBGC file no. 9262, an immigrant father who wanted his children to have a good education; and no. 9253, a widowed mother who worked at housecleaning and hoped the clinic could convince her daughter to stay in school. Alternative attitudes are discussed in Smith, "Italian Mothers, American Daughters."

50. Elder, *Children of the Great Depression*, pp. 26–27.

51. Ibid., p. 28.

52. Lynd and Lynd, *Middletown*, p. 133.

53. Thom, "Guiding the Adolescent," p. 53.

54. Dale Carnegie, *How to Win Friends and Influence People* (New York: Simon and Schuster, 1936), p. 18.

55. Healy, *The Individual Delinquent*, pp. 694–708.

56. Winifred Richmond, *The Adolescent Girl: A Book for Parents and Teachers* (New York: Macmillan Co., 1928), p. 53.

57. Leo Kanner, *Child Psychiatry* (Springfield, Ill.: Charles C. Thomas, 1935), pp. 36–38.

58. Leta Hollingworth used the term "psychological weaning" in *The Psychology of the Adolescent* (New York: D. Appleton and Co., 1929), pp. 36–58.

59. Healy, *The Individual Delinquent*, p. 712.

60. For example, see JBGC file no. 1643 and case no. 1659. See also Judge Baker Foundation, *Case Studies, Series I*, "Case no. 2–3," p. 35-a; and "Case no. 9," p. 15-a. The subject was discussed in S. Spafford Ackerly, "Rebellion and Its Relation to Delinquency and Neurosis in 60 Adolescents," *AJO* 3 (1933): 147–160.

61. Defined in Healy, *The Individual Delinquent*, p. 766–767. See also Judge Baker Foundation, "Case no. 15," *Case Studies, Series I*, p. 24-a.

62. Although Healy followed Hall's characterization of the years of puberty as a time of erratic behavior, he lacked Hall's reverence for adolescence. Hall called the teen years "the apical stage of human development" (*Adolescence*, vol. 2., p. 361, quoted in Dorothy Ross, *G. Stanley Hall: The Psychologist as Prophet* (Chicago: University of Chicago Press, 1972), p. 332). Healy, in contrast, saw adolescence as a problem stage to be outgrown, not a stage of highest development that only degenerated with maturity. On perceptions of "normal" adolescence during the years of child guidance professionalization, see Leta S. Hollingworth, *The Psychology of the Adolescent* (New York: D. Appleton and Co., 1929); and Frankwood E. Williams, *Adolescence: Studies in Mental Hygiene* (New York: Farrar and Rinehart, 1930).

63. Other cases of adolescent rebellion included JBGC case nos. 9246, 9266, and 9209.

64. Thom, "Guiding the Adolescent," p. 37. See also Frankwood Williams, "Confronting the World: The Adjustments of Later Adolescence," in Child Study Association of America, ed., *Concerning Parents: A Symposium* (New York: New Republic, 1929), pp. 137–138. Williams believed that the adolescent had to face two major hurdles: emancipation from home, and the establishment of heterosexuality.

65. See also JBGC case no. 9246. The clinic team noted that the father in this case had little understanding of an adolescent girl's needs, consequently they called the girl's resentments entirely justified.

66. Alice D. Kelly, "Why Adolescence Is Hard on Parents," *Parents' Magazine* 6 (December 1931): 52.

67. The psychiatrist Ira S. Wile took this attitude to the extreme when he adopted the voice of the child in a radio talk, reprinted as "Adolescence—Its Challenges," *AJO* 11 (1941): 599–602. "Accept the world of youth and recognize that adolescents have a world of their own," Wile's adolescent told its elders (p. 600).

68. Thom, "Guiding the Adolescent," pp. 87–88.

69. Katharine Whiteside Taylor, *Do Adolescents Need Parents?* (New York: D. Appleton-Century Co., 1938). Thom makes the same point in "Guiding the Adolescent."

70. A good summary of child guidance views can be found in Bird T. Baldwin, "Bridging the Gap between Our Knowledge of Child Nature and the Training

of Children," in M. V. O'Shea, ed., *The Child: His Nature and His Needs* (New York: Children's Foundation, 1924), pp. 13–30. See John B. Watson, *Behaviorism,* rev. ed. (Chicago: University of Chicago Press, 1930), and Watson, *The Psychological Care of the Infant* (New York: W. W. Norton, 1928). For the psychoanalytic perspective, see J. C. Flügel, *The Psycho-Analytic Study of the Family* (1921; reprint, London: Hogarth Press and the Institute for Psycho-Analysis, 1960). The Jungian viewpoint was represented by Frances G. Wickes, *The Inner World of Childhood: A Study in Analytical Psychology* (New York: D. Appleton and Co., 1930). The influence of these two perspectives on child rearing is discussed in Elizabeth M. R. Lomax et al., *Science and Patterns of Child Care* (San Francisco: W. H. Freeman and Co., 1978); and Geoffrey H. Steere, "Freudianism and Child-Rearing in the Twenties," *American Quarterly* 20 (1968): 759–765.

71. Peter Stearns, *American Cool,* chaps. 4–8, pp. 95–264.

72. The popularization literature is filled with discussions of these needs. A good starting point, and a quasi-professional account of the emotional needs of the child, is Mary Buell Sayles, *The Problem Child at Home: A Study in Parent-Child Relationships* (New York: Commonwealth Fund, 1932), pp. 3–13. An explicit statement based on experiences at the Judge Baker Foundation was by Augusta Bronner, "Emotional Problems of Adolescents," in Chicago Association for Child Study and Parent Education, ed., *The Child's Emotions, Proceedings of the Midwest Conference on Character Development* (Chicago: University of Chicago Press, 1930), pp. 214–230.

73. Douglas Thom, *The Everyday Problems of the Everyday Child* (New York: D. Appleton and Co., 1927), p. 200.

74. Sayles, *The Problem Child at Home,* p. 5. See also Blanchard and Manasses, *New Girls for Old,* pp. 15–21.

75. Leo Kanner, in his textbook *Child Psychiatry,* noted that "environment" constituted more than the child's immediate surroundings. Even he, however, assumed that "it is only natural that the home looms first and foremost among the situational factors which contribute to the molding of the child's personality" (p. 87). Kanner cited two cases where national events influenced the "psychiatric office hour," one of which was the fear of kidnapping engendered by the Lindbergh case. In discussing "environmental" causes of misbehavior and maladjustment, Kanner began with the home, which he followed with shorter sections on the neighborhood and school. In the discussion of schools, a subheading indicated parental interference as one aspect of the educational environment, suggesting that parental attitudes infiltrated even the larger definition of environment. Kanner was by no means a Freudian in 1935, yet here, too, the family was seen as the instrument of the child's emotional failings. *Child Psychiatry,* pp. 86–112.

76. Thom, *Everyday Problems of the Everyday Child,* pp. 193, 206.

77. Ibid., pp. 201–206. Among adolescent girls insecurity was thought to account for sexual escapades. See Blanchard and Manasses, *New Girls for Old,* pp. 57, 20. See also Thomas, *The Unadjusted Girl,* pp. 1–40. Thomas identified four "wishes," or "forces which impel action" (p. 4), as the desire for new experience, the desire for security, the desire for response (or love), and the desire for recognition. Thwarting the desires resulted in sexual promiscuity among the adolescents he studied.

78. On Adler and the inferiority complex, see Paul Stepansky, *In Freud's Shadow: Adler in Context* (Hillside, N.J.: Analytic Press, 1983), pp. 206–211. A good summary of the American understanding of the concept can be found in Lawson Lowrey, "Competitions and the Conflict over Difference: The 'Inferiority Complex' in the Psychopathology of Childhood," *MH* 12 (1928): 316–330; see also Kanner, *Child Psychiatry,* p. 8. The relationship between physical defects and feelings of inferiority was described in William E. Carter, "Physical Findings in Problem Children," *MH* 10 (1926): 75–84. On Adler's influence in the clinic, see the interview with S. Spafford Ackerly, a psychiatrist who worked with Healy and Bronner at the Judge Baker clinic, in the Milton Senn Child Guidance Oral History Collection, History of Medicine Division, National Library of Medicine, Bethesda, Md.

79. Lowrey, "Competitions and Conflict over Difference," pp. 320–321.

80. Two clear statements of this position can be found in John Levy, "The Impact of Cultural Forms upon Children's Behavior," *MH* 16 (1932): 203–220, and Ira S. Wile, "The Challenge of Childhood," *MH* 19 (1935): 44.

81. William Healy and Augusta Bronner, *New Light on Delinquency and Its Treatment* (New Haven: Yale University Press for the Institute of Human Relations, 1936), pp. 4–5.

82. A summary of his views can be found in James S. Plant, *Personality and the Cultural Pattern* (New York: Commonwealth Fund, 1937).

83. Linda Gordon, *Pitied but Not Entitled: Single Mothers and the History of Welfare, 1890–1935* (New York: Free Press, 1994). The White House Conference on Child Health and Protection, meeting during 1930, did produce a "Bill of Rights" for children. This document begins: "1. Every child is entitled to be understood, and all dealings with him should be based on the fullest understanding of the child." It concluded with a call for more public services for children. The title, however, seems to represent a formulaic usage of rights rather than a reconceptualization of needs. "The White House Conference Drafts a Bill of Rights for the American Child," *MH* 15 (1931): 208–210.

6. Children and Child Guidance

1. Joseph F. Kett, *Rites of Passage: Adolescence in America, 1790 to the Present* (New York: Basic Books, 1977), is just one example of the objectification of children

in historical literature. See "Introduction," in N. Ray Hiner and Joseph M. Hawes, eds., *Growing up in America: Children in Historical Perspective* (Urbana: University of Illinois Press, 1985), pp. xiii–xxv, for a critique of this view.

2. See Harvey J. Graff, *Conflicting Paths: Growing Up in America* (Cambridge: Harvard University Press, 1997) for a history of young people that makes "the young people, themselves, their voices . . . central" to the story (pp. 5–6). For the problems of the age group that drove the interests of the child guiders, see Grace Palladino, *Teenagers: An American History* (New York: Basic Books, 1996). Other studies of children as historical agents include John Gillis, *Youth and History: Tradition and Change in European Age Relations, 1770–Present* (New York, Academic Press, 1974); William M. Tuttle, Jr., *"Daddy's Gone to War": The Second World War in the Lives of America's Children* (New York: Oxford University Press, 1993); David Nasaw, *Children of the City: At Work and at Play* (Garden City, N.Y.: Anchor Press/Doubleday, 1985); E. Anthony Rotundo, "Boy Culture: Middle-Class Boyhood in Nineteenth-Century America," in Mark C. Carnes and Clyde Griffen, eds., *Meanings of Manhood: Constructions of Masculinity in Victorian America* (Chicago: University of Chicago Press, 1990); and Elliott West and Paula Petrik, eds., *Small Worlds: Children and Adolescents in America, 1850–1950* (Lawrence: University Press of Kansas, 1992). The influential behavior of adolescent girls has become a part of the literature of women's history. See the work of Joan Jacobs Brumberg, *Fasting Girls: The Emergence of Anorexia Nervosa as a Modern Disease* (Cambridge: Harvard University Press, 1988); Kathy Peiss, *Cheap Amusements: Working Women and Leisure in Turn-of-the-Century New York* (Philadelphia: Temple University Press, 1986); and Mary E. Odem, *Delinquent Daughters: Protecting and Policing Adolescent Female Sexuality in the United States, 1885–1920* (Chapel Hill: University of North Carolina Press, 1995).

3. Voluntary cases split about evenly, but the juvenile court continued to send more boys than girls for evaluation.

4. This heading is borrowed from Frederick H. Allen, "The Child as the Therapist Sees Him," *Bulletin of the State University of Iowa*, Child Welfare Pamphlets no. 50, Iowa City, 23 November 1935.

5. "Symposium: Certain Aspects of Treatment in Psychiatric Work with Children," *AJO* 3 (1933): 310–336; "Symposium on Child Psychiatry," *AJP* 94 (1937): 643–707; "Trends in Therapy: The Evolution and Present Status of Treatment Approaches to Behavior and Personality," *AJO* 9 (1939): 669–760. At the 1940 meeting, the American Orthopsychiatric Association presented yet another "Symposium: Techniques of Treatment," *AJO* 10 (1940): 651–697. Discussants presented case histories followed by general discussion.

6. Lawson G. Lowrey, "Treatment of Behavior Problems. Part I: Some Illustrations of Variations in Treatment Approach," *AJO* 4 (1934): 121.

7. Lawson G. Lowrey made this observation during the 1939 symposium on

treatment. "Evolution, Status, and Trends," part 1 of "Trends in Therapy: The Evolution and Present Status of Treatment Approaches to Behavior and Personality Problems," *AJO* 9 (1939): 670.

8. Transference, as Healy and Bronner defined it in their source book of psychoanalysis, referred to the "shifting of feelings of love . . . from one object or person to another." William Healy, Augusta F. Bronner, and Anna Mae Bowers, *The Structure and Meaning of Psychoanalysis as Related to Personality and Behavior* (New York: Alfred A. Knopf, 1930), p. 204. Samuel W. Hartwell, "Symposium: The Treatment of Behavior and Personality Problems in Children. A. The Psychiatrist," *AJO* 1 (1930): 5.

9. Samuel W. Hartwell, *Fifty-Five "Bad" Boys* (New York: Alfred A. Knopf, 1931), p. 269.

10. Sheldon Glueck and Eleanor T. Glueck, *One Thousand Juvenile Delinquents: Their Treatment by Court and Clinic* (Cambridge: Harvard University Press, 1934); and Helen Leland Witmer, "A Comparison of Treatment Results in Various Types of Child Guidance Clinics," *AJO* 5 (1935): 351–360. Witmer's article was a comprehensive report of investigations undertaken by students from Smith College School of Social Work during the previous four years. See also Marjorie Stauffer, "Some Aspects of Treatment by Psychiatrist and Psychiatric Social Worker," *AJO* 2 (1932): 152–161; Ruth M. Hubbard and Christine F. Adams, "Factors Affecting the Success of Child Guidance Clinic Treatment," *AJO* 6 (1936): 81–102; and William I. Thomas and Dorothy Swain Thomas, discussing social worker Porter Lee's account of the Bureau of Child Guidance in New York City, in *The Child in America: Behavior Problems and Programs* (New York: Alfred A. Knopf, 1928), p. 149.

11. David Levy, "Comment," *AJO* 3 (1933): 334.

12. Dr. G. S. Amsden made these remarks in the discussion following a paper by Lawson G. Lowrey. The paper and discussion were reprinted as "Some Principles in the Treatment of Behavior Problems in Children," *Archives of Neurology and Psychiatry* 25 (1931): 883–894, quote p. 891.

13. Frederick H. Allen, of the Philadelphia child guidance center, suggested this in "Participation in Therapy," *AJO* 9 (1939): 737.

14. Another example of a boy who entered into the spirit of the clinic (at least until his father interfered) is in JBGC case no. 9241.

15. JBGC case nos. 9202, 9205, 9212, and 9244.

16. Psychiatrists usually requested that older children make independent visits to the clinic, part of a plan to promote adolescent independence.

17. Philip Davis, "Preliminary Report on the Study of the Boy Problem," *Proceedings of the National Conference of Charities and Corrections* 42 (1915): 202–203.

18. Forbush and others are discussed in Michael Kimmel, *Manhood in America: A Cultural History* (New York: Free Press, 1996), pp. 157–188. On the culture's

concern about masculinity, see Gail Bederman, *Manliness and Civilization: A Cultural History of Gender and Race in the United States, 1880–1917* (Chicago: University of Chicago Press, 1995).

19. Brother Barnabas, "The Prevention of Delinquency: Boy Guidance—The New Profession," *Proceedings of the National Conference of Social Work* (1924): 157–160; and Brother Barnabas, "Boyology," *Proceedings of the National Conference of Social Work* (1926): 172–174. See also "Boyology—A New and All-Important Study," *Playground* 19 (March 1926): 670. On the founder's life and work, see "Brother Barnabas Dies in New Mexico," *New York Times* (24 April 1929): 29.

20. "Special Bulletin of the University of Notre Dame, Courses in Boys' Work" August 1931. A copy is located in Notre Dame Printed Materials (PNDP) 1212–Boy, Archives of the University of Notre Dame, Notre Dame, Ind.

21. The basic elements of Freud's ideas can be found in a collection of his essays, *The Sexual Enlightenment of Children*, ed. Philip Reiff (New York: Collier Books, 1963). I have used also the description provided by Healy, Bronner, and Bowers in *The Structure and Meaning of Psychoanalysis*, pp. 128–165. A helpful contemporary summary of American psychoanalysis in the 1930s was found in Horace M. Kallen, "Psychoanalysis," in Edwin R. A. Seligman, ed., *Encyclopaedia of the Social Sciences*, vol. 12 (New York: Macmillan Co., 1934), pp. 580–588.

22. Not all child guidance psychiatrists adhered strictly to Freudian constructs of personality development. Leo Kanner, for example, a disciple of Adolf Meyer's psychobiology, dismissed the Oedipus complex as another "ready-made formula," applied without diagnostic evidence; its use, he felt, was akin to calling troublesome behavior "badness," or neurotic tendencies "just imagination." Leo Kanner, *Child Psychiatry* (Springfield, Ill.: Charles C. Thomas, 1935), pp. 15, 76–77, 81.

23. Helen T. Wooley, "A Review of Recent Literature on the Psychology of Sex," *Psychological Bulletin* 7 (1910): 335–342, was critical of the idea; Leta S. Hollingworth, "Comparison of the Sexes in Mental Traits," *Psychological Bulletin* 15 (1918): 427–432, reviewed findings in this field to date. Hollingworth herself had contributed studies in this area; her role is discussed by Rosalind Rosenberg, "Leta Hollingworth: Toward a Sexless Intelligence," in Miriam Lewin, ed., *In the Shadow of the Past: Psychology Portrays the Sexes, a Social and Intellectual History* (New York: Columbia University Press, 1984), pp. 77–96. See also Rosenberg's larger study, *Beyond Separate Spheres: The Intellectual Roots of Modern Feminism* (New Haven: Yale University Press, 1982). Cynthia Eagle Russett, *Sexual Science: The Victorian Construction of Womanhood*, (Cambridge: Harvard University Press, 1989), provides background for this debate.

24. Beth L. Wellman, "Sex Differences," in Carl Murchison, ed., *A Handbook of Child Psychology*, 2d ed. rev. (New York: Russell and Russell, 1933), p. 626. The

subject was so pervasive that, in their textbook *Child Psychology* (New York: Macmillan Co., 1934), George E. Stoddard and Beth Wellman indicated sex differences for virtually every topic covered. While the term "sex differences" was indexed by the authors, neither race nor class differences were deemed equally important.

25. Percival M. Symonds, "Sex Differences in the Life Problems and Interests of Adolescents," *School and Society* 43 (30 May 1936): 752. Emphasis in original.

26. Girls show more aesthetic appreciation: Harvey C. Lehman and Paul A. Witty, "Play Interests as Evidence of Sex Differences in Aesthetic Appreciation," *American Journal of Psychology* 40 (1928): 449–457. William F. Book and John L. Meadows, "Sex Differences in 5925 High School Seniors in Ten Psychological Tests," *Journal of Applied Psychology* 12 (1928): 56–81, found differences in special mental abilities; boys excelled on tests using mathematical abilities and practical information while girls surpassed boys on word completion and logical memory tests. On gangs and groups, see Florence L. Goodenough, *Developmental Psychology: An Introduction to the Study of Human Behavior* (New York: D. Appleton-Century Co., 1934), pp. 474–475.

H. Hart and E. Olander, "Sex Differences in Character as Indicated by Teachers' Ratings," *School and Society* 20 (1924): 381–382, used the phrase "sex halo" to describe the differential ratings teachers gave to boys and girls. Girls received higher grades, these researchers contended, because teachers found girls more sincere, earnest, energetic, and kind than boys. E. A. Lincoln, in *Sex Differences in the Growth of American School Children* (Baltimore: Warwick and York, 1927), found evidence that girls were brighter than boys up to age fourteen or fifteen, and attributed the cause to the different rates of physical maturity. Using college students as subjects, Roswell H. Whitman found no difference in rates of introversion and extroversion, but did find differences in "kind." "Sex and Age Differences in Introversion-Extroversion," *Journal of Abnormal Psychology* 24 (1929): 207–211. Sarah Janet Bassett, "Sex Differences in History Retention," *School and Society* 29 (23 March 1929): 397–398.

Lehman and Witty also reported that "boys obtain greater pleasure than do girls from participation in activities which require a high degree of mechanical ability or motor skill"; "Sex Differences: Interest in Tasks Requiring Mechanical Ability and Motor Skill," *Journal of Educational Psychology* 21 (1930): 243. In the same article, these researchers concluded that the differences measured "acquired abilities" based on experience rather than on innate differences. Paul L. Boynton, "Are Girls Superior to Boys in Visual Memory," *Journal of Social Psychology* 2(1931): 496–500, concluded: "This study would seem to indicate that, while it is possible to show that girls are superior to boys in visual memory, it is also possible to show that girls are not superior to boys in visual memory [depending on the materials used in measurement]" (p. 500). Arthur

E. Traxler, "Sex Differences in Rate of Reading in the High School," *Journal of Applied Psychology* 19 (1935): 351–352, found that boys read faster but this was not necessarily an indicator of intelligence. Boys were less punctual than girls: L. A. Lockwood, "Causes of Tardiness," *School Review* 38 (1930): 538–543; and boys were more punctual than girls: George J. Dudycha, "Sex Differences in Punctuality," *Journal of Social Psychology* 8 (1937): 355–363. On the question of lying, Byrne J. Horton reported that "GIRLS are more truthful than boys . . . The greatest deceivers are the boys in the high school" (p. 399). "The Truthfulness of Boys and Girls in Public and Private Schools," *Journal of Abnormal Psychology* 31 (1937): 398–405.

In addition to Beth Wellman's review essay, other comprehensive discussions include: William H. Burnham, "Sex Differences in Mental Ability," *Educational Review* 62 (1921):273–284; Chauncey N. Allen, "Studies in Sex Differences," *Psychological Bulletin* 24 (1927): 294–304; Allen, "Recent Studies in Sex Differences," *Psychological Bulletin* 27 (1930): 394–407; Allen, "Recent Research on Sex Differences," *Psychological Bulletin* 32 (1935): 343–354; and Winifred B. Johnson and Lewis M. Terman, "Some Highlights in the Literature of Psychological Sex Difference Published since 1920," *Journal of Psychology* 9 (1940): 327–336.

27. Lewis M. Terman et al., *The Promise of Youth: Follow-up Studies of a Thousand Gifted Children*, vol. 3 of *Genetic Studies of Genius* (Stanford: Stanford University Press, 1930), pp. 153–161.

28. Lewis M. Terman and Catharine Cox Miles, *Sex and Personality: Studies in Masculinity and Femininity* (New York: Russell and Russell, 1936).

29. The entire test is reprinted in appendix 4 of Terman and Miles, *Sex and Personality*, pp. 482–530. On the M-F test, see Henry L. Minton, *Lewis M. Terman: Pioneer in Psychological Testing* (New York: New York University Press, 1988), pp. 168–178; and Miriam Lewin, "'Rather Worse than Folly?' Psychology Measures Femininity and Masculinity, 1: From Terman and Miles to the Guilfords," in Lewin, ed., *In the Shadow of the Past*, pp. 155–178.

30. Miles and Terman noted that they were not interested "at present" in "demonstrating a superiority of one sex with corresponding inferiority of the other . . . Rather, the concern is with an evaluation of the available, experimentally demonstrated findings which may contribute to an understanding of present development under existing conditions" (p. 161); "Sex Difference in the Association of Ideas," *American Journal of Psychology* 41 (1929): 165–206. Cynthia Fuchs Epstein's discussion of the uses of analytical distinctions in social science research is particularly helpful in interpreting the sex differences research of the 1920s and 1930s; see *Deceptive Distinctions: Sex, Gender, and the Social Order* (New Haven: Yale University Press, 1988).

31. On the changing composition of the work force, see Lynn Y. Weiner, *From*

Working Girl to Working Mother: The Female Labor Force in the United States, 1820–1980 (Chapel Hill: University of North Carolina Press, 1985), pp. 84–88, 100–110. See also Lois Scharf, *To Work and to Wed: Female Employment, Feminism, and the Great Depression* (Westport, Conn.: Greenwood Press, 1980). Scharf discusses opposition in Massachusetts to work-force participation by married women (pp. 55–56). On homosexuality, see George Chauncey, *Gay New York: Gender, Urban Culture, and the Making of the Gay Male World, 1890–1940* (New York: Basic Books, 1994). Terman believed the M-F Test could diagnose serious sex-identification problems, including homosexuality (*Sex and Personality,* pp. 9–10). Henry L. Minton, "Femininity in Men and Masculinity in Women: American Psychiatry and Psychology Portray Homosexuality in the 1930s," *Journal of Homosexuality* 13 (1986): 1–21.

32. Kimmel, *Manhood in America,* pp. 191–221; Jessie Bernard, "The Good-Provider Role: Its Rise and Fall," *American Psychologist* 36 (1981): 1–12; Robert Griswold, *Fatherhood in America: A History* (New York: Basic Books, 1993), pp. 143–160.

33. What E. Anthony Rotundo has called, in another context, a "boy culture." "Boy Culture: Middle-Class Boyhood in Nineteenth-Century America," in Carnes and Griffen, eds., *Meanings of Manhood,* pp. 15–36.

34. "Abnormal sexualism" was from William Healy, *The Individual Delinquent* (Boston: Little, Brown and Co., 1915), p. 400. Healy used the term to refer to masturbation, early sex experiences, hypersexualism, and homosexuality. Popularized child guidance books on adolescence focused much more attention on boy-girl relationships. Douglas Thom, in "Guiding the Adolescent" (U.S., Department of Labor, Children's Bureau Publication no. 225 [Washington, D.C.: Government Printing Office, 1933]), talked about the impact of coeducation and followed up with a discussion of petting. See the chapter on "Attitudes toward Sex," pp. 12–20. The term "petting" did not appear in any of the case files from 1935. The psychologist Winifred Richmond, in *The Adolescent Boy: A Book for Parents and Teachers* (New York: Farrar and Rinehart, 1933), explained that a teenager's feelings were not apt to be directed to girls (this was "the gang stage *par excellence*"). But a boy's sex feelings were awakening at this stage of life, and therefore homosexuality could develop (pp. 50–51). Then again, Richmond also wrote that "the thing of greatest importance in the life of the average adolescent boy is his relationship with the opposite sex" (p. 187). She apparently saw no contradiction.

35. There were exceptions. In case no. 9440, a sixteen-year-old boy was asked directly about sex with girls. "It is rather unfortunate," the staff reported in its treatment recommendation, "that the boy did not return [to the clinic] because he told frankly of being recently in sex episodes with girls and it may be that he has had more conflict and that this may play some part in his behavior. Family

apparently know nothing about this, and boy would undoubtedly profit by some discussion of sex interests." This boy, the son of immigrants, had stolen a belt from a local store, an act the clinic staff dismissed as not very serious.

36. Stephen Habbe, "Nicknames of Adolescent Boys," *AJO* 7 (1937): 371–377.

37. See the chapter entitled "Deviance," in Clyde W. Franklin II, *Men and Society* (Chicago: Nelson-Hall, 1988), pp. 123–155.

38. Derivation of the term "sissy" is discussed in Peter N. Stearns, "Girls, Boys, and Emotions: Redefinitions and Historical Change," *Journal of American History* 80 (1993): 48–49. Chauncey, in *Gay New York,* explains the terms "fairy," "faggot," "queer," and "pansy" (pp. 13–23). As each author points out, the sexual worries and the nomenclature were not new to the 1930s, but professional interest certainly grew more intense at that time. On medical researchers' interest in homosexuality, see Henry L. Minton, "Community Empowerment and the Medicalization of Homosexuality: Constructing Sexual Identities in the 1930s," *Journal of the History of Sexuality* 6 (1996): 435–458.

39. "Sophisticated" was equally bad, for it implied a "sex teacher" who introduced other boys to noxious habits, or a lad with an unusual degree of sexual experience. Sophisticated, however, was an adjective more often applied to girls.

40. JBGC case nos. 9277, 9205, 9220, 9183, 9272, and 9249.

41. Allan M. Brandt, *No Magic Bullet: A Social History of Venereal Disease in the United States since 1880* (New York: Oxford University Press, 1987); John Burnham, "The Progressive Era Revolution in American Attitudes toward Sex," *Journal of American History* 59 (1973):885–908; Bryan Strong, "Ideas of the Early Sex Education Movement in America, 1890–1920," *History of Education Quarterly* 12(1972): 129–161; and James R. Cook, "The Evolution of Sex Education in the Public Schools of the United States, 1900–1970" (Ph.D. diss., Southern Illinois University, 1971).

42. Parent discomfort with sex education was reported by Robert S. Lynd and Helen Merrell Lynd, *Middletown: A Study in American Culture* (New York: Harcourt, Brace and Co., 1929), pp. 145–146. See, for example, JBGC case no. 9261, involving the mother of a sixteen-year-old boy. She knew her son "[knew] things," but because his father would not discuss the topic, she wanted the male doctor to give the boy information. Mary Buell Sayles, *The Problem Child at Home: A Study in Parent-Child Relationships* (New York: Commonwealth Fund, 1928), advised parents that physicians were their "natural confidants and advisers" when "facing problems of sex education or sex habits in their children, and . . . child guidance clinics receive the confidences of many an anxious parent" (pp. 93–94).

43. A similar story is in JBGC case no. 9302.

44. Social workers had begun by the mid-1930s to encourage adults to talk about their own sexual difficulties, and hoped to find here insights into the behavioral

problems of the children. JBGC case no. 9215 is an example of such a discussion.

45. JBGC case no. 9183 was another instance of a foster mother upset by the clinic's "sex talk." The staff made plans to discuss the boy's psychotherapy with her to allay her fears.

46. In JBGC case no. 9216, Skinner recommended further sex education, but this was a court case—one interview—and there was no evidence in the file that the clinic followed up on the recommendation.

47. The book was Karl de Schweinitz, *Growing Up: The Story of How We Become Alive, Are Born, and Grow Up* (New York: Macmillan Co., 1928). This simple text with many photographs was frequently recommended to parents at the clinic and was one of the standards on bibliographies published by the Child Study Association of America. Pavenstedt also read *Growing Up* to another mixed-up ten-year-old (9437). This was a child whose neighbors had been reporting signs of neglect and abuse for at least three years. They described the girl's search for food in garbage cans, and the fact that she was used as a "slavey" at home to scrub floors and perform other menial tasks. She was reported to be in poor physical condition, with fewer clothes than the boys in the family. Her mother, however, reported that the child was a chronic masturbator who was teaching her younger brothers bad sex habits. In this case the profession seems to have focused on what it could change, not the root of the problem.

48. The cases treated by Eleanor Pavenstedt, who was at the clinic for only a short while in 1935, were the exception. This psychologist considered sex education important. Case no. 9453: "Another attempt was made to find out how much sex information she had. She thinks that babies come from hospitals and so this also was taken up—informing her as to the fact of motherhood. No further attempt was made to orientate her." Case no. 9454: In this case the interviewer read *Growing Up* to a girl whose mother had decided against giving her sex information until the girl was nearer age twelve. Pavenstedt provided the information and told the girl it was unnecessary for her to tell her mother, unless she wanted to do so.

49. Sex delinquency was still a category of juvenile crime in 1935. On the parents' observations, see the mothers in JBGC case nos. 9442 and 9288.

50. See Elizabeth Lunbeck, *Psychiatric Persuasion: Knowledge, Gender, and Power in Modern America* (Princeton: Princeton University Press, 1994), pp. 295–300; and Lillian Faderman, *Odd Girls and Twilight Lovers: A History of Lesbian Life in Twentieth-Century America* (New York: Penguin Books, 1991), pp. 62–138.

51. The Children's Bureau reported in 1926 that 8.6 percent of Massachusetts children (aged ten to fifteen) were "engaged in gainful occupations." (Only 0.2 percent were doing agricultural work.) U.S., Department of Labor, "Child

Labor in the United States: Ten Questions Answered," Children's Bureau Publication no. 114 (Washington, D.C.: Government Printing Office, 1926), p. 10. In 1935, however, the clinic staff did not advocate child labor or work to help support the family. In JBGC case no. 9239, parents expected their son to bring home his earnings; this the clinic did not condone. Control over a child's earnings was also an issue in case nos. 9251 and 9255. The clinic distinguished between "child labor" and legitimate child work, which provided a form of mental discipline and an appropriate use of leisure time. Douglas Thom, in "Guiding the Adolescent," stated the child guidance requirements for work: "work during adolescence under proper conditions is a means of keeping young boys and girls wholesomely occupied, helping them to use up some of the abundant energy that is constantly seeking an outlet, and teaching them that work itself is an excellent antidote for all kinds of dissatisfactions, sorrows, and tribulations" (p. 51). See Viviana A. Zelizer, "From Child Labor to Child Work: Redefining the Economic World of Children," chap. 3 of *Pricing the Priceless Child: The Changing Social Value of Children* (New York: Basic Books, 1985), pp. 73–112.

52. Lindbergh also figured in these stories as a cause of fear. At least two children reported being scared by or having dreams about the man who kidnapped the Lindberghs' baby. JBGC case nos. 9225, 9231.

53. JBGC case nos. 9287, 9263. Flying was to be not as farfetched as the Judge Baker staff presumed since many of these boys eventually found their way into military service during World War II. In 1935, however, the staff believed aviation outside the reach of most Judge Baker boys.

54. Ester Loring Richards, *Behaviour Aspects of Child Conduct* (New York: Macmillan Co., 1932), p. 209. Winifred Richmond made the same point in *The Adolescent Boy.* Teenagers should be encouraged but not pushed.

55. A good summary of vocational guidance in the 1930s can be found in John T. Brewer, "Vocational Guidance," in *Encyclopaedia of the Social Sciences,* vol. 15, pp. 276–279. On child guidance contributions, see Harry M. Tiebout, "Psychiatric Phases in Vocational Guidance," *MH* 10 (1926): 102–112.

56. In this instance, the clinic urged the agency to give the boy his lead. If he faltered in the aviation course, the agency was advised to prepare him carefully for an alternative, since the goal "means so much to b[oy]" (9222).

57. In cases from early in the Depression I found scattered references to boys who asked their Judge Baker contacts for employment references, but in the 1935 files the only references supplied by the clinic were in response to military inquiries years later during World War II. Perhaps this dearth of reactions existed because psychologists, not known for recording lengthy or detailed accounts of interviews, performed the actual testing and much of the advising.

58. JBGC case nos. 9422, 9455, 9433, and 9305.

59. Harvey C. Lehman and Paul A. Witty, "Sex Differences in Vocational Attitudes," *Journal of Applied Psychology* 20 (1936): 576–585.
60. Occasionally, as in JBGC case no. 9209, the psychiatrist offered a child advice on how to handle a difficult parent. Samuel Hartwell, in *Fifty-Five Bad Boys* (pp. 75–77), explained to a JBF boy why mothers worry too much (after Hartwell decided that this mother was not likely to change under the clinic's supervision).
61. Frederick H. Allen, "Evolution of a Treatment Philosophy in Child Guidance," *MH* 14 (1930): 6.

7. The Critique of Motherhood

1. Helen Leland Witmer, *Psychiatric Clinics for Children* (New York: Commonwealth Fund, 1940), p. 345.
2. Ethel Sturges Dummer to Ester Loring Richards, 4 February 1920, Dummer Papers.
3. In his study of motherhood, Levy reported that "selfish, demanding, undisciplined" youngsters had begun to form a significant part of child guidance caseloads. David M. Levy, *Maternal Overprotection* (New York: Columbia University Press, 1943), p. 160; John B. Watson, *Psychological Care of Infant and Child* (New York: W. W. Norton, 1928), p. 69. For Ernest R. Groves and Gladys H. Groves this was a theme of their work, but see particularly *Parents and Children* (Philadelphia: J. B. Lippincott Co., 1928), p. 116. A good summary of contemporary thinking about the role of family dynamics on juvenile behavior is Percival Symonds, *The Psychology of Parent-Child Relationships* (New York: D. Appleton-Century Co., 1939).
4. J. M. Flügel, *The Psycho-Analytic Study of the Family* (1921; reprint, London: Hogarth Press and the Institute of Psycho-Analysis, 1960), p. 46. American researchers referenced Flügel more frequently than Freud. See, for example, the credit given to Flügel in Symonds, *Parent-Child Relationships*, p. 5. In this same passage Flügel also condemned authoritarian fathers; I discuss child guidance perceptions of fathers later in this chapter.
5. Peter N. Stearns, *American Cool: Constructing a Twentieth-Century Emotional Style* (New York: New York University Press, 1994); Ann Douglas, *Terrible Honesty: Mongrel Manhattan in the 1920s* (New York: Farrar, Straus and Giroux, Noonday Press, 1995); Susan Contratto, "Mother: Social Sculptor and Trustee of the Faith," in Miriam Lewin, ed., *In the Shadow of the Past: Psychology Portrays the Sexes—a Social and Intellectual History* (New York: Columbia University Press, 1984), pp. 226–255; Julia Weiss, "Womanhood and Psychoanalysis: A Study of Mutual Construction in Popular Culture, 1920–1963" (Ph.D. diss., Brown University, 1990); Barbara Ehrenreich and Deirdre English,

For Her Own Good: 150 Years of the Experts' Advice to Women (Garden City, N.Y.: Anchor Press/Doubleday, 1979); Robyn Muncy, *Creating a Female Dominion in American Reform, 1890–1935* (New York: Oxford University Press, 1991); and Molly Ladd-Taylor, *Mother-Work: Women, Child Welfare, and the State, 1890–1930* (Urbana: University of Illinois Press, 1994).

6. Ellen Ross, "New Thoughts on 'the Oldest Vocation': Mothers and Motherhood in Recent Feminist Scholarship," *Signs* 20 (1995): 402; Linda W. Rosenzweig, *The Anchor of My Life: Middle-Class American Mothers and Daughters, 1880–1920* (New York: New York University Press, 1993); and Ellen Ross, *Love and Toil: Motherhood in Outcast London, 1870–1918* (New York: Oxford University Press, 1993). See also the exploration of the tensions between professional representations of motherhood and its personal meanings in Meryle Mahrer Kaplan, *Mothers' Images of Motherhood* (New York: Routledge, 1992).

7. See Paula J. Caplan and Ian Hall-McCorquodale, "Mother-blaming in Major Clinical Journals," *AJO* 55 (1985): 345–353; Caplan's popularized work, *Don't Blame Mother: Mending the Mother-Daughter Relationship* (New York: Harper and Row, 1989); and Diane E. Eyer, *Motherguilt: How Our Culture Blames Mothers for What's Wrong with Society* (New York: Times Books/Random House, 1996).

8. See, for example, JBGC case no. 1999, an insignificant incident of peddling without a license. The boy's mother, living, according to the social worker's report, on "insufficient income," sent the boy out to sell lemons.

9. JBGC case nos. 1660, 1683, and 1800 are examples of failure to supervise.

10. JBGC case nos. 1612, 1733, and 1800 are specific examples of these terms and the mother who lacked information.

11. On the interest among Boston welfare workers in foster parenting and its usefulness as a "treatment" for delinquency, see William Healy et al., *Reconstructing Behavior in Youth: A Study of Problem Children in Foster Families* (New York: Alfred A. Knopf, 1929). These mothers of delinquents were the wives of workers or the unemployed, or sometimes single parents. Linda Gordon, "Single Mothers and Child Neglect," *American Quarterly* 37 (1985): 173–192, discusses the predilection among welfare workers to find single mothers guilty of child neglect.

12. Groves and Groves, *Parents and Children*, p. 116; Watson, *Psychological Care of Infant and Child*, pp. 81–82; Ernest R. Groves and Gladys H. Groves, *Wholesome Parenthood* (Boston: Houghton Mifflin Co., 1929), p. 244; U.S., Department of Labor, "Child Management," by Douglas A. Thom, Children's Bureau Publication no. 143 (Washington, D.C.: Government Printing Office, 1925), p. 3; Anna Wolf, *The Parents' Manual* (New York: Simon and Schuster, 1941), p. 285.

13. One of the founding members of the American Orthopsychiatric Association,

Levy was interested in the scientific testing of Freudian theories. When the Institute for Child Guidance opened in 1927 with financing from the Commonwealth Fund, its director Lawson Lowrey agreed to the creation of a special research unit, headed by Levy, to identify and study the treatment of "pathological mother-child relationships." Lawson G. Lowrey and Geddes Smith, *The Institute for Child Guidance, 1927–1933* (New York: Commonwealth Fund, 1933), p. 58. Brief biographical sketches of David M. Levy (1892–1977) can be found in "David M. Levy, Samuel W. Hamilton Memorial Lecturer, 1954," in Paul H. Hoch and Joseph Zubin, eds., *Psychopathology of Childhood* (New York: Grune and Stratton, 1955), pp. ix–x; and William Goldfarb, "In Memoriam: David M. Levy, 1892–1977," *AJO* 134 (1977): 934. Levy's papers are located in the History of Psychiatry Section, Department of Psychiatry, New York Hospital–Weill Medical College of Cornell University.

Maternal Overprotection was Levy's best-known work, but see also see his earlier reports on motherhood, including: "A Method of Integrating Physical and Psychiatric Examinations with Special Studies of Body Interest, Over-Protection, Response to Growth and Sex Differences," *AJP* 86 (1929): 121–194; "Maternal Overprotection and Rejection," *Archives of Neurology and Psychiatry* 25 (1931): 886–889; "On the Problem of Delinquency," *AJO* 2 (1932): 197–211; and "Relation of Maternal Overprotection to School Grades and Intelligence Tests," *AJO* 3 (1933): 26–34. Levy's ideas were further tested and developed by social work students from Smith College; their thesis work, some of which is cited below, was published regularly in *Smith College Studies in Social Work.*

14. Levy, *Maternal Overprotection,* pp. 36–38; "Maternal Overprotection and Rejection," p. 886.

15. Levy, *Maternal Overprotection,* pp. 213, 117.

16. Ibid., pp. 112–150.

17. Judith Silberpfennig, "Mother Types Encountered in Child Guidance Clinics," *AJO* 11 (1941): 475–484. Also characteristic of the categorizing of mothers was Emma Joan Bergel, "Problem Mothers at a Child Guidance Clinic" (M.S. thesis, Boston University School of Social Work, 1942).

18. Defined by Margaret Figge, a social work student, in "Some Factors in the Etiology of Maternal Rejection," *Smith College Studies in Social Work* 2 (1932): 237.

19. H. W. Newell, "The Psycho-dynamics of Maternal Rejection," *AJO* 4 (1934): 387–401; Percival Symonds, in his review of the literature on parent-child relations (*The Psychology of Parent-Child Relationships,* 1939), noted that definitions of rejecting behavior were still scarce.

20. David Levy, "Primary Affect Hunger," *AJP* 94 (1937): 643–52; *Maternal Overprotection,* p. 18.

21. Newell, "The Psycho-dynamics of Maternal Rejection," p. 390.

22. Figge, "Etiology of Maternal Rejection," pp. 253–254.

23. See, for example, JBGC case no. 9274, in which the staff identified a mother's overt rejection of a "fat, unlovable" female adolescent. In the 1930s clinicians labeled many more mothers overprotective than they did rejecting, however, rejection often appeared among the cases of adoptive children or those with stepmothers.

24. Frederick Rosenheim, a psychiatrist at the Judge Baker Guidance Center in the early 1940s, concluded as much in "Character Structure of a Rejected Child," *AJO* 12 (1942): 486–494.

25. Lowrey and Geddes, *The Institute for Child Guidance,* p. 44; Levy, *Maternal Overprotection,* p. 35; Figge, "Etiology of Maternal Rejection," p. 253; H. W. Newell, "Further Study of Maternal Overprotection," *AJO* 6 (1936): 580; and Christine Brunk, "Effects of Maternal Over-Protection on the Early Development and Habits of Children," *Smith College Studies in Social Work* 2 (1932): 263.

26. Douglas Thom, *The Everyday Problems of the Everyday Child* (New York: D. Appleton and Co., 1927), pp. 46–47, 49.

27. Mildred Burgum, "The Father Gets Worse: A Child Guidance Problem," *AJO* 12 (1942): 474–485, noted that there were only "occasional murmurs" in the field pointing to the father's role in etiology and in the treatment of troublesome behavior. See also Levy's limited discussion of fathers in *Maternal Overprotection,* pp. 150–155. On fatherhood in the early twentieth century, see Robert L. Griswold, *Fatherhood in America: A History* (New York: Basic Books, 1993); and Ralph Larossa, *The Modernization of Fatherhood: A Social and Political History* (Chicago: University of Chicago Press, 1997).

28. Charles S. Lamson, "Boy Trouble," *Journal of the Association of American Medical Colleges* 15 (1940): 32–48. I am indebted to Charlotte G. Borst for bringing this play to my attention.

29. Levy, *Maternal Overprotection,* pp. 136–137; the idea is also discussed in Mary Buell Sayles, *The Problem Child at Home: A Study in Parent-Child Relationships* (New York: Commonwealth Fund, 1932).

30. The needs of the children had, as the historian Sonya Michel has suggested in the context of expert opinion on day care, superseded the rights of mothers. "Children's Interests/Mothers' Rights: Women, Professionals, and the American Family, 1920–1945" (Ph.D. diss., Brown University, 1986).

31. Levy, *Maternal Overprotection,* pp. 121–126; Figge, "Etiology of Maternal Rejection," pp. 247–248; Ernest R. Groves and Gladys H. Groves, "24 Rules for Happiness in Marriage," *Parents' Magazine* 6 (December 1931), 13. A good starting point for the study of professional attitudes toward the family is the college text by the sociologists Ernest R. Groves and William F. Ogburn, *American Marriage and Family Relations* (New York: Henry Holt and Co., 1928). On

the development of family sociology, see Ronald L. Howard, *A Social History of American Family Sociology, 1865–1940*, ed. John Mogey (Westport, Conn.: Greenwood Press, 1981).

32. H. Meltzer, "Children's Attitudes to Parents," *AJO* 5 (1935): 263. See also Meltzer's later studies: "Economic Security and Children's Attitudes to Parents," *AJO* 6 (1936): 590–608; "Sex Differences in Children's Attitudes to Parents," *Journal of Genetic Psychology* 62 (1943): 311–326; and "Sex Differences in Parental Preferences Patterns," *Journal of Personality* 10 (1941): 114–128. In this last article Meltzer concluded, "The distribution of labor between parents in the present economic order is to a large extent responsible for the differences in parental preferences between the sexes," rather than "any universal 'complex' or 'fixation'" (p. 127). Other parent preference studies include: Meyer F. Nimkoff, "The Child's Preference for Father or Mother," *American Sociological Review* 7 (1942): 517–524; and H. W. Newell, "Family Attitudes as Revealed by the Psychiatric Examinations of 107 Juvenile Delinquents," *AJO* 2 (1932): 377–383. Robert Griswold also uses the parent preferences research to make a similar argument in "'Ties That Bind and Bonds That Break': Children's Attitudes toward Fathers, 1900–1930," in Paula Petrick and Elliott West, eds., *Small Worlds: Children and Adolescents in America, 1850–1950* (Lawrence: University Press of Kansas, 1992), pp. 255–274.

33. Another, commenting on his parents' separation, noted that he understood "just how his F. feels about his M's continual nagging" (9439).

34. Lois Meredith French, a psychiatric social worker, used the term "errand girl" to describe the social worker's lowly status in "Some Trends in Social Work" (1936), an essay published in French's book, *Psychiatric Social Work* (New York: Commonwealth Fund, 1940), p. 203. Roy Lubove, *The Professional Altruist: The Emergence of Social Work as a Career, 1880–1930* (Cambridge: Harvard University Press, 1965), is still the most easily accessible account of the transformation of social work. See also John H. Ehrenreich, *The Altruistic Imagination: A History of Social Work and Social Policy in the United States* (Ithaca: Cornell University Press, 1985); Daniel J. Walkowitz, "The Making of a Feminine Professional Identity: Social Workers in the 1920s," *American Historical Review* 95 (1990): 1051–1075; Regina G. Kunzel, *Fallen Women, Problem Girls: Unmarried Mothers and the Professionalization of Social Work, 1890–1945* (New Haven: Yale University Press, 1993); and Elizabeth Lunbeck, *The Psychiatric Persuasion: Knowledge, Gender, and Power* (Princeton: Princeton University Press, 1994). Margo Horn, "The Moral Message of Child Guidance, 1925–1945," *Journal of Social History* 18 (1984): 25–36, offers an alternative view representing the social worker as more passive and less moralistic.

35. "General Organization of Psychiatric Social Work in the United States," typescript, 1928. National Association of Social Workers (NASW) Records, Social

Welfare History Archives, University of Minnesota, Minneapolis, Minn., box 69, folder 763. Membership lists for the new organization can also be found in the NASW Records.

36. Solomon's address was reprinted as "Annual Address: Section on Psychiatric Social Work, American Association of Hospital Social Workers," *Journal of Abnormal and Social Psychology* 21 (1927): 422–433, NASW Records, Box 69, folder 764. The social worker Bertha Reynolds offered a fanciful, tongue-in-cheek description of the skewed relationship between Dr. Psychiatry ("who comes from a well-to-do medical family who give the impression that they despise him . . . He considers them crude in the way they treat people, and they say he is visionary and wastes time on ne'er-do-wells") and P.S.W. (who "is said to come from a family so associated with poverty that she has been loath to admit her connection") in "The Relationship between Psychiatry and Psychiatric Social Work," *The News-Letter of the American Association of Psychiatric Social Workers* 3 (May 1934):1–4, NASW Records, ephemera.

37. Porter R. Lee and Marion E. Kenworthy, *Mental Hygiene and Social Work* (New York: Commonwealth Fund, 1929), p. 152.

38. Porter Lee's comment was reprinted in "Symposium: The Treatment of Behavior and Personality Problems in Children," *AJO* 1 (1930): 47. By 1931 the American Psychiatric Association had a standing committee to explore "aspects of the common field of interest" of the two groups. Creation of the committee was announced in "American Psychiatric Association Standing Committee on Psychiatric Social Work," *The [AAPSW] News Letter* 17 (February 1931), p. 3. *The News Letter* (copies of which can be found in the NASW Records) printed a committee report (5 [March 1934]) in which the psychiatrists supported the "interrelationship" of the fields, but felt it "best assured when: . . . the psychiatrist retains full responsibility for the activities of the psychiatric social worker" (p. 7). The issue, of course, was more pressing for the psychiatric social workers seeking to expand their responsibilities, and it was more fully discussed in their professional meetings. For example, at the AAPSW annual meeting in San Francisco in June 1929, participants listened to a roundtable discussion of the "Coordination of Work between Psychiatrist and Social Worker"; at a business meeting in Boston held the next year, a psychiatrist read a paper on "intensive psychotherapy with Children in a Child Guidance Clinic," which elicited much discussion of the relationship between psychiatrists and social workers. Accounts of the meetings can be found in the NASW Records, box 69, folder 763.

39. "Symposium: The Treatment of Behavior and Personality Problems in Children," pp. 3–60. Another statement of the division of responsibilities is by Marjorie Stauffer, "Some Aspects of Treatment by Psychiatrist and Psychiatric Social Worker," *AJO* 2 (1932): 152–161.

40. JBGC case no. 9302. Helen Leland Witmer's study of Judge Baker cases from

1932 and 1933 corroborates this finding. See Witmer, "Parental Behavior as an Index to the Probable Outcome of Treatment in a Child Guidance Clinic," *AJO* 3 (1933): 431–444.

41. This was a unique child guidance contribution to professional development and work with children. Helen Witmer, in her report on services for children, noted that the compromise worked out in the child guidance clinic sometimes generated misunderstanding in other psychiatric settings. Witmer, *Psychiatric Clinics for Children,* pp. 349–350.

42. Margaret Mahler-Schoenberger, for example, did so in her "Discussion of 'Mother Types Encountered in Child Guidance Clinics' by Judith Silberpfennig," *AJO* 11 (1941): 484.

43. Amelia Bush was not alone. From the popular press, see Dorothy Hazeltine Yates, *Psychological Racketeers* (Boston: Richard G. Badger, Gorham Press, 1932); and from the professionals see Bernard Sachs and Louis Hausman, *Nervous and Mental Disorders from Birth through Adolescence* (New York: Paul B. Hoeber, 1926), pp. 730–744.

44. William Healy, Augusta F. Bronner, and Anna Mae Bowers define "resistance" in *The Structure and Meaning of Psychoanalysis* (New York: Alfred A. Knopf, 1930), pp. 446–449. Although published later, Gordon Hamilton's description of "resistance" and "transference" in *Psychotherapy in Child Guidance* (New York: Columbia University Press, 1947), pp. 127–131, 134–136, applied as well to child guidance during the 1930s.

45. Betsy Mazur, "Mothers Who Refuse Treatment: A Follow-up Study of Cases Accepted for and Refusing Treatment in a Child Guidance Clinic" (M.S. thesis, Boston University School of Social Work, 1955), pp. 30–38. One mother specifically told the interviewer that to improve the clinic, "the Center should not blame parents for children's problems" (p. 46). Writing from within the child guidance frame, Mazur concluded that the situations improved because the mothers changed, probably with some outside help. See also Helen Leland Witmer, "A Comparison of Treatment Results in Various Types of Child Guidance Clinics," *AJO* 5 (1935): 351–360; and Linda M. Johnson, "Parents' Perceptions of Their Experience with a Child Guidance Clinic" (MSW thesis, Smith College School of Social Work, 1972).

46. See especially Margo Horn's study ("The Moral Message of Child Guidance") of mothers and social workers in a Philadelphia child guidance clinic. Horn identifies "three impressionistic categories of intervention," loosely defined as "correction and instruction," "support and reassurance," and "psychodynamic." She suggests that correction and instruction (with "no psychological content") characterized the mid-1920s, while a psychodynamic approach was more representative of the late 1930s, a change she relates to the development of a "therapeutic stance" (more passive, less moralistic) among social work

professionals. While Horn suggests that social workers in Philadelphia were nondirective and nonjudgmental, records from the Judge Baker clinic cast doubt on such a benign view of the social worker's intervention. Perhaps it reflects the peculiar ideological stance of the Philadelphia clinic. Philadelphia served as the home base of the social workers Jessie Taft and Virginia Robinson, two influential leaders in the development of a "functionalist" school of nondirective social work. The Judge Baker student social workers whose comments are reflected in the 1935 case records followed a much more eclectic approach than Horn discovered in Philadelphia. Moreover, the sympathy for the mothers that Horn found among the Philadelphia social workers should not necessarily be equated with an absence of desire to intervene and alter what they perceived to be unhealthy parent-child relationships. On the split in social work theory in the 1930s and the impact of the functionalists, see Ehrenreich, *The Altruistic Imagination,* pp. 102–138.

My discussion of treatment in case records at the Judge Baker Guidance Clinic follows categories devised by David Levy. See Constance Rathbun, "An Evaluation of Factors Determining Outcome of Treatment in a Child Guidance Clinic" (M.S. thesis, Smith College School for Social Work, 1938), p. 42. Rathbun's work was a survey of eleven theses discussing treatment and based on Judge Baker case records.

47. See Horn, "The Moral Message of Child Guidance," and the works of the Philadelphia social workers Jessie Taft and Virginia Robinson, including Taft's summary in *A Functional Approach to Family Case Work* (Philadelphia: University of Pennsylvania Press, 1944).

48. In JBGC case no. 9284 the social worker's specific goal with the mother was "reassurance." See also no. 9294, where, over several months of meetings, the social worker reported she had "sympathized" with a mother who had to cope with much aggravation from her sixteen-year-old son.

49. George S. Stevenson and Geddes Smith, *Child Guidance Clinics: A Quarter Century of Development* (New York: Commonwealth Fund, 1934), p. 91.

50. David Levy, "Attitude Therapy," *AJO* 7 (1937): 111. Porter R. Lee and Marion Kenworthy also discussed the need for "insight," in *Mental Hygiene and Social Work,* pp. 106–109. (At the time their training book was published, Lee and Kenworthy were associated with Levy at the Institute for Child Guidance in New York City.)

51. Levy, "Attitude Therapy," p. 103. See also Stevenson and Smith, *Child Guidance Clinics,* pp. 92–93; and Lee and Kenworthy, *Mental Hygiene and Social Work,* pp. 123–139. An "ideal" example of attitude therapy was prepared for the 1935 annual meeting of the American Association of Psychiatric Social Workers. The patient was a rejecting mother who lacked affection for her daughter, who, at age four, showed symptoms of "feeding difficulties." Uncharacteristically, this

woman was an immigrant, a expert dressmaker who did not work after marriage, and who was dissatisfied with her husband's allowance to her. She also
felt thwarted educationally. After 115 interviews the patient is described as
having conquered the emotions that kept her from accepting her child and
"adjusting to the realities of life with her husband." "A Case of Attitude Therapy," NASW Records, ephemera, AAPSW 1926–1928.

52. Burgum, "The Father Gets Worse: A Child Guidance Problem," presented
several case studies showing the dynamics of intra-familial relationships in
which the mother "gets better" during treatment, while the father "gets worse,"
that is, as an aggressive and domineering mother developed a better relationship with her child, the child's relationship with the dependent, immature,
inadequate father grew worse.

53. William Healy and Augusta F. Bronner, *Treatment and What Happened Afterward* (Boston: Judge Baker Guidance Center, 1939), p. 46.

54. See, for example, JBGC case no. 9229.

55. Ralph Larossa, *The Modernization of Fatherhood,* discusses the new interpretation of the father's role in child rearing that developed during the 1920s and
1930s. It is ironic, then, that in these JBGC cases it was the girls who turned to
social work, psychology, and nursing as professional aspirations. None of the
boys showed any desire to follow in their new "pal's" vocational footsteps.

56. Healy and Bronner, *Treatment and What Happened Afterward,* pp. 25, 44.
Margo Horn tabulated successes and failures for the Philadelphia clinic and
concluded that failures represented only 14 percent of a sample of cases drawn
from records kept between 1925 and 1944. Many cases were withdrawn, however, and many more were recorded as simply "services rendered." Added
together, Horn concludes that "nearly half (45 percent) of the cases had outcomes that were inconclusive as to the effectiveness of the treatment, even as
defined by the staff." *Before It's Too Late: The Child Guidance Movement in the
United States, 1922–1945* (Philadelphia: Temple University Press, 1989), p. 160.

57. One of the few fathers who spoke for themselves thanked the clinic for helping
his marriage (by working with his wife); "as far as the boy is concerned," this
father reported, "there has not been any real change yet [though] the home
situation has improved considerably" (9314).

58. Katherine Moore, "A Specialized Method in the Treatment of Parents in a Child
Guidance Clinic," paper read at the annual meeting of the American Psychiat-
ric Association, Boston, June 1, 1933. Quoted in Stevenson and Smith, *Child
Guidance Clinics,* p. 92.

59. The mother of case no. 9314 "said that she has felt she had no one to confide in.
Even her one friend she does not like to talk about marital difficulties with.
Feels it would be much more safe to do it in the clinic. Said she looks upon
coming to the clinic as recreation." This woman was clearly ill at ease in her

therapeutic relationship, for, despite her confession of need, when asked to schedule the next appointment, she demurred, citing the problems involved in changing maids, and proposed to call in a week. The mother of no. 9342, when asked what benefits she thought she had derived from her year of therapy, "spontaneously" replied, "'I got to think below the surface.' Bec. she cannot talk with their neighbors, she likes to come to the clinic."

60. The term "companionate" is often used to describe the new ideals of marriage—the notion that marriage represented romance and sexuality and focused on the relationship between husband and wife rather than between parents and children. Ben Lindsey and Wainwright Evans used the term (*The Companionate Marriage* [New York: Boni and Liveright, 1927]) to describe a trial marriage, based on contraception and easily dissolved. This was not the expectation found among the women at the Judge Baker clinic, where perhaps "companionable" would better describe their hopes for marriage. "Democratic" is the description used in family sociology texts such as Groves and Ogburn, *American Marriage and Family Relationships,* p. 32. For a description of the new ideals, see their chapters 3 and 4, "The Husband," and "The Wife," pp. 30–58.

61. The mother in JBGC case no. 9288 also complained of having a very restricted social life.

62. Levy, "Attitude Therapy," p. 106.

63. Ibid., p. 103.

8. The Limits of Psychiatric Authority

1. See, for example, Judge Baker Guidance Center, *Straightening the Twig: Work of the Judge Baker Foundation, Child Guidance Center* (Boston: Judge Baker Guidance Center, 1931). The novelist Dorothy Canfield (Fisher) used the image in *The Bent Twig* (New York: Henry Holt and Co., 1915; discussed in chap. 5); so did psychiatrist Leslie B. Hohman, *As the Twig Is Bent* (New York: Macmillan Co., 1940). Hohman warned parents not to take the new psychological theories too far. "We must keep our wits about us—never blindly apply old sayings, such as, 'children should be seen and not heard,' nor blindly apply new sayings like 'no repression' . . . Our child-training should be directed by common sense, reinforced by the unconfusing, understandable principles all the substantial schools of modern psychology can offer" (p. 7).

2. Healy to Ethel S. Dummer, 27 June 1944, Dummer Papers.

3. Lawson Lowrey, "Psychiatry for Children," *AJO* 101 (1944): 375–388.

4. On wartime psychiatry, see Ellen Herman, *The Romance of American Psychology: Political Culture in the Age of Experts* (Berkeley: University of California Press, 1995); Gerald N. Grob, *From Asylum to Community: Mental Health Policy*

in Modern America (Princeton: Princeton University Press, 1991), pp. 5–23; Johannes C. Pols, "Managing the Mind: The Culture of American Mental Hygiene, 1910–1950" (Ph.D. diss., University of Pennsylvania, 1997); and Rebecca Schwartz Greene, "The Role of the Psychiatrist in World War II" (Ph.D. diss., Columbia University, 1977). Both William M. Tuttle, Jr., *"Daddy's Gone to War": The Second World War in the Lives of America's Children* (New York: Oxford University Press, 1993), and James Gilbert, *A Cycle of Outrage: America's Response to the Juvenile Delinquent in the 1950s* (New York: Oxford University Press, 1986), describe psychiatric advice on child rearing during wartime.

5. Franz G. Alexander and Sheldon T. Selesnick, *The History of Psychiatry: An Evaluation of Psychiatric Thought and Practice from Prehistoric Times to the Present* (New York: Harper and Row, 1966), p. 383.

6. Edward A. Strecker, *Their Mothers' Sons: The Psychiatrist Examines an American Problem* (Philadelphia: Lippincott, 1946), pp. 30–31.

7. Leo Kanner, "Autistic Disturbance in Affective Contact," *Nervous Child* 2 (1942–43): 217–250; "Early Infantile Autism," *Journal of Pediatrics* 25 (1944): 211–217; and "Foreword," in Bernard Rimland, *Infantile Autism: The Syndrome and Its Implications for a Neural Theory of Behavior* (New York: Appleton-Century-Crofts, 1964), p. v. Accolades to Kanner appeared in "The Child Is Father," *Time Magazine* (25 July 1960), p. 78.

8. Jacob Kasanin, Elizabeth Knight, and Priscilla Sage, "The Parent-Child Relationship in Schizophrenia: I. Over-Protection-Rejection," *Journal of Nervous and Mental Disease* 79 (1934): 249, 261.

9. Frieda Fromm-Reichmann, "Notes on the Mother Role in the Family Group," *Bulletin of the Menninger Clinic* 4 (1940): 132–148; and "Notes on the Development of Treatment of Schizophrenia by Psychoanalytic Psychotherapy," *Psychiatry* 11 (1948): 263–273. On the intellectual background of Fromm-Reichmann's ideas and their subsequent adaptations, see Carol Eadie Ishikawa, "The Genesis, Transmutation, and Demise of the Schizophrenogenic Mother: An Historical Analysis of a Concept within Psychiatry" (Master of Liberal Arts in Extension Studies thesis, Harvard University, 1993). I am indebted to Anne Harrington for bringing this study to my attention.

10. René A. Spitz, "Hospitalism," *Psychoanalytic Study of the Child* 1 (1945): 53–74; R. A. Spitz and K. M. Wolf, "Anaclitic Depression: An Inquiry into the Genesis of Psychiatric Conditions in Early Childhood: II," *Psychoanalytic Study of the Child* 2 (1946): 313–342.

11. John Bowlby's report to the World Health Organization appeared in popularized form in the United States as *Child Care and the Growth of Love* (Baltimore: Penguin Books, 1953). Bowlby's influence is discussed in Denise Riley, *War in the Nursery: Theories of the Child and the Mother* (London: Virago Press, 1983).

12. On the problem of latchkey children, see Tuttle, *"Daddy's Gone to War,"* pp. 69–90. On popularized versions of this advice, see Claudia Ann Miner, "What

about the Children? Americans' Attitudes toward Children and Childhood during the 1950s" (Ph.D. diss, Washington State University, 1986).

13. Stella Chess, "Editorial: Mal de Mère," *AJO* 34 (1964): 613–614. Michael Rutter, *Maternal Deprivation Reassessed* (Middlesex: Penguin Books, 1972). See also Lawrence Casler, "Maternal Deprivation: A Critical Review of the Literature," *Monographs of the Society for Research in Child Development* 26, no. 2 (1961). Lauretta Bender, "Childhood Schizophrenia," *Nervous Child* 1 (1941–42): 138–140; Bender, "Schizophrenia in Childhood: Its Recognition, Description, and Treatment," *AJO* 26 (1956): 499–506; quote is from Bender, "Childhood Schizophrenia: Clinical Study of One Hundred Schizophrenic Children," *AJO* 17 (1947): 52.

14. Stella Chess, "The 'Blame the Mother' Ideology," *International Journal of Mental Health* 11 (1982): 95–107.

15. Molly Ladd-Taylor and Lauri Umansky, "Introduction," in Molly Ladd-Taylor and Lauri Umansky, eds., *"Bad" Mothers: The Politics of Blame in Twentieth-Century America* (New York: New York University Press, 1998), p. 23.

16. For a general discussion of postwar expectations of family life, see Elaine Tyler May, *Homeward Bound: American Families in the Cold War Era* (New York: Basic Books, 1988). Both Robert L. Griswold, *Fatherhood in America: A History* (New York: Basic Books, 1993), pp. 108–126; and Ralph Larossa, *The Modernization of Fatherhood: A Social and Political History* (Chicago: University of Chicago Press, 1997), pp. 144–176, note that fathers as well as mothers consulted parenting advisers. Each cites letters from fathers to newspaper columnist Angelo Patri. Tuttle, *"Daddy's Gone to War,"* pp. 212–230, discusses fathers returning from military service, as does Griswold, *Fatherhood in America,* pp. 176–182.

17. JBGC case nos. 13966, 13541, 13465.

18. From 40 to 50 percent of American mothers were deemed either rejecting, overprotecting, or dominating, according to the psychiatrist Marynia F. Farnham and her coauthor Ferdinand Lundberg in *Modern Woman: The Lost Sex* (New York: Grosset and Dunlap, 1947), a widely quoted postwar treatise on the psychological failings of contemporary women.

19. JBGC case nos. 13969, 13971, 13972, 13974, and 13970.

20. The anti–comic book crusade is usually associated with the publication of Fredric Wertham's *Seduction of the Innocent* (1954). An earlier article by Lauretta Bender and Reginald S. Lourie, "The Effect of Comic Books on the Ideology of Children," *AJO* 11 (1941): 540–550, denied the significance of comic book violence. These authors concluded, "It is evident from our case studies that whatever anxiety, aggression or confusion was attributable to comic books could be traced further back to the basic traumatic factors within the children's background" (p. 547).

21. Hillary Rodham Clinton, *It Takes a Village: And Other Lessons Children Teach*

Us (New York: Simon and Schuster, 1996). On maternal thinking, see Carol Gilligan, *In a Different Voice: Psychological Theory and Women's Development* (Cambridge: Harvard University Press, 1982); and in particular, Sara Ruddick, *Maternal Thinking: Toward a Politics of Peace* (Boston: Beacon Press, 1989).

22. "Minutes of a Meeting of a Group of Child Psychiatrists, Atlantic City, N.J., February 24, 1952;" and "Proceedings: Organization Meeting of the American Academy of Child Psychiatry," Atlantic City, N.J., 24 February 1952, Gardner Collection. "The History of the American Academy of Child Psychiatry," *Journal of the American Academy of Child Psychiatry* 1 (1962): 196–202; George Tarjan, "The American Academy of Child Psychiatry; Our 25th Anniversary," *Journal of the American Academy of Child Psychiatry* 17 (1978): 561–564. On the significance of specialization, see Rosemary Stevens, *American Medicine and the Public Interest* (New Haven: Yale University Press, 1971).

23. See, for example, Richard R. J. Lewine, "Parents: The Mental Health Professionals' Scapegoat," in *Changing Families,* ed. Irving E. Sigel and Luis M. Laosa (New York: Plenum Press, 1983), pp. 267–289.

24. The quotation and the description of the origins of the Joint Commission, are from Reginald S. Lourie (President, Joint Commission on Mental Health of Children), "Introduction" in Irving N. Berlin, ed., *Advocacy for Child Mental Health* (New York: Brunner/Mazel, 1975), p. x.

25. Joint Commission on Mental Health of Children, *Crisis in Child Mental Health: Challenge for the 1970s* (New York: Harper and Row, 1969, 1970). Quote from pp. xviii–xix.

26. The commission also called for the creation of a child advocacy system and the development of programs to foster family and community involvement in child welfare. Joint Commission, *Crisis in Child Mental Health,* p. 194.

27. Punishing parents is not a new idea. During the 1950s FBI director J. Edgar Hoover endorsed a similar argument and similar solution. See Miner, "What about the Children?" pp. 164–165.

28. On the Chicago sociologists, see Robert E. L. Faris, *Chicago Sociology, 1920–1932* (1967; reprint, Chicago: University of Chicago Press, 1979), and Martin Bulmer, *The Chicago School of Sociology: Institutionalization, Diversity, and the Rise of Sociological Research* (Chicago: University of Chicago Press, 1984).

29. The two major "Chicago school" delinquency studies were Clifford Shaw and Henry D. MacKay, *Social Factors in Juvenile Delinquency* (Washington, D.C.: U.S. Government Printing Office, 1931); and Clifford Shaw, *Delinquency Areas* (Chicago: University of Chicago Press, 1929). On Shaw and MacKay, see Robert M. Mennel, *Thorns and Thistles: Juvenile Delinquents in the United States, 1825–1940* (Hanover: University Press of New England, 1973), pp. 181–195; and Jon D. Snodgrass, "American Criminological Tradition: Portraits of the Men and Ideology in a Discipline" (Ph.D. diss., University of Pennsylvania, 1972), pp. 125–216.

30. Clifford Shaw, *The Jack-Roller: A Delinquent Boy's Own Story* (Chicago: University of Chicago Press, 1930), pp. 54, 34–35. Shaw published two additional case studies, *The Natural History of a Delinquent Career* (1931) and *Brothers in Crime* (1936).

31. Ernest Burgess, "Discussion," in Shaw, *The Jack-Roller*, p. 196. "Thrasher" refers to Frederic M. Thrasher, *The Gang: A Study of 1,313 Gangs in Chicago* (Chicago: University of Chicago Press, 1927).

32. As explained by Ernest Burgess, Joseph Lohman, and Clifford Shaw, "The Chicago Area Project," National Probation Association, *Yearbook, 1937*, pp. 8–10. Quoted in Steven Schlossman, Gail Zellman, and Richard Shavelson, *Delinquency Prevention in South Chicago: A Fifty Year Assessment of the Chicago Area Project* (Santa Monica, Calif.: Rand Corporation, 1984), p. 1. See also Snodgrass, "American Criminological Tradition," pp. 203–216.

33. Schlossman, Zellman, and Shavelson call this project the "first systematic challenge to the dominance of psychology and psychiatry in public and private programs for the prevention and treatment of juvenile delinquency." Schlossman, Zellman, and Shavelson, *Delinquency Prevention in South Chicago*, p. 2.

34. Gilbert, *Cycle of Outrage*, pp. 63–78, discusses the generation and exaggeration of this fear by public officials.

35. On the role of child guidance and the child psychiatrist, see Stuart M. Finch, "The Psychiatrist and Juvenile Delinquency," *Journal of the American Academy of Child Psychiatry* 1 (1962): 619–635. Finch cites the Judge Baker's unpublished report to the National Institutes of Health. Directions from the Rockefeller Fund can be found in the Rockefeller Foundation Archives, Record Group 1.1, Box 96, Projects, Series 200 United States, folder 1156: "Judge Baker Guidance Center (Child Psychiatry) 1944–1952," Rockefeller Archive Center, Sleepy Hollow, N.Y.

36. William McCord and Joan McCord, *Origins of Crime: A New Evaluation of the Cambridge-Somerville Youth Study* (New York: Columbia University Press, 1959), p. 19.

37. Lee N. Robins, *Deviant Children Grown Up: A Sociological and Psychiatric Study of Sociopathic Personality* (Baltimore: Williams and Wilkins Co., 1966), pp. 160, 300–309, 292.

38. Joseph M. Hawes, *The Children's Rights Movement: A History of Advocacy and Protection* (Boston: Twayne Publishers, 1991), pp. 96–121, is a brief introduction to current issues.

39. Boston Child Council, *Juvenile Delinquency in Massachusetts as a Public Responsibility* (Boston: Boston Child Council, 1939), pp. 87–90, 181.

40. I am grateful to Linda A. Szymanski of the National Center for Juvenile Justice and Piper L. Durrell of Student Legal Services at Virginia Tech for providing this information and copies of the relevant Massachusetts and Virginia statutes.

41. U.S., Department of Labor, "Controlling Juvenile Delinquency: A Community Program," Children's Bureau Publication no. 301 (Washington, D.C.: Government Printing Office, 1943), p. 24.

42. Gilbert, *Cycle of Outrage*, pp. 54–55.

43. Frederick Allen, director of the Philadelphia Child Guidance clinic, assessed the impact of the Mental Health Act on child psychiatry in "Developments in Child Psychiatry in the United States," *American Journal of Public Health* 38 (1948): 1201–1209. See also Jeanne L. Brand, "The National Mental Health Act of 1946: A Retrospect," *Bulletin of the History of Medicine* 39 (1965): 231–245.

44. Tatara Toshio, "1400 Years of Japanese Social Work from Its Origins through the Allied Occupation, 552–1952" (Ph.D. diss., Bryn Mawr College, 1975), pp. 434–442.

45. Elizabeth M. Costello et al., "Psychiatric Disorders in Pediatric Primary Care: Prevalence and Risk Factors," *Archives of General Psychiatry* 45 (1988): 1107–1116. The study was reported in the *New York Times* by Daniel Goleman, "Pioneering Studies Find Surprisingly High Rate of Mental Ills in Young" (10 January 1989), p. C1.

Index

Abbott, Edith, 47–48, 59
Abbott, Mrs. T. Grafton, 108
Addams, Jane, 31, 32, 34, 39, 43
Adler, Alfred, 143
Adolescence: cultural changes and, 121–125, 135; leisure time and, 123, 126–129; sexuality and, 129–131; social suggestibility and, 130–131, 136–137; adolescent rebellion, 138–139; emotional needs, 140–147
Adolescence: Its Psychology and its Relations to Physiology, Anthropology, Sociology, Sex, Crime, Religion, and Education (Hall), 51–52
Advertising, 92–93, 96, 102–103
Advice literature, 94–105; mothers and, 99–100, 184–185; child guidance principles in, 100–101; Children's Bureau pamphlets, 103–104
Alexander, Franz, 210
Alienists, 17–18, 24
Allen, Frederick H., 173
American Academy of Child Psychiatry, 217
American Association of Clinical Psychologists, 71
American Association of Psychiatric Social Workers, 190
American Journal of Insanity, 19, 21
American Orthopsychiatric Association (AOA), 2, 90, 190, 217
American Pediatric Society, 25
Anorexia nervosa, 19
"Are You Training Your Child to Be Happy?," 104

Asylums. *See* Mental asylums; Reformatories; Training schools
Attitude therapy, 197–200, 203
Authority, 3, 5–6, 83–89, 95, 208–210; parent education movement and, 107–108
Autism, 211
Auto-suggestion for Mothers, 101

Baker, Harvey H., 9, 34, 56, 57
Barnabas, Brother, 157
Beers, Clifford, 53
Behaviorism, 94, 101
Bender, Lauretta, 212–213, 218
Bent Twig, The (Canfield), 127
Blamelessness of children, 29, 30, 84, 89
Blanton, Dorothy Gray, 99
Blanton, Smiley, 99
Boston Habit Clinic, 94
Boston House of Reformation, 30
Boston Psychopathic Hospital, 5, 53, 79
Bowlby, John, 212
Boyology, 157
Boy Problem, The (Forbush), 157
Boys: masturbation and, 1–24, 26, 131, 165, 167–168; weak character and, 73, 80, 133; sexuality and, 76–77, 131, 162–168; gender issues and, 150–151, 156–162; boyhood culture, 162–165; vocational guidance and, 169–171
"Boy Trouble," 184
Brandt, Allan, 166
Breckinridge, Sophonisba P., 47–48
Brennemann, Joseph, 114–115

303